Principles of
Experimental
Psychopathology

Principles of Experimental Psychopathology

Essays in Honor of Brendan A. Maher

Edited by Mark F. Lenzenweger and Jill M. Hooley

American Psychological Association • Washington, DC

Published by
American Psychological Association
750 First Street, NE
Washington, DC 20002
www.apa.org

To order   Tel: (800) 374-2721; Direct: (202) 336-5510
APA Order Department   Fax: (202) 336-5502; TDD/TTY: (202) 336-6123
P.O. Box 92984   Online: www.apa.org/books/
Washington, DC 20090-2984   Email: order@apa.org

In the U.K., Europe, Africa, and the Middle East, copies may be ordered from
American Psychological Association
3 Henrietta Street
Covent Garden, London
WC2E 8LU England

Typeset in Century Schoolbook by PageGrafx, Inc., St. Simon's Island, GA

Printer: United Book Press, Inc., Baltimore, MD
Cover Designer: Naylor Design, Washington, DC
Technical/Production Editor: Jennifer L. Zale

The opinions and statements published are the responsibility of the authors,
and such opinions and statements do not necessarily represent the policies of
the American Psychological Association.

Library of Congress Cataloging-in-Publication Data
Principles of experimental psychopathology: essays in honor of Brendan A. Maher /
edited by Mark F. Lenzenweger and Jill M. Hooley.
    p. cm.
   Includes bibliographical references and index.
   ISBN 1-55798-928-1 (alk. paper)
   1. Schizophrenia—Research. 2. Delusions—Research. 3. Psychology,
Pathological—Research. 4. Psychiatry—Research. I. Maher, Brendan A. (Brendan
Arnold), 1924– II. Lenzenweger, Mark F. III. Hooley, Jill M. IV. Series. V. Series: APA
science volumes

RC514 .P689 2002
616.89'027—dc21   2002018560

British Library Cataloguing-in-Publication Data
A CIP record is available from the British Library.

Printed in the United States of America
First Edition

APA Science Volumes

Attribution and Social Interaction: The Legacy of Edward E. Jones

Best Methods for the Analysis of Change: Recent Advances, Unanswered Questions, Future Directions

Cardiovascular Reactivity to Psychological Stress and Disease

The Challenge in Mathematics and Science Education: Psychology's Response

Changing Employment Relations: Behavioral and Social Perspectives

Children Exposed to Marital Violence: Theory, Research, and Applied Issues

Cognition: Conceptual and Methodological Issues

Cognitive Bases of Musical Communication

Cognitive Dissonance: Progress on a Pivotal Theory in Social Psychology

Conceptualization and Measurement of Organism–Environment Interaction

Converging Operations in the Study of Visual Selective Attention

Creative Thought: An Investigation of Conceptual Structures and Processes

Developmental Psychoacoustics

Diversity in Work Teams: Research Paradigms for a Changing Workplace

Emotion and Culture: Empirical Studies of Mutual Influence

Emotion, Disclosure, and Health

Evolving Explanations of Development: Ecological Approaches to Organism–Environment Systems

Examining Lives in Context: Perspectives on the Ecology of Human Development

Global Prospects for Education: Development, Culture, and Schooling

Hostility, Coping, and Health

Measuring Patient Changes in Mood, Anxiety, and Personality Disorders: Toward a Core Battery

Occasion Setting: Associative Learning and Cognition in Animals

Organ Donation and Transplantation: Psychological and Behavioral Factors

APA Decade of Behavior Volumes

Contents

Contributors

Xavier F. Amador, PhD, Columbia University
Crystal R. Blyler, PhD, Substance Abuse and Mental Health Services Administration
Bernard P. Chang, AM, Harvard University
Pearl H. Chiu, AB, Harvard University
Richard J. Chung, Harvard University
Scott C. Clark, MD, Faculty of Medicine, University of New South Wales
Patrica J. Deldin, PhD, Harvard University
Robert H. Dworkin, PhD, University of Rochester School of Medicine and Dentistry
Don C. Fowles, PhD, University of Iowa
Jack M. Gorman, MD, Columbia University
Irving I. Gottesman, PhD, University of Virginia
Staci A. Gruber, EdM, MS, Harvard Medical School and McLean Hospital
Philip S. Holzman, PhD, Harvard University and McLean Hospital
Jill M. Hooley, DPhil, Harvard University
Jerome Kagan, PhD, Harvard University
Junghee Lee, MA, Vanderbilt University
Mark F. Lenzenweger, PhD, Harvard University
Brendan A. Maher, PhD, Harvard University
Dara S. Manoach, PhD, Harvard Medical School and Beth Israel-Deaconess Hospital
Theo C. Manschreck, MD, MPH, Harvard Medical School
Richard J. McNally, PhD, Harvard University
Elna M. Nagasako, PhD, University of Rochester School of Medicine and Dentistry
Ken Nakayama, PhD, Harvard University
Sohee Park, PhD, Vanderbilt University
James L. Reilly, MA, University of Virginia
Avgusta Y. Shestyuk, BS, Harvard University
Milton E. Strauss, PhD, Case Western Reserve University
Ann Summerfelt, BA, Maryland Psychiatric Research Center
William C. Wirshing, MD, University of California at Los Angeles
Lyman C. Wynne, MD, University of Rochester School of Medicine and Dentistry
Deborah A. Yurgelun-Todd, PhD, Harvard Medical School and McLean Hospital

Foreword

In early 1988, the American Psychological Association (APA) Science Directorate began its sponsorship of what would become an exceptionally successful activity in support of psychological science—the APA Scientific Conferences program. This program has showcased some of the most important topics in psychological science and has provided a forum for collaboration among many leading figures in the field.

The program has inspired a series of books that have presented cutting-edge work in all areas of psychology. At the turn of the millennium, the series was renamed the Decade of Behavior Series to help advance the goals of this important initiative. The Decade of Behavior is a major interdisciplinary campaign designed to promote the contributions of the behavioral and social sciences to our most important societal challenges in the decade leading up to 2010. Although a key goal has been to inform the public about these scientific contributions, other activities have been designed to encourage and to further collaboration among scientists. Hence, the series that was the "APA Science Series" has continued as the "Decade of Behavior Series." This represents one element in APA's efforts to promote the Decade of Behavior initiative as one of its endorsing organizations. For additional information about the Decade of Behavior, please visit http://www.decadeofbehavior.org.

Over the course of the past years, the Science Conference and Decade of Behavior Series has allowed psychological scientists to share and explore cutting-edge findings in psychology. The APA Science Directorate looks forward to continuing this successful program and to sponsoring other conferences and books in the years ahead. This series has been so successful that we have chosen to extend it to include books that, although they do not arise from conferences, report with the same high quality of scholarship on the latest research.

We are pleased that this important contribution to the literature was supported in part by the Decade of Behavior program. Congratulations to the editors and contributors of this volume on their sterling effort.

Kurt Salzinger, PhD
Executive Director for Science

Virginia E. Holt
*Assistant Executive Director
for Science*

Brendan A. Maher

Brendan A. Maher

A Biographical Sketch

Mark F. Lenzenweger

This book examines the work of Professor Brendan A. Maher, a primary architect of experimental psychopathology, leading scholar in schizophrenia research, teacher and mentor for many, and academic statesman-at-large. It consists of chapters written by scholars who have had the opportunity to work with Brendan as colleagues, collaborators, and former students. All individuals who contributed to this volume have come to know the scientific rigor, professional wisdom, and lasting friendship of Professor Maher. Brendan's life and travels throughout the academy have provided him with a wealth of academic, clinical, and other professional adventures, which have inspired many an anecdote or story that all of us who know Brendan relish. What follows is a succinct biographical sketch to round out this volume.

Brendan A. Maher was born in Widnes, Lancashire, England, on October 31, 1924. His parents had come from the County Tipperary in Ireland. He attended De La Salle College, Manchester, from which he matriculated in 1940. During World War II, Maher served in the Royal Navy, enlisting as an Ordinary Seaman in 1942. He was promoted through the commissioned ranks and was discharged in 1947 as Lieutenant. He was the navigating officer in the lead minesweeper in the assault of Sword Beach in Normandy on D-Day, June 6, 1944. He was later wounded sweeping mines in Holland and spent more than a year in the hospital before his discharge from the service. He recounted this period in *A Passage to Sword Beach: Minesweeping in the Royal Navy* (Maher, 1996).

After the war, Maher was free to actively pursue his advanced education. He completed his BA (with honors) at the University of Manchester. His graduate education brought him to the United States as a Fulbright Scholar at Ohio State University. There, Maher entered the world of psychological science with the helpful guidance of his adviser, George Kelly. Maher would later edit a collection of Kelly's major scientific papers (Maher, 1969). He received his MA in 1951 and his PhD in 1954, both from Ohio State University. In 1950 at Ohio State, Maher met Winifred Barbara Brown, who would become his wife and partner in life in 1952. As part of his doctoral training in clinical psychology, he completed his clinical internship at the Illinois Neuropsychiatric Institute, an affiliate of the University of Illinois Medical School. There he had the opportunity to work in the department under the direction of David Shakow, who was actively pursuing empirical investigations into the nature of schizophrenia.

On completing his PhD in 1954, Maher took his first post as a clinical psychologist in H.M. Prison in Wakefield, England. Maher then returned the following year to Ohio State University as an instructor in psychology. Maher took an assistant professorship post at Northwestern University in 1956 and then moved on to Louisiana

State University as an associate professor and the director of clinical training at the university. In 1960 he accepted a lecturer position in the Department of Psychology at Harvard University, where he also served as the chair of the Center for Research in Personality. He left Harvard in 1964 to assume a professorship at the University of Wisconsin–Madison, where he stayed until he returned to the East in 1967 to assume a named chair in the Department of Psychology at Brandeis University, where he was soon to serve as both dean of the graduate school and then dean of the faculty.

In 1972, Maher returned to Harvard as a professor of psychology, and he has remained there for the past 30 years. At Harvard he has served in numerous positions of leadership, including chairing the Department of Psychology twice, serving as dean of the Graduate School of Arts and Sciences, and even serving a 1-year tour of duty as acting chair of the Department of Linguistics. At Harvard, Maher has held an endowed chair—the Edward C. Henderson Professor of the Psychology of Personality—for 20 years, and he has been a continuous and critical influential force in the direction of the Harvard experimental psychopathology research and training group since 1972.

Many people know Maher through his influence as a teacher, and they can attest to his genuine concern for education and professional development in addition to scientific training. His concern for education, which extends well beyond the field of psychology, has most recently been in evidence through the comprehensive evaluation of doctoral programs across the nation that was completed in the mid-1990s. This major undertaking resulted in an already well-known compendium of information titled *Research-Doctorate Programs in the United States: Continuity and Change* (which Maher coedited with M. L. Goldberger and P. E. Flattau, 1995). Maher has mentored many students across his career, and a large proportion of those students, many of whom have contributed to this volume, have gone on to make distinguished contributions to experimental psychopathology and other areas of psychological science. In addition to his many contributions to the education of generations of students, at both the undergraduate and graduate levels, Maher has maintained long-term productive collaborative relationships. One of the most productive has been with Theo C. Manschreck of the Harvard Medical School. Maher and Manschreck, together, have probed deeply and carefully the various aspects of cognitive and motor anomalies in schizophrenia over a period of 25 years.

That Maher has made numerous substantial contributions to the study of psychopathology, principally schizophrenia, as well as to design and methodology, is abundantly evident. He has produced more than 200 publications, including 9 monographs or edited volumes, numerous journal articles, and many book chapters. However, Maher has not just contributed to the empirical study of psychopathology; he also can be viewed as a primary architect of the discipline of experimental psychopathology. Indeed, his classic 1966 monograph, *Principles of Psychopathology: An Experimental Approach*, is widely viewed in the field as the landmark publication that articulated the meaning and intentions of an experimental approach to the study of psychopathology. *Principles of Psychopathology*, reprinted numerous times and in multiple languages, is generally regarded as the seminal statement and vision that established experimental psychopathology as a recognized subdiscipline in psychological science.

In addition to his own scholarly contributions to the study of psychopathology, Maher has served important leadership roles in the field at the national and international levels. He has served on American Psychological Association (APA) task forces on research and training in clinical psychology as well as on the advisory board of the APA's Committee on Standards for Tests and Measures. He served as the editor of the *Journal of Consulting and Clinical Psychology* from 1973 to 1978. He was also the senior editor for *Progress in Experimental Personality Research* from 1964 to 1989. Maher is one of those scientists whose collective vision led to the formation of the leading scholarly society in psychopathology research, the Society for Research in Psychopathology. He served as the charter president of the society in 1986, guiding the newly founded organization through its first critical year. He received the esteemed Joseph Zubin Award for Distinguished Research in Psychopathology from the society in 1998.

It is difficult to summarize in a succinct manner Maher's specific scientific accomplishments and innovations and his impact. Indeed, a volume of his collected papers would have a better chance of success in conveying his range and depth of scientific contributions. Nonetheless, one can clearly see Maher's impact in at least four major areas within the scientific study of psychopathology. First, his work on the language disturbances in schizophrenia (and their quantitative analysis) is readily evident. Maher's (1972) article "The Language of Schizophrenia: A Review and Interpretation," which appeared in the *British Journal of Psychiatry*, remains a standard reference point for all studies of the language of schizophrenia. Second, Maher has devoted a considerable effort to the careful dissection of delusional processes and the formation of delusional beliefs. This work, which was begun in the early 1970s and continues to this day, has been described in numerous publications, including Maher's own chapter in this volume. Maher's (1988) account of delusional formations that follow on anomalous experiences provides one of the few accounts of the processes or mechanisms that both seeks to explain the emergence of delusional thoughts and is amenable to experimental research (see also Oltmanns & Maher, 1988).

Third, a consistent emphasis throughout nearly all of Maher's scholarly papers is the very palpable concern with moving the study of psychopathology, particularly schizophrenia, beyond the purely descriptive verbal–behavioral arena of study to rigorous quantitative assessments. In short, Maher has always suggested that it is better to count things rather than to rate or describe them. His work on motor behavior and laterality in relation to schizophrenia exemplifies this principle of psychopathology research, a principle that was stated clearly in *Principles of Psychopathology* (Maher, 1966). Fourth, Maher has maintained for nearly 50 years an ongoing intellectual passion, namely, the examination of problems of method and measurement in psychopathology research in general, including a concern for understanding the patient's experience.

A listing of Maher's major contributions and intellectual passions would be incomplete without mention of one other major scholarly interest. This great interest, which he has pursued with vigor in collaboration with his wife, Winifred Barbara Maher, is the exploration of historical contexts surrounding the scientific problem areas in psychopathology. Brendan and Barbara have published nine papers and chapters on the history of psychopathology. Both have felt that a knowledge of the history of previous attempts to answer questions still current in psychopathology is an essential part of the search for answers—for the Mahers, this has not just been a kind of decorative (and therefore dispensable) scholarly addition to contemporary empirical and theoretical research effort; it has also been a source of considerable intellectual enjoyment.

Finally, Maher—known clearly as a scientist and scholar of the first rank—is known also, most importantly, as a diplomat and sage citizen in the university environment, whose scope of vision, interpersonal sensitivity, and honesty are admired throughout the academic world of psychological science and beyond. The complexities and pitfalls of academic life are well known; however, the most effective, fair, and humane way to navigate those tempestuous waters is known by relatively few in the world of the university. Maher has been an able navigator in those complicated straits and has provided wise counsel to many at Harvard and beyond when a colleague, department chair, university administrator, or student found himself or herself in turbulent seas.

Brendan and Barbara Maher live in the Boston area and are the proud parents of five children as well as five grandchildren. Maher is currently the Edward C. Henderson Research Professor of the Psychology of Personality in the Department of Psychology at Harvard, where he continues to pursue his psychopathology research, mentor students, participate in the university community, and enrich the lives of those around him.

References

Goldberger, M. L., Maher, B. A., & Flattau, P. E. (Eds.). (1995). *Research-doctorate programs in the United States: Continuity and change*. Washington, DC: National Academy Press.

Maher, B. A. (1966). *Principles of psychopathology: An experimental approach*. New York: McGraw-Hill.

Maher, B. A. (Ed.). (1969). *Clinical psychology and personality: Selected papers of George Kelly*. New York: Wiley.

Maher, B. A. (1972). The language of schizophrenia: A review and interpretation. *British Journal of Psychiatry, 120*, 3–17.

Maher, B. A. (1988). Anomalous experience and delusional thinking. In T. F. Oltmanns & B. A. Maher (Eds.), *Delusional beliefs* (pp. 15–33). New York: Wiley.

Maher, B. A. (1996). *A passage to Sword Beach: Minesweeping in the Royal Navy*. Annapolis, MD: Naval Institute Press.

Oltmanns, T. F., & Maher, B. A. (1988). *Delusional beliefs*. New York: Wiley.

Principles of
Experimental
Psychopathology

Introduction

Mark F. Lenzenweger and Jill M. Hooley

The various forms of psychopathology—particularly the most severe conditions, such as schizophrenia and other psychoses—have been slow to yield their secrets to both researchers and clinicians alike. As is well known, the pioneers of this field (Emil Kraepelin, Eugen Bleuler, Karl Jaspers, and others) provided rich, carefully detailed descriptions of the conditions that many would study and treat in the ensuing 100 years. They offered some initial speculations regarding the fundamental nature of a given pathology and made preliminary theoretical conjectures regarding potential etiological factors. It was soon realized, however, that to fully probe psychopathology in an effort to make the various disorders divulge clues to their etiology and underlying pathophysiology, the study of psychopathology needed to move from a form of analysis that was primarily descriptive to the methods of the experimental laboratory. In the experimental laboratory one can use the methods of experimental psychology and allied disciplines to move beyond description, all the while benefiting from the power of the experimental method as applied to conditions assigned by nature, as it were. Despite the appeal of moving to the experimental laboratory in the quest to understand psychopathology, psychopathology researchers were faced with the harsh reality that the subject of concern was not the ubiquitous (and reasonably cooperative) white rat or the equally ubiquitous (and reasonably cooperative) college sophomore, both of whom have served the purposes of psychological science so dutifully. Psychopathology researchers seeking to use experimental methods needed to learn rather quickly that the complexities of the subject matter would always pose rather vexing challenges in the design of experiments. One needed to anticipate that matters of a methodological nature in the study of psychopathology would quickly rise to the surface in any scientific endeavor. In short, the *methods*, in many instances, would require nearly as much, if not more, consideration than substantive issues for the proper execution of a study. Nonetheless, as Maher (1966) noted, the fundamental methods needed to illuminate psychopathology were not somehow new or qualitatively different. Rather, as he suggested 35 years ago, one "may proceed effectively with those principles that have been worked out in the experimental laboratory (Maher, 1966, p. ix)." In these words, and through the influence of his classic volume *Principles of Psychopathology: An Experimental Approach* (Maher, 1966), the field of experimental psychopathology was established as a fruitful subdiscipline of psychological science.

Since 1966, spectacular advances have been made in researchers' and clinicians' understanding of cognition, emotion, neurobiology, genetics, and psychosocial processes. These advances have helped to deepen knowledge of the nature of psychopathology, the territory that remains to be traversed in the quest for a full understanding of etiology and pathogenesis, for any given disorder is expansive by any measure. With increasing sophistication, researchers can now gather glimpses of the functioning brain using the evolving methods of neuroimaging, better dissect complex multivariate data through the use of well-developed statistical procedures, and define more precisely the diagnostic entities they wish to study through the use of refined nomenclatures and assessment techniques. Nonetheless, despite the advances in various substantive areas that bear on an understanding of psychopathology, as well as the ever-increasing number of analytic tools at researchers' disposal, psychopathologists are always faced with a critically important question in pursuing any empirical study of psychopathology: "How does one conduct this study?" More to the point, what method is to be used in a given study, and how will the phenomenon of interest be measured? This volume, which represents a tribute to the seminal influence of Brendan A. Maher on the development of experimental psychopathology, is organized in the spirit of these issues: methods and measurement in an experimental approach to psychopathology. We believe that Maher's vision for a scientific, laboratory-based dissection of psychopathology has now guided several generations of scholars in experimental psychopathology, influencing not only students, of course, but also peers, contemporaries, and colleagues, both inside and outside of psychopathology research.

Following this brief introduction, this volume is divided into five parts. The first part is devoted to chapter 1, by Maher, in which he discusses the origins of his views on the formation of delusional thought as well as the methodological approach he has taken in the study of delusional beliefs. Embodied in this chapter are the various methodological principles that have guided Maher's work for nearly four decades, and he states these principles in a manner that is useful to all readers. The second part of this volume contains chapters in which a selection of scholars examine schizophrenia, one of the most devastating illnesses known to humankind (Lenzenweger & Dworkin, 1998), from a number of alternative methodological vantage points. In the first chapter in this section (chapter 2), Irving I. Gottesman and James L. Reilly explore the complicated and ever-changing landscape of the genetics of schizophrenia. They suggest a variety of dimensions that should be at the foreground of any discussion of genetic influences in schizophrenia, and they provide important suggestions as to how to evaluate the various forms of evidence that support the now well-established genetic component to this illness. In chapter 3, Theo C. Manschreck provides a detailed and compelling overview of the evidence, drawn from laboratory studies, that suggests a nontrivial role for motor dysfunction in the emergence and development of schizophrenia. Robert H. Dworkin and his colleagues continue this focus on neuromotor abnormalities in chapter 4 through a review of their laboratory work, which has drawn on both clinical and electromechanical measures of neuromotor abnormalities in schizophrenia patients as well as the offspring of schizophrenia-affected individuals. Dworkin et al. argue for the greater sensitivity of electromechanical measures relative to clinical ratings in identifying individuals with a vulnerability to develop schizophrenia. In chapter 5, Sohee Park and Junghee Lee describe in overview an elegant program of research aimed at the careful examination of spatial working memory; they discuss frontal-lobe dysfunction in schizophrenia, models of human working memory, neural correlates of working memory in animals, and the results of a series of laboratory investigations of spatial working memory in relation to schizophrenia. Moving from the within-individual level of analysis, Crystal R. Blyler provides in chapter 6 an overview of her current research in schizophrenia, which has focused on an evaluation of the effectiveness of various models of vocational support programs for helping individuals with severe mental disorders find and maintain employment, a life task that is inherently interpersonal in many instances. Overall, the chapters contained in Part II illustrate the multiple facets of schizophrenia that remain to be fully understood as well as the utility of rigorous empirical methods, often deriving from laboratory investigations, for probing this complex disorder.

Part III of the volume includes chapters that have a distinct methodological focus, and each of these chapters illustrates the methodological issue of interest within the context of schizophrenia research. Milton E. Strauss and Ann Summerfelt provide in chapter 7 a framework for the study of neuropsychological functions in schizophrenia as a blueprint for improving psychopathologists' understanding of brain–behavior relations in the disorder. Strauss and Summerfelt urge greater attention to issues of construct validity and generalized deficit and provide an argument for the use of experimental control of performance levels in the study of brain function. In chapter 8, Mark F. Lenzenweger and his colleagues detail the development of a vector of research that seeks to dissect somatosensory dysfunction in schizotypy and schizophrenia. Drawing on the rich clinical observations of multiple pioneers in schizophrenia research, these investigators describe a series of studies that has yielded a signal detection based assessment of exteroceptive sensitivity for use in laboratory studies. In chapter 9, Jill M. Hooley and Richard J. Chung examine the issue of pain insensitivity in the relatives of individuals with either schizophrenia or bipolar illness. They focus on pain thresholds and pain tolerances in their laboratory studies and point to a useful avenue for future research in schizophrenia.

Part IV of this volume consists of chapters that speak to a variety of more general methodological issues in psychopathology research. In chapter 10, Philip S. Holzman offers a perspective on reductivism in psychopathology research and how this approach may be used to parse complex behaviors and cognitions in the laboratory study of pathological processes. He uses his own extensive program of research on eye movement dysfunction as a template for this discussion, which has broader implications for all areas of psychopathology. The great utility of the psychophysiology research perspective is illustrated in the research studies on memory biases in depression discussed in chapter 11, authored by Patricia J. Deldin and her colleagues. These investigators emphasize the value in seeking physiologically based markers of cognitive processes, markers that transcend clinical signs and symptoms. Deborah A. Yurgelun-Todd and Staci A. Gruber provide in chapter 12 a useful overview of several state-of-the-art techniques in neuroimaging in relation to psychopathology research. They not only provide an exciting window on the ever-emerging and -developing neuroimaging approach, but they also provide a sobering assessment of the issues that could affect such research and lead investigators astray by producing potentially ambiguous findings. In chapter 13, Dara S. Manoach continues a focus on neuroimaging through a careful review of imaging research on working memory deficits in schizophrenia. Manoach urges readers to realize that the deficits observed in a complex process such as working memory are much more likely the result of a dysfunctional neural circuit rather than a pathology at a single site. Taken together, the chapters of Part IV are exemplary in their focus on technologically advanced methods of inquiry coupled with a temperate view of the limits of such approaches.

The chapters in Part V address issues related to temperament and cognition in experimental psychopathology and developmental psychological science. In chapter 14, Jerome Kagan offers a rich perspective on the function of semantic structures, schematic representation of experience, and the emergence of cognitive uncertainty. Kagan uses data from the many laboratory-based studies of highly reactive children he has conducted to illustrate his conceptual framework and specific hypotheses. In chapter 15, Don C. Fowles elucidates the power of investigations into electrodermal processes in conjunction with observed temperaments in children. He depicts the potential utility of this line of work through extension to a discussion of the behavioral inhibition system, with special reference to the development of psychopathy. Chapter 16, by Richard J. McNally, concludes this volume. McNally reveals the leverage to be gained through the use of laboratory-based investigations of memory processes in individuals reporting recovered memories of abusive events alleged to have happened in the past. The recovered memory controversy is indeed volatile, and the value of laboratory-based research to the memory processes at issue is well illustrated in the work of McNally and his colleagues and is indeed welcome.

Thirty-five years ago, Maher urged psychopathologists to bring psychopathology into the laboratory with the hope that the power of experimental methods, which had proven so useful in experimental psychology, might help researchers resolve more clearly a variety of fundamental processes in the study of mental illness. In so doing, his vision helped transform the manner in which psychopathology research was carried out. It continues to implicitly guide the manner in which experimental psychopathology research is conducted, regardless of one's specific focus. We believe the chapters in this volume celebrate the spirit and implementation of that seminal vision.

References

Lenzenweger, M. F., & Dworkin, R. H. (Eds.). (1998). *Origins and development of schizophrenia: Advances in experimental psychopathology.* Washington, DC: American Psychological Association.

Maher, B. A. (1966). *Principles of psychopathology: An experimental approach.* New York: McGraw-Hill.

Part I _____

Experimental Psychopathology of Delusions

1

Psychopathology and Delusions: Reflections on Methods and Models

Brendan A. Maher

During my first year of graduate study at The Ohio State University I was housed in a dormitory that consisted of a camp of wooden huts formerly used by the military. The accommodation was austere, and the walls were very thin. I had not been there many days when I became aware that the occupant of the next room had set his alarm clock to wake him up every 4 hours during the night. The bell would ring, muffled shuffling sounds would be heard, a door closed, and then silence. Awhile later the door would open again, more shuffling, and more silence.

The pattern was annoying. However, it was only after several nights of broken sleep that I finally chanced to meet my neighbor during the daylight hours. I inquired more or less politely as to the reason for these nocturnal episodes. He informed me that he was a doctoral student in astronomy and that his dissertation required that he make a radio-telescopic reading in the observatory every 4 hours for a period of a sidereal year. He apologized for the disruption. This was 1950, and there were no computers available, and he had no choice but to do what he was doing.

Over the years since then, this incident has come to mind many times. It left a permanent impression. It might be summed up as "Now I know why astronomers' predictions are precise and accurate while ours so often are not. They have the patience to take the pains that are necessary to get their measurements right. We don't." One of the consequences of this has been the development of the conviction that we have paid too little attention to the problems of the measurement of details, too little attention to the fine-grained analysis of the phenomena that we study, and been too ready to take group differences (or the lack of them) as a source of definitive answers to important questions.[1]

In this chapter I first consider some of the methodological problems that confront research pathologists. After that I examine the phenomena of delusions. I do so partly as an illustration of methodological principles that are crucial to the investigation of any form of psychopathology and partly because delusions present

---

[1]While I was serving as cochair of the National Research Council committee planning the 1995 survey of doctoral programs (Goldberger, Maher, & Flattau, 1995) a colleague (an astronomer) asked me to explain the meaning of a standard score, saying that he had never heard of it before. I explained it, and a look of benevolent understanding crossed his face: "Oh, I see. It's a statistical concept. We don't use statistics much in astronomy." He was, perhaps, exaggerating a little, but I suspect not.

special difficulties to research investigators, but most of all because delusions have long been regarded as the core feature of madness.

Critical Methodological Issues

For the most part, research into psychopathology begins with patients who already present manifest anomalies of behavior sufficient to lead them to seek professional help or to lead others to induce them to do so. In trying to reconstruct the origin and development of the present pathology, we are faced with difficulties. If we turn to relatives for information about the premorbid behavior of the future patient we encounter serious problems. Veridical recall of the past behavior of others is unreliable even when the recall is unaffected by any dramatic later development in the life of the person whose behavior is being described. This problem becomes significantly more severe when memory is selectively influenced by the knowledge that the individual is currently displaying manifest psychopathology.

Furthermore, the timing and unfolding sequence of the appearance of the various elements of the manifest pathology (even if described accurately) do not necessarily correspond to the sequential timing of the underlying pathological processes themselves. Causes do not always become apparent before their consequences do. People often die from heart disease without any prior symptoms, the underlying pathology becoming evident only after the final fatal fact. The preferred solution to this problem—namely, the premorbid investigation of populations believed to be at some high risk of later pathology—is complex and difficult. It requires very shrewd ideas about the kinds of precursor variables that should be examined premorbidly and, of course, requires good epidemiological bases for the selection of high-risk participants. Given that in schizophrenia, for example, there is a predicted morbidity of approximately 16% for the offspring of mothers known to have schizophrenia, the base sample necessary to ensure the emergence of an adequately large sample of future actual patients is prohibitively large and correspondingly expensive. Prospective longitudinal studies using a variety of strategies now exist in some number (e.g., Cornblatt, Obuchowski, Andreasen, & Smith, 1998; Erlenmeyer-Kimling et al., 1998; Walker, Baum, & Diforio, 1998). We may expect that the outcomes of these studies will change conceptions of the schizophrenias in important ways.

Adaptive Atypical Behavior and the Default Hypothesis

Patterns of atypical behavior that elicit the diagnosis of psychopathology are generally an amalgam of primary pathological factors plus behavior that has arisen adaptively to cope with the distresses that the primary pathology produces. To these are added behavior that has arisen as a result of the diagnosis and hospitalization and the reaction of others to all of this. The peculiar limping walk of a person with a sprained ankle is an adaptive response that serves to reduce the pain that arises when walking normally. Some withdrawn patients with schizophrenia may be withdrawn because they are seeking escape from the intolerable stresses of a noisy environment in which impaired attentional focusing has made organized behavior impossible and not because they have a primarily pathology of "withdrawal." Patients with paranoia who regard other people with suspicion may do so, at least in part, because other people were responsible for their incarceration, and they have now learned to trust no one.

The heart of this analysis lies in the question "What would I do if I were experiencing the conscious phenomena that this patient is facing? In fact, what do I do when surrounded by intense environmental input that I cannot terminate at will, noise that prompts me to say 'I can't hear myself think in here. I must find somewhere quiet to get away from it.'" Like the patient, I withdraw.

Primary and reactive components of the clinical picture unfortunately do not come labeled as such. However, a strategy for discriminating between them might be based on two initial methodological principles. The first is to adopt a "default hypothesis" that some at least of what the patient is doing is reacting normally to an environment experienced in ways that differ substantially from the experience of the observer. Applying this to delusions, Reed (1974) put it this way:

> Given the necessary information, the observer can empathize with the subject; if he himself were to have such an unusual experience he would express beliefs about it which would be just as unusual as those of the subject. . . . [Delusions] can occur in anybody who experiences disturbing phenomena, while retaining the ability to think clearly enough to be able to devise explanations of those phenomena. (Reed, 1974, p. 154)

One might extend this to suggest that *a first strategy toward understanding instances of pathological behavior might be to assume that the behavior is adaptive to something that has not yet been identified and that one way to find out what that might be is to ask the patients why they are doing what they are doing.* This would be the default hypothesis.

It will help to remember that there are instances in the research literature in which patients who were presumed to have a deficit that impairs reality contact showed a more accurate contact than did normal control individuals. A good example is the case of *depressive realism*, the superior perception of reality by patients with depression (e.g., Dykman, Horowitz, Abramson, & Usher, 1991; Layne, 1986; Lobitz & Post, 1979). Another is the greater accuracy of patients with paranoid schizophrenia in detecting the affect in genuine, nonposed photographs of people but reduced accuracy in the case of artificially posed photographs (Davis & Gibson, 2000; LaRusso, 1978). The second part of these findings may, of course, reflect not so much an inability to interpret facial expressions but a superior sensitivity to the artificiality of the expression in posed photographs. It would be interesting to know what the actual emotions of the people portraying the posed emotion were; perhaps the paranoid patients' "errors" were correct estimates of the actual emotions felt by the posing individuals.

A third example comes from studies of reasoning in deluded and nondeluded patients. In the often-cited study of Huq, Garety, and Hemsley (1988), patients with delusions required less information to reach correct conclusions in a probability inference task than did control patients. Their implicit probability level was the same as that found in most research studies (i.e., below .05). In spite of the finding that in this task the patients with delusions were better reasoners than were control patients, Huq et al. rejected their own finding. They concluded instead that "although the deluded sample's response . . . appears more 'Bayesian' . . . it is not possible to argue that deluded people are better reasoners" (Huq et al., 1988, p. 810). Subsequent studies (e.g., Garety & Hemsley, 1994) replicated Huq et al.'s general finding, with the added observation that the hypotheses of the patients with delusions were more subject to modification in the face of counterevidence than was the case with control patients. Putting both studies together, it appears that patients with delusions were both superior in a reasoning task and more responsive to counterevidence than were those in normal control comparison groups. Perhaps a more plausible conclusion is that this kind of experimental approach has limited ecological validity when applied to the clinical phenomena of delusions.

Studies such as these remind us that we generally expect that diagnosed patients are likely to perform worse than control individuals in almost any task and are highly unlikely to perform better. On the other hand, if we begin with the default hypothesis that patients are human beings trying to adapt to very unusual circumstances, we will be less surprised to find that the process of adaptation sometimes results in the acquisition of superior performance.

A second methodological principle is that *close fine-grained examination of the components of the clinical picture will reveal differences between a specific kind of behavior when it is the primary pathology and when the same behavior is a secondary reaction*. In effect, this implies that a general category, such as social withdrawal, is likely to be heterogeneous in the range of behavior that it encompasses and will include some patients for whom the presence of other people is basically aversive and others for whom it is not aversive, but the noise of several people talking at the same time is. Careful analysis of the detailed characteristics of the withdrawal and the exact circumstances in which it appears is likely to reveal differences in detail between the two cases.

One of the tasks of the experimental psychopathologist is to sort out the subcategories by improved methods of measuring behavior and by the identification of the environmental features that produce one or the other kind of response. The capacity to do this is determined in large part by the power of the method of measurement to detect small differences. Continuous ratio scale measures are likely to be much more sensitive than rating scales to small but crucial differences and should be preferred wherever they are available. Where they are not available, it is part of the task of the experimental psychopathologist to develop them.

Heterogeneity

Implicit in these admonitions is the recognition that any specific pattern of human behavior is likely to be heterogeneous, that is, it may arise from several causes. For example, a sequence of disorganized verbal utterances may arise as an unavoidable consequence of particular kinds of neuropathology, as an episodic consequence of the disruptive effect of strong emotion (or a strong drink), as an avoidance response intended to deter others from social contact, and so on. The belief that one is being plagued by microwave transmissions may arise as a delusional explanation of strange experiences or as a veridical description of an uncommon but real event. There is no need to extend this discussion with additional examples; the important point is that much research into psychopathology necessarily begins with the observation of manifest behavior, with consequences and not with causes. To the extent that we hope to establish the etiology of a particular syndrome, we are therefore faced with the always-dubious task of arguing backward from consequences to causes. This is a problem, and it requires solutions.

We may approach the solution with certain assumptions, almost equivalent to scientific "acts of faith." One of these is that although different etiologies may produce similar manifest pathologies at the gross categorical level, the similarity is likely to be somewhat superficial, and detailed analysis of the pathology will likely reveal fine differences missed at the grosser level.

An example of an attempt to do this can be seen in work by me and my colleagues (Maher, Manschreck, Hoover, & Weisstein, 1987). We examined in detail the characteristics of the actual language utterances of patients who had been classified by rating as demonstrating Derailment, deficient Understandability, deficient Logic, and Poverty of Content, as assessed in the Schedule for Affective Disorders and Schizophrenia (SADS; Spitzer & Endicott, 1977). We found that the counted repetitions of words and phrases (a ratio scale measure) in samples of speech from patients with schizophrenia obtained at a different time correlated significantly with the rated levels of each of the rated variables in the SADS. What the patients were not doing was showing a "richness of content"; what the patients were doing, at least in part, was repeating and perseverating in speech. This observation directs us to search for the positive determinants of repetition and perseveration. The question "What factors lead to repetitiousness?" is a more definable research problem than the question "Where did the content go?"

Distinctions between superficially similar manifest phenomena require the kind of fine-grained microanalysis of differences in detail that have been found to be essential in scientific classification across other disciplines. Whenever we can detect these detailed differences within a single gross category and relate them to differences in the specific etiologies that underlie them, we will have succeeded in reducing the constraints that multiple causation has created.

One of the main obstacles to this kind of analysis is that it is a tedious drudgery, as indeed is much measurement in science when it is necessary to take many observations and to submit each observation to a detailed metric. My dormitory neighbor in astronomy knew that, and Ivan Pavlov emphasized it at the close of his life. To the aspiring scientist he said

> *Firstly*, gradualness. About this most important condition of fruitful scientific work, I never can speak without emotion. Gradualness, gradualness and gradualness. From the very beginning of your work, school yourselves to severe gradualness in the accumulation of knowledge.
>
> Learn the ABC of science before you try to ascend to its summit. Never begin the subsequent without mastering the preceding. Never attempt to screen an insufficiency of knowledge even by the most audacious surmise and hypothesis. . . . School yourselves to demureness and patience. Learn to inure yourselves to drudgery in science. Learn, compare, collect the facts.
>
> (Pavlov, 1935, cited in Curtis & Greenslet, 1962, p. 98)

This advice could well be applied to our own approaches. We have too often preferred the simpler technique of rating behavior along gross dimensions, trusting clinical judgment to provide the separation of magnitudes that could be obtained more laboriously, but more accurately, by counting. In so doing we have laid a self-imposed limit on the possibility of finding important discoveries that require more sensitive methods of detection. The methodological principle here is *Wherever possible, use a ratio scale method in preference to a rating scale. If a ratio scale does not exist, consider what is necessary to develop one.*

Primary Heterogeneity and Secondary Homogeneity

Certain forms of deviant behavior are found in connection with a wide variety of etiologies, the validity of which has been established independently. An outstanding example is to be found in the case of delusions. Delusions have been reported in connection with more than 70 disorders (Manschreck, 1979). This fact alone argues that they are clearly most likely to be secondary consequences of quite different basic pathologies. Their presence in connection with other symptoms, such as ambivalence, looseness of association, and autism, is likely to sustain a diagnosis of schizophrenia, but it is clear that the delusion *per se* is not pathognomonic for any specific disorder. Although, like hallucination, delusion is one of the most common symptoms seen in patients bearing the diagnosis of schizophrenia, it is unlikely that its presence or absence will provide a clue to the pathology of any particular subtype of schizophrenia. Note that it is quite possible that a detailed analysis of typological differences within the corpus of schizophrenic delusions will provide such clues, but mere presence or absence of a delusion will not. By the same token, the search for a single general genetic marker for schizophrenia (or any other heterogeneous disorder) seems likely to be disappointing (see, e.g., Gottesman & Moldin, 1998) and likely to discover, at best, an index of a secondary process that can be initiated by the different pathologies of each of several genotypes.

This issue creates a paradox: *Those behavioral features that distinguish most completely between members of one general diagnostic group and members of some other groups, including normal controls, are least likely to lead us to the components of the fundamental spectrum of pathologies that underlie the heterogeneity of that general diagnostic group.*

The Ambiguous Legacy of Francis Galton

Of the many contributions to psychology for which Francis Galton is known was his promotion of the Gaussian (or bell-shaped) distribution as evidence of the intentions of nature. A keystone in Galtonian eugenics was the notion that the mean of a distribution gave us an indication of what nature had intended to be the ideal value for a group whose scores were spread around it in a symmetrical distribution.[2] Actual cases falling on either side of the mean were "error." Galton was referring not to errors of measurement but to errors of development, to people whom he regarded

---

[2]In this spirit, Galton once attempted to make a composite photograph of the faces of "lunatics" at a London psychiatric hospital, hoping to discover the prototypical physiognomy of people with mental illnesses. The attempt was terminated when the patients became uncooperative.

as deviating from "nature's ideal" much as imperfect products rejected by quality control inspectors are relegated to the category of "seconds" to be devalued down to bargain prices or, if too defective, to be destroyed.

This had been expressly stated by Quételet, as cited by Galton (1892), who stated that it was "as if they were errors of Nature in her attempt to mould individual men of the same race according to some ideal pattern" (p. 28). The idea, then, was that all deviations from the mean value for any human variable, such as height, weight, chest size, and "intelligence," were essentially errors of nature. If one wishes to know nature's true intentions, one should look at the means.

Galton embraced this interpretation literally. He discussed it at some length in the introduction to *Hereditary Genius* (Galton, 1892), citing data provided by Quételet on the height of 100,000 conscripts into the French army. Inspection ironically revealed that the data were not symmetrical, there being a very much larger number of men at the lower end of the scale than at the corresponding upper end. As this contradicted Galton's assumption that the normal curve was a law of nature, he concluded that some proportion of men in the lower range were really taller than reported but had fraudulently managed to get themselves mismeasured so as to avoid military service. In short, as some of the actual data did not fit the theory, Galton invented a reason to reject them while retaining the data that did fit the theory. Intrinsic to all of this was the assumption that what defined the boundaries of any one of nature's groups was intuitively obvious to the observer. Galton's "natural" groups, for example, included "criminals," "the insane," and officers of the Royal Engineers of the British Army, among others.

Apart from the serious defects in Galton's assumptions, they encourage us to focus primarily on mean values and to ignore the realities of heterogeneity in groups of actual human beings classified together within the gross categories of diagnostic system. These differences are tacitly ignored as reflecting an expected range of "error variance" and as being sufficiently described by reporting the standard deviation. There is no compulsion to examine the data in detail.

Many phenomena, of course, are not distributed in Gaussian fashion. The distribution of earthquakes, floods, and other natural disasters does not follow a bell-shaped curve. If we accept Quételet's actual data, height is not exactly normally distributed. Income is not normally distributed, neither are accident proneness, voting preferences, life expectancy, reaction times, lateral preference, and many other variables.[3]

Reflection on this gives rise to the following methodological principle: *Varance is not "error." Always look at all of the data in numerical and scattergram form before deciding how to analyze it and what it means. Pay particular attention to the cases that fall in the "wrong" corner of the chi-square or depart most visibly from the regression line in a correlation. These are hints of heterogeneity and the possible source of new hypotheses.*

---

[3]In 1998, I examined an entire year's issues of *Science* in search of published normal distributions in the biological sciences. I found none but did find many examples of skewed distributions. It seems clear that the Gaussian curve is not defensible as the presumed default distribution of attributes of natural phenomena.

With these principles in mind, I now turn to the major questions surrounding the psychopathology of delusions.

Delusions

The Problem of Definition

The first set of problems centers on the definition of *delusion*. There are many minor variants in different definitions, but they generally have in common certain elements. These are that *delusion* is a term to be applied to "false beliefs" arising from a defect of inference; delusions are held by the patient in the face of "evidence sufficient to refute them," and they are not held by a number of other members of the culture in which the patient is found. Some definitions have added in other criteria, such as the degree to which the patient is preoccupied with the belief and behaves in ways that are determined by the belief.

It is important to look at the applicability of the definition to the real-world circumstances in which beliefs are formed or abandoned and in which delusions are actually diagnosed.

Falsity

Turning to the first criterion, that of falsity, we encounter the fact that many beliefs regarded as delusional are, strictly speaking, not amenable to being falsified. For example, the belief that one is being spied on can be falsified only by demonstrating a negative, namely, that the individual is not being spied on in any way by anyone. Such a demonstration is in practice impossible to achieve. Instead, one might want to argue that the belief is extremely improbable and that the evidence adduced by the believer is insufficient to justify the belief. However, this means that the issue has become a matter of opinion and not of incontrovertible fact.

At this point we have passed from applying a fixed objective criterion to making a judgment. In daily life the question of how much evidence justifies a belief on which one might act is generally dependent on the real-world consequences of rejecting a true conclusion or accepting a false one. The practical consequences of making a Type I or a Type II error play a central role. If the false belief is that oneself is being threatened, then the costs of avoiding a nonexistent threat may be very much less than the costs of ignoring a real threat, and one may be well advised to take avoidant action. Knowledge of the general base-rate probability that the chances that the threat is real are very low may play an insignificant part in the judgment. In short, the p value that warrants accepting or rejecting a belief depends on a real-world cost–benefit factor, not on a table of conventional levels of statistical significance.

Some delusions, of course—notably those described as bizarre—appear to be self-refuting, as, for example, the delusion that one is already dead or that some body part has turned into a foreign substance ("My heart has turned into lead"). I discuss later the question of how such a belief can develop and be maintained.

Other delusions are not self-refuting but are by definition impossible to falsify. The belief that one has lived one or more previous lives is resistant to practical test and does not fit easily into the categories of true or false. It belongs instead in the

Popperian category of nonfalsifiable propositions (Popper, 1979) and therefore is, in a scientific sense, meaningless.

Counterevidence

What constitutes "evidence"? Personal primary experience is an irrefutable source of evidence. Consider the case of the phantom limb. If a patient whose leg has been amputated feels pain in the missing leg, no amount of cognitive restructuring can remove the actual experience of pain or the localization of the pain in the missing leg. It might convince the patient that, logically speaking, the pain cannot be originating from the leg, and this can open the way for the patient to understand the objective explanation of the actual origin of the pain. However, until the experience of the pain finally disappears, the quality of the experience remains unchanged. For the naive external observer, the patient's description of the pain is incorrect and, in that respect, irrational. How can one really experience pain in a leg that is not there? From this it is a short step to conclude that if the patient cannot be experiencing pain in the leg then the patient is not really experiencing pain in the leg. For the patient to believe such a thing, in spite of its blatant illogicality, looks like evidence that there is something wrong with the patient's inferential processes. The point of this example is that what constitutes primary firsthand evidence for the patient is not the same as the evidence available to the observer. The kind of evidence brought to refute the patient's belief—namely, that the patient cannot be experiencing pain in the nonexistent leg—is necessarily much less persuasive to the patient than the fact that he or she is experiencing it.

Because the neurophysiological basis of the phenomenon of the phantom-limb experience is reasonably well understood, the trained clinician has an explanation to offer that does not deny the quality of the experience but explains it as "normal" under the circumstances. The patient's reasoning is not regarded as deviant; the pain can be controlled by analgesics and will ultimately vanish. The question of delusional thinking does not arise. It does not arise because the clinician accepts the patient's description of the experience but puts it into a valid biomedical context. Now the patient has an explanation of the pain that does not demand denying the quality of the experience.

When a patient presents a belief based on an unusual personal experience that currently has no adequate biomedical explanation, the observer—clinician or otherwise—has no valid counterexplanation to offer. The temptation to focus on the patient's inferential processes is the main alternative strategy. This brings us to the next component of the definition.

Defective Inference

The phrase *arising from a defect of inference* suggests strongly that the "defect of inference" has a causative role in producing the subsequent delusion. One may reasonably assume that the phrase is not circular and redundant, that is, that it does not mean that because the delusion is a false belief, and any false belief is ipso facto evidence of faulty inference, the simple presence of the delusion is sufficient evidence of a defective reasoning process. Instead, the implication is that the patient has a defect of the inferential processes that can be demonstrated independently of the delusional topic. In other words, the patient has a fundamental cognitive defect.

Methodological requirements for demonstrating a defect of inference in a group of patients diagnosed as delusional have been proposed as follows (Maher, 1992b): (a) The defect of reasoning must be demonstrated in some range of topics that are not direct derivatives of the delusional belief. For example, it would be insufficient to establish a basic defect by showing that a patient who believes that he or she is being spied on by powerful agencies believes that it is probable that more people are also being spied on than is generally believed. (b) The defects must be different from, or more pronounced than, those found in samples of patients without delusions and the normal population. In this latter connection the mere demonstration that patients with delusions make errors of formal logic or of Bayesian (statistical–probabilistic) inference is unhelpful without comparison with the error types and frequencies found in control groups. The proper standard of comparison is not a textbook of logic or a textbook of statistical procedures; it is the actual, frequently faulty, reasoning found in the general population. (c) The defect demonstrated must be one that leads to erroneous conclusions. If the "defect" is such that the patient with delusions reaches correct conclusions as frequently as, but sooner than, controls do, there is no compelling reason to believe that this characteristic is responsible for the development of false beliefs.

Studies of reasoning in patients with delusions necessarily begin with patients who are already expressing delusional beliefs sufficient to bring them to the notice of clinicians. As far as can be ascertained, there are no published prospective studies of the premorbid reasoning of individuals who later developed delusions. Measures of syllogistic or of Bayesian reasoning do not appear to have been included in high-risk studies of schizophrenia, for example. As a consequence, studies that have been reported have been compelled to rely on correlational strategies. This leaves open the question of whether atypical cognitive processes (if found) in the patient with delusions antedate and create the later delusional belief or whether the set of events that occur after the delusional belief has been developed and been diagnosed have disruptive effects on cognitive processes.

It seems particularly important to consider the difficulties surrounding the abandonment of a publicly stated belief the assertion of which has cost the believer many unpleasant consequences in his or her life. One cost, of course, is the inevitable tacit admission that one was mad to have believed such a thing. Another is that the many other consequences, such as loss of employment and social rejection by friends and family, may not easily be restored by a simple renunciation of the belief. When we consider that it is not unknown for scientists and scholars to fabricate evidence, and suppress actual evidence, in order to maintain a hypothesis with which they have become closely identified, it may seem less surprising that other mortals might defend their delusions with similar dedication.

The Irrelevance of Formal Rationality in the Real World

The development of what we tem the *scientific method* represents a distinct and crucial departure from normative patterns of inference. Cognitive processes evolved in the same way that other processes have evolved, namely, along lines that improved the chances of survival. I expressed this principle elsewhere as follows:

Illogical thinking is not selected against unless it leads to maladaptive behavior. Maladaptive behavior is always selected against regardless of the conformity to the rule of thinking that led to it. The burglar who commits the fallacy that goes: "Policemen wear blue uniforms; that man coming down the street is wearing a blue uniform; therefore he is a policeman and I should get away" will spend fewer years in prison than the one who thinks only according to the formal rules of syllogistic deduction, and whose behavior is thus influenced by the possibility that the man might be a fireman, a naval officer, an airline pilot or any other of the host of people who wear blue uniforms. (Maher, 1990, pp. 75–76)

The same general principle is true of normative Bayesian reasoning. Adaptive behavior is adaptive in a specific environment. Scientific observation is usually aimed at making generalizations of relevance to a broad spectrum of environments, and for this reason scientists are understandably critical of conclusions based on small samples. In the real world of the individual, experience is limited to small samples, and it is to these small samples that individuals must adapt. For an individual who has been held up and robbed at gunpoint in a city to which he has just moved, the fact that the citywide probability that it will ever happen to anybody is 0.01% is irrelevant. For the victim, the experienced probability is 100%, and it is this probability that will affect his future behavior. Avoidant self-protective behaviors of various kinds are likely to appear even though, rationally considered, they will seem to others to be phobic and unnecessary. The victim may well understand and recite what the objective probabilities are, but his behavior is likely to reflect his experience and not somebody else's calculations.

A patient with schizophrenia who has been engaged in an ongoing account of his experiences to me recently provided a good example of the primacy of direct experience over cognitive structuring of the experience. The patient had frequent auditory hallucinations that had been woven into a delusional scheme, involving transmissions from powerful others intent on controlling his behavior. During one meeting in which the patient was being continually interrupted by auditory hallucinations, I asked him where the voice was coming from. He pointed to a location a few feet above and behind his head. I asked him to stand up and to turn 90 degrees to his right. He did so. I then asked him where the voices were now, and he indicated a new location, still a few feet above and still behind his head. I said nothing more about it, and we resumed our discussion. At the next meeting he began by saying, "The voice must have been inside my head. When I turned, it turned with me, so it must be somewhere in my head."

This created an opportunity to discuss his previous delusional interpretation, and he spontaneously offered the conclusion that he must have been mistaken. The voices must, in some way, emanate from his own brain. My satisfaction at this turn of events disappeared not long afterward, when he remarked "I know that it seems that they must be inside my head, but they don't sound like anything inside my head; they sound like voices that are clearly outside my head." The quality of the auditory experience was more convincing than conclusions arrived at by reasoning. His experience had refuted his own reasoning. It has remained that way for the rest of our many discussions.

The central implication of all this is that the reason why evidence presented by others to refute the delusion is not sufficient to do so may well be that the patient has a different and more compelling kind of evidence to support it, unavailable to direct observation by others, namely, firsthand personal conscious experience. Even the patient's own insight into the irrationality of his or her beliefs may not be sufficient to refute them.

Resistance to Counterevidence in Individuals Without Delusions

An important implication of the definition is that individuals without delusions do change their beliefs quite readily when presented with evidence sufficient to refute them. Experience with the reaction of those holding a particular scientific hypothesis to evidence that contradicts it suggests that rarely do investigators conduct research motivated to disprove their own hypotheses. This fortunately is not fatal to the progress of science, as there will be many other investigators motivated to defend their own hypotheses by disproving rival alternatives.

The literature on reasoning indicates that this is also the case in most individuals. Wason and Johnson-Laird (1972) reported the existence of a "confirmation bias" in the scrutiny of evidence relevant to the individual's beliefs. Evidence favorable to the belief is noticed and used. Unfavorable evidence is either ignored, dismissed as inadequate, or reinterpreted post hoc in ways that make it appear to be confirmative. Similar findings have been reported by Einhorn and Hogarth (1978); Lord, Lepper, and Ross (1979); and Ross and Anderson (1982).

Whether the dismissal is of counterevidence of such substance that it would effectively falsify the hypothesis or is of evidence that merely reduces without eliminating the probability that it is correct is unclear. Incidentally, the work of Garety and Hemsley (1994), mentioned earlier, demonstrated that in a comparative study of individuals with and without delusions, the control individuals were more resistant to the effects of counterevidence than were the individuals with delusions. In short, the question of whether delusional beliefs are more incorrigible than normal beliefs is far from resolved. The beliefs of both groups of individuals do not appear to be very different with respect to their modification by counterevidence; what difference there is seems to point to greater incorrigibility in individuals without delusions.

The Anomalous-Experience Hypothesis

Thirty years ago I offered an alternative hypothesis (Maher, 1970): that delusions are not generally a consequence of a primary reasoning defect that impairs the comprehension of normal experience. They are, instead, a consequence of personal experiences of an anomalous nature; thus, if we are to understand delusions we must first focus on the patients' experiences rather than on their inferential processes. Extended versions of the original article were published later (Maher, 1974a, 1974b).

An observation made in the Laboratory of Psychology at the University of Copenhagen provided the stimulus to the hypothesis that began to form. A young researcher, Tosten Ingemar Nielsen, was conducting a study of what he described as the "threshold of free will." The question he had in mind was to define the point at which the magnitude of the discrepancy between an intended motor movement and the movement as actually executed would lead the participant to explain the discrepancy in terms that did not refer to his or her own "error." By a complex arrangement of the apparatus (see Nielsen, 1963), on certain trials the experimenter could cause an artificial hand to move in synchrony with the actual movement. The participant's hand was hidden from view, and the artificial hand was projected visually to the correct location. From time to time, the participants received conflicting information about their own movement, the visual input being discrepant with the kinesthetic input from their own hand. Nielsen was interested in the magnitude of the discrepancy at which the participants' explanations began to invoke something other than their own error.

The participants, adult Danes with no history of psychiatric disorder, gave explanations including the following:

> It seems my hand was moved by magnetism or electricity.
>
> My hand took over, and my mind was not able to control it.
>
> I looked to see if there were any electrodes on my hand, but I could not see any; they were there, but I was deceived about them.
>
> My hand was controlled by an outside physical force—I don't know what it was, but I could feel it. (T. I. Nielsen, personal communication, February 1967)

Out of 28 participants, only 2 hypothesized the existence of an artificial hand. Many of the participants stated that they could feel their own hand being moved against their will.

Scrutiny of these explanations produced an immediate insight that their content was remarkably similar to those found in delusions of control. An anomalous experience produced explanations that referred to invisible and mostly unidentified external forces. This anomalous experience was brief and occurred against a background of no prior history of strikingly unusual experiences. Neither was there any basis for suspecting that the participants had any abnormal reasoning defect. The default hypothesis applied very clearly; these were normal individuals responding adaptively to a seemingly inexplicable experience—namely, they were trying to explain it.

As is so often the case with ideas that seemed new at the time, the anomalous-experience hypothesis has a prior history. Much credit goes to E. E. Southard, who published a series of case studies of delusions during the period 1912–1916 in which the biopathological origin of the patients' anomalous experiences was established. Unfortunately for the patients, this vindication of their descriptions of their experiences did not generally occur until autopsy revealed the truth. Southard's approach is well exemplified in one of his many articles (Southard, 1916) on the role of the patient's experience in the genesis of delusions.

I have worked to develop the implications of this view over a period of 30 years (Maher, 1970, 1974a, 1974b, 1988a, 1988b, 1988c, 1990, 1991a, 1991b, 1992a, 1992b, 1999, 2001; Maher & Ross, 1983; Maher & Spitzer, 1992). Over that period, the study of anomalous experience has gradually expanded (e.g., Cardeña, Lynn, & Krippner, 2000; Reed, 1974; Zimbardo, 1999). At the same time, the concept of anomalous experience has undergone both refinement and expansion. At this point it might be helpful to discuss the assumptions that underlie the concept and the criteria that define it.

There are two basic assumptions. One is that the vivid directness of personal experience cannot be refuted by cognitive processes; cognitive processes may serve to reduce the tension that such experiences would otherwise create, but they do not and cannot alter the actual experience. The second is that conscious experience of all kinds is accompanied by, and dependent on, neural activity. Although this neural activity is normally a consequence of external input (external, in this case, includes input from bodily states), it can be created by direct activation of the neural substrate itself. Direct activation can rise from neuropathology, whether structural, neurochemical, or from other sources. Experience produced in this way is not necessarily distinguishable from the same kind of experience arising from external stimulation.

The sequence of activities that arise following an anomalous experience will be much the same regardless of the origin of that experience. These include a state of increased arousal (often experienced as anxiety or general tension) and a search for the external source of the experience, accompanied by the development of hypotheses about the probable sources. When and if the source is accurately located, there is a reduction in arousal with resulting feelings of relief. If the identification of the source is incorrect, the arousal state is partially but not completely reduced, and the search for confirmatory evidence of its correctness may continue. Challenges to the erroneous identification exacerbate the state of arousal. If the anomalous experience is brief and is neither continuous nor repeated, it may be left unexplained or interpreted as strange but of no great importance. For example, sounds heard at night that might be made by somebody trying to break in will prompt a search to check if this is the case. If nothing is found, and the sounds do not occur again, the incident is dismissed as noises coming perhaps from the central heating unit, or an animal prowling around outside, and so on. We see an interesting example of this process in the memoirs of Daniel Schreber (the case on which Freud based his theory of paranoid delusions). If one undertakes a fine-grained analysis of what Schreber himself said about his illness, one notices a number of items that are omitted in Freud's summary of the case. Schreber described the beginning of his mental illness as follows:

> It was then that an extraordinary event occurred. During several nights when I could not get to sleep, a recurrent crackling noise in the wall of our bedroom became noticeable at shorter or longer intervals; time and time again it woke me as I was about to go to sleep. Naturally we [himself and his wife] thought of a mouse although it was very extraordinary that a mouse should have found its way to the first floor of such a solidly built house. But having heard similar noises innumerable times since then, and still hearing them around me every day in day time and at night I have come to recognize them as . . . interferences. (Schreber, 1903/1988, p. 64)

Schreber went on to conclude that the explanation of the noises might then lie in their consequences. Because Schreber had been experiencing insomnia for some time, and the effect of the noises had been to interrupt his sleep, then perhaps the purpose of the noise was to disrupt his sleep. Now the search had changed from the unsuccessful hunt for the exact physical origin of the noises themselves to the identification of who might have an interest in disrupting his sleep and what his or her purpose might be. From this stage onward, Schreber proceeded to develop a complex delusion, which became the focus of Freud's interest. Schreber's personal history was to influence the content of the delusion, especially the views of his father, who was a well-known advocate of stern methods in the rearing of children.

Schreber was at first puzzled by the noises and offered a possible hypothesis, namely that it might be the noise of mice, a hypothesis that his wife considered plausible even though she did not hear the sounds. They doubted, however, that mice were the cause, because of the way the wall was built, and Schreber rejected the hypothesis when the noise became continual and frequent in the daytime and the nighttime, that is, when it was no longer consistent with the mouse hypothesis. He then turned to a different explanatory strategy, deducing causes from effects, and was on the way to developing a delusional scheme. We do not know what the noises were. They could have been minor background noise being heard by an individual whose capacity to inhibit background noises was pathologically defective. They could have been the concomitant of internal neural activity, possibly in the temporal area. Whatever their origin, it seems that Schreber sought out normal external explanations for them, and failing to find such explanations and continuing to hear the noises, he turned to an explanation that would be diagnosed as delusional.

The core element of anomalous experiences is that they involve a disruption of expectations that normally follow from the immediately prior experience. Expectations about sequential probabilities arise on the basis of past learning about the environment in which the individual lives. In parts of the world in which earthquakes are common, the experience that a building has begun to vibrate is less anomalous than it would be in a place where earthquakes have never happened before. Put another way, an anomalous experience might be defined as one that has a very low probability—even a zero probability—of occurrence in the circumstances in which it is experienced. The kinds of experience that appear in connection with delusions are quite varied. Some of the most common types are listed here. The list is not intended to be exhaustive.

- Sensory anomalies arising in connection with undiagnosed sensory defect in the peripheral sensory organ (see, e.g., Cooper, 1976; Cooper & Curry, 1976; Cooper & Porter, 1976).
- Sensory anomalies attributable to biopathology in the central nervous system, while the peripheral organs are intact. These include accentuated visual and auditory "vividness," changes in depth perception, loss of the perceptual constancies, and so on. The relevant biopathology may be associated with defects in attentional mechanisms, such as the inability to inhibit irrelevant input when responding to a limited aspect of the environment (e.g., MacDonald, 1960; McGhie & Chapman, 1961).
- Conflicting inputs from two sensory systems (e.g., between visual and pain inputs, as in the phantom-limb experiences). Hallucinations of all kinds fall into this classification.
- Conflicting input from external input and internal feeling states, for example, the lack of recognition of a very familiar face while visual comparison with photographs, for example, indicates that recognition should occur (e.g., Ellis & Young, 1990).
- Biopathological activation, or failure of normal activation, of conscious experiences of feeling, such as feelings of surprise, feelings that something has changed, feelings of significance, and so on, in the absence of any relevant external input (e.g., Maher, 1999). Feelings described as "mystical" would be classed under this heading.

- The experienced discrepancy between an intended act (e.g., a speech utterance, a motor movement) and the actual execution of the act. This is the condition created in Nielsen's (1963) investigation, described earlier. I examined the implications for discrepancies between intended speech utterances and the actual words spoken (Maher, 1988c).

Some of these experiences may have an interactive relationship. Thus, a biopathological condition that accentuates the vividness of visual experiences (as has often been described by both patients with schizophrenia and users of psychedelic substances) may lead to feelings of "significance" for the same reasons that very bright lights and fluorescent colors in the external environment serve to attract attention and thereby indicate the alleged importance of the object that they illuminate.

The Delusions of Schizophrenia

To the extent that abnormal experiences are due to endogenous neuropathology, one might reasonably expect that patients with circumscribed delusions who are relatively free from other psychotic symptoms would exhibit circumscribed neuropathological lesions. Patients with more diffuse neuropathology, with involvement of many loci, may exhibit not only a broad spectrum of delusions but also an array of other disturbances of behavior. Patients with schizophrenia exhibit delusions with a wide array of content. These include the passivity delusions of thought insertion and thought broadcasting and other delusions of control, Capgras and other delusional misidentification syndromes, somatic delusions, systematized delusions of persecution, Cotard's syndrome, and so forth. Patients with schizophrenia also exhibit a wide array of neuropathologies both of structure and of neurochemical function (e.g., DeLisi, 1991; Dewan, 1987; Green, 1998).

Given what is known about the heterogeneity of schizophrenia, none of this is surprising. It also raises the strong possibility that the unusual experiences produced by some of the neuropsychological defects interact with and contribute to the development of the delusion. The well-known difficulty that some patients with schizophrenia have with perceiving the figurative or metaphorical meaning of utterances, including their own, is a case in point. Chapman (1960), for example, reported that, compared with control groups, patients with schizophrenia significantly more often responded to the literal meaning of a word or phrase that had been uttered in a figurative sense. Much the same phenomenon can be seen in the many reports of the tendency of patients with schizophrenia to respond to the concrete rather than the abstract meanings of proverbs and in other tasks in which this distinction is relevant. The English language is replete with common folk metaphors for describing psychological or physical states. Thus, one's heart is "as heavy as lead" or is "broken," there are "butterflies" in one's stomach, one's bones feel "like jelly," one's itching skin feels like there are "insects crawling under it," and so on. If a person uses these phrases when talking to a clinician, they will be understood as metaphors and translated into appropriate medical terms. Should examination fail to discover a physical cause for these sensations, the patient is left with the sensation but no explanation for it other than his or her own metaphor. For normal individuals, the result is perhaps some frustration, but the metaphor is still understood as a metaphor. For patients with schizophrenia, the concrete meaning of the metaphor that first came to mind when describing the sensation may tend to dominate their explanation of it. Now there is a basis for a somatic delusion in which the heart is believed to have really been turned into lead, with the accompanying necessity of developing an explanation of how and why that came to pass. In short, one basic pathology in schizophrenia—the inability to inhibit the literal concrete meaning of words—combines with another—the experience of unexplained somatic sensations—to produce a delusion. The belief cannot be readily undone by counterevidence unless the patient can be helped to understand it metaphorically and can be given some other correct explanation of the origin of the sensations that initiated the sequence.

Parenthetically, an unusual treatment of a somatic delusion, reported from India by Gangdev, Joshi, Sinorwala, and Agarwal (1988), used the tactic of "confirming" the truth of the literal meaning of a somatic delusion. The patient, a 50-year-old woman, had many vague symptoms, which she attributed to there being an iron bar in her abdomen. She had received various forms of psychiatric treatment without success. Her own opinion was that she would get better only if the iron bar were removed surgically. Finally, the clinicians performed mock surgery on her abdomen, and—in collaboration with her son—assured her that she had been correct, as they had all seen the bar as it was removed. The report asserts that the patient improved rapidly and remained so on later follow-up. A similar treatment was applied to a woman who believed that snakes had invaded her body. Gangdev et al. interpreted their procedure as a method for refutation of the delusion: "You can't still have an iron bar(/snakes) in your abdomen because it(/they) has been taken out."

Conclusion

What might now be done to further the understanding of the genesis of delusions? One step might be to develop detailed descriptions of the sequential development of delusions in individuals whose condition is clearly due to external factors rather than to a developing psychosis. Delusions in the toxic conditions, transient delusions of the kind that often follow major surgery, and delusions in individuals following the onset of AIDS are some of the possibilities. There would be no a priori reason to believe that the delusion was due to some preexisting defect of reasoning, and it might be possible to gain retrospective accounts that would be less affected by other ongoing psychotic processes.

Another possibility is to look at the various measures of cognitive bias or inferential processes within samples of deluded patients with a view to detecting what, if any, components of the delusions and the associated clinical picture are significantly correlated with the quality of performance on these measures. What is known about the heterogeneity of schizophrenia, for example, suggests that simple comparison of means between groups defined as deluded or not deluded will not carry us very far in our understanding of delusions. Discovery of the differences in delusions between patients with normal or superior performance in information-processing tasks and patients with inferior performance could go some distance toward resolving the role, if any, of inferential defect in the genesis of delusions.

Whatever direction we take, it will be important to keep in mind that the experimental method gives us precision of observation and measurement but cannot give us the same kind of information that we can get by trying to understand the nature of patients' experiences. Both sorts of information are vitally necessary if our understanding of the pains of psychopathology is to advance in ways that will permit us to reduce those pains.

References

Cardeña, E., Lynn, S. J., & Krippner, S. (Eds.). (2000). *Varieties of anomalous experience: Examining the evidence*. Washington, DC: American Psychological Association.

Chapman, L. J. (1960). Confusion of figurative and literal usages of words by schizophrenics and brain damaged patients. *Journal of Abnormal Psychology, 60,* 412–416.

Cooper, A. F. (1976). Deafness and psychiatric illness. *British Journal of Psychiatry, 129,* 216–226.

Cooper, A. F., & Curry, A. R. (1976). The pathology of deafness in the paranoid and affective psychoses of later life. *Journal of Psychosomatic Research, 20,* 97–105.

Cooper, A. F., & Porter, R. (1976). Visual acuity and ocular pathology in the paranoid and affective psychoses of later life. *Journal of Psychosomatic Research, 20,* 107–114.

Cornblatt, B. A., Obuchowski, M., Andreasen, A., & Smith, C. (1998). High-risk research in schizophrenia: New strategies, new designs. In M. F. Lenzenweger & R. H. Dworkin (Eds.), *Origins and development of schizophrenia* (pp. 349–384). Washington, DC: American Psychological Association.

Curtis, C. P., & Greenslet, F. (1962). *The practical cogitator.* Boston: Houghton Mifflin.

Davis, P. J., & Gibson, M. G. (2000). Recognition of posed and genuine facial expressions of emotion in paranoid and nonparanoid schizophrenia. *Journal of Abnormal Psychology, 109,* 445–450.

DeLisi, L. E. (1991). Brain imaging studies of cerebral morphology and activation in schizophrenia. In S. R. Steinhauer, J. H. Gruzelier, & J. Zubin (Eds.), *The handbook of schizophrenia: Vol. 5. Neuropsychology, psychophysiology, and information processing* (pp. 147–160). Amsterdam: Elsevier.

Dewan, M. J. (1987). Cerebral structure and symptomatology. In P. Harvey & W. Walker (Eds.), *Positive and negative symptoms in psychosis: Description, research, and future directions* (pp. 216–242). Hillsdale, NJ: Erlbaum.

Dykman, B. M., Horowitz, L. M., Abramson, L. Y., & Usher, M. (1991). Schematic and situational determinants of depressed and nondepressed students' interpretation of feedback. *Journal of Abnormal Psychology, 100,* 45–55.

Einhorn, H. J., & Hogarth, R. M. (1978). Confidence in judgement: Persistence of the illusion of validity. *Psychological Review, 85,* 395–416.

Ellis, H., & Young, A. W. (1990). Accounting for delusional misidentification. *British Journal of Psychiatry, 157,* 239–248.

Erlenmeyer-Kimling, L., Roberts, S. A., Rock, D., Adamo, U. H., Shapiro, B. M., & Pape, S. (1998). Prediction from longitudinal assessments of high-risk children. In M. F. Lenzenweger & R. H. Dworkin (Eds.), *Origins and development of schizophrenia* (pp. 427–446). Washington, DC: American Psychological Association.

Galton, F. (1892). *Hereditary genius* (2nd ed.). London: Macmillan.

Gangdev, P., Joshi, V., Sinorawala, A., & Agarwal, M. (1988). Non-conventional treatment of somatic delusions. *Journal of Commonwealth Psychiatry, 11,* 9–11.

Garety, P. A., & Hemsley, D. R. (1994). *Delusions: Investigations into the psychology of delusional reasoning.* Oxford, England: Oxford University Press.

Goldberger, M. L., Maher, B. A., & Flattau, P. E. (Eds.). (1995). *Research-doctorate programs in the United States: Continuity and change.* Washington, DC: National Academy Press.

Gottesman, I. I., & Moldin, S. O. (1998). Genotypes, genes, genesis, and pathogenesis in schizophrenia. In M. F. Lenzenweger & R. H. Dworkin (Eds.), *Origins and development of schizophrenia* (pp. 5–26). Washington, DC: American Psychological Association.

Green, M. F. (1998). *Schizophrenia from a neurocognitive perspective.* Boston: Allyn & Bacon.

Huq, S. F., Garety, P. A., & Hemsley, D. R. (1988). Probabilistic judgements in deluded and non-deluded subjects. *Quarterly Journal of Experimental Psychology, 40A,* 801–812.

LaRusso, L. (1978). Sensitivity of paranoid patients to nonverbal cues. *Journal of Abnormal Psychology, 87,* 463–471.

Layne, C. (1986). Painful truths about depressives' cognitions. *Journal of Clinical Psychology, 39,* 848–853.

Lobitz, W. C., & Post, R. D. (1979). Parameters of self-reinforcement and depression. *Journal of Abnormal Psychology, 88,* 33–41.

Lord, C., Lepper, M. R., & Ross, L. (1979). Biased assimilation and attitude polarization: The effects of prior theories on subsequently considered evidence. *Journal of Personality and Social Psychology, 37,* 2098–2110.

MacDonald, N. (1960). Living with schizophrenia. *Canadian Medical Journal, 82,* 218–221, 678–681.

Maher, B. A. (1970, September). *The psychology of delusions.* Paper presented at the 78th Annual Convention of the American Psychological Association, Miami Beach, FL.

Maher, B. A. (1974a). Delusional thinking and cognitive disorder. In R. Nisbet & H. London (Eds.), *Thought and feeling: Cognitive alteration of feeling states* (pp. 85–103). Chicago: Aldine.

Maher, B. A. (1974b). Delusional thinking and perceptual disorder. *Individual Psychology, 30,* 98–113.

Maher, B. A. (1988a). Anomalous experience and delusional thinking. In T. H. Oltmanns & B. A. Maher (Eds.), *Delusional beliefs* (pp. 15–33). New York: Wiley.

Maher, B. A. (1988b). Delusions as the product of normal cognitions. In T. H. Oltmanns & B. A. Maher (Eds.), *Delusional beliefs* (pp. 333–336). New York: Wiley.

Maher, B. A. (1988c). Language disorders in psychoses and their impact on delusions [Sprachstörungen bei Psychotikern und ihre Relevanz für Wahnphänomene]. In M. Spitzer, F. A. Uehlein, & G. Oepen (Eds.), *Psychopathology and philosophy* (pp. 109–120). Berlin, Germany: Springer-Verlag.

Maher, B. A. (1990). The irrelevance of rationality in adaptive behavior. In M. Spitzer & B. A. Maher (Eds.), *Philosophy and psychopathology* (pp. 73–85). New York: Springer-Verlag.

Maher, B. A. (1991a). Deception, rational man, and other rocks on the road to a personality psychology of real people. In W. Grove & D. Cicchetti (Eds.), *Thinking clearly about psychology* (Vol. 2, pp. 72–88). Minneapolis: University of Minnesota Press.

Maher, B. A. (1991b). Delusions. In *Medical and health annual* (pp. 437–440). Chicago: Encyclopædia Britannica.

Maher, B. A. (1992a). Delusions: Contemporary etiological hypotheses. *Psychiatric Annals, 22,* 260–268.

Maher, B. A. (1992b). Models and methods for the study of reasoning in delusions. *Revue européenne de Psychologie Appliquée, 42,* 97–102.

Maher, B. A. (1999). Anomalous experience in everyday life: Its significance for psychopathology. *The Monist, 82,* 547–570.

Maher, B. A. (2001). Delusions. In P. Sutker & H. Adams (Eds.), *Comprehensive handbook of psychopathology* (3rd ed., pp. 309–339). New York: Kluwer Academic.

Maher, B. A., Manschreck, T. C., Hoover, T., & Weisstein, C. (1987). Thought disorder and measured features of language production in schizophrenia. In P. Harvey & E. Walker (Eds.), *Positive and negative symptoms in psychosis: Description, research, and future directions* (pp. 195–215). Hillsdale, NJ: Erlbaum.

Maher, B. A., & Ross, J. (1983). Delusions. In H. Adams & P. Sutker (Eds.), *Comprehensive handbook of psychopathology* (pp. 383–409). New York: Plenum.

Maher, B. A., & Spitzer, M. (1992). Delusions. In P. Sutker & H. Adams (Eds.), *Comprehensive handbook of psychopathology* (2nd ed., pp. 263–293). New York: Plenum.

Manschreck, T. C. (1979). The assessment of paranoid features. *Comprehensive Psychiatry, 20,* 370–377.

McGhie, A., & Chapman, J. (1961). Disorders of attention and perception in early schizophrenia. *British Journal of Medical Psychology, 34,* 103–117.

Nielsen, T. I. (1963). Volition: A new experimental approach. *Scandinavian Journal of Psychology, 4,* 225–230.

Popper, K. (1979). *Objective knowledge: An evolutionary approach* (Rev. ed.). Oxford, England: Oxford University Press.

Reed, G. (1974). *The psychology of anomalous experience: A cognitive approach.* Boston: Houghton Mifflin.

Ross, L., & Anderson, C. A. (1982). Shortcomings in the attribution process: On the origins and maintenance of erroneous social assessment. In D. Kahneman, P. Slovic, & A. Tversky (Eds.), *Judgement under uncertainty: Heuristics and biases* (pp. 129–152). New York: Cambridge University Press.

Schreber, D. P. (1988). *Memoirs of my nervous illness* (I. MacAlpine & R. A. Hunter, Trans.). Cambridge, MA: Harvard University Press. (Original work published 1903)

Southard, E. E. (1916). On descriptive analysis of manifest delusions from the subject's point of view. *Journal of Abnormal Psychology, 11,* 189–202.

Spitzer, R., & Endicott, J. (1977). *Schedule for affective disorders and schizophrenia.* New York: Biometrics Research.

Walker, E. F., Baum, K. M., & Diforio, D. (1998). Developmental changes in the behavioral expression of vulnerability for schizophrenia. In M. F. Lenzenweger and R. H. Dworkin (Eds.), *Origins and development of schizophrenia* (pp. 427–446). Washington, DC: American Psychological Association.

Wason, P. C., & Johnson-Laird, P. N. (1972). *Psychology of reasoning: Structure and content.* Cambridge, MA: Harvard University Press.

Zimbardo, P. G. (1999). Discontinuity theory: Cognitive and social searches for rationality and normality—may lead to madness. In M. Zanna (Ed.), *Advances in experimental social psychology* (Vol. 31, pp. 345–486). San Diego, CA: Academic Press.

Part II _____

Schizophrenia as Seen From the Experimental Psychopathology Vantage Point

2

Strengthening the Evidence for Genetic Factors in Schizophrenia (Without Abetting Genetic Discrimination)

Irving I. Gottesman and James L. Reilly

A quest for a man for all seasons by Irving I. Gottesman ended in 1960 when he met Brendan A. Maher, who was, like himself, in the pile of new hires in the Department of Social Relations at Harvard University, entitled, temporarily, to visit Olympus and rub minds with the resident gods. As both had been naval officers in recent wars and both recently had received doctoral training in clinical psychology at two enormous land grant universities in the Midwest—Ohio State University and the University of Minnesota—they seemed to draw replenishment for the oxygen needed to work efficiently at that altitude from their shared experiences with a wide range of humanity under stress and from their shared values in both scientific empiricism and dry humor. Maher was invited by Norman Ellis to contribute a chapter to a new handbook of mental deficiency that would emphasize biological aspects, and the former invited Gottesman to join him to add a genetic perspective; when each of their sections grew unwieldy, they agreed to each produce their own complementary chapters. The interchange of viewpoints, and, more important, of scientific values, has continued into each of their formal retirements, against a background of controversy that has characterized the discipline(s) of psychology in the United States.

The essence of the controversy arises from the cleavage between perceiving, accurately, the discipline of psychology as a social science and as a natural science simultaneously. This controversy has paradoxically led to intellectual skirmishes and extreme discomfort not only within the discipline but also at both ends, where psychology merges into sociology and the humanities on the left and into biology and genetics on the right. Some participants have opted for divorces or all-out excommunication, whereas others, including Maher, have, soberly and wisely, counseled mediation and reconciliation. The latter strategy has guided the program of research described in this chapter; it has also led to a distinction among what Maher, in privately published essays stimulated by being dean of the Graduate School of Arts and Sciences at Harvard, has termed "facts, Irish facts, [and] mythofacts." The theme of one such essay focuses on the definition of *evidence* and the need for appropriate and uniform standards of scholarship. Maher argues persuasively that overly cathected moral values ought not to be allowed to trump over counterevidence in the search for scientific facts. In the spirit of reconciliation, we offer the efforts described in this chapter that attempt to synthesize some of the evidence that bears on understanding the causes of schizophrenia.

Evidence from classical genetic epidemiology—population, family, twin, and adoption studies—has repeatedly substantiated the plain fact that there are major genetic components in the distal causes of schizophrenia (Faraone, Tsuang, & Tsuang, 1999; Gottesman & Moldin, 1998; Kendler, 2000). Advances in molecular genetic strategies implicating certain gene regions and candidate genes (Baron, 2001; Levinson & Mowry, 2000; Moises & Gottesman, 2001; Riley & McGuffin, 2000) have complemented the findings from traditional studies, further suggesting that particular genetic regions (not yet genes per se) and genes-qua-genes will be identified "soon." But don't hold your breath. Despite the accumulation of substantial evidence for the role of genetic factors underlying the schizophrenic phenotype (Gottesman, 2001), the nature of the genetic diathesis, the proteins produced (Cravchik & Goldman, 2000; Stoltenberg & Burmeister, 2000), and the nature of their interactions with environmental and experiential factors over the course of pre- and postnatal development remain uncertain. Furthermore, the roles of epigenetic factors (Petronis, 2001; Petronis et al., 2000) and stochastic events (Woolf, 1997) over the course of development continue to gain footing in an understanding of schizophrenia's baffling unfolding. The term *epigenetic factors* refers to various demonstrated and speculative mechanisms that control the expression and the suppression of genes (cf. Petronis, 2001), ranging from methylation at the molecular level to the physiological reactions triggered by feeling stressed. *Stochastic* is a more formal descriptor of the unsystematic or random encounters endured by organisms.

Given such lack of closure, the loyal opposition as well as doubters and ideologues of various persuasions and motivations continue to command a hearing, each claiming a significant piece of the causal pie. They deserve an informed hearing, such as the forum for examining ideas in experimental psychopathology exemplified in Maher's (1966) classic textbook, updated by using the strategies for giving proper weights (effect sizes) to any competing claims (cf. Heinrichs, 2001). A multigenic–multifactorial threshold model (Gottesman & Shields, 1967; McGue & Gottesman, 1989; Moldin, 1994), enriched by a neurodevelopmental context (Cicchetti & Cannon, 1999; Erlenmeyer-Kimling, 2000; Marenco & Weinberger, 2000), remains the leading conceptual schema for best synthesizing the complexity of the transmission of schizophrenia as well as its epigenesis. Such thinking has speeded progress on other such complex genetic diseases as Type I and II diabetes (Gottesman & Shields, 1967; Todd & Wicker, 2001) and coronary artery disease (Sing, Zerba, & Reilly, 1994). A schematic cartoon of an overriding systems approach engendered by such thinking is presented in Figure 2.1—not for schizophrenia, as that is not yet ready for such a treatment, but for the complex human trait of cognitive ability, as a relevant analogy (Gottesman, 1997; cf. Sing et al., 1994).

The advantages of such a systems approach include the facilitation of clear thinking about the different levels of contributors to a final phenotype, the possibilities of complexity and interaction at each level, and the possibilities for intervention at different stages of the processes involved between the distal influences of genes and their proteins and regulators and the proximal contributors such as stressors and protectors. In the example shown for cognitive ability, genes and quantitative trait loci (Flint & Mott, 2001) have been identified and named from studies with fruit flies, mice, and humans with mental retardation or Alzheimer's disease.

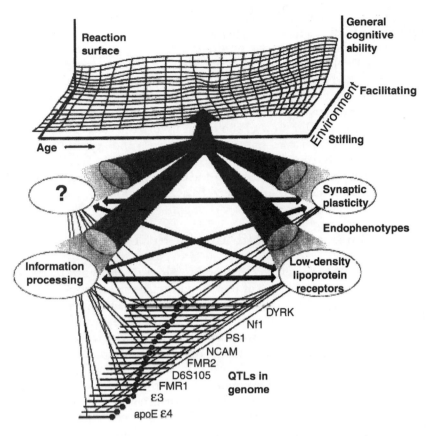

Figure 2.1. Illustration of a complex systems approach schema showing the sequential and concurrent influences of genes, environment, chance, and time on the development of general cognitive ability, analogous to their usage in research on coronary artery disease, and recommended for understanding major psychopathologies (cf. Sing et al., 1994; Gottesman, 1997). QTLs = quantitative trait loci; apoEε4, D6S105, DYRK, ε3, FMR1, FMR2, NCAM, Nf1, and PS1 are specific genes. From "Twins: En Route to QTLs for Cognition," by I. I. Gottesman, 1997, *Science, 276* (June 6), p. 1523. Copyright 1997 by the American Association for the Advancement of Science. Adapted with permission.

Sampling the Contributors to Liability

Parallel with advances in the genetics of schizophrenia, considerable ground has been made implicating the role of other factors in the causal chains leading to the clinical manifestation of schizophrenia-related psychosis (SRP) and its spectrum of related conditions. Among these, support for disturbed neurodevelopment has been mounting (Cornblatt & Malhotra, 2001; Erlenmeyer-Kimling, 1996; Marenco & Weinberger, 2000; Weinberger, 1995) since Barbara Fish first drew attention to such issues from her sensitive clinical observations of babies born to mothers with schizophrenia (Fish & Alpert, 1962). We present a perspective on the complex genetics of schizophrenia, focusing, regrettably not in depth, on contributions made by recent family and twin studies. We conclude by calling for the continual theoretical and empirical integration of genetic findings with other substantiated, schizophrenia-specific or schizophrenia-indicating contributory factors, and then we provide an example of misapplied knowledge about prediction of schizophrenia with bioethical implications. To these ends, we speculate about the integration of the current genetic perspective with some of the evidence implicating neurodevelopmental disturbances in schizophrenia. Our view of the latter favors the concept of developmental instability, as indexed by excess homozygosity across the genome (Markow, 1992) complemented by stochastic (Gottesman & Bertelsen, 1989; Woolf, 1997) and epigenetic inputs (Petronis, 2001) that allow for Genotype × Environment interaction for complex adaptive systems (Zerba, Ferrell, & Sing, 2000).

Confirming Familiality of Schizophrenia

It is too easy for skeptics to dismiss the solid foundation (Rosenthal, 1970; Slater & Cowie, 1971; Zerbin-Ruedin, 1967) of increased familial risk for SRP and spectrum disorders on the grounds that the studies were conducted before criteria from the *Diagnostic and Statistical Manual of Mental Disorders* (3rd ed. [*DSM–III*], American Psychiatric Association, 1980) were used for diagnosis; the studies of relatives were not blindfolded enough; the control groups, using the same objective criteria as for probands, were nonexistent; and the researchers had some kind of genetic axe to grind. Kendler (2000) provided a summary of family studies conducted worldwide that dispels such criticisms. He found 11 studies (1980–1995) of first-degree relatives (2 only were of offspring) using blind diagnoses, contemporary criteria, and screened or unscreened local control individuals. In sum, except for 1 study, the differences in morbid risk (i.e., age corrected) were highly reliable statistically, and the heritabilities of the liability to developing schizophrenia ranged nominally from .50 to 1.0.

Die-hard critics still find it easy to disparage twin studies of schizophrenia, perhaps because the findings so clearly support strong genetic inferences about a strong role for genes as distal causes in all 12 instances since 1928 (Gottesman, 1991). Studies of monozygotic (MZ) and dizygotic (DZ) twins have been central, but never sufficient, to the establishment of a genetic contribution to the etiology of schizophrenia. Continued support for a major heritable component to the liability for developing schizophrenia is now available from a surprising five new studies (1996–1999), in which were used diagnostic criteria from Research Diagnostic Criteria (Spitzer, Endicott, & Robins, 1978), *DSM–III–R* (American Psychiatric Association, 1987), and *International Classification of Diseases* (*ICD-10*; World Health Organization, 1992); structured and blinded interviews; sound sampling strategies; and sophisticated genetic modeling. In the new studies reviewed by Cardno and Gottesman (2000), and as shown in Figure 2.2, similar patterns of probandwise concordance rates (i.e., rates for MZ twins are always greater than twice the rates for DZ twins) were reported in twin pairs ascertained from clinical as well as population samples. Consistent heritability estimates upwards of 80% clearly confirm a substantial genetic component among the distal causes of schizophrenia. Results from biometric model fitting support this conclusion, with the remaining contribution

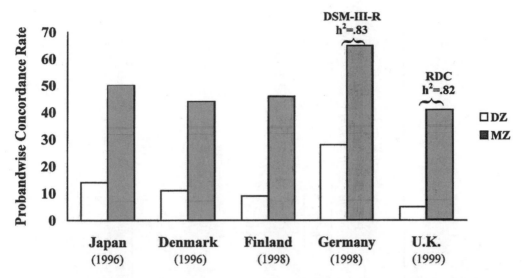

Figure 2.2. Probandwise concordance rates from recent twin studies of schizophrenia by country (for specific references see Cardno & Gottesman, 2000, p. 13). Heritability estimates (h2) are provided if general population risks were reported in the original study. DSM–III–R = *Diagnostic and Statistical Manual of Mental Disorders* (3rd. ed., rev.; American Psychiatric Association, 1987); RDC = Research Diagnostic Criteria (Spitzer, Endicott, & Robins, 1978); DZ = dizygotic; MZ = monozygotic. From A. G. Cardno and I. I. Gottesman, personal communication, July 27, 1999. Copyright 1999 by A. G. Cardno and I. I. Gottesman. Adapted with permission.

to liability attributable to idiosyncratic, rather than shared, environmental factors (Cardno & Gottesman, 2000; cf. Turkheimer & Waldron, 2000).

Although traditional twin studies of schizophrenia have been important for the big picture, reductionistic studies of MZ twin pairs who are discordant for schizophrenia have provided the potential for identifying some of the intervening mechanisms of the multifactorial etiology suggested in Figure 2.1. Furthermore, studies of the offspring of discordant MZ pairs indicate comparable risks for SRPs in the offspring of both the affected and unaffected cotwins (Gottesman & Bertelsen, 1989; Kringlen & Cramer, 1989). This indicates that the specific genetic factors conferring susceptibility to schizophrenia are transmitted, but that they may not be expressed, as evidenced by the normal MZ cotwins with affected offspring.

Another powerful element in our thinking about the causal chain involved in schizophrenia is provided by the fruition of the prospective high-risk strategies that begin with the young children born to mothers and fathers with schizophrenia and follow them for the many years required to observe mental illness and health outcomes. The outcomes contribute to the picture of familiality, and the neurobehavioral assessments, conducted on the way there, encourage a focusing on attention, information processing, and motor development as endophenotypes (Gottesman & Shields, 1972) worthy of close scrutiny. Erlenmeyer-Kimling (2000) updated this body of research, and in Table 2.1 we abstract some of the SRP prevalence data from

Table 2.1. Offspring of Schizophrenic Parents: Fruition of Longitudinal High-Risk Projects

Variable	New York Infant Study (Fish, 1984)	Copenhagen High-Risk Project (Cannon et al., 1993)	Israeli High-Risk Study (Ingraham et al., 1995)	New York High-Risk Project (Erlenmeyer-Kimling et al., 1995)		Jerusalem Infant Development Study (Hans et al., 1999)
				Sample A	Sample B	
Participant information						
Age at start of study (years)	Birth	9–20	5–8	7–12	7–12	Birth,[a] 8–13[b]
Age at last diagnostic assessment (years)	20–26	39–42	21–27	36.6	27.1	14–21
N						
Schizophrenia risk	12	207	50	63	46	19[a], 10[b]
Normal controls	12	104	50	100	65	19,[a] 7[b]
Prevalence (SE) of SRP						
Offspring of parents with schizophrenia	8.5% (8.0)	20.8% (2.8)	8.0% (3.8)	18.5% (4.8)	7.7% (3.9)	4.1% (3.7)[c]
Offspring of normal controls	0.0% (—)	2.9% (1.6)	0.0% (—)	1.1% (1.0)	0.0% (—)	0.0% (—)[c]

Note. See Erlenmeyer-Kimling (2000) for details on these five projects. SRP = schizophrenia-related psychosis. Adapted from "Psychopathology Through a Life Span–Genetic Prism," by I. I. Gottesman, 2001, *American Psychologist, 56,* p. 872. Copyright 2001 by the American Psychological Association.
[a]Targets. [b]Siblings. [c]Targets and siblings.

studies in New York City, New York State, Denmark, and Israel. Pointers to the neurodevelopmental indicators of risk for offspring can be found in Erlenmeyer-Kimling et al.'s (2000) article, whereas those in MZ cotwins can be found in Torrey, Bowler, Taylor, and Gottesman's (1994) book. We develop some of these ideas next.

Ever mindful of the simple fact that familiality cannot be equated with an exclusive role for genetic factors, we would be remiss to not update the information available about the refinements in the well-known adoption strategies applied to the biological and adoptive relatives of people with schizophrenia. The goal of such designs is to move toward disentangling experiential from genetic contributions to a phenotype by removing one of the elements of experience: being reared by disturbed parents. The recent loss of Seymour S. Kety (Sokoloff, 2000) to this field was mourned worldwide. Ingraham and Kety (2000) reminded us that the strategy used for the Copenhagen sample was expanded to include all adoptees in Denmark who developed schizophrenia, and the excess risk continued to show up among the biological relatives who had little contact with the adoptees, even when *DSM–III* criteria were applied. They concluded that "Adoption studies of schizophrenia have convincingly demonstrated a significant role for genetic factors in schizophrenia" (Ingraham & Kety, 2000, p. 21). Continuing refinements in the Finnish adoption study, led by P. Tienari and L. Wynne, in which the adopted-away offspring of mothers with schizophrenia in a nationwide cohort are being examined (Tienari et al., 2000), now include *DSM–III–R* diagnoses. Tienari et al. (2000) concluded that "the genetic liability to 'typical' *DSM–III–R* schizophrenia is decisively confirmed" (p. 433), and the risk of 8.1% rises when a broad spectrum of SRPs is included.

Proportionality in Weighting Risk Factors

In a major methodological leap forward, R. Walter Heinrichs (2001) escalated the utility of meta-analytic approaches by conducting meta-analyses of the 54 English language meta-analyses for a broad field of factors implicated one way or another in the differences observed by neuroscientists between individuals with schizophrenia and control individuals without major mental disorders. The yields of such a perspective are presented in terms of effect sizes or Cohen's d. The results complement those obtained from looking at odds ratios, and both approaches can be used within or without a family context. Given the sample sizes available in the literatures for the two decades beginning 1980, Heinrichs also was able to provide invaluable 95% confidence intervals on the effect sizes for many of the same factors in which we are interested here. Between effect sizes and odds ratios (Jablensky, 1999, 2000; McGuffin & Gottesman, 1999; Moises & Gottesman, 2001), a careful researcher can detect the most promising roads to successful outcomes as well as the dead ends. A sampling of the results are shown in Table 2.2. It is clear that some of the most highly touted factors suggested in the literature to explore as possibly causal and important may have highly reliable statistical significance levels, but they have trivial usefulness in advancing knowledge. An effect size of $d = 1.0$ between schizophrenic cases and control cases without major mental disorders implies that 50% (only) of individuals with schizophrenia are characterized by the marker; an effect size of $d = 3.0$ would be a powerful indicator implying 97% of cases characterized by the marker. Likewise, an odds ratio of 1.1 means that the marker conveys a risk 10%

Table 2.2. Estimated Odds Ratios and Effect Sizes (d) for Some Risk Factors in Schizophrenia

Risk factor	OR	d (95% CI)	N Studies	Comments
MZ cotwin ill	50		~17	Cardno & Gottesman (2000)
Parent ill	13		7	
Sibling ill	9.6		9	SRP
P50		1.55 (1.21–1.89)	20	Evoked brain potential (best neuroscience OR)
Low IQ		1.10 (0.86–1.34)	35	
Continuous Performance Test		1.04 (0.90–1.18)	29	Cornblatt & Erlenmeyer-Kimling (1985)
Frequency in eye tracking saccade		1.03 (0.56–1.50)	14	
Hippocampal volume (MRI)		0.41 (0.25–0.57)	22	
Lower SES	3.0		17	Explained by downward drift (Jablensky, 1999)
Obstetric complications (various)	2.0	0.32 (0.20–0.44)	10 (OR) 15 (d)	OR = 3.7 for OC ≥ 7 (Hultman et al., 1997)
Stressful life events	1.5		3	
Maternal influenza	1.1	0.02 (0.00–0.04)	9 (OR) 4 (d)	Morgan et al. (1999)

Note. All data on effect sizes are from Heinrichs (2001); data on odds ratios are from Jablensky (1999, 2000) and Moises and Gottesman (2001). OR = odds ratio; CI = confidence interval; MZ = monozygotic; SRP = schizophrenia-related psychosis; P50 = an evoked brain potential; MRI = magnetic resonance imaging; SES = socioeconomic status; OC = obstetric complications. Adapted from "Psychopathology Through a Life Span—Genetic Prism," by I. I. Gottesman, 2001, *American Psychologist, 56,* p. 873. Copyright 2001 by the American Psychological Association. Adapted with permission.

greater than average; thus, instead of a risk of schizophrenia equal to the general population risk of 1%, it is 1.1% for those infants who were exposed to maternal influenza or experienced a winter birth. Such an increase in risk is in sharp contrast to the risk experienced by the MZ cotwins of *DSM–III–R* schizophrenic patients, which was 50 times the base rate of 1% (Cardno & Gottesman, 2000).

Toward a Synthesis: From Genes Through Aberrant Neurodevelopment and Developmental Instability to Schizophrenia

Given the early hints implicating some kind of neurointegrative defect in those infants at a higher risk of developing schizophrenia, and given the evidence reviewed earlier, it is time to seek a resting spot for synthesis. There is no single neurodevelopmental theory of schizophrenia; neither is there any single pathognomonic indicator of aberrant neurodevelopment, yet lines of evidence have converged to support the role of disturbed neurodevelopmental processes in the etiology of schizophrenia (Erlenmeyer-Kimling, 1996; Marenco & Weinberger, 2000; Weinberger, 1995). Dysmorphology (Green, Satz, Gaier, Ganzell, & Kharabi, 1989; O'Callaghan et al., 1995), dermatoglyphic variants (Markow & Gottesman, 1989; Reilly & Gottesman, 1999; Van Os, Fananas, Cannon, Macdonald, & Murray, 1997), and possible increases in obstetric and birth complications (see Table 2.2 and references) in schizophrenia imply schizophrenia- or psychosis-specific pre- and perinatal developmental disturbances. Such disturbances lead, in a proportion of cases, to neurobehavioral and neuroanatomical variants that may be detectable premorbidly. A major limitation to the evidence that supports a neurodevelopmental theory to schizophrenia is the lack of specificity of this evidence for schizophrenia, small effect sizes between patients and control individuals, and the failure to integrate these findings into a broad, genetically informed context.

We can provide only a brief introduction to the concept of developmental stability as one possible framework under which neurodevelopmental theories of schizophrenia can be incorporated with our current understanding of the complex genetics of schizophrenia. Waddington (1957) introduced the concept of developmental stability as the capacity of an individual to properly carry out his or her developmental program despite environmental and genetic perturbations, through an "epigenetic landscape" model of development (cf. Gottesman, 1974, for a behavioral application). Lerner (1958) kept the ball rolling with his exegesis of genetic homeostasis. These schema were forerunners of the ideas in Figure 2.1 and the ones used by Sing and his colleagues (e.g., Sing et al., 1994) to talk about complex adaptive systems in coronary artery disease (Zerba et al., 2000). Since its inception, the concept of developmental stability has been used by developmental biologists and population geneticists studying experimental organisms, although its application to human traits and development has only recently been emphasized (Markow, 1992; Markow & Gottesman, 1993; Woolf, 1997). The underlying genetic basis of developmental stability is theorized to reside in genomewide levels of heterozygosity (i.e., two different alleles at one locus) and the maintenance of coadapted gene complexes throughout the genome (Clark, 1993; Zerba et al., 2000). Fluctuating asymmetry, the unsigned right-versus-left difference between an individual's paired bilateral traits, is a useful indicator of developmental stability (Fraser, 1994; Palmer & Strobeck, 1986) and occurs when environmental factors impede the execution of a developmental program equally on both sides.

Developmental stability and its converse, developmental instability, provide a compelling framework under which neurodevelopmental findings can be integrated with epigenetic explanations. Intriguing partial models of developmental instability and schizophrenia consistent with neurodevelopmental theories have been offered by Gottesman and Shields (1967), Markow (1992), Markow and Gottesman (1993), and Woolf (1997). Individual trajectories for developing schizophrenia will vary because of dynamic interactions between genotype and environment. Therefore, we would predict an associated systemic increase in the level of developmental instability in those individuals whose developmental trajectories lead them beyond the liability threshold. Underlying these increasing levels of developmental instability, the specific genetic factors predisposing to schizophrenia are superimposed on a genome that varies in the degree to which it can buffer environmental perturbations. In support of developmental instability as a framework under which the complex genetics of schizophrenia and suggested neurodevelopmental disturbances can be integrated, evidence has suggested that increasing levels of developmental instability are associated with both greater genetic liability to schizophrenia (Reilly & Gottesman, 1999) and to indirect markers of atypical neurodevelopment (Reilly et al., 2001). Although developmental instability itself is not a specific cause of schizophrenia, indicators of its presence as a background characteristic in individuals with schizophrenia highlight the importance of dynamic interactions between those genotypes more susceptible to environmental disturbance and relevant, often idiosyncratic, stressors.

Misapplied Genetic Reasoning and Human Rights

We end with a tale in which the strength of genetic factors, as understood by one group of contemporaries, was overstated to the detriment of human rights of three men who happened to be the offspring of parents with a chart diagnosis of schizophrenia. We hope we have made clear so far that our goal is to highlight evidence-based weighting for the various risk factors involved in the liability, course, and phenomenology of schizophrenia. Gottesman was invited to participate as one of three expert witness in a foreign country where the law deemed that anyone with a mentally ill parent, regardless of his or her own present status on all dimensions relevant to employment by the government in an occupation involving public safety, was not employable because such a person had a "substantial risk of developing mental illness." Given the conflict of rights, one part of the government charged with ensuring equal opportunities and nondiscrimination in employment sued another part of the government that was trying to avoid any risk of mental illness in employees in stress-filled occupations; the case was settled in court after expert witnesses on both sides testified.

The information arrays presented in Figure 2.3 were instrumental in the judge's decision to find for the plaintiffs, three young men who had met the standards for the jobs, each of whom happened to have a parent with an alleged diagnosis of paranoid or undifferentiated schizophrenia. Although the average risk of developing schizophrenia for the offspring of people with schizophrenia is shown to be 13%, for an odds ratio of 13.0, further examination shows that not only are 87% of the offspring free of SRP as adults but also that fully 11% of the offspring have a lower liability for developing schizophrenia than 50% of the members in the general population. When the average risk was decomposed into individually appropriate risk classes as a function of both the severity of the parental illness and as a function of the risk period already survived for a disorder with a variable age of onset, the evidence-based estimates of risks for developing schizophrenia were greatly reduced (Gottesman, 1991; McGuffin, Owen, O'Donovan, Thapar, & Gottesman, 1994). Our best estimates in each case ranged from 5% to 7%, mostly influenced by the severity and age-survived factors, but allowing for any information presented on the risk factors in Table 2.2 above and their weights. A careful clinical examination by one of our experts versed in *DSM* and *ICD* criteria showed that none of the plaintiffs had any hints of schizophrenia-spectrum disorders, further bolstering our confidence in the estimates provided to the court.

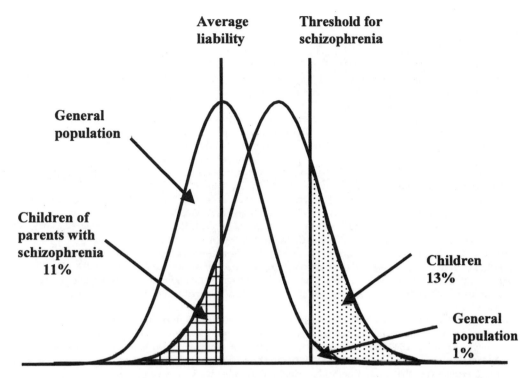

Figure 2.3. Distributions of the liabilities to developing schizophrenia in the general population (g.p.; (left side of figure) and in the offspring born to parents with schizophrenia (right side of figure) showing 1% of the g.p. affected and 13% of the offspring also above the threshold. Note that 11% of children are to the left of the average liability of the g.p. and thus have even less liability than 50% of the g.p. From I. I. Gottesman and P. McGuffin, personal communication, January 15, 2000. Copyright 2000 by I. I. Gottesman and P. McGuffin. Adapted with permission.

Conclusion

The search for the causes of schizophrenia continues, using all available useful suggestions from every manner of scientist. We have suggested some strategies and schemas for evaluating the weights to be accorded to current findings and to those that continue to be presented from the mushrooming field of molecular genetics. The answers will not come easily, as the disorder is truly complex whether viewed thorough the lens of the clinical investigator or the lens of the molecular geneticist (Rao & Province, 2001); all will benefit from a flexible stance that constantly strives toward integration of evidence, properly weighted, and then recursively pruned as a consequence of new information, and seen from the perspective of a complex adaptive systems "engineer."

References

American Psychiatric Association. (1980). *Diagnostic and statistical manual of mental disorders* (3rd ed.). Washington, DC: Author.

American Psychiatric Association. (1987). *Diagnostic and statistical manual of mental disorders* (3rd ed., rev). Washington, DC: Author.

Baron, M. (2001). Genetics of schizophrenia and the new millennium: Progress and pitfalls. *American Journal of Human Genetics, 68*, 299–312.

Cannon, T. D., Mednick, S. A., Parnas, J., Schulsinger, F., Praestholm, J., & Vestergaard, A. (1993). Developmental brain abnormalities in the offspring of schizophrenic mothers: I. Contributions of genetic and perinatal factors. *Archives of General Psychiatry, 50*, 551–564.

Cardno, A. G., & Gottesman, I. I. (2000). Twin studies of schizophrenia: From bow-and-arrow concordances to Star Wars Mx and functional genomics. *American Journal of Medical Genetics (Neuropsychiatric Genetics), 97*, 12–17.

Cicchetti, D., & Cannon, T. D. (1999). Neurodevelopmental processes in the ontogenesis and epigenesis of psychopathology. *Development and Psychopathology, 11*, 375–393.

Clark, G. M. (1993). The genetic basis of developmental stability: I. Relationships between stability, heterozygosity, and genomic coadaptation. *Genetica, 89*, 15–23.

Cornblatt, B. A., & Erlenmeyer-Kimling, L. (1985). Global attentional deviance in children at risk for schizophrenia: Specificity and predictive validity. *Journal of Abnormal Psychology, 94*, 470–486.

Cornblatt, B. A., & Malhotra, A. K. (2001). Impaired attention as an endophenotype for molecular genetic studies of schizophrenia. *American Journal of Medical Genetics (Neuropsychiatric Genetics), 105*, 11–15.

Cravchik, A., & Goldman, D. (2000). Neurochemical individuality: Genetic diversity among human dopamine and serotonin receptors and transporters. *Archives of General Psychiatry, 57*, 1105–1114.

Erlenmeyer-Kimling, L. (1996). A look at the evolution of developmental models of schizophrenia. In S. Matthysse, D. Levy, J. Kagan, & F. M. Benes (Eds.), *Psychopathology: The evolving science of mental disorders* (pp. 229–252). Cambridge, England: Cambridge University Press.

Erlenmeyer-Kimling, L. (2000). Neurobehavioral deficits in offspring of schizophrenic parents: Liability indicators and predictors of illness. *American Journal of Medical Genetics (Neuropsychiatric Genetics), 97*, 65–71.

Erlenmeyer-Kimling, L., Rock, D., Roberts, S. A., Janal, M., Kestenbaum, C., Cornblatt, B., et al. (2000). The New York High-Risk Project: Attention, memory, and motor skills as childhood predictors of schizophrenia. *American Journal of Psychiatry, 157*, 1416–1422.

Erlenmeyer-Kimling, L., Squires-Wheeler, E., Adamo, U. H., Bassett, A. S., Cornblatt, B. A., Kestenbaum, C. J., et al. (1995). The New York High-Risk Project. Psychoses and cluster A personality disorders in offspring of schizophrenic parents at 23 years of follow-up. *Archives of General Psychiatry, 52*, 857–865.

Faraone, S. V., Tsuang, M. T., & Tsuang, D. W. (1999). *Genetics of mental disorders.* New York: Guilford Press.

Fish, B. F. (1984). Characteristics and sequelae of the neurointegrative disorder in infants at risk for schizophrenia. In N. F. Watt, E. J. Anthony, L. C. Wynne, & J. Rolf (Eds.), *Children at risk for schizophrenia: A longitudinal perspective* (pp. 423–439). New York: Cambridge University Press.

Fish, B., & Alpert, M. (1962). Abnormal states of consciousness and muscle tone in infants born to schizophrenic mothers. *American Journal of Psychiatry, 119*, 439–445.

Flint, J., & Mott, R. (2001). Finding the molecular basis for quantitative traits: Successes and pitfalls. *Nature Reviews: Genetics, 2*, 437–445.

Fraser, F. C. (1994). Developmental instability and fluctuating asymmetry in man. In T. A. Markow (Ed.), *Developmental instability: Its origins and evolutionary applications* (pp. 319–334). Dordrecht, The Netherlands: Kluwer Academic.

Gottesman, I. I. (1974). Developmental genetics and ontogenetic psychology: Overdue detente and propositions from a matchmaker. In A. Pick (Ed.), *Minnesota Symposium on Child Psychology* (pp. 55–80). Minneapolis: University of Minnesota Press.

Gottesman, I. I. (1991). *Schizophrenia genesis: The origins of madness.* New York: Freeman.

Gottesman, I. I. (1997). Twins—En route to QTLs for cognition. *Science, 276*, 1522–1523.

Gottesman, I. I. (2001). Psychopathology through a life span–genetic prism. *American Psychologist, 56*, 864–878.

Gottesman, I. I., & Bertelsen, A. (1989). Confirming unexpressed genotypes for schizophrenia. *Archives of General Psychiatry, 46,* 867–872.

Gottesman, I. I., & Moldin, S. O. (1998). Genotypes, genes, genesis, and pathogenesis in schizophrenia. In M. Lenzenweger & R. Dworkin (Eds.), *The pathogenesis of schizophrenia: An experimental psychopathology perspective* (pp. 5–25). Washington, DC: American Psychological Association.

Gottesman, I. I., & Shields, J. (1967). A polygenic theory of schizophrenia. *Proceedings of the National Academy of Science, 58,* 199–205.

Gottesman, I. I., & Shields, J. (1972). *Schizophrenia and genetics: A twin study vantage point.* New York: Academic Press.

Green, M. F., Satz, P., Gaier, D. J., Ganzell, S., & Kharabi, F. (1989). Minor physical anomalies in schizophrenia. *Schizophrenia Bulletin, 15,* 91–99.

Hans, S. L., Marcus, J., Nuechterlein, K. H., Asarnow, R. F., Styr, B., & Auerbach, J. G. (1999). Neurobehavioral deficits at adolescence in children at risk for schizophrenia: The Jerusalem Infant Development Study. *Archives of General Psychiatry, 56,* 741–748.

Heinrichs, R. W. (2001). *In search of madness: Schizophrenia and neuroscience.* New York: Oxford University Press.

Hultman, C. M., Ohman, A., Cnattingius, S., Wieselgren, I. M., & Lindstrom, L. H. (1997). Prenatal and neonatal risk factors for schizophrenia. *British Journal of Psychiatry, 170,* 128–133.

Ingraham, L. J., & Kety, S. S. (2000). Adoption studies of schizophrenia. *American Journal of Medical Genetics (Neuropsychiatric Genetics), 97,* 18–22.

Ingraham, L. K., Kugelmass, S., Frenkel, E., Nathan, M., & Mirsky, A. F. (1995). Twenty-five year follow-up of the Israeli High-Risk Study: Current and lifetime psychopathology. *Schizophrenia Bulletin, 21,* 183–192.

Jablensky, A. (1999). The 100-year epidemiology of schizophrenia. In W. F. Gattaz & H. Hafner (Eds.), *Search for the causes of schizophrenia: Vol. 4. Balance of the century* (pp. 3–19). Darmstadt, Germany: Steinkopff.

Jablensky, A. (2000). Epidemiology of schizophrenia: The global burden of disease and disability. *European Archives of Psychiatry and Clinical Neuroscience, 250,* 274–285.

Kendler, K. S. (2000). Schizophrenia: Genetics. In B. J. Sadock & V. A. Sadock (Eds.), *Kaplan & Sadocks's comprehensive textbook of psychiatry* (Vol. 1, pp. 1147–1159). Philadelphia: Lippincott, Williams & Wilkins.

Kringlen, E., & Cramer, G. (1989). Offspring of monozygotic twins discordant for schizophrenia. *Archives of General Psychiatry, 46,* 873–877.

Lerner, I. M. (1958). *The genetic basis of selection.* New York: Wiley.

Levinson, D. F., & Mowry, B. J. (2000). Genetics of schizophrenia. In D. W. Pfaff (Ed.), *Genetic influences on neural and behavioral functions* (pp. 47–82). Boca Raton, FL: CRC Press.

Maher, B. A. (1966). *Principles of psychopathology: An experimental approach.* New York: McGraw-Hill.

Marenco, S., & Weinberger, D. R. (2000). The neurodevelopmental hypothesis of schizophrenia: Following a trail of evidence from cradle to grave. *Development & Psychopathology, 12,* 501–527.

Markow, T. A. (1992). Genetics and developmental stability: An integrative conjecture on aetiology, and neurobiology of schizophrenia. *Psychological Medicine, 22,* 295–305.

Markow, T. A., & Gottesman, I. I. (1989). Fluctuating dermatoglyphic asymmetry in psychotic twins. *Psychiatry Research, 29,* 37–43.

Markow, T. A., & Gottesman, I. I. (1993). Behavioral phenodeviance: A Lerneresque conjecture. *Genetica, 89,* 297–305.

McGue, M., & Gottesman, I. I. (1989). Genetic linkage in schizophrenia: Perspectives from genetic epidemiology. *Schizophrenia Bulletin, 15,* 453–464.

McGuffin, P., & Gottesman, I. I. (1999). Risk factors for schizophrenia [Letter]. *New England Journal of Medicine, 341,* 370–371.

McGuffin, P., Owen, M., O'Donovan, M., Thapar, A., & Gottesman, I. I. (1994). *Seminars in psychiatric genetics.* Washington, DC: American Psychiatric Press.

Moises, H. W., & Gottesman, I. I. (2001). Genetics, risk factors, and personality factors. In F. Henn, H. Helmchen, H. Lauter, & N. Sartorius (Eds.), *Contemporary psychiatry* (pp. 47–59). Heidelberg, Germany: Springer-Verlag.

Moldin, S. O. (1994). Indicators of liability to schizophrenia: Perspectives from genetic epidemiology. *Schizophrenia Bulletin, 20,* 169–184.

Morgan, V., Castle, D., Page, A., Fazio, S., Gurrin, L., Burton, P., et al. (1999). Influenza epidemics and incidence of schizophrenia, affective disorders, and mental retardation, in Western Australia: No evidence of a major effect. *Schizophrenia Research, 26*, 25–39.

O'Callaghan, E., Buckley, P., Madigan, K., Redmond, O., Stack, J. P., Kinsella, A., et al. (1995). The relationship of minor physical anomalies and other putative indices of developmental disturbance in schizophrenia to abnormalities of cerebral structure on magnetic resonance imaging. *Biological Psychiatry, 38*, 516–524.

Palmer, A. R., & Strobeck, C. (1986). Fluctuating asymmetry: Measurement, analysis, patterns. *Annual Review of Ecological Systems, 15*, 479–499.

Petronis, A. (2001). Human morbid genetics revisited: Relevance of epigenetics. *Trends in Genetics, 17*, 142–146.

Petronis, A., Gottesman, I. I., Crow, T. J., DeLisi, L. E., Klar, A. J., Macciardi, F., et al. (2000). Psychiatric epigenetics: A new focus for the new century. *Molecular Psychiatry, 5*, 342–346.

Rao, D. C., & Province, M. A. (Eds.). (2001). *Advances in genetics: Vol. 42. Genetic dissection of complex traits.* San Diego, CA: Academic Press.

Reilly, J. L., & Gottesman, I. I. (1999). Dermatoglyphic fluctuating asymmetry, homozygosity, and liability to schizophrenia. *Biological Psychiatry, 45*, 8S.

Reilly, J. L., Murphy, P., Byrne, M., Gill, M., Larkin, C., O'Callaghan, E., et al. (2001). Dermatoglyphic fluctuating asymmetry and atypical handedness in schizophrenia. *Schizophrenia Research, 50*, 159–168.

Riley, B. P., & McGuffin, P. (2000). Linkage and associated studies of schizophrenia. *American Journal of Medical Genetics (Neuropsychiatric Genetics), 97*, 23–44.

Rosenthal, D. (1970). *Genetic theory and abnormal behavior.* New York: McGraw-Hill.

Sing, C. F., Zerba, K. E., & Reilly, S. L. (1994). Traversing the biological complexity in the hierarchy between genome and CAD endpoints in the population at large. *Clinical Genetics, 46*, 6–14.

Slater, E., & Cowie, V. A. (1971). *The genetics of mental disorders.* New York: Oxford University Press.

Sokoloff, L. (2000). Seymour Kety, MD, 1915–2000. *American Journal of Medical Genetics (Neuropsychiatric Genetics), 96*, 585–589.

Spitzer, R. L., Endicott, J., & Robins, E. (1978). Research diagnostic criteria: Rationale and reliability. *Archives of General Psychiatry, 35*, 773–782.

Stoltenberg, S. F., & Burmeister, M. (2000). Recent progress in psychiatric genetics—Some hope but no hype. *Human Molecular Genetics, 9*, 927–935.

Tienari, P., Wynne, L. C., Moring, J., Laksy, K., Nieminen, P., Sorri, A., et al. (2000). Finnish Adoptive Family Study: Sample selection and adoptee *DSM–III–R* diagnoses. *Acta Psychiatrica Scandinavica, 101*, 433–443.

Todd, J. A., & Wicker, S. (2001). Genetic protection from the inflammatory disease Type 1 diabetes in humans and animal models. *Immunology, 15*, 387–395.

Torrey, E. F., Bowler, A. E., Taylor, A. H., & Gottesman, I. I. (1994). *Schizophrenia and manic depressive disorder.* New York: Basic Books.

Turkheimer, E., & Waldron, M. (2000). Nonshared environment: A theoretical, methodological, and quantitative review. *Psychological Bulletin, 126*, 78–108.

Van Os, J., Fananas, L., Cannon, M., Macdonald, A., & Murray, R. (1997). Dermatoglyphic abnormalities in psychosis: A twin study. *Biological Psychiatry, 41*, 624–626.

Waddington, C. H. (1957). *The strategy of the genes.* New York: Macmillan.

Weinberger, D. R. (1995). Schizophrenia as a neurodevelopmental disorder. In S. R. Hirsch & D. R. Weinberger (Eds.), *Schizophrenia* (pp. 293–323). Cambridge, MA: Blackwell Science.

Woolf, C. M. (1997). Does the genotype for schizophrenia often remain unexpressed because of canalization and stochastic events during development? *Psychological Medicine, 27*, 659–668.

World Health Organization. (1992). *ICD-10 classification of mental and behavioral disorders: Clinical descriptions and diagnostic guidelines.* Geneva, Switzerland: Author.

Zerba, K. E., Ferrell, R. E., & Sing, C. F. (2000). Complex adaptive systems and human health: The influence of common genotypes of the apolipoprotien E (Apo E) gene polymorphism and age on the relational order within a field of lipid metabolism traits. *Human Genetics, 107*, 466–475.

Zerbin-Ruedin, E. (1967). Endogene psychosen [Endogenous psychoses]. In P. E. Becker (Ed.), *Humangenetik, ein kurzes handbuch* (Vol. 2, pp. 446–577). Stuttgart, Germany: Thieme.

3

The Role of Motor Behavior in the Pathogenesis of Schizophrenia

Theo C. Manschreck

In the mid-1970s, I was a chief resident in psychiatry at Massachusetts General Hospital. I invited Brendan Maher, whom I did not know at all, to present a conference to first-year residents on schizophrenia and language. At the time, schizophrenia research had become preoccupied with dopamine; diagnosis was in shambles; and the phenomenology of thinking, hallucinations, and delusions in the disorder, which I found fascinating, was of little interest to most colleagues.

Maher gave his famous talk on "the language of schizophrenia": a breath of fresh air; practical; down to earth; and, although inspired by theory, empirical to the core. His proposals concerning the nature of formal thought disorder, connecting this defining feature of the illness to a disturbance of focus and selection in attention, were appealing at many levels: They were testable, and they related mind to brain. The presentation demonstrated his storytelling teaching style, humor, and an ever-present respect for data. The meeting became a turning point in my training and my life. Sensing my interest, Maher invited me to Cambridge, where, over the ensuing months, we planned a tutorial and eventually launched our joint studies. These soon led to the formation of the Laboratory for Clinical and Experimental Psychopathology at Massachusetts General Hospital. We weathered years of limited resources but managed to be productive. Maher maintained his involvement throughout. His generosity and ability to connect intellectually with people with widely ranging scientific backgrounds provided inspiration to the laboratory's staff. Maher's special talents—for finding the blood in stones and turnips, for using data to generate insights rather than to fit prior theories or models, and for brilliant creativity in a field that has been conspicuously reserved about adopting new paradigms—built excitement and awe for the research enterprise.[1] A large number of individuals trained and contributed in the laboratory; many have distinguished themselves in psychopathology research and related endeavors (see Exhibit 3.1).

---

[1]It has been my special fortune to have worked with Brendan all these years. We have taught together; discussed endlessly psychopathology, methods, philosophy of science, and almost everything else; and forged a wonderful friendship that has extended to both our families. To be sure, along the way, we enjoyed many entertaining and relaxed moments as well. Brendan has been an extraordinary mentor, collaborator, and friend.

Exhibit 3.1. Associates of the Laboratory for Clinical and Experimental Psychopathology

Deborah Ader	Barbara Hinchman	Jason Rock
Scott Beaudette	Toni Hoover	Melissa Rosato
Jon Berner	Victoria Jackson-Moreno	Jill Rosenthal
Crystal Blyler	Nancy Keuthen	Mary Rucklos
Roger Boshes	Craig Latham	Margaret Schneyer
Steve Candela	Judy Laughery	Laura Seavy
Brooks Casas	Jacob Linnet	Melinda Solomon
Teresa Celada	Dana Manoach	Manfred Spitzer
Paul Collins	Frank Marzinzik	Ming Tsuang
Wendy Coons	Jamie Milavetz	Don Vereen
Claude Curran	Christine Miller	Nils Waller
Patricia Deldin	Phoebe Myhill	Cecily Weisstein
Rod Fernandez	Kerry Pimental	Laura Winzig
Jennifer Ferreira	Mariann Popoli	Donna (Ames) Wirshing
Meredith Hanrahan-Boshes	Ann Pulver	Deborah Yurgelun-Todd
	Deborah Redmond	

The Laboratory for Clinical and Experimental Psychopathology

I first met Maher while I was a chief resident in psychiatry at the Massachusetts General Hospital. I had organized a series of presentations on psychopathology for first-year psychiatry residents and had invited Maher to speak about language in schizophrenia. His intellectually exciting presentation on information theory, cognition, and speech analysis intrigued me; and I was curious to learn more. Happily, Maher's generosity extended to psychiatrists. Following the talk we arranged a meeting to discuss mutual interests. This led to further meetings, later a tutorial on the vocabulary and methods of experimental psychopathology, and eventually, a research collaboration that has endured for over 20 years.

The collaboration resulted in the founding of a laboratory to conduct studies based on careful observation and measurement of clinical features and astute application of theory, the Laboratory for Clinical and Experimental Psychopathology. The laboratory was first located at the Massachusetts General Hospital and the Erich Lindemann Mental Health Center. Later there was a move to Dartmouth (1990–1994), to Brown (1994–1996), and then back to Harvard. In the laboratory, many valued associates (undergraduate, graduate, and medical students; fellows in psychology and in psychiatry; and advanced students, distinguished colleagues, and collaborators in experimental psychopathology) have received training, assisted in our research (or carried out their own), and launched careers (see Exhibit 3.1).

The laboratory remains a center for new studies and collaborations, and it continues its record of innovation, careful measurement and analysis of schizophrenic features, and cutting-edge theoretical development. A special respect for research methods, particularly certain principles that Maher has championed, has inspired the work. Maher has been a wise advisor and thoughtful consultant to all; and for me a dear friend as well as close collaborator.

Motor Behavior in Schizophrenia: Methodologic Hurdles

In this chapter I discuss the context that influenced the direction and methods of the laboratory's research.

Definitions and Measures

The late 19th century presented similar challenges to those faced today (see Exhibit 3.2) concerning the puzzling phenomena of mental illness. For centuries, the formidable hurdle of defining mental disorder had not been scaled successfully. Emil Kraepelin (1919) recognized that without rigorous causal explanations for psychopathologic disorders, classification was tentative and offered limited practical or therapeutic value. His attempt to classify mental disorders scientifically on the basis of etiology went only so far, because the majority of psychiatric cases had no known causes.

Kraepelin (1919) skillfully navigated around this problem. He proposed that, lacking causal knowledge, the validation of psychiatric nosology required systematic characterization of outcome. In other words, understanding natural history offered a limited anchor for definitions to distinguish psychiatric conditions until the discovery of etiology (Robins & Guze, 1970).

Now, in a new century, psychopathology researchers confront opportunities made possible by technologies that permit direct examination of brain function and structure. However, methodological hurdles constrain orderly scientific progress. For example, determination of causes for mental disorders remains unachieved and elusive. No laboratory test provides definitive help in diagnosis. On the other hand, there has been progress and a shift in emphasis in the assessment of psychopathology: Repeated demonstrations of deficiency in diagnostic reliability in the 1960s and 1970s stimulated the development of research-oriented classification schemes and, ultimately, the third version of the *Diagnostic and Statistical Manual of Mental Disorders* (*DSM–III*; American Psychiatric Association, 1980). These classification systems encouraged rigorous clinical assessment and codified Kraepelin's (1919) proposals by improving the soundness of clinical symptom definition and incorporating better characterized features of natural history. Structured-interviewing techniques and a plethora of rating scales were created. Research benefited from the selection of patient groups that are more diagnostically homogeneous. Nevertheless, the limits of standard clinical assessment techniques abound. Structured

Exhibit 3.2. Methodologic Hurdles in Schizophrenia Research

- A rigorous causal explanation (definition)
- Measures free of human judgment
- Brain loci for abnormal behavior
- Parsimony in explanatory strategies
- Presumption of heterogeneity

interviews for diagnosis and assessment of symptoms, even side effect scales, still depend fundamentally on ratings. Although they are clearly an advance over unsystematized description, rating approaches have disadvantages. For example, reliance on fallible judgment to make ratings and to discriminate magnitudes of each level of rating can be risky. The rater is fundamentally being asked to make assumptions about the distribution underlying the phenomenon to be rated. The division of ratings into discontinuous units (e.g., mild, moderate, severe, or extreme) compounds difficulty. Even when grounded in operational criteria, ratings are seldom based on counting or quantitatively describable observations; hence their sensitivity to detecting potentially critical differences is low. Such ratings generate special problems for statistical evaluation as well, for example, because of their poor transfer to parametric analysis.

Maher has tirelessly promoted the goal of refining and quantifying measurements. The achievement of precise quantifiable measures marks the maturation of a scientific discipline. To move from reliance on ratings when quantification is possible to minimal dependence on judgment has been a methodologic goal in our studies. We have also embraced a preference for quantitative over qualitative measures, that is, for that which can be counted. For example, in contrast to a rating that calls for judgment regarding how slow or rigid movement in an extremity is, one could operationalize such judgments using a stopwatch and a strain gauge. With the development of electronic equipment designed to detect motor movements—such as tremor, bradykinesia, and so on—at levels not detectable clinically, the prospects for fine-grained evaluation have become brighter.

Refined measurement permits researchers to improve definitions in the absence of causal knowledge in a manner similar to Kraepelin's (1919) strategy—that is, precise measurement advances the characterization of both psychopathology and natural history; it also makes possible a range of additional advances, including the detection of important connections that may point to etiologic or pathogenetic insights, obscured or lost in the imprecision of ratings or unstructured clinical observation.

Behavior and Brain

The leading hypothesis about schizophrenia in the 1970s was the *dopamine hypothesis*, namely, that excess dopamine activity led to the emergence and maintenance of psychosis (Carlsson, 1978). This proposal was consistent with psychopharmacologic studies and was a beacon for investigations of neurotransmitter function in schizophrenia. As a corollary, dopamine-blocking agents were predicted to reverse the psychosis and other clinical manifestations of the illness. Yet treatment response was more complicated. Many patients improved, but few became well, when they took the dopamine-blocking antipsychotic agents. It took years before this fundamental result was appreciated: The new agents were generally effective in treating psychosis per se, regardless of cause, but they had no particular specificity for schizophrenia. Problems in the measurement of clinical psychopathology—especially low reliability and inadequate definitions for differential diagnosis—helped delay discovery of these connections between brain disturbance and abnormal behavior.

In addition to improved measures, at that time there was also a need for bridging hypotheses (i.e., proposals that could relate dopamine biology to the clinical phenomena in specific ways or to the phenomena captured in peripheral measures, such as reaction time to brain physiology). Elsewhere I have referred to such hypotheses as *midrange theorizing*, in this case to connect behavior to the brain (Manschreck & Kleinman, 1979). A strong candidate in the 1970s was information-processing theory, later succeeded by the emergence of cognitive neuroscience as a framework for relevant theoretical concepts. Information-processing theory drew from evolutionary and psychological concepts as well as from computer science. Maher laid out a synthesis of this theoretical perspective concerning speech deviances of schizophrenic patients in his classic article "The Language of Schizophrenia: A Review and Interpretation," which appeared in the *British Journal of Psychiatry* in 1972. According to this view, oddities in the verbal behavior in schizophrenia arise from a breakdown in information-processing capacities manifested in compromised attention. This proposal outlined a map for further investigation of speech with the implicit assumption that there was a biology underlying these phenomena.

The principle here, often neglected in research in the frenzied analysis of correlations among cognitive and clinical measures, is to recognize and understand the fundamental association of behavior and anatomy (or physiology). In contrast to the largely meaningless attempts to justify the concept of "functional" disorder in psychopathology (Slavney & McHugh, 1987), this concept serves as a foundation for scientific hypothesizing about psychopathology. It also reminds researchers that although the process of inference in psychopathology has relied on the logic of correlation, it has often been assumed that relationships among measured variables are linear. In fact, it is known from studies of biological systems that the underlying relationships may be curvilinear. Detecting associations between clinical features and structural underpinnings is another means of circumventing the problem of not knowing causes; such associations provide a framework for refining definitions and pointing to important etiologic or pathogenetic possibilities.

Parsimony

The principle of parsimony, that there is value in simplicity of scientific explanation, has provided an important guidepost. An explanation involving one pathology for understanding schizophrenia is to be preferred over another involving several. Given findings of clinical, cognitive, and neurological abnormality in schizophrenia, and the troubling puzzles inherent in the heterogeneity issue, the idea that one pathology might explain schizophrenia seems absurd, yet the time-proven value of parsimony remains. In effect, it points out the hypothesis: namely, to seek connections in the varied abnormalities of this disorder as a means of testing for a common pathogenesis. This in turn might help researchers understand how seemingly distinct brain functions are integrated and how they break down. For example, that abnormalities from domains of behavior as distinct as motor response and memory could arise from a common underlying pathology has called for thinking creatively and designing experimental strategies in new ways, and such a search might result in effective subtyping strategies when empirical support for common mechanisms is not to be found. This would involve researchers in the heterogeneity challenge anew.

Heterogeneity

The presumption of heterogeneity has also governed researchers' strategy of study. Clinical heterogeneity—the variety of possible presentations to be found within the confines of diagnostic criteria—is easily observed and accepted. Etiologic heterogeneity is in fact an assumption, albeit one that is consistent with numerous observations within the field. It suggests that, despite surface similarities, specific subsets of cases of schizophrenia arise from different causes. This leads to problems in research: No matter how reliable one's diagnostic strategy, there is likely to be some level of heterogeneity of etiology (pathology) within one's samples. This underlying heterogeneity doubtless contributes (along with the crudeness of some measures) to the phenomenon of great variability in the performance of schizophrenic individuals (Van der Velde, 1976). It may also account for the routine observation that many cases within the schizophrenic group fail to be distinguishable from controls on some important variable, or that correlations are more modest than one might desire, or that mean differences may be significant but the distribution of measures overlaps considerably. The challenge of etiologic heterogeneity is that modest differences or correlations may or may not be trivial. Careful analysis of the components that give rise to the mean differences and the correlations will permit researchers to form hypotheses about the plausible candidates for etiology.

Examining the Data

Given the problems of diagnosis, the imprecision of most clinical measures, and the presumption of etiologic heterogeneity, there is virtue in experimental psychopathology in "looking at the data"—that is, visualizing the raw distribution patterns of measured variables, as in scatter plots, before crunching the numbers. This starting point in data analysis gives the investigator a feel for the data and permits insight into the phenomenon being measured.

Maher once expressed this principle poetically:

> Here is my law, for woman and man,
> In any assessment some can't and some can
> Some couldn't, some could, some wouldn't, some would
> The way the twigs are bent doesn't bias the bud.

> Turn away from the mean, and examine the spread
> Dim down the computer and switch on your head
> Were it not for the variance where would we be
> If you can't make a t-test, you can't take a p.

> Now this is a comfort, not grounds for complaint
> Thank God for the fact that some are and some ain't.
> From the data of variance pleasure derive
> It's one of the things that helps us survive.

> (excerpted from Maher's "Bale's Law of Invariant Variability,"
> personal communication, 1997)

What They Are Doing

Many observations in schizophrenia focus on deficits. These include avolition, alo-gia, anhedonia, and so forth. This emphasis has obscured awareness of what the patients are able to do either at a superior level to controls (as has been illustrated by studies of semantic priming and incidental learning; e.g., Manschreck et al., 1988) or of what they are doing rather than not doing (i.e., what is occurring when one sees something lacking). For example, *alogia*, or poverty of content, a dimension of formal thought disorder, refers to a reduction in the color and richness of utterances. Examination of utterance has led to the finding that individuals with schizophrenia who exhibit such poverty actually produce significantly different (higher) levels of repetition of words and phrases. They fail to produce rich content, but they do produce much repetition (Manschreck, Maher, Waller, Ames, & Latham, 1985).

In summary, establishment of the Laboratory for Clinical and Experimental Psychopathology in the late 1970s occurred during a period of significant challenges. Methodologic problems, diagnostic issues, and a poverty of theory slowed advances in experimental psychopathology. In the following sections I describe approaches to these issues that we at the laboratory have found useful. It was in this context that many of the observations and studies on the role of motor behavior in schizophrenia arose.

Motor Behavior Research in Schizophrenia

Our investigations initially focused on deviant speech in schizophrenia, so-called *formal thought disorder*, Bleuler's (1911/1950) "loosened associations." The attention-deficit hypothesis purported to explain these disturbances in comprehensibility. In his seminal article in 1972 Maher used information theory to generate hypotheses about the mechanism for speech deviances. Much early work in this laboratory attempted to test these proposals. We observed that a division of schizophrenic individuals into those with and without clinically rated formal thought disorder helped detect associations for the former with a range of quantifiable features in speech (i.e., predictability, Manschreck, Maher, Rucklos, & White, 1979; and repetitiousness, Manschreck, Maher, Hoover, & Ames, 1984) and memory (i.e., greater failure to take advantage of contextual characteristics in verbal recall; Maher, Manschreck, & Rucklos, 1980, and Manschreck, Maher, Rosenthal, & Berner, 1991).

The challenge facing researchers committed to exploring the attention-deficit hypothesis as a comprehensive model for schizophrenia was the extent to which this hypothesis was useful in understanding psychopathologic phenomena other than speech (the principle of parsimony). In numerous discussions, Maher and I began to view the study of motor behavior as a promising way to further test this hypothesis. Moreover, there was the advantage of avoiding the methodologic confounds (such as relying on verbal behavior to assess verbal deviance) that limited progress on the study of verbal pathology. This led to study of the motor dimension of schizophrenia.

Motor abnormalities have long been observed and commented on, often with excellent descriptions (Berrios, 1981; Bleuler, 1911/1950; Kahlbaum, 1874/1973; Kraepelin, 1919; Manschreck, 1986; Rogers, 1992). These abnormalities fall into various subcategories, including posture, gait, and voluntary and involuntary motor movements; the variety is depicted in Exhibit 3.3. Despite the rich clinical lore, motor abnormalities were neglected during much of the early 20th century and have not been adequately explained (Manschreck, 1983; Rogers, 1992).

This neglect was shortsighted. Not only did 19th-century psychiatrists identify motor abnormalities in schizophrenia but also case records from that era enriched understanding of their relationship to schizophrenia. For example, Kraepelin (1919) described features in dementia praecox indistinguishable from contemporary accounts of tardive dyskinesia (Crow et al., 1982; Crow, Owens, Johnstone, Cross, & Owen, 1983). Turner (1992) creatively examined casebooks from Ticehurst House Asylum from 1845 to 1890. As part of this study, he counted movement abnormalities when they were clearly recorded and unambiguously present (see Exhibit 3.4). He also estimated the probable diagnosis of the cohort using the Research Diagnostic Criteria (Spitzer, Endicott, & Robins, 1978), and he was able to

Exhibit 3.3.   Abnormalities of Spontaneous Motor Behavior in Schizophrenia

Decreased Motor Activity	*Increased Motor Activity*	*Postural Disturbance*
Diffuse	Diffuse	Diffuse
Retardation	Restlessness	Rigidity
Poverty of movement	Excitement	Catalepsy
Stupor	Patterned	Stereotypic/manneristic
Patterned	Tremor	postures
Motor blocking	Stereotypies/mannerisms	Clumsiness
Cooperation	Spasms	Patterned
Opposition	Choreiform movements	Motor blocking
Automatic obedience	Athetoid movements	Cooperation
Negativism	Parakinesia	Opposition
Ambitendency	Myoclonic movements	Automatic obedience
	Perseverative movements	Negativism
	Impulsive movements	Ambitendency
	Carphologic movements	
	Agitation	
	Tics	
	Mannerisms	

Exhibit 3.4.   Persistent or Recurrent Movement Abnormalities as Recorded at the Ticehurst House Asylum, 1845–1890

"Ugly grimaces"
"Constant fidgeting"
"Adopts all sorts of positions"
"Extraordinary attitudes"
"Jerky"

From "A Diagnostic Analysis of the Casebooks of Ticehurst House Asylum, 1845–1890" by T. H. Turner, 1992, *Psychological Medicine, 21*(Suppl.), pp. 15, 21. Copyright 1992 by Cambridge University Press. Adapted with permission.

Table 3.1.   Movement Disorders, Ticehurst House Asylum (1845–1890)

RDC diagnosis	Patients with a movement/posture anomaly (%)
Schizophrenia	28.5
Indefinite diagnosis	22
Manic depressive	0.5
Organic disorder	3.6

Note. RDC = Research and Diagnostic Criteria (Spitzer et al., 1978). From "A Diagnostic Analysis of the Casebooks of Ticehurst House Asylum, 1845–1890" by T. H. Turner, 1992, *Psychological Medicine*, *21*(Suppl.), p. 22. Copyright 1992 by Cambridge University Press. Adapted with permission.

characterize certain broad categories of outcome associated with the presence of motor abnormalities.

The findings are instructive. Well before the advent of neuroleptic treatment, abnormal movements were observed and recorded. These movements were particularly concentrated among patients with diagnoses of schizophrenia and, in striking contrast, virtually absent among patients with other brain disorders (see Table 3.1). Far from being incidental findings, these features were associated with several natural-history variables (see Exhibit 3.5), notably a poorer prognosis and limited social recovery.

Another characteristic of motor abnormality that drew our attention was the striking overlap of descriptive terms for verbal and motor pathology in schizophrenia (see Exhibit 3.6), such as poverty of movement and poverty of speech or motor

Exhibit 3.5.   Characteristics of Ticehurst Patients With Movement Disorders

- Poor prognosis (only 1/5 "relieved" or "recovered")
- Hospital stay >5 years
- Tendency toward violence, other psychopathology
- Single marital status

Note. From "A Diagnostic Analysis of the Casebooks of Ticehurst House Asylum, 1845–1890" by T. H. Turner, 1992, *Psychological Medicine*, *21*(Suppl.), p. 22. Copyright 1992 by Cambridge University Press. Adapted with permission.

Exhibit 3.6.   Phenomenologic Overlap of Motor and Speech Abnormalities in Schizophrenia

- Stereotypies
- Perseveration
- Blocking
- Echo phenomena (echopraxia and echolalia)
- Mannerisms (associative intrusions)
- Poverty of movement (poverty of speech)
- Last-minute responses
- Rigidity (mutism)
- Clumsiness (stilted speech)

blocking and thought blocking. This phenomenologic correspondence suggested that motor abnormalities might be associated with verbal deviances in ways not yet understood, and this suggested a possible hypothesis: that formal thought disorder and motor pathology might be related in schizophrenia.

There were, however, barriers (see Exhibit 3.7) that made research difficult. The first was a lack of measurement units for motor behavior. What is a unit of motor activity? Spontaneous motor behavior does not lend itself easily to a description in discrete units of activity. Descriptive commentary was plentiful, but seldom was there evidence of quantifiability in measurements (King, 1954, 1976). This was in contrast to speech, which can be broken down into individual words, word frequencies, pauses, clauses and sentences, and so forth. A further barrier had to do with Bleuler's (1911/1950) emphasis on loosening of associations. Identification of this feature as a basic symptom and the linchpin of the pathogenesis of schizophrenia elevated verbal pathology to a preeminence that diminished the potential significance of motor anomalies. The popularity of psychoanalytic ideas encouraged the formulation that motor abnormalities could be understood as symbolic expressions of unconscious conflict (i.e., a reaction to the disorder rather than a part of it).

Another feature that contributed to reduced interest in motor abnormality was the lowered incidence of catatonia and catatonic schizophrenia in particular (Barnes, Saunders, Walls, Saunders, & Kirk, 1986; Fricchione, 1985; Guggenheim & Babigian, 1974; Mahendra, 1981). Catatonic presentations of stupor and posturing, as well as waxy flexibility, were dramatic, frequent, and well described in the past but had become unusual.

However, the most important barrier to study of motor behavior had to do with the prevalent view that most if not all motor features in schizophrenia result from neuroleptic drug effects. Specifically, the array of Parkinsonian and other extrapyramidal features observed since the earliest use of the neuroleptic agents in the 1950s seemed to encourage the belief that all such behavior was the result of treatment rather than an intrinsic part of the disorder. Daniel Rogers (1985) referred to this belief as one of many biases operating in observations of motor behavior. The collision of biases creates a conflict of paradigms and much disagreement about what one does and does not see in specific motor features. Indeed, there are many possible sources of motor disturbance in schizophrenia, including the disease itself, reaction to the disease, treatment of the disease, environmental factors, and combinations of these sources.

These barriers, although numerous, we believed could be overcome, and the assessment of motor behavior we felt could be organized to answer key questions in an

Exhibit 3.7.   Barriers in Motor Behavior Research

- Lack of measurement units
- Bleuler's (1911/1950) emphasis on "loosening of associations"
- Functional disorder
- Catatonic phenomena
- Neuroleptic drug effects
- Conflict of paradigms

Exhibit 3.8.   Tasks of Motor Research in Schizophrenia

- Kinds and frequencies of abnormalities
- Relationship to schizophrenia: intrinsic, drug induced, or ?
- Relationship to other features of schizophrenia
- Refinement of measurement, especially laboratory-based measures
- Response to treatment
- Connection to the brain (i.e., loci of pathology)
- Contribution to heterogeneity

unbiased manner. Certain issues needed to be addressed in motor behavior research in schizophrenia to begin to establish connection to the verbal pathology associated with the disorder (Manschreck, 1983; see Exhibit 3.8).

The first of these was to determine the kinds and frequencies of such abnormalities, their specificity in relation to schizophrenia, and their association to other psychopathologic features. Our approach has involved the use of structured clinical techniques and the development and application of laboratory measures.

Clinical Studies of Motor Behavior in Schizophrenia

My colleagues and I investigated the nature of clinical motor anomaly in a hospital sample of 37 patients with schizophrenia and 16 patients with mood disorders diagnosed according to *DSM–III* and the Research Diagnostic Criteria (Manschreck, Maher, Rucklos, & Vereen, 1982). The assessment included a 1-hr examination of spontaneous motor activity using a rating scale designed to identify abnormalities reported in the literature. A further 10-min examination of simple and complex motor tasks judged according to level of disorganization, delayed response, length of completion, and persistence was undertaken to elicit abnormalities (see Exhibit 3.9; DeJong, 1967; Freeman, 1969; Luria, 1966). Drug-induced effects were evaluated with the Abnormal Involuntary Movement Scale (National Institute of Mental

Exhibit 3.9.   Techniques Used to Elicit Motor Disturbances

- General motility
    Shake head
    Open and then close eyes
    Clasp hands three times
    Grasp examiner's hand three times
- Ozeretski's Test
- First-Ring Test
- First-Edge-Palm Test
- Tests of coordination
- Station and gait

Health, 1974) and a rating scale of extrapyramidal symptoms (EPS; Wojcik, Gelenberg, LaBrie, & Berg, 1980). The main findings were as follows:

1. Thirty-six of 37 patients with schizophrenia showed disturbed voluntary movements. There was some tendency for the paranoid phenomenologic subtype cases to show somewhat less severe levels of abnormality. The shorter (elicitation) examination demonstrated better sensitivity than the spontaneous examination.
2. The patients with mood disorders showed less frequent and less severe evidence of abnormality.
3. Voluntary motor disturbances were associated with formal thought disorder, emotional blunting, and nonlocalizing neurologic signs. Furthermore, they were not associated with evidence of drug-induced motor effects. Indeed, the analysis supported the conclusion that antipsychotic medication had a marginally positive impact, reducing the occurrence of such movements.

In fact, the forms of motor disturbance detected were not characteristic of drug-induced motor effects. Rather, these disturbances fell into three general categories: (a) disruption in the smoothness and coordination of movements, (b) intermittent repetitive movements (e.g., stereotypies), and (c) disturbances in performing sequential actions. Motor abnormalities were frequent, but they were seldom dramatic in their presentation. They could easily be missed without careful examination. Certain unusual catatonic behaviors, for example, were not observed; on the other hand, stereotyped and manneristic behaviors were common.

The motor abnormalities identified correlated with formal thought disorder. In other words, speech deviance was associated with deviance in the motor sphere. As hypothesized, we identified a possible connection between formal thought disorder and motor anomalies (Manschreck et al., 1982). The major finding, however, was the extent to which we could tease out the presence of intrinsic schizophrenia motor abnormality when most researchers believed that motor features resulted from neuroleptic medication. In fact, in an editorial, Marsden (1982), a proponent of such views, repeated them but admitted that these findings could not be dismissed.

The next step in establishing the connection between motor abnormality and formal thought disorder was to examine that relationship using quantifiable measures of speech deviance. For some years we had examined various quantitative methods of measuring thought disorder and had arrived at the use of the type–token ratio, a measure of the concentration of word repetitiousness or speech disorganization also known as the *TTR*. With drug effects controlled for by specific assessment, we found that thought-disordered patients with schizophrenia showed more motor disturbance than non-thought-disordered patients with schizophrenia and patients with mood disorders (Manschreck, Maher, & Ader, 1981). In addition, the motor disturbance correlated ($r = -.58$, $p < .01$, $df = 20$) with speech deviance as measured by the type–token ratio. Thus, motor anomaly was associated with speech disorganization. However, an important limitation had to do with the fact that we did not yet have a quantitative laboratory-based measure of motor abnormality to compare with the speech indexes. This inspired a new development in the study of motor behavior.

Motor Synchrony

A useful theoretical construct in studies of speech deviance and memory function in schizophrenia is that, in contrast to normal individuals, patients with schizophrenia fail to take advantage of the predictable (or redundant) features of behavior (Cromwell, 1968; Maher, 1972; Maher et al., 1980; Manschreck et al., 1979; Shannon, 1948). This hypothesis about the nature of schizophrenic behavior guided the creation of a laboratory task to measure the ability to take advantage of redundancy (see Exhibit 3.10). In the task, participants attempt to finger-tap a key synchronously with uniform computer-generated acoustic (tremolo) stimuli presented at different rates. To reduce the impact of motivation and related variables, the accuracy of the rate is checked compared with the computer stimulus. The main measure of this rhythmic tapping is an index of the uniformity of the participant's *interresponse intervals*, defined as the standard deviation around the response mean interval. We discovered that patients with schizophrenia synchronized tapping as well as controls at most rates but exhibited marked deficiency in synchronization in a relatively narrow range of rates around 40–80 beats per minute (Manschreck, Maher, Rucklos, Vereen, & Ader, 1981). We also found that antipsychotic medication tends to improve motor synchrony in schizophrenia, suggesting that the abnormality is part of the disorder itself.

Further work has elaborated the connection of deficient motor synchrony to schizophrenia (Manschreck et al., 1985). The correlation between deficient motor synchrony and ratings of clinical motor disturbance in schizophrenia was significant ($r = -.53, p < .005$) and indicates a valid relationship between the clinical phenomenon and the laboratory measure. Also, as predicted, deficient motor synchrony was associated with formal thought disorder ($r = -.50, p < .005$). Similarly, negative symptoms were associated with deficient motor synchrony (Manschreck et al., 1985; range of $rs = .59 -.65, p < .05$). Also, a recent study (Manschreck et al., 2000) found that deficient motor synchrony was associated with failure in context memory in patients with schizophrenia ($r = -.47, p < .02$). We had previously found that failure in context memory was related to changes in relative magnetic resonance imaging (MRI) volume in the frontal areas (Maher, Manschreck, Woods, Yurgelun-Todd, & Tsuang, 1995). Further investigation found that MRI volumetric indices from the frontal areas, particularly the dorsal lateral division of the frontal lobes, were associated with deficient motor synchrony ($r = .54, p < 05$; Manschreck et al., 2000).

Exhibit 3.10.   Motor Synchrony

Guidepost (theory): Schizophrenic patients have difficulty in taking advantage of predictable features of behavior (redundancy).

Task: Tapping synchronously to uniform acoustic stimuli presented at different rates.

Measure: Uniformity of interresponse intervals (rhythmic tapping).

General finding: Schizophrenic patients synchronize tapping as well as controls do at most rates but exhibit deficient motor synchrony at 40–80 beats per minute. Medication tends to improve motor synchrony performance.

We at the laboratory have attempted to use a variation of the Wing–Kristofferson (1973) model for distinguishing the roles of central (central nervous system [CNS] pathology) versus peripheral (e.g., neuromuscular conduction, muscular pathology) influences on tapping responses in the motor synchrony task (Ivry, Keele, & Diener, 1988; Keele & Margolin, 1984). These observations led us to conclude that the main effects on motor behavior arise from central sources but that there are peripheral contributions. Hence, motor abnormalities may arise not simply from CNS (brain) pathology but from a more widespread set of disorders (cf. Crayton, Stalberg, & Hilton-Brown, 1977; Goode, Manning, Middleton, & Williams, 1981; Goode, Meltzer, Crayton, & Mazura, 1977; Meltzer, 1976; Schneider & Grossi, 1979).

Motor Laterality and Precision

Another line of research led to the development of an additional strategy of measuring motor abnormality in schizophrenia. The rationale arose in part from findings concerning nonlocalizing ("soft") neurologic signs in schizophrenia that replicated the observation that almost all patients with schizophrenia (88% [n = 53]) show evidence of motor abnormality (Manschreck & Ames, 1984). In addition, motor disturbance was associated with both poor recall and formal thought disorder, which also replicated earlier findings. In these observations, the consistency of lateralization of function (eye, hand, and foot preference) had been examined in patients who were schizophrenic compared with controls, and a phenomenon called *anomalous laterality* was identified.

Anomalous laterality refers to the presence of inconsistency in the lateral preferences of eyedness, handedness, and footedness. An anomalous-laterality participant might, for example, be right-handed and right-eyed but would kick with the left foot. This simple division of anomalous versus consistent laterality was an important distinguishing variable: Patients with anomalous laterality had even greater motor, thought, and cognitive disturbances than patients with schizophrenia who were consistently lateralized. This observation suggested that laterality may have an important pathogenetic connection to motor abnormality and speech disturbance in schizophrenia.

For years there has been a view that left-handedness—in this case, pathological left-handedness—has a disproportionately heightened prevalence among patients with schizophrenia (Boklage, 1977; Piran, Bigler, & Cohen, 1982). Left-handedness is distributed normally in the population in a range of 7%–10%, so a higher prevalence suggests that lateralization has been modified, perhaps because of disease or CNS damage (i.e., pathological).

Manoach, Maher, and Manschreck (1988) found heightened levels of formal thought disorder among left-handed patients with schizophrenia compared with right-handed patients with schizophrenia. Later, Manschreck, Maher, Redmond, Miller, and Beaudette (1996) examined the relationship between handedness and context memory performance among patients with schizophrenia. Gains in memory performance when context is increased had been described for years as lower among patients with schizophrenia compared with normal individuals and other controls (Maher et al., 1980; Manschreck et al., 1991; Miller & Selfridge, 1950). Manschreck et al. (1996) investigated 21 left-handed and 21 right-handed patients with schizophrenia individually matched for age, gender, rote memory, education, and age of onset to determine the relationship between handedness and context memory performance. Left-handed patients with schizophrenia performed more poorly on context memory. This finding, and that of the U.K. Child Development Study (Crow, Done, & Sacker, 1996), suggested that low lateralization of performance was associated with a higher risk for adult schizophrenia and indicated that relationships between lateralization and the phenomena of schizophrenia warranted further study.

Yet the measurement of handedness itself as an index of lateralization has problems. The evaluation of handedness as in, for example, the Annett Scale (Annett, 1967) depends on preference rather than performance; that is, respondents are asked to provide preferences for specific actions such as writing, throwing a ball, opening a jar, cutting with scissors, and so on. The result of such probes is an estimate of right-, left-, or mixed-handedness, a discontinuous measure presumed to be related to cerebral lateralization. However, an evaluation of actual performance ability in such activities offers the advantage of a more sensitive assessment and generates a continuous quantitative measure. Maher has developed a method for measuring performance differences in a manual task: the line drawing task.

The line drawing task is simple, places minimal demand on understanding of instructions or on previously learned skills, and is designed to give an estimate of laterality based on performance differences between hands (Blyler, Maher, Manschreck, & Fenton, 1997). The task is portable and brief. The respondent is asked to draw, freehand, four straight lines, two with each hand, running at a 45° direction from one corner of a 2-in (5-cm) square to another. One line is drawn from bottom right to upper left, and one is drawn from bottom left to upper right. The lines are each scanned into a computer graphic format, which in turn is digitized into a series of x–y pairs. The pairs are analyzed by linear regression, for which the resulting root-mean-square (RMS) residual becomes the error score. A perfect straight line would produce no error (RMS = 0). These four scores (one for each line) are used to assess performance differences (asymmetries), through an equation that subtracts the RMS sum for right-hand lines from that derived from left-hand lines and then divides this result by the sum of RMS for all four lines. Thus, by combining the performance on lines drawn with each hand, measures of lateralization can be generated on the basis of the relative level of straightness of lines drawn with either hand. Normal right-handed individuals tend to draw lines with the right hand substantially straighter (lower RMS) than those drawn with the left hand.

Applying this measure to samples that include individuals with schizophrenia has led to interesting findings. For example, individuals with schizophrenia are considerably less lateralized than controls. This means that they draw lines with similar straightness with either hand regardless of their stated preference. Individuals with low levels of lateralization are referred to as *poorly lateralized*. Those with schizophrenia with poor lateralization have an earlier age of onset and more negative symptoms and mannerisms and Parkinsonian features than controls (Manschreck, Maher, Candela, & Winzig, 2002). This set of observations linking one aspect of brain function associated with the hemispheric dominance and clinical features suggests a connection between deviant cerebral development and the occurrence of certain psychopathological features in schizophrenia. Specifically, poor lateralization, early onset, and both voluntary and involuntary motor abnormalities appear to be linked among some individuals with schizophrenia.

We at the laboratory have noted another interesting characteristic of the line drawing results. If one examines the total RMS (sum of RMS for each of the four lines), which we might tentatively identify as an index of motor precision or coordination, then other potentially important observations can be made. For example, there is an even more robust correlation ($r = .425$, $n = 65$, $p < .002$) between age of onset and RMS, corrected for age (Manschreck et al., 2002). This suggests that poor motor coordination and earlier age of onset are related.

Involuntary Motor Abnormalities

There are now several forms of motor abnormalities known to be associated with schizophrenia (see Exhibit 3.11). The connection among the different forms has not been sufficiently explored. One form, which can be addressed here only briefly, is oculomotor disturbance, specifically, smooth pursuit eye tracking and optokinetic nystagmus associated tracking (see chap. 10, this volume; Latham, Holzman, Manschreck, & Tole, 1981). In an unpublished study conducted in the laboratory, my colleagues and I determined that opticokinetic-nystagmus-related tracking disturbances (measured quantitatively) were associated with clinical motor abnormalities, suggesting that a generalized disturbance in motor systems operation is at work (Manschreck & Latham, 1983).

On the other hand, we have been able to continue to investigate the role of involuntary motor movements (e.g., tremors, dyskinesia, EPS, etc.) in schizophrenia. For many years all such movements were believed to be the result of medication, but numerous observations challenge this view (Manschreck, 1989; Owens, Johnstone, & Frith, 1982; Turner, 1992). For example, studies indicate that neuroleptic naive patients with schizophrenia have a base rate of 7%–50% involuntary-movement prevalence that often is Parkinsonian in nature (Caligiuri, Lohr, & Jeste, 1993; Fenton, Blyler, Wyatt, & McGlashan, 1997; McCreadie & Ohaeri, 1994). Many such movements were described in the literature of 19th-century psychiatry (see Exhibit 3.3). These movements often are typical extrapyramidal features such as bradykinesia or rigidity similar to those assessed for drug side effects. In addition, the incidence of drug-induced EPS is associated with the later onset of tardive dyskinesia. Moreover, drug-induced EPS and tardive dyskinesia are associated with negative

Exhibit 3.11.   Motor Abnormalities Related to Schizophrenia

- Repetitive movements
- Clumsiness (awkwardness) of bodily movement
- Disturbances in sequential motor actions
- Lateralization disturbances
- Oculomotor disturbances
- Involuntary movements

symptoms and cognitive changes (Waddington, 1995; Waddington & Youssef, 1986, 1996). These observations certainly suggest that abnormal involuntary movements have a pathophysiology related to the syndrome of schizophrenia (Crow et al., 1983; Iager, Kirch, Jeste, & Wyatt, 1986; Manschreck, 1989).

Manschreck et al. (1990) studied patients with schizophrenia with and without evidence of unambiguous abnormal involuntary movements and found no differences in age, chronicity, education, or drug treatment that would distinguish the two groups. Patients with abnormal involuntary movements had greater evidence of voluntary motor abnormality, greater evidence of formal thought disorder, negative symptoms, and memory disturbance. It is interesting that patients with abnormal involuntary movements also showed lower premorbid intellectual ability. This study is certainly consistent with others (e.g., Waddington, 1995) that have indicated the complexity of abnormal involuntary motor features in schizophrenic disorders. Their presence suggests profound changes in cognition, lower likelihood of recovery, and greater severity of psychopathologic features among such patients.

Toward a Comparative Pathology for Schizophrenia

In schizophrenia a linkage exists among three features: cognitive deficits, motor abnormality, and psychosis. The association of these three characteristics is not unique to schizophrenia; indeed, a number of different neurologic and psychiatric disorders (e.g., Parkinson's disease, Huntington's disease, and bipolar disorder) share these elements (McHugh, 1989; Rogers, 1990). There is reason to believe that the coincidence of these features is not fortuitous (Bowman & Lewis, 1980; Farran-Ridge, 1926; Graybiel, 1984; Heimer, Switzer, & Van Hoesen, 1982; Javoy-Agid & Agid, 1980; McKenna, Lund, Mortimer, & Biggins, 1991). Indeed, researchers may unravel the underlying structural and physiologic factors that induce these disorders and demonstrate that their anatomic pathologies, although distinct, may arise in proximity to each other. For example, the basal ganglia and nearby structures (e.g., ventral–striatal–pallidal nuclear complex) may be a good candidate for a common anatomic region of pathology for these conditions (Albin, Young, & Pennery, 1989; Alexander, 1986; Nauta & Domesick, 1984). The basal ganglia is a dense set of neurons and neuronal tracts whose complex anatomy could be associated with the occurrence of these common features and other distinctive patterns based on relatively small differences in localization of pathology (Graybiel, Aosaki, Flaherty, & Kimura, 1994; McHugh, 1989). This proposal is consistent with frontal and cerebellar influences as well as the formulation that disrupted brain circuits contribute to schizophrenic pathology (Taylor, 1991). It merely underscores the importance of studying the comparative psychopathology and neuropathology of the disorders affecting various areas (Denny-Brown, 1950, 1958; Ojemann, 1982).

Discussion

The role of motor behavior in the pathogenesis of schizophrenia is not yet fully understood; however, it clearly does have a role. Motor abnormalities constitute part of the psychopathology, not simply an epiphenomenon such as a drug treatment effect.

Furthermore, motor abnormalities are related in various ways, some of which are clearly complex, to other aspects of the disorder, including speech deviance, memory performance, neurologic signs, emotional responsivity, and natural history, including outcome (Walker, Savoie, & Davis, 1995; Yarden & Discipio, 1971). This rich array of interconnections has been complemented by attempts to understand the structural correlates of motor disturbance in schizophrenia. By using assessments such as the motor synchrony examination (and, more recently, the line drawing task), my colleagues and I have been able to detect specific connections between motor anomaly and brain structure, for example, MRI volumes. It appears that frontal areas are associated with these motor abnormalities. The evidence also suggests that motor lateralization is poorly developed and may be a marker for a delay or deviation in normal brain development in schizophrenia, specifically a reduction or absence of normal hemispheric structural asymmetries. A plausible role for basal ganglia pathology is evident because of the coincidence of cognitive deficits, motor anomalies, and psychosis.

Motor anomalies suggest more severe pathology, a poorer prognosis, and a more severe level of cognitive impairment. Further studies guided by this knowledge could focus on a variety of issues, including the relationship between motor abnormality and drug treatment response; motor abnormality and the presence of other psychopathologic features, such as delusion or hallucination; and motor abnormality and prognosis.

Summary

Motor abnormalities play an important if not fully understood role in the pathogenesis of schizophrenia. Abnormal voluntary movements (AVMs) are frequent in schizophrenia. They are different phenomenologically and can be reliably distinguished from drug-induced movements. AVMs are related to other specific psychopathologic features, including memory, thinking, emotional blunting, nonlocalizing neurologic signs, and imaging characteristics. In addition, AVMs appear to be associated with a breakdown in the capacity to use redundancies in behavior, a characteristic that may account for their connection to other superficially different aspects of the disorder.

Lateralization of motor performance is reduced in schizophrenia and is associated with increased thought disorder, memory disturbances, and an earlier age of onset. Similarly, measures of precision (coordination of movement) are associated with age of onset in schizophrenia: less precision and earlier onset.

Involuntary movements are also frequent and have been associated with drug treatment, aging, and the disease process of schizophrenia itself. Such movements are associated with the same pattern of psychopathologic features but at a more severe level than the movements that are described as "voluntary" movements.

The coincidence of abnormal involuntary and voluntary movements, cognitive deficits, and psychosis suggests a possible role of the basal ganglia and related systems in the pathogenesis of schizophrenia. This connection is further supported by the presence of other disorders with basal ganglia abnormalities that share the same features. Finally, a satisfactory account of schizophrenia must ultimately provide an explanation for all forms of deviant motor movements associated with it.

References

Albin, R. L., Young, A. B., & Pennery, J. B. (1989). The functional anatomy of basal ganglia disorders. *Trends in Neurosciences, 12,* 366–375.

Alexander, G. E. (1986). Parallel organization of functionally segregated circuits linking basal ganglia and cortex. *Annual Review of Neurosciences, 9,* 357–381.

American Psychiatric Association. (1980). *Diagnostic and statistical manual of mental disorders* (3rd ed.). Washington, DC: Author.

Annett, M. (1967). The binomial distribution of right, mixed, and left-handedness. *Quarterly Journal of Experimental Psychology, 19,* 327–333.

Barnes, M. P., Saunders, M., Walls, T. J., Saunders, I., & Kirk, C. A. (1986). The syndrome of Karl Ludwig Kahlbaum. *Journal of Neurology, Neurosurgery and Psychiatry, 49,* 991–996.

Berrios, G. E. (1981). Stupor: A conceptual history. *Psychological Medicine, 11,* 677–688.

Bleuler, E. (1950). *Dementia praecox or the group of schizophrenias.* New York: International Universities Press. (Original work published 1911)

Blyler, C. R., Maher, B. A., Manschreck, T. C., & Fenton, W. F. (1997). Line drawing a possible measure of lateralized motor performance in schizophrenia. *Schizophrenia Research, 26,* 15–23.

Boklage, C. E. (1977). Schizophrenia, brain asymmetry development, twinning: Cellular relationship with etiologic and possibly prognostic implications. *Biological Psychiatry, 12,* 19–35.

Bowman, M., & Lewis, M. S. (1980). Sites of subcortical damage in diseases which resemble schizophrenia. *Neuropsychologia, 18,* 597–601.

Caligiuri, M. P., Lohr, J. B., & Jeste, D. V. (1993). Parkinsonism in neuroleptic naïve schizophrenic patients. *American Journal of Psychiatry, 150,* 1343–1348.

Carlsson, A. (1978). Antipsychotic drugs, neurotransmitters, and schizophrenia. *American Journal of Psychiatry, 135,* 164–173.

Crayton, J. W., Stalberg, E., & Hilton-Brown, P. (1977). The motor unit in psychotic patients: A single fibre EMG study. *Journal of Neurology, Neurosurgery, and Psychiatry, 40,* 455–463.

Cromwell, R. L. (1968). Stimulus redundancy in schizophrenia. *Journal of Nervous and Mental Disease, 146,* 360–375.

Crow, T. J., Cross, A. J., Johnstone, E. C., Owen, F., Owens, D. G. C., & Waddington, J. L. (1982). Abnormal involuntary movements in schizophrenia: Are they related to the disease process or its treatment? Are they associated with changes in dopamine receptors? *Journal of Clinical Psychopharmacology, 2,* 336–340.

Crow, T. J., Done, D. J., & Sacker, A. (1996). Cerebral lateralization is delayed in children who later develop schizophrenia. *Schizophrenia Research, 22,* 181–185.

Crow, T. J., Owens, D. G. C., Johnstone, E. C., Cross, A. J., & Owen, F. (1983). Does tardive dyskinesia exist? *Modern Problems in Pharmacopsychiatry, 21,* 206–219.

DeJong, R. (1967). *The neurological examination.* New York: Harper & Row.

Denny-Brown, D. (1950). Disintegration of motor function resulting from cerebral lesions. *Journal of Nervous and Mental Disease, 112,* 1–45.

Denny-Brown, D. (1958). The nature of apraxia. *Journal of Nervous and Mental Disease, 126,* 9–32.

Farran-Ridge, C. (1926). Some symptoms referable to the basal ganglia occurring in dementia praecox and epidemic encephalitis. *Journal of Mental Science, 72,* 513–523.

Fenton, W. S., Blyler, C. R., Wyatt, R. J., & McGlashan, T. H. (1977). Prevalence of spontaneous dyskinesia in schizophrenia and non-schizophrenic patients. *British Journal of Psychiatry, 171,* 265–268.

Freeman, T. (1969). *Psychopathology of the psychoses.* New York: International Universities Press.

Fricchione, G. L. (1985). Neuroleptic catatonia and its relationship to psychogenic catatonia. *Biological Psychiatry, 20,* 304–313.

Goode, D. J., Manning, A. A., Middleton, J. F., & Williams, B. (1981). Fine motor performance before and after treatment in schizophrenia and schizoaffective patients. *Psychiatry Research, 5,* 247–255.

Goode, D. J., Meltzer, H. Y., Crayton, J. W., & Mazura, T. A. (1977). Physiologic abnormalities of the neuromuscular system in schizophrenia. *Schizophrenia Bulletin, 3,* 121–138.

Graybiel, A. M. (1984). Neurochemically specified subsystems in the basal ganglia. In D. Evered & M. O'Connor (Eds.), *Functions of the basal ganglia* (pp. 114–149). London: Pitman.

Graybiel, A. M., Aosaki, T., Flaherty, A. W., & Kimura, M. (1994). The basal ganglia and adaptive motor control. *Science, 165*, 1826–1831.

Guggenheim, F. G., & Babigian, H. M. (1974). Catatonic schizophrenia: Epidemiology and clinical course. *Journal of Nervous and Mental Disease, 158*, 291–305.

Heimer, L., Switzer, R. D., & Van Hoesen, G. W. (1982). Ventral striatum and ventral pallidum: Components of the motor system? *Trends in Neurosciences, 5*, 83–87.

Iager, A. C, Kirch, D. G., Jeste, D. V., & Wyatt, R. J. (1986). Defect symptoms and abnormal involuntary movements in schizophrenia. *Biological Psychiatry, 21*, 751–755.

Ivry, R. B., Keele, S. W., & Diener, H. W. (1988). Dissociation of the lateral and medial cerebellum in movement timing and movement execution. *Experimental Brain Research, 73*, 167–180.

Javoy-Agid, F., & Agid, Y. (1980). Is the mesocortical dopaminergic system involved in Parkinson's disease? *Neurology, 30*, 1326–1331.

Kahlbaum, K. (1973). *Catatonia* (Y. Levij & T. Priden, Trans.). Baltimore: Johns Hopkins University Press. (Original work published 1874)

Keele, S., & Margolin, D. I. (1984). Motor disorder and the timing of repetitive movements. *Annals of the New York Academy of Sciences, 423*, 183–192.

King, H. E. (1954). *Psychomotor aspects of mental disease: An experimental study.* Cambridge, MA: Harvard University Press.

King, H. E. (1976). Psychomotor correlates of behavior disorder. In M. L. Kietzman, S. Sutton, & J. Zubin (Eds.), *Experimental approaches to psychopathology* (pp. 421–450). New York: Academic Press.

Kraepelin, E. (1919). *Dementia praecox and paraphrenia* (R. Barclay, Trans.). Edinburgh, Scotland: Livingstone.

Latham, C., Holzman, P., Manschreck, T. C., & Tole, J. (1981). Optokinetic nystagmus and smooth pursuit eye movements in schizophrenia. *Archives of General Psychiatry, 38*, 997–1003.

Luria, A. R. (1966). *Higher cortical function in man.* New York: Basic Books.

Mahendra, B. (1981). Where have all the catatonics gone? *Psychological Medicine, 11*, 669–671.

Maher, B. A. (1972). The language of schizophrenia: A review and interpretation. *British Journal of Psychiatry, 120*, 3–17.

Maher, B. A., Manschreck, T. C., & Rucklos, M. (1980). Contextual constraint and the recall of verbal material in schizophrenia: The effect of thought disorder. *British Journal of Psychiatry, 137*, 69–73.

Maher, B. A., Manschreck, T. C., Woods, B. T., Yurgelun-Todd, D. A., & Tsuang, M. T. (1995). Frontal brain volume and context effects in short term recall in schizophrenia. *Biological Psychiatry, 37*, 144–150.

Manoach, D. S., Maher, B. A., & Manschreck, T. C. (1988). Left-handedness and thought disorder in the schizophrenias, *Journal of Abnormal Psychology, 97*, 97–99.

Manschreck, T. C. (1983). Psychopathology of motor behavior in schizophrenia. In B. A. Maher (Ed.), *Progress in experimental personality research* (Vol. 12, pp. 53–99). New York: Academic Press.

Manschreck, T. C. (1986). Motor abnormalities in schizophrenic disorders. In H. Nasrallah & D. Weinberger (Eds.), *The neurology of schizophrenia: Vol. 1. Handbook of schizophrenia* (pp. 65–96). Amsterdam: Elsevier–North Holland.

Manschreck, T. C. (1989). Motor and cognitive disturbances in schizophrenic disorders. In C. Tamminga & S. C. Schulz (Eds.), *Schizophrenia: Scientific progress* (pp. 372–380). New York: Oxford University Press.

Manschreck, T. C., & Ames, D. (1984). Neurological features and psychopathology in schizophrenic disorders. *Biological Psychiatry, 19*, 703–719.

Manschreck, T. C., Keuthen, N. J., Schneyer, N. L., Celada, M. T., Laughery, J., & Collins, P. (1990). Abnormal involuntary movements and chronic schizophrenic disorders. *Biological Psychiatry, 27*, 150–158.

Manschreck, T. C., & Kleinman, A. (1979). Psychiatry's identity crisis: A critical rational remedy. *General Hospital Psychiatry, 1*, 166–173.

Manschreck, T. C., & Latham, C. (1983). [Optokinetic nystagmus and voluntary motor disorder in schizophrenia]. Unpublished raw data.

Manschreck, T. C., Maher, B. A., & Ader, D. (1981). Formal thought disorder, the type–token ratio and disturbed voluntary motor behavior in schizophrenia. *British Journal of Psychiatry, 139*, 7–15.

Manschreck, T. C., Maher, B. A., Candela, S. F., Redmond, D., Yurgelun-Todd, D., & Tsuang, M. (2000). Impaired verbal memory is associated with impaired motor performance in schizophrenia: Relationship to brain structure. *Schizophrenia Research, 43*, 21–32.

Manschreck, T. C., Maher, B. A., Candela, S. F., & Winzig, L. L. (2002). *Poorly lateralized and imprecise motor performances are associated with an earlier age of onset in schizophrenia.* Manuscript submitted for publication.

Manschreck, T. C., Maher, B. A., Hoover, T., & Ames, D. (1984). The type–token ratio in schizophrenic disorders: Clinical and research value. *Psychological Medicine, 14,* 151–158.

Manschreck, T. C., Maher, B. A., Milavetz, J., Ames, D., Weisstein, C., & Schneyer, M. L. (1988). Semantic priming in thought-disordered schizophrenic patients. *Schizophrenia Research, 1,* 61–66.

Manschreck, T. C., Maher, B. A., Redmond, D., Miller, C., & Beaudette, S. M. (1996). Laterality, memory, and thought disorder in schizophrenia. *Neuropsychiatry, Neuropsychology, and Behavioral Neurology, 9,* 1–7.

Manschreck, T. C., Maher, B. A., Rosenthal, J., & Berner, J. (1991). Reduced primacy and related features in schizophrenia. *Schizophrenia Research, 5,* 35–41.

Manschreck, T. C., Maher, B. A., Rucklos, M. E., & Vereen, D. R. (1982). Disturbed voluntary motor activity in schizophrenic disorder. *Psychological Medicine, 12,* 73–84.

Manschreck, T. C., Maher, B. A., Rucklos, M. E., Vereen, D. R., & Ader, D. N. (1981). Deficient motor synchrony in schizophrenia. *Journal of Abnormal Psychology, 90,* 321–328.

Manschreck, T. C., Maher, B. A., Rucklos, M. E., & White, M. (1979). The predictability of thought disordered speech in schizophrenic patients. *British Journal of Psychiatry, 134,* 595–601.

Manschreck, T. C., Maher, B. A., Waller, N. G., Ames, D., & Latham, C. A. (1985). Deficient motor synchrony in schizophrenic disorders: Clinical correlates. *Biological Psychiatry, 20,* 990–1002.

Marsden, C. D. (1982). Motor disorders in schizophrenia. *Psychological Medicine, 12,* 13–15.

McCreadie, R. G., & Ohaeri, J. U. (1994). Movement disorder in never and minimally treated Nigerian schizophrenia patients. *British Journal of Psychiatry, 164,* 184–189.

McHugh, P. R. (1989). The neuropsychiatry of basal ganglia disorders. *Neuropsychiatry, Neuropsychology, and Behavioral Neurology, 2,* 239–247.

McKenna, P. J., Lund, C. E., Mortimer, C. E., & Biggins, C. A. (1991). Motor, volitional and behavioral disorders in schizophrenia. 2: The conflict of paradigms hypothesis. *British Journal of Psychiatry, 158,* 328–336.

Meltzer, H. (1976). Neuromuscular dysfunction in schizophrenia. *Schizophrenia Bulletin, 2,* 106–135.

Miller, G., & Selfridge, J. (1950). Verbal context and the recall of meaningful material. *American Journal of Psychology, 63,* 176–185.

National Institute of Mental Health. (1974). *Abnormal Involuntary Movement Scale* (U.S. Public Health Service Publication No. MH-9-17). Washington, DC: U.S. Government Printing Office.

Nauta, W. J., & Domesick, V. B. (1984). Afferent and efferent relationships of the basal ganglia. In D. Evered & M. O' Conner (Eds.), *Functions of the basal ganglia* (pp. 3–29). London: Pitman.

Ojemann, G. A. (1982). Interrelationships in the localisation of language, memory, and motor mechanisms in human cortex and thalamus. In R. A. Thomson & J. R. Green (Eds.), *New perspectives in cerebral localisation* (pp. 157–175). New York: Raven Press.

Owens, D. G. C., Johnstone, E. C., & Frith, C. D. (1982). Spontaneous involuntary disorders of movement: Their prevalence, severity, and distribution in chronic schizophrenics with and without treatment with neuroleptics. *Archives of General Psychiatry, 39,* 452–461.

Piran, N., Bigler, E. D., & Cohen, D. (1982). Motor laterality and eye dominance suggest a unique pattern of cerebral organization in schizophrenia. *Archives of General Psychiatry, 39,* 1006–1010.

Robins, E., & Guze, S. (1970). Establishment of diagnostic validity in psychiatric illnesses: Its application to schizophrenia. *American Journal of Psychiatry, 126,* 983–987.

Rogers, D. (1985). The motor disorders of severe psychiatric illness: A conflict of paradigms. *British Journal of Psychiatry, 147,* 221–232.

Rogers, D. (1990). Psychiatric consequences of basal ganglia disease. *Seminars in Neurology, 10,* 262–266.

Rogers, D. (1992). *Motor disorder in psychiatry.* Chichester, England: Wiley.

Schneider R. D., & Grossi, V. (1979). Differences in muscle activity before, during and after responding in a simple reaction time task: Schizophrenics vs. normals. *Psychiatry Research, 1,* 141.

Shannon, C. E. (1948). A mathematical theory of communication. *Bell System Technology Journal, 379,* 623–656.

Slavney, P. R., & McHugh, P. R. (1987). *Psychiatric polarities.* Baltimore: Johns Hopkins University Press.

Spitzer, R., Endicott, J., & Robins, E. (1978). *Research diagnostic criteria.* New York: New York State Psychiatric Institute.

Taylor, M. A. (1991). The role of the cerebellum in the pathogenesis of schizophrenia. *Neuropsychiatry, Neuropsychology, and Behavioral Neurology, 4,* 251–280.

Turner, T. H. (1992). A diagnostic analysis of the casebooks of Ticehurst House Asylum, 1845–1890. *Psychological Medicine, 21*(Suppl.), 1–70.

Van der Velde, C. D. (1976). Variability in schizophrenia, reflection of a regulatory disease. *Archives of General Psychiatry, 33,* 489–496.

Waddington, J. L. (1995). Psychopathological and cognitive correlates of tardive dyskinesia in schizophrenia and other disorders treated with neuroleptic drugs. *Behavioral Neurology of Movement Disorders, 65,* 211–229.

Waddington, J. L., & Youssef, H. A. (1986). Late onset involuntary movements in chronic schizophrenia: Relationship of tardive dyskinesia to intellectual impairment and negative symptoms. *British Journal of Psychiatry, 149,* 616–620.

Waddington, J. L., & Youssef, H. A. (1996). Cognitive dysfunction in chronic schizophrenia followed perspectively over 10 years and its longitudinal relationship to the emergence of tardive dyskinesia. *Psychological Medicine, 26,* 681–688.

Walker, E. F., Savoie, T., & Davis, D. (1995). Neuromotor precursors of schizophrenia. *Schizophrenia Bulletin, 20,* 441–451.

Wing, A. M., & Kristofferson, A. B. (1973). Response delays and the timing of discrete motor responses. *Perception and Psychophysics, 14,* 5–12.

Wojcik, J., Gelenberg, A., LaBrie, R. A., & Berg, M. (1980). Prevalence of tardive dyskinesia in an outpatient population. *Comprehensive Psychiatry, 21,* 370–379.

Yarden, P. E., & Discipio, W. J. (1971). Abnormal movements and prognosis in schizophrenia. *American Journal of Psychiatry, 128,* 317–323.

4

Negative Symptoms, Neuromotor Abnormalities, and Vulnerability to Schizophrenia

Robert H. Dworkin, Elna M. Nagasako, Scott C. Clark, William C. Wirshing, Xavier F. Amador, Jack M. Gorman, and Lyman C. Wynne

The research discussed in this chapter has its origins in the first research project I conducted after becoming one of Brendan Maher's graduate students. This study, begun in 1973, arose out of vigorous discussions of the role of genetic influences in the development of schizophrenia that occurred in Brendan's graduate student proseminar. During these discussions, Brendan recalled that Irving Gottesman had conducted a twin study of normal personality in adolescents in the Boston area in the early 1960s, and he somewhat offhandedly suggested that it would be worthwhile to conduct a follow-up study of these twins, who would now be in their late 20s. Barbara Winstead and I rose to the bait, and with Brendan's encouragement and tutelage, and Irv Gottesman's expertise in behavior genetics provided from afar, we relocated 42 pairs of the twins.

In studying these twins during their adolescence, Irv had administered the Minnesota Multiphasic Personality Inventory and the California Personality Inventory, and our follow-up study consisted of a series of Saturdays spent readministering these measures and providing refreshments to one or two twins at a time in a conference room outside Brendan's office. Although a very small sample of twins by today's standards, this was the first longitudinal twin study of normal personality (Dworkin, Burke, Maher, & Gottesman, 1976, 1977). I became intrigued with the role of genetic influences in both normal personality and psychopathology; having identified Brendan as a doctoral committee chair equally fascinated by this question and having found a willing sample of adult twins, I examined in my dissertation research genetic influences on person–situation interactions, the animus of personality research at the time (Dworkin, 1978, 1979).

The original impetus for the follow-up study of these twins, however, had been to identify genetic aspects of normal personality that might play a role in the development of schizophrenia. It was here that Brendan's influence was again piv-

The research described in this chapter was supported in part by National Institute of Mental Health Grant MH-51791. We are indebted to Stephanie White Bateman, Crystal Blyler, Rachel Levy, and Harriet Oster for their assistance with data collection and to Raymond Goetz for his invaluable help with management of the New York State Psychiatric Institute data.

otal. The idea that an individual's vulnerability to developing schizophrenia could be a consequence of extremes of normal personality—that is, that individuals with schizophrenia were quantitatively rather than qualitatively different from normal—had been a recurring theme in the discussions that occurred almost 30 years ago between Brendan and his graduate students. These discussions, and Brendan's mentorship in experimental research on personality and psychopathology, were not only the sources of my enduring belief in the validity of a dimensional approach to psychopathology; they also provided the conceptual and methodological foundation for the ongoing research program discussed in this chapter.

—Robert H. Dworkin

A dimensional approach is particularly apt in considering the negative symptoms of schizophrenia, such as anhedonia and affective blunting, which are psychological processes that even minimally astute observers of human behavior can recognize vary widely among normal individuals. In 1983, Robert H. Dworkin and Mark F. Lenzenweger initiated a program of research in which genetic influences and other aspects of positive and negative symptoms were examined in case histories from twin studies of schizophrenia that were rated for a large number of demographic and clinical characteristics.

Two important conclusions were reached from this research. One was that negative symptoms were more closely associated with the genetic predisposition to develop schizophrenia than were positive symptoms (e.g., Dworkin & Lenzenweger, 1984; Dworkin, Lenzenweger, Moldin, Skillings, & Levick, 1988). The second conclusion was that negative symptoms represented a dimension of schizophrenia symptomatology that was independent of both positive symptoms and social functioning (e.g., Dworkin, 1990; Lenzenweger & Dworkin, 1996; Lenzenweger, Dworkin, & Wethington, 1989).

These conclusions were further supported by a series of studies in which positive and negative symptoms and social competence were investigated in the offspring of parents with schizophrenia and mood disorder by Dworkin in collaboration with Barbara Cornblatt and Nikki Erlenmeyer-Kimling (e.g., Dworkin et al., 1990, 1991, 1993). In these studies, two key negative symptoms—affective flattening and poverty of speech—were examined, and the results indicated that the adolescent offspring of parents with schizophrenia had significantly greater affective flattening and poverty of speech than the adolescent offspring of parents with mood disorders and normal comparison parents.

Genetic Influences on Negative Symptoms

The results of these studies suggested that negative symptoms—and affective deficits in particular—reflect important processes in the pathogenesis of schizophrenia. The results of research conducted by other investigators during the past 15 years have been generally consistent with the results of these studies. A number of different research designs have been used to explore the relationship between genetic influences in schizophrenia and both negative symptoms and the *deficit syndrome*, a subtype of schizophrenia characterized by the presence of enduring negative symptoms.

The results of an increasing number of studies have suggested that the presence of either prominent negative symptoms or the deficit syndrome in individuals with schizophrenia is associated with an increased risk of schizophrenia in their relatives (Berenbaum, Oltmanns, & Gottesman, 1990; T. Cannon, Mednick, & Parnas, 1990; Castle, Sham, Wessely, & Murray, 1994; Dollfus et al., 1998; Dollfus, Ribeyre, & Petit, 1996; Gottesman, McGuffin, & Farmer, 1987; Kendler, McGuire, Gruenberg, & Walsh, 1994; Kirkpatrick, Buchanan, Ross, & Carpenter, 2001; Kirkpatrick, Castle, Murray, & Carpenter, 2000; Malaspina et al., 2000; McGuffin, Farmer, & Gottesman, 1987; Van Os et al., 1997; Verdoux et al., 1996; cf. Baron, Gruen, & Romo-Gruen, 1992; Cardno et al., 1997). A recent study of high-density schizophrenia families also addressed the role of genetic influences in negative symptoms; in this study, affected individuals from families with evidence of linkage to chromosome 8p were found to have significantly greater "affective deterioration" (Kendler et al., 2000).

Other studies have examined whether negative symptoms are more common among relatives of individuals with schizophrenia than among relatives of normal individuals or of individuals with other psychiatric disorders. The results of several family studies have suggested that negative symptoms and affective deficits such as flat affect and anhedonia discriminate the relatives of individuals with schizophrenia (Bassett, Collins, Nuttall, & Honer, 1993; Clementz, Grove, Katsanis, & Iacono, 1991; Craver & Pogue-Geile, 1999; Franke, Maier, Hardt, & Hain, 1993; Grove et al., 1991; Katsanis, Iacono, & Beiser, 1990; Kendler, McGuire, Gruenberg, & Walsh, 1995; Kendler, Thacker, & Walsh, 1996; Torgersen, Onstad, Skre, Edvardsen, & Kringlen, 1993; Tsuang, 1993; Tsuang, Gilbertson, & Faraone, 1991) and the deficit syndrome (Kirkpatrick, Ross, Walsh, Karkowski, & Kendler, 2000) from other groups.

Negative symptoms have also been found to be correlated between individuals with schizophrenia and their first-degree relatives (Burke, Murphy, Bray, Walsh, & Kendler, 1996; Fanous, Gardner, Walsh, & Kendler, 2001; Hwu et al., 1997; Kendler et al., 1997; Tsuang, 1993; cf. Cardno et al., 1999), and this correlation may be greater than the corresponding correlation for positive symptoms (Tsuang, 1993). Similarly, the results of one recent study indicated that sibling pairs with schizophrenia significantly resembled each other with respect to whether they had the deficit syndrome or not (Ross et al., 2000).

In addition, a number of twin and family studies have found evidence of genetic influences on affective deficits, anhedonia, and other negative symptoms in normal individuals as well as in individuals with schizophrenia (e.g., Berenbaum & McGrew, 1993; Berenbaum et al., 1990; Dworkin & Saczynski, 1984; Kendler & Hewitt, 1992; Kendler et al., 1991); these data are consistent with the suggestion that negative symptoms reflect the genetic predisposition to develop schizophrenia. Moreover, recent studies of normal adolescents with elevated levels of anhedonia have found a greater risk of psychotic illnesses, schizophrenia spectrum disorders, and schizotypal symptoms at follow-up assessments 10 years later (Chapman, Chapman, Kwapil, Eckblad, & Zinser, 1994; Kwapil, 1998; Kwapil, Miller, Zinser, Chapman, & Chapman, 1997). Although not directly relevant to genetic influences on negative symptoms, these results provide additional support for the conclusion that negative symptoms have an important role to play in understanding in the pathogenesis of schizophrenia.

Affective Deficits and Neuromotor Abnormalities

> Indeed, for many observers the motor symptoms occupy an important place in the symptomatology. . . . The coordination of arm and leg movements is often disturbed. . . . In the women's division of the hospital in Rheinau, many patients were able to circulate freely in a rather large garden. . . . From certain positions one saw the patients only up to the knee. Yet in many of them, one could make the diagnosis simply from their will-o'-the-wisp-like gait; it did not lose this peculiarity even when the patients were moving toward a definite goal. (Bleuler, 1911/1950, pp. 170–171)

Dworkin and colleagues' studies of twins and the offspring of individuals with schizophrenia required that negative symptoms be reliably rated from published case histories and from videotaped clinical interviews. In developing standardized procedures for rating affective deficits, it became increasingly clear that very little attention had been devoted to considering the nature of affective deficits in schizophrenia. The specific behaviors that had been included in measures of affective flattening—for example, facial expressiveness, vocal inflection, and eye contact—were all interpersonal behaviors that serve to facilitate communication among people. Individuals with schizophrenia may well lack these interpersonal behaviors because they suffer from an affective deficit. However, as Dworkin (1992) proposed, diminished facial expressiveness or vocal inflections, for example, may occur in schizophrenia not because of an affective deficit but because individuals with schizophrenia suffer from neuromotor abnormalities or social skills deficits (see also Berenbaum & Rotter, 1992; Bermanzohn & Siris, 1992; Knight & Valner, 1993).

As the quoted material at the beginning of this section indicates, neuromotor abnormalities have been a readily observable characteristic of individuals with schizophrenia from the time of Bleuler (1911/1950) to the present (e.g., Chatterjee et al., 1995; Fenton, Wyatt, & McGlashan, 1994; Flashman, Flaum, Gupta, & Andreasen, 1996; Gervin et al., 1998; Gupta et al., 1995; Kinney, Yurgelun-Todd, & Woods, 1993; Manschreck, 1989, 1993; Woods, Kinney, & Yurgelun-Todd, 1986). Indeed, the results of studies conducted by Theo C. Manschreck and Maher suggest that affective flattening is associated with neuromotor deficits in schizophrenia (Manschreck, Maher, Rucklos, & Vereen, 1982; Manschreck, Maher, Waller, Ames, & Latham, 1985). These findings provided one of the bases for a study in which Dworkin et al. (1993) found that neuromotor dysfunction in childhood predicted affective flattening in adolescents at risk for schizophrenia.

Considered together with the results of the earlier studies by Manschreck and Maher, the results of this study of high-risk adolescents suggested that affective flattening in schizophrenia might reflect, at least in part, the neuromotor dysfunction found in individuals with the disorder. Studies with normal individuals had found that there are significant relationships between the facial expression of emotion and subjective emotional experience (e.g., Ekman, Friesen, & Ancoli, 1980), and so Dworkin, Clark, Amador, and Gorman (1996) hypothesized that the affective flattening observed in schizophrenia reflects both neuromotor dysfunction and an affective deficit. Because associations between extrapyramidal side effects and ratings of negative symptoms had been reported (Mayer, Alpert, Stastny, Perlick, & Empfield, 1985; Prosser et al., 1987; see also Blanchard & Neale, 1992), Dworkin et al. (1996) focused their research on patients who had been withdrawn from all neuroleptics, irrespective of whether these medications were typical or atypical. Although the results of recent studies have suggested that atypical neuroleptics are associated with fewer extrapyramidal symptoms than typical neuroleptics are, they may lead to significant improvement in negative symptoms (e.g., Tollefson et al., 1997; Tollefson & Sanger, 1997). If any reduction in facial expressiveness caused by neuroleptics was "confounded by an increase in facial activity during improvement, two opposing tendencies would exist" (Schneider et al., 1992, p. 238).

As hypothesized, Dworkin et al.'s (1996) results suggested that the measures of affective flattening they examined reflected not only affective deficits but also neuromotor dysfunction. They concluded that individuals with schizophrenia may manifest flat affect not only because their experience of emotion is reduced but also because the motoric expression of their emotions is compromised.

Neuromotor Abnormalities in Patients With Schizophrenia

The measure of neuromotor dysfunction used in Dworkin et al.'s (1996) study, however, did not fulfill what Dworkin remembered as Maher's most aphoristic injunction to his graduate students about conducting research: "Whenever possible, *count* behaviors, don't rate them." Dworkin et al. (1996) used a brief rating scale of neurological signs (Clark, Malaspina, Hasan, Koeppel, & Gorman, 1993); although reliable and able to discriminate individuals with schizophrenia from normal individuals, such measures did not seem to have great promise as a sensitive means of identifying relatives and other individuals with a vulnerability to developing schizophrenia. Indeed, many investigators have argued that continued progress in research on the etiology of schizophrenia is dependent on improved measures of the schizophrenia phenotype and of putative markers of the schizophrenia genotype (e.g., Faraone et al., 1995; Goldman-Rakic, 1995; Matthysse et al., 1992; Matthysse & Parnas, 1992; Tsuang, Stone, & Faraone, 2000).

Manschreck and Maher had been conducting a program of research that counted motor behaviors as well as rated them (e.g., Manschreck et al., 1982; Manschreck et al., 1985; Manschreck, Maher, Rucklos, Vereen, & Ader, 1981), and this research provided a model for the two studies we discuss in the remainder of this chapter (see also Caligiuri, Lohr, & Jeste, 1993; Caligiuri, Lohr, & Ruck, 1997; Vrtunski, Simpson, & Meltzer, 1989). To further examine neuromotor abnormalities in schizophrenia, we used a comprehensive clinical neurological examination that was developed by Scott C. Clark and a set of electromechanical measures that was developed by William C. Wirshing.

Study Participants

The participants were 11 inpatients from the Schizophrenia Research Unit of the New York State Psychiatric Institute and 34 normal controls. The mean age of the 11 patients was 34.0 years (range: 20–55 years), and 4 were female. All patients fulfilled the criteria for schizophrenia or schizoaffective disorder from the *Diagnostic and Statistical Manual of Mental Disorders*, fourth edition (American Psychiatric Association, 1994). Research diagnoses were based on past records and the information provided in a semistructured interview by a trained and reliable master's- or greater level clinician using the Diagnostic Interview for Genetic Studies (Nurn-berger et al., 1994). A consensus diagnosis was arrived at by the rater and Xavier F. Amador, a senior clinician. Patients were screened to exclude those who had a history of neurological insult or illness and current substance abuse or a history of substance abuse that would obscure the diagnosis of schizophrenia. At the time of testing, patients had been withdrawn from all neuroleptic medications for at least 2 weeks.

The control participants were 34 individuals recruited by means of posters placed throughout Columbia–Presbyterian Medical Center in New York City. Individuals who were older than 55 years of age, who currently had any major medical illness, who were taking any psychotropic medications, or who had any Axis I diagnosis (except simple phobia) or a history of substance abuse within the past 6 months were excluded from participation in the research. The mean age of the 34 control participants was 33.1 years (range: 18–57 years), and 16 were female.

Measures

Clinical and electromechanical measures of motor abnormalities were adminis-tered to all participants by trained doctoral-level clinical psychologists. The clinical neurological examination was designed to comprehensively assess soft and hard neurological symptoms and signs using a structured format. Summary scores were derived from the ratings of total motor abnormalites and total sensory abnor-malities. Extrapyramidal symptoms were assessed with the Abnormal Involuntary Movement Scale (Guy, 1976), the Simpson–Angus Extrapyramidal Symptom Rating Scale (Simpson & Angus, 1970), and the Barnes Akathisia Scale (Barnes, 1989), which were administered to all participants at the same time as the neurological examination.

The electromechanical measures used to examine neuromotor abnormalities as-sessed resting and action tremor, muscle rigidity, and bradykinesia. Resting tremor was measured using a resting hand platform device (Kern, Green, Satz, & Wirsh-ing, 1991; Wirshing, Cummings, Dencker, & May, 1991; Wirshing, Freidenberg, Cummings, & Bartzokis, 1989). The hand is fully supported by an 8-cm diameter platform resting on a load cell. The load cell measures the amount of force exerted by the hand as a function of time. This signal was differentiated (i.e., the force per unit of time was calculated) and sent to a data acquisition board with a sampling rate of 100 Hz. Six 20-s intervals were recorded for each hand. The data from each epoch were averaged and Fourier transformed. Action tremor was measured using the resting hand platform device and an analog meter that displayed the amount of force exerted on the platform of the device. Instead of resting the hand on the platform, participants were instructed to press down with their index finger on the center of the platform with sufficient force (1.5 lbs [0.68 kg]) to keep the analog meter needle in the center of the display. The desired force magnitude was indicated on the ana-log meter with a target. Two 20-s intervals were recorded for each hand. The data acquired were sampled at 100 Hz and subsequently Fourier transformed.

For both the resting and action tremor assessments the spectra obtained were used to calculate two parameters to quantify the degree of tremor present. The first parameter reflects the amount of activity in the 3–6 Hz range, the Parkinsonian tremor band (Wirshing et al., 1989), and the second parameter reflects the amount of activity in the 6–12 Hz range. Each parameter was calculated by defining the maximum amplitude (A_{max}) and the average amplitude (A_{avg}) in the specified frequency range. The number reported is equal to $\sqrt{(A_{max}^2/A_{avg})}$.

Rigidity was measured using a rotating disk. This device consists of a 46-cm diameter horizontally mounted rotating circular disk with a handle perpendicular to the disk surface. The disk apparatus is mounted on a set of four load cells arranged in a square. The cells are paired diagonally, defining two orthogonal axes. The difference between the output of the two cells on a given axis is a measure of the force exerted in that direction. The combined output of the four load cells is thus a measure of the magnitude and direction of the force exerted on the disk handle. This force was measured at 32 evenly spaced points in the disk's rotation. The participants were instructed to grip the disk's handle while otherwise leaving the test arm as relaxed as possible. The disk was then rotated with variable speed through eight rotations, and the average force magnitude for all eight rotations was calculated. The average of one set of eight rotations performed for each arm with the participant's contralateral arm at rest was calculated.

Bradykinesia was assessed using a doorknob attached to a rotation sensor. The output from this sensor was sampled at 100 Hz. In this task, participants were instructed to rotate the doorknob back and forth as quickly as possible. Two 10-s epochs were recorded for each hand. The "count" parameter calculated from the data is equal to the average for both hands of the total number of revolutions swept out by the participant, multiplied by 1,024.

In addition to this set of electromechanical measures of motor abnormalities, the Purdue Pegboard test (Tiffin, 1968) was administered to provide another quantitative measure of motor coordination that has been used frequently in neuropsychological studies of schizophrenia (e.g., Flashman et al., 1996).

Results

Table 4.1 presents the mean scores for each of the clinical measures of neurological and motor abnormalities. As can be seen from table, patients with schizophrenia

Table 4.1. Clinical Measures of Neurological Signs and Symptoms and Motor Abnormalities in Schizophrenia Patients and Control Participants

Measure	Schizophrenia patients			Control participants			t	df
	M	SD	n	M	SD	n		
Neuromotor symptoms	3.00	1.12	7	1.10	1.07	34	4.24***	39
Neurosensory symptoms	0.71	0.70	7	0.35	0.55	33	1.52	38
Extrapyramidal Rating Scale	1.00	1.32	7	1.13	1.35	30	−0.24	35
Akathisia Scale	3.00	2.00	7	0.65	1.38	31	3.75***	36
Abnormal Involuntary Movement Scale	3.29	4.72	7	0.90	1.81	31	1.32[a]	6.41

[a]Assumes unequal variances.
***$p < .001$, two-tailed.

who had been withdrawn from all neuroleptic medication had significantly greater neuromotor symptoms and akathisia. Table 4.2 presents the mean scores for each of the electromechanical measures and for the Purdue Pegboard time. The patients with schizophrenia had significantly greater resting and action 3–6 Hz tremor, greater muscle rigidity, and slower Purdue Pegboard performance. These data are consistent with previous reports of neuromotor abnormalities in neuroleptic-naive patients with schizophrenia, in which both clinical and electromechanical methods of assessment have been used (e.g., Caligiuri et al., 1993; Chatterjee et al., 1995; Gupta et al., 1995).

Neuromotor Abnormalities in Offspring of Individuals With Schizophrenia

The results of this study of patients withdrawn from all neuroleptic medication provide support for the validity of the electromechanical measures of neuromotor abnormalities. Our primary aim in assessing neuromotor function using electromechanical instruments, however, was not only to determine whether they were sensitive enough to detect abnormalities intrinsic to schizophrenia but also to attempt to identify abnormalities that reflect the vulnerability to develop the disorder. Neuromotor abnormalities in schizophrenia are associated with a family history of psychosis (Woods, Yurgelun-Todd, & Kinney, 1987), and studies of first-degree relatives of individuals with schizophrenia have found that neurologic signs—especially neuromotor abnormalities—discriminate their siblings, parents, and offspring from various comparison samples (e.g., Clementz, Sweeney, Hirt, & Haas, 1990; Dworkin et al., 1993; Grove et al., 1991; Holzman et al., 1974; Holzman, Solomon, Levin, & Waternaux, 1984; Ismail, Cantor-Graae, & McNeil, 1998; Kinney, Woods, & Yurgelun-Todd, 1986; Kinney, Yurgelun-Todd, & Woods, 1991; McNeil, Harty, Blennow, & Cantor-Graae, 1993). In addition, the results of a recent study of individuals with schizophrenia-spectrum personality disorders suggested that spontaneous dyskine-

Table 4.2. Electromechanical and Purdue Pegboard Measures of Motor Abnormalities in Schizophrenia Patients and Control Participants

Measure	Schizophrenia patients			Control participants			t	df
	M	SD	n	M	SD	n		
Resting tremor (3–6 Hz)	3.67	1.63	8	2.30	1.70	33	2.06*	39
Resting tremor (6–12 Hz)	76.79	39.07	8	74.40	30.89	33	0.19	39
Action tremor (3–6 Hz)	7.21	1.36	8	5.16	1.20	33	4.21***	39
Action tremor (6–12 Hz)	6.57	2.49	8	6.11	1.98	33	0.57	39
Muscle rigidity	386.94	123.06	8	232.51	116.02	33	3.34**	39
Bradykinesia count	$1.54e^4$	$6.93e^3$	8	$1.76e^4$	$5.61e^3$	33	−0.97	39
Purdue Pegboard time	93.86	30.18	11	69.83	9.44	32	2.60[a]*	10.68

[a]Assumes unequal variances.
*$p < .05$, two-tailed. **$p < .01$, two-tailed. ***$p < .001$, two-tailed.

sia and dyskineticlike movements are common in schizotypal personality disorder (Cassady, Adami, Moran, Kunkel, & Thaker, 1998).

Neuromotor abnormalities in first-degree relatives of individuals with schizophrenia have also been found to be associated with affective deficits (e.g., Dworkin et al., 1993) and social–interpersonal abnormalities (e.g., Clementz, Sweeney, Hirt, & Haas, 1991). To provide a basis for examining the relationship between affective and neuromotor deficits in individuals with a vulnerability to developing schizophrenia, we administered the clinical neurological examination and electromechanical measures described previously to a sample of adult offspring of patients with schizophrenia.

Study Participants

In 1972, Lyman Wynne and his colleagues began the University of Rochester Child and Family Study (URCAFS), a prospective investigation of the sons of hospitalized patients with a diagnosis of functional psychiatric disorder (e.g., Wynne, 1984; Wynne, Cole, & Perkins, 1987). To be eligible for enrollment in the study, the sons of patients had to be 4, 7, or 10 years of age and not receiving any psychiatric treatment at the time the study began. Although the parents had originally been diagnosed on the basis of *DSM–II* criteria (American Psychiatric Association, 1968) criteria, they were rediagnosed when *DSM–III* (American Psychiatric Association, 1980) became available.

To examine neuromotor function in first-degree relatives of individuals with schizophrenia, we conducted a follow-up of URCAFS index sons and their siblings whose parents had received a *DSM–III* rediagnosis of schizophrenia or schizoaffective disorder. To date, we have studied 20 of these adult offspring; their mean age is 32.2 years (range: 18–44 years), and 10 are female.

The URCAFS had been designed to identify differences between sons of parents with schizophrenia and depression and did not include a comparison group of sons of normal parents. We therefore have recruited a sample of 14 adults to serve as control participants in our follow-up study of the URCAFS sons and their siblings. These nonpatient control participants were recruited by means of posters placed throughout the University of Rochester Medical Center. Individuals who were older than 45 years of age, who had more than 16 years of schooling, who currently had any major medical illness or a history of a neurological disorder or a head injury with loss of consciousness, who were taking any psychotropic medications, or who had any Axis I diagnosis or history of substance abuse were excluded from participation in the research. Also excluded from participation were any individuals who had a first-degree relative with a history of psychiatric hospitalization or a first-, second-, or third-degree relative who had been diagnosed with schizophrenia. The mean age of these 14 control participants is 25.6 years (range: 19–43 years), and 9 are female.

Measures

The same clinical and electromechanical measures of motor abnormalities described earlier were administered to URCAFS offspring and control participants by a trained graduate student research associate.

Results

Table 4.3 presents the mean scores for each of the measures of neurological and motor abnormalities based on the clinical neurological examination. As can be seen from the table, the adult offspring of parents with schizophrenia did not differ significantly on any of these clinical measures from the control participants. Table 4.4 presents the mean scores for each of the electromechanical measures and for the Purdue Pegboard time. The offspring of patients with schizophrenia had significantly greater action tremor in the 3–6 Hz and 6–12 Hz bands as well as greater muscle rigidity compared with control participants.

Conclusion

We found that both clinical and electromechanical measures of neuromotor abnormalities significantly discriminated patients with schizophrenia who had been withdrawn from all neuroleptic medication from control participants, whereas only electromechanical measures significantly discriminated the adult offspring of patients with schizophrenia from control participants. This pattern of findings provides preliminary support for our expectation that electromechanical measures would have greater sensitivity than clinical ratings in identifying individuals with a vulnerability to develop schizophrenia. In forthcoming analyses, we will examine the relationships between these clinical and electromechanical measures of neuromotor abnormalities and comprehensive assessments of affective deficits in individuals with schizophrenia and in their first-degree relatives (Dworkin, Oster, Clark, & White, 1998).

It would be valuable in future research on neuromotor abnormalities in schizophrenia to supplement clinical and electromechanical assessments with evaluations of motor performance in the participants' daily environments. A recent study of elementary school records reported that poor performance in sports and in handicrafts

Table 4.3. Clinical Measures of Neurological Signs and Symptoms and Motor Abnormalities in Offspring of Patients With Schizophrenia and Control Participants

Measure	Offspring of patients with schizophrenia			Control participants			t	df
	M	SD	n	M	SD	n		
Neuromotor symptoms	1.70	1.72	20	1.61	0.98	14	0.18	32
Neurosensory symptoms	0.73	1.01	20	0.86	1.13	14	−0.36	32
Extrapyramidal Rating Scale	1.10	1.26	20	1.46	1.53	14	−0.76	32
Akathisia Scale	0.75	1.29	20	0.29	0.83	14	1.28[a]	31.81
Abnormal Involuntary Movement Scale	0.60	1.64	20	0.36	0.74	14	0.52	32

[a]Assumes unequal variances.

Table 4.4. Electromechanical and Purdue Pegboard Measures of Motor Abnormalities in Offspring of Patients With Schizophrenia and Control Participants

Measure	Offspring of patients with schizophrenia			Control participants			t	df
	M	SD	n	M	SD	n		
Resting tremor (3–6 Hz)	2.16	0.42	19	2.14	0.79	14	0.10[a]	18.30
Resting tremor (6–12 Hz)	56.32	37.25	19	45.63	18.26	14	0.99	31
Action tremor (3–6 Hz)	5.87	1.65	19	4.74	0.62	14	2.74[a]*	24.32
Action tremor (6–12 Hz)	5.19	1.46	19	3.94	0.92	14	2.83**	31
Muscle rigidity	309.56	178.72	19	174.51	77.83	14	2.94[a]**	26.07
Bradykinesia count	$2.42e^4$	$5.39e^3$	18	$2.31e^4$	$4.04e^3$	13	0.61	29
Purdue Pegboard time	65.00	15.54	20	62.50	7.68	14	0.55	32

[a]Assumes unequal variances.
*$p \leq .05$, two-tailed. **$p < .01$, two-tailed.

during childhood was more common in children who developed adult schizophrenia than in an age-matched control group, and the authors suggested that these findings may reflect deficits in motor coordination (M. Cannon et al., 1999). Studies of such real-world manifestations of neuromotor abnormalities have the potential to complement clinical and laboratory assessments by identifying the impacts of such abnormalities on the individual's function, an approach that has been used in studies of the consequences of cognitive deficits in schizophrenia (Green, 1996).

The studies we have reviewed and other data provide considerable support for Tsuang's (1993) conclusion that "a growing body of evidence . . . points to the significance of negative symptoms as indicators of the genetic and neurobiological underpinnings of schizophrenia" (p. 305). Within the constellation of negative symptoms, neuromotor abnormalities would seem to play a prominent role. Liddle (1987) recognized the motor aspects of both flat affect and poverty of speech in naming his negative-symptom factor *Psychomotor Poverty*, and Faraone et al. (1995) found that neuromotor impairments were one of the few putative indicators of the schizophrenia genotype that would contribute to analyses of genetic linkage. Nevertheless, it is important to conclude by emphasizing that despite considerable evidence that negative symptoms and neuromotor abnormalities in schizophrenia are associated with etiologic processes (Faraone, Green, Seidman, & Tsuang, 2001; Tsuang et al., 2000), they are undoubtedly components of what will ultimately be a multidimensional characterization of the schizophrenia phenotype and of individuals with the predisposition to develop the disorder (Dworkin & Cornblatt, 1995).

References

American Psychiatric Association. (1968). *Diagnostic and statistical manual of mental disorders* (2nd ed.). Washington, DC: Author.
American Psychiatric Association. (1980). *Diagnostic and statistical manual of mental disorders* (3rd ed.). Washington, DC: Author.

American Psychiatric Association. (1994). *Diagnostic and statistical manual of mental disorders* (4th ed.). Washington, DC: Author.

Barnes, T. R. E. (1989). A rating scale for drug-induced akathisia. *British Journal of Psychiatry, 154,* 672–676.

Baron, M., Gruen, R. S., & Romo-Gruen, J. M. (1992). Positive and negative symptoms: Relation to familial transmission of schizophrenia. *British Journal of Psychiatry, 161,* 610–614.

Bassett, A. S., Collins, E. J., Nuttall, S. E., & Honer, W. G. (1993). Positive and negative symptoms in families with schizophrenia. *Schizophrenia Research, 11,* 9–19.

Berenbaum, H., & McGrew, J. (1993). Familial resemblance of schizotypic traits. *Psychological Medicine, 23,* 327–333.

Berenbaum, H., Oltmanns, T. F., & Gottesman, I. I. (1990). Hedonic capacity in schizophrenics and their twins. *Psychological Medicine, 20,* 367–374.

Berenbaum, H., & Rotter, A. (1992). The relationship between spontaneous facial expressions of emotion and voluntary control of facial muscles. *Journal of Nonverbal Behavior, 16,* 179–190.

Bermanzohn, P. C., & Siris, S. G. (1992). Akinesia: A syndrome common to Parkinsonism, retarded depression, and negative symptoms of schizophrenia. *Comprehensive Psychiatry, 33,* 221–232.

Blanchard, J. J., & Neale, J. M. (1992). Medication effects: Conceptual and methodological issues in schizophrenia research. *Clinical Psychology Review, 12,* 345–361.

Bleuler, E. (1950). *Dementia praecox or the group of schizophrenias* (J. Zinkin, Trans.). New York: International Universities Press. (Original work published 1911)

Burke, J. G., Murphy, B. M., Bray, J. C., Walsh, D., & Kendler, K. S. (1996). Clinical similarities in siblings with schizophrenia. *American Journal of Medical Genetics (Neuropsychiatric Genetics), 67,* 239–243.

Caligiuri, M. P., Lohr, J. B., & Jeste, D. V. (1993). Parkinsonism in neuroleptic-naïve schizophrenic patients. *American Journal of Psychiatry, 150,* 1343–1348.

Caligiuri, M. P., Lohr, J. B., & Ruck, R. K. (1997). Scaling of movement velocity: A measure of neuromotor retardation in patients with psychopathology. *Psychophysiology, 35,* 431–437.

Cannon, M., Jones, P., Huttunen, M. O., Tanskanen, A., Huttunen, T., Rabe-Hesketh, S., et al. (1999). School performance in Finnish children and later development of schizophrenia: A population-based longitudinal study. *Archives of General Psychiatry, 56,* 457–463.

Cannon, T. D., Mednick, S. A., & Parnas, J. (1990). Antecedents of predominantly negative- and predominantly positive-symptom schizophrenia in a high-risk population. *Archives of General Psychiatry, 47,* 622–632.

Cardno, A. G., Holmans, P. A., Harvey, I., Williams, M. B., Owen, M. J., & McGuffin, P. (1997). Factor-derived subsyndromes of schizophrenia and familial morbid risks. *Schizophrenia Research, 23,* 231–238.

Cardno, A. G., Jones, L. A., Murphy, K. C., Sanders, R. D., Asherson, P., Owen, M. J., et al. (1999). Dimensions of psychosis in affected sibling pairs. *Schizophrenia Bulletin, 25,* 841–850.

Cassady, S. L., Adami, H., Moran, M., Kunkel, R., & Thaker, G. K. (1998). Spontaneous dyskinesia in subjects with schizophrenia spectrum personality. *American Journal of Psychiatry, 155,* 70–75.

Castle, D. J., Sham, P. C., Wessely, S., & Murray, R. M. (1994). The subtyping of schizophrenia in men and women: A latent class analysis. *Psychological Medicine, 24,* 41–51.

Chapman, L. J., Chapman, J. P., Kwapil, T. R., Eckblad, M., & Zinser, M. C. (1994). Putatively psychosis-prone subjects 10 years later. *Journal of Abnormal Psychology, 103,* 171–183.

Chatterjee, A., Chakos, M., Koreen, A., Geisler, S., Sheitman, B., Woerner, M., et al. (1995). Prevalence and clinical correlates of extrapyramidal signs and spontaneous dyskinesia in never-medicated schizophrenic patients. *American Journal of Psychiatry, 152,* 1724–1729.

Clark, S. C., Malaspina, D., Hasan, A., Koeppel, C., & Gorman, J. M. (1993). Non-localizing neurological abnormalities in schizophrenia. *Schizophrenia Research, 9,* 96.

Clementz, B. A., Grove, W. M., Katsanis, J., & Iacono, W. G. (1991). Psychometric detection of schizotypy: Perceptual aberration and physical anhedonia in relatives of schizophrenics. *Journal of Abnormal Psychology, 100,* 607–612.

Clementz, B. A., Sweeney, J. A., Hirt, M., & Haas, G. (1990). Pursuit gain and saccadic intrusions in first-degree relatives of probands with schizophrenia. *Journal of Abnormal Psychology, 99,* 327–335.

Clementz, B. A., Sweeney, J. A., Hirt, M., & Haas, G. (1991). Phenotypic correlations between oculomotor functioning and schizophrenia-related characteristics in relatives of schizophrenic probands. *Psychophysiology, 28,* 570–578.

Craver, J. C., & Pogue-Geile, M. F. (1999). Familial liability to schizophrenia: A sibling study of negative symptoms. *Schizophrenia Bulletin, 25,* 827–839.

Dollfus, S., Germain-Robin, S., Chabot, B., Brazo, P., Delamillieure, P., Langlois, S., et al. (1998). Family history and obstetric complications in deficit and non-deficit schizophrenia: Preliminary results. *European Psychiatry, 13,* 270–272.

Dollfus, S., Ribeyre, J. M., & Petit, M. (1996). Family history and deficit form in schizophrenia. *European Psychiatry, 11,* 260–262.

Dworkin, R. H. (1978). Genetic influences on cross-situational consistency. In W. E. Nance (Ed.), *Twin research: Psychology and methodology* (pp. 49–56). New York: Liss.

Dworkin, R. H. (1979). Genetic and environmental influences on person–situation interactions. *Journal of Research in Personality, 13,* 279–293.

Dworkin, R. H. (1990). Patterns of sex differences in negative symptoms and social functioning consistent with separate dimensions of schizophrenic psychopathology. *American Journal of Psychiatry, 147,* 347–349.

Dworkin, R. H. (1992). Affective deficits and social deficits in schizophrenia: What's what? *Schizophrenia Bulletin, 18,* 59–64.

Dworkin, R. H., Bernstein, G., Kaplansky, L. M., Lipsitz, J. D., Rinaldi, A., Slater, S. L., et al. (1991). Social competence and positive and negative symptoms: A longitudinal study of children and adolescents at risk for schizophrenia and affective disorder. *American Journal of Psychiatry, 148,* 1182–1188.

Dworkin, R. H., Burke, B. W., Maher, B. A., & Gottesman, I. I. (1976). A longitudinal study of the genetics of personality. *Journal of Personality and Social Psychology, 34,* 510–518.

Dworkin, R. H., Burke, B. W., Maher, B. A., & Gottesman, I. I. (1977). Genetic influences on the organization and development of personality. *Developmental Psychology, 13,* 164–165.

Dworkin, R. H., Clark, S. C., Amador, X. F., & Gorman, J. M. (1996). Does affective blunting in schizophrenia reflect affective deficit or neuromotor dysfunction? *Schizophrenia Research, 20,* 301–306.

Dworkin, R. H., & Cornblatt, B. A. (1995). Predicting schizophrenia. *The Lancet, 345,* 139–140.

Dworkin, R. H., Cornblatt, B. A., Friedmann, R., Kaplansky, L. M., Lewis, J. A., Rinaldi, A., et al. (1993). Childhood precursors of affective vs. social deficits in adolescents at risk for schizophrenia. *Schizophrenia Bulletin, 19,* 563–577.

Dworkin, R. H., Green, S. R., Small, N. E., Warner, M. L., Cornblatt, B. A., & Erlenmeyer-Kimling, L. (1990). Positive and negative symptoms and social competence in adolescents at risk for schizophrenia and affective disorder. *American Journal of Psychiatry, 147,* 1234–1236.

Dworkin, R. H., & Lenzenweger, M. F. (1984). Symptoms and the genetics of schizophrenia: Implications for diagnosis. *American Journal of Psychiatry, 141,* 1541–1546.

Dworkin, R. H., Lenzenweger, M. F., Moldin, S. O., Skillings, G. F., & Levick, S. E. (1988). A multidimensional approach to the genetics of schizophrenia. *American Journal of Psychiatry, 145,* 1077–1083.

Dworkin, R. H., Oster, H., Clark, S. C., & White, S. R. (1998). Affective expression and affective experience in schizophrenia. In M. F. Lenzenweger & R. H. Dworkin (Eds.), *Origins and development of schizophrenia: Advances in experimental psychopathology* (pp. 385–424). Washington, DC: American Psychological Association.

Dworkin, R. H., & Saczynski, K. (1984). Individual differences in hedonic capacity. *Journal of Personality Assessment, 48,* 620–626.

Ekman, P., Friesen, W. V., & Ancoli, S. (1980). Facial signs of emotional experience. *Journal of Personality and Social Psychology, 39,* 1125–1134.

Fanous, A., Gardner, C., Walsh, D., & Kendler, K. S. (2001). Relationship between positive and negative symptoms of schizophrenia and schizotypal symptoms in nonpsychotic relatives. *Archives of General Psychiatry, 58,* 669–673.

Faraone, S. V., Green, A. I., Seidman, L. J., & Tsuang, M. T. (2001). "Schizotaxia": Clinical implications and new directions for research. *Schizophrenia Bulletin, 27,* 1–18.

Faraone, S. V., Kremen, W. S., Lyons, M. J., Pepple, J. R., Seidman, L. J., & Tsuang, M. T. (1995). Diagnostic accuracy and linkage analysis: How useful are schizophrenia spectrum phenotypes? *American Journal of Psychiatry, 152,* 1286–1290.

Fenton, W. S., Wyatt, R. J., & McGlashan, T. H. (1994). Risk factors for spontaneous dyskinesia in schizophrenia. *Archives of General Psychiatry, 51,* 643–650.

Flashman, L. A., Flaum, M., Gupta, S., & Andreasen, N. C. (1996). Soft signs and neuropsychological performance in schizophrenia. *American Journal of Psychiatry, 153,* 526–532.

Franke, P., Maier, W., Hardt, J., & Hain, C. (1993). Cognitive functioning and anhedonia in subjects at risk for schizophrenia. *Schizophrenia Research*, *10*, 77–84.

Gervin, M., Browne, S., Lane, A., Clarke, M., Waddington, J. L., Larkin, C., et al. (1998). Spontaneous abnormal involuntary movements in first-episode schizophrenia and schizophreniform disorder: Baseline rate in a group of patients from an Irish catchment area. *American Journal of Psychiatry*, *155*, 1202–1206.

Goldman-Rakic, P. S. (1995). More clues on "latent" schizophrenia point to developmental origins. *American Journal of Psychiatry*, *152*, 1701–1703.

Gottesman, I. I., McGuffin, P., & Farmer, A. (1987). Clinical genetics as clues to the "real" genetics of schizophrenia (a decade of modest gains while playing for time). *Schizophrenia Bulletin*, *13*, 23–47.

Green, M. F. (1996). What are the functional consequences of neurocognitive deficits in schizophrenia? *American Journal of Psychiatry*, *153*, 321–330.

Grove, W. M., Lebow, B. S., Clementz, B. A., Cerri, A., Medus, C., & Iacono, W. G. (1991). Familial prevalence and coaggregation of schizotypy indicators: A multitrait family study. *Journal of Abnormal Psychology*, *100*, 115–121.

Gupta, S., Andreasen, N. C., Arndt, S., Flaum, M., Schultz, S. K., Hubbard, W. C., et al. (1995). Neurological soft signs in neuroleptic-naive and neuroleptic-treated schizophrenic patients and in normal comparison subjects. *American Journal of Psychiatry*, *152*, 191–196.

Guy, W. (Ed.). (1976). *ECDEU assessment manual for psychopharmacology* (Publication ADM 76-338). Washington, DC: U.S. Department of Health, Education, and Welfare.

Holzman, P. S., Proctor, L. R., Levy, D. L., Yasillo, N. J., Meltzer, H. Y., & Hurt, S. W. (1974). Eye-tracking dysfunctions in schizophrenic patients and their relatives. *Archives of General Psychiatry*, *31*, 143–151.

Holzman, P. S., Solomon, C. M., Levin, S., & Waternaux, C. S. (1984). Pursuit eye movement dysfunctions in schizophrenia: Family evidence for specificity. *Archives of General Psychiatry*, *41*, 136–139.

Hwu, H., Wu, Y., Lee, S. F., Yeh, L., Gwo, S., Hsu, H., et al. (1997). Concordance of positive and negative symptoms in coaffected sub-pairs with schizophrenia. *American Journal of Medical Genetics (Neuropsychiatric Genetics)*, *74*, 1–6.

Ismail, B., Cantor-Graae, E., & McNeil, T. F. (1998). Neurological abnormalities in schizophrenic patients and their siblings. *American Journal of Psychiatry*, *155*, 84–89.

Katsanis, J., Iacono, W. G., & Beiser, M. (1990). Anhedonia and perceptual aberration in first-episode psychotic patients and their relatives. *Journal of Abnormal Psychology*, *99*, 202–206.

Kendler, K. S., & Hewitt, J. (1992). The structure of self-report schizotypy in twins. *Journal of Personality Disorders*, *6*, 1–17.

Kendler, K. S., Karkowski-Shuman, L., O'Neill, F. A., Straub, R. E., MacLean, C. J., & Walsh, D. (1997). Resemblance of psychotic symptoms and syndromes in affected sibling pairs from the Irish Study of High-Density Schizophrenia Families: Evidence for possible etiologic heterogeneity. *American Journal of Psychiatry*, *154*, 191–198.

Kendler, K. S., McGuire, M., Gruenberg, A. M., & Walsh, D. (1994). Clinical heterogeneity in schizophrenia and the pattern of psychopathology in relatives: Results from an epidemiologically-based family study. *Acta Psychiatrica Scandinavica*, *89*, 294–300.

Kendler, K. S., McGuire, M., Gruenberg, A. M., & Walsh, D. (1995). Schizotypal symptoms and signs in the Roscommon Family Study: Their factor structure and familial relationship with psychotic and affective disorders. *Archives of General Psychiatry*, *52*, 296–303.

Kendler, K. S., Myers, J. M., O'Neill, F. A., Martin, R., Murphy, B., MacLean, C. J., et al. (2000). Clinical features of schizophrenia and linkage to chromosomes 5q, 6p, 8p, and 10p in the Irish Study of High-Density Schizophrenia Families. *American Journal of Psychiatry*, *157*, 402–408.

Kendler, K. S., Ochs, A. L., Gorman, A. M., Hewitt, J. K., Ross, D. E., & Mirsky, A. F. (1991). The structure of schizotypy: A pilot multitrait twin study. *Psychiatry Research*, *36*, 19–36.

Kendler, K. S., Thacker, L., & Walsh, D. (1996). Self-report measures of schizotypy as indices of familial vulnerability to schizophrenia. *Schizophrenia Bulletin*, *22*, 511–520.

Kern, R. S., Green, M. F., Satz, P., & Wirshing, W. C. (1991). Patterns of manual dominance in patients with neuroleptic-induced movement disorders. *Biological Psychiatry*, *30*, 483–492.

Kinney, D. K., Woods, B. T., & Yurgelun-Todd, D. (1986). Neurologic abnormalities in schizophrenic patients and their families: II. Neurologic and psychiatric findings in relatives. *Archives of General Psychiatry*, *43*, 665–668.

Kinney, D. K., Yurgelun-Todd, D., & Woods, B. T. (1991). Hard neurologic signs and psychopathology in relatives of schizophrenic patients. *Psychiatry Research, 39,* 45–53.

Kinney, D. K., Yurgelun-Todd, D., & Woods, B. T. (1993). Neurological hard signs in schizophrenia and major mood disorders. *Journal of Nervous and Mental Disease, 181,* 202–204.

Kirkpatrick, B., Buchanan, R. W., Ross, D. E., & Carpenter, W. T., Jr. (2001). A separate disease within the syndrome of schizophrenia. *Archives of General Psychiatry, 58,* 165–171.

Kirkpatrick, B., Castle, D., Murray, R. M., & Carpenter, W. T., Jr. (2000). Risk factors for the deficit syndrome of schizophrenia. *Schizophrenia Bulletin, 26,* 233–242.

Kirkpatrick, B., Ross, D. E., Walsh, D., Karkowski, L., & Kendler, K. S. (2000). Family characteristics of deficit and nondeficit schizophrenia in the Roscommon Family Study. *Schizophrenia Research, 45,* 57–64.

Knight, R. A., & Valner, J. B. (1993). Affective deficits in schizophrenia. In C. G. Costello (Ed.), *Symptoms of schizophrenia* (pp. 145–200). New York: Wiley.

Kwapil, T. R. (1998). Social anhedonia as a predictor of the development of schizophrenia-spectrum disorders. *Journal of Abnormal Psychology, 107,* 558–565.

Kwapil, T. R., Miller, M. B., Zinser, M. C., Chapman, J., & Chapman, L. J. (1997). Magical ideation and social anhedonia as predictors of psychosis proneness: A partial replication. *Journal of Abnormal Psychology, 106,* 491–495.

Lenzenweger, M. F., & Dworkin, R. H. (1996). The dimensions of schizophrenia phenomenology? Not one or two, at least three, perhaps four. *British Journal of Psychiatry, 168,* 432–440.

Lenzenweger, M. F., Dworkin, R. H., & Wethington, E. (1989). Models of positive and negative symptoms in schizophrenia: An empirical evaluation of latent structures. *Journal of Abnormal Psychology, 98,* 62–70.

Liddle, P. F. (1987). The symptoms of chronic schizophrenia: A re-examination of the positive–negative dichotomy. *British Journal of Psychiatry, 151,* 145–151.

Malaspina, D., Goetz, R. R., Yale, S., Berman, A., Friedman, J. H., Tremeau, F., et al. (2000). Relation of familial schizophrenia to negative symptoms but not to the deficit syndrome. *American Journal of Psychology, 157,* 994–1003.

Manschreck, T. C. (1989). Motor abnormalities and the psychopathology of schizophrenia. In B. Kirkcaldy (Ed.), *Normalities and abnormalities in human movement* (pp. 100–127). Basel, Switzerland: Karger.

Manschreck, T. C. (1993). Psychomotor abnormalities. In C. G. Costello (Ed.), *Symptoms of schizophrenia* (pp. 261–290). New York: Wiley.

Manschreck, T. C., Maher, B. A., Rucklos, M. E., & Vereen, D. R. (1982). Disturbed voluntary motor activity in schizophrenic disorder. *Psychological Medicine, 12,* 73–84.

Manschreck, T. C., Maher, B. A., Rucklos, M. E., Vereen, D. R., & Ader, D. N. (1981). Deficient motor synchrony in schizophrenia. *Journal of Abnormal Psychology, 90,* 321–328.

Manschreck, T. C., Maher, B. A., Waller, N. G., Ames, D., & Latham, C. A. (1985). Deficient motor synchrony in schizophrenic disorders: Clinical correlates. *Biological Psychiatry, 20,* 990–1002.

Matthysse, S., & Parnas, J. (1992). Extending the phenotype of schizophrenia: Implications for linkage analysis. *Journal of Psychiatric Research, 26,* 329–344.

Matthysse, S., Levy, D. L., Kinney, D., Deutsch, C., Lajonchere, C., Yurgelun-Todd, D., et al. (1992). Gene expression in mental illness: A navigation chart to future progress. *Journal of Psychiatric Research, 26,* 461–473.

Mayer, M., Alpert, M., Stastny, P., Perlick, D., & Empfield, M. (1985). Multiple contributions to clinical presentation of flat affect in schizophrenia. *Schizophrenia Bulletin, 11,* 420–426.

McGuffin, P., Farmer, A., & Gottesman, I. I. (1987). Is there really a split in schizophrenia? The genetic evidence. *British Journal of Psychiatry, 150,* 581–592.

McNeil, T. F., Harty, B., Blennow, G., & Cantor-Graae, E. (1993). Neuromotor deviation in offspring of psychotic mothers: A selective developmental deficiency in two groups of children at heightened psychiatric risk? *Journal of Psychiatric Research, 27,* 39–54.

Nurnberger, J. I., Blehar, M. C., Kaufmann, C. A., York-Cooler, C., Simpson, S. G., Harkavy-Friedman, J., et al. (1994). Diagnostic interview for genetic studies: Rationale, unique features, and training. *Archives of General Psychiatry, 51,* 849–859.

Prosser, E. S., Csernansky, J. G., Kaplan, J., Thiemann, S., Becker, T. J., & Hollister, L. E. (1987). Depression, Parkinsonian symptoms, and negative symptoms in schizophrenics treated with neuroleptics. *Journal of Nervous and Mental Disease, 175,* 100–105.

Ross, D., Kirkpatrick, B., Karkowski, L. M., Straub, R. E., MacLean, C. J., O'Neill, F. A., et al. (2000). Sibling correlation of deficit syndrome in the Irish Study of High-Density Schizophrenia Families. *American Journal of Psychiatry, 157,* 1071–1076.

Schneider, F., Ellgring, H., Friedrich, J., Fus, I., Beyer, T., Heimann, H., et al. (1992). The effects of neuroleptics on facial action in schizophrenic patients. *Pharmacopsychiatry, 25,* 233–239.

Simpson, G. M., & Angus, J. W. S. (1970). A rating scale for extrapyramidal side effects. *Acta Psychiatrica Scandinavica, 212*(Suppl.), 11–19.

Tiffin, J. (1968). *Purdue pegboard: Examiner manual.* Chicago: Science Research Associates.

Tollefson, G. D., Beasley, C. M., Jr., Tran, P. V., Street, J. S., Krueger, J. A., Tamura, R. N., et al. (1997). Olanzapine versus haloperidol in the treatment of schizophrenia and schizoaffective and schizophreniform disorders: Results of an international collaborative trial. *American Journal of Psychiatry, 154,* 457–465.

Tollefson, G. D., & Sanger, T. M. (1997). Negative symptoms: A path analytic approach to a double-blind, placebo- and haloperidol-controlled clinical trial with olanzapine. *American Journal of Psychiatry, 154,* 466–474.

Torgersen, S., Onstad, S., Skre, I., Edvarsen, J., & Kringlen, E. (1993). "True" schizotypal personality disorder: A study of co-twins and relatives of schizophrenic probands. *American Journal of Psychiatry, 150,* 1661–1667.

Tsuang, M. T. (1993). Genotypes, phenotypes, and the brain: A search for connections in schizophrenia. *British Journal of Psychiatry, 163,* 299–307.

Tsuang, M. T., Gilbertson, M. W., & Faraone, S. V. (1991). Genetic transmission of negative and positive symptoms in the biological relatives of schizophrenics. In A. Marneros, N. C. Andreasen, & M. T. Tsuang (Eds.), *Negative versus positive schizophrenia* (pp. 265–291). Berlin, Germany: Springer-Verlag.

Tsuang, M. T., Stone, W. S., & Faraone, S. V. (2000). Toward reformulating the diagnosis of schizophrenia. *American Journal of Psychiatry, 157,* 1041–1050.

Van Os, J., Marcelis, M., Sham, P., Jones, P., Gilvarry, K., & Murray, R. (1997). Psychopathological syndromes and familial morbid risk of psychosis. *British Journal of Psychiatry, 170,* 241–246.

Verdoux, H., Os, J. V., Sham, P., Jones, P., Gilvarry, K., & Murray, R. (1996). Does familiality predispose to both emergence and persistence of psychosis? *British Journal of Psychiatry, 168,* 620–626.

Vrtunski, P. B., Simpson, D. M., & Meltzer, H. Y. (1989). Voluntary movement dysfunction in schizophrenics. *Biological Psychiatry, 25,* 529–539.

Wirshing, W. C., Cummings, J. L., Dencker, S. J., & May, P. R. A. (1991). Electromechanical characteristics of tardive dyskinesia. *Journal of Neuropsychiatry and Clinical Neurosciences, 3,* 10–17.

Wirshing, W. C., Freidenberg, D. L., Cummings, J. L., & Bartzokis, G. (1989). Effects of anticholinergic agents on patients with tardive dyskinesia and concomitant drug-induced Parkinsonism. *Journal of Clinical Psychopharmacology, 9,* 407–411.

Woods, B. T., Kinney, D. K., & Yurgelun-Todd, D. (1986). Neurologic abnormalities in schizophrenic patients and their families: I. Comparison of schizophrenic, bipolar, and substance abuse patients and normal controls. *Archives of General Psychiatry, 43,* 657–663.

Woods, B. T., Yurgelun-Todd, D., & Kinney, D. K. (1987). Relationship of neurological abnormalities in schizophrenics to family psychopathology. *Biological Psychiatry, 21,* 325–331.

Wynne, L. C. (1984). The University of Rochester Child and Family Study: Overview of research plan. In N. F. Watt, E. J. Anthony, L. C. Wynne, & J. E. Rolf (Eds.), *Children at risk for schizophrenia: A longitudinal perspective* (pp. 335–347). Cambridge, England: Cambridge University Press.

Wynne, L. C., Cole, R. E., & Perkins, P. (1987). University of Rochester Child and Family Study: Risk research in progress. *Schizophrenia Bulletin, 13,* 463–476.

5

Spatial Working Memory Function in Schizophrenia

Sohee Park and Junghee Lee

Brendan Maher loves mysteries of all kinds, and psychosis is one of the greatest unsolved mysteries of all ages. So it is not surprising that he is one of the creators of the field of experimental psychopathology, which provides the scientific framework for investigating the seemingly intangible world of schizophrenia. I was initiated into experimental psychopathology by Brendan during graduate school. He taught me directly and indirectly three essential principles that I have carried with me ever since. First, he emphasized the importance of looking for differences in patterns of behavior rather than a simple deficit. Patients with schizophrenia have deficits in a wide range of domains; the more interesting questions are *how* their patterns of behavior diverge from the normal range and whether pockets of *better* performance can be found. To answer these questions, one may need to search for the imperceptible clues in the background rather than the foreground. For example, it may be more informative to see what people do *after* they make errors rather than counting the errors themselves. The second Maher principle has to do with cognitive flexibility: See the forest rather than the trees most of the time, but do pay attention to the trees when the forest begins to move. I found this to be very useful advice not only for research but for all aspects of my life (and Macbeth would have been wiser had he listened to Brendan). The third principle concerns generosity toward the next generation. Brendan was always the champion of the lost causes and lost students. In my own small ways, I have tried to follow his principles, and I have both succeeded and failed. However, even failures seem useful to me, because I apply his first principle and see what happens after one fails at something. There just might be interesting data.

—Sohee Park

This chapter focuses on a subset of cognitive deficits displayed by patients with schizophrenia that closely resembles dysfunctions of the prefrontal cortex. Deficits of executive functions, such as distractibility, perseveration, and an inability to

This work was supported by the National Alliance for Research in Schizophrenia and Depression, Human Frontiers of Science, the Swiss National Science Foundation, Scottish Rite, and the National Institute of Mental Health. We thank Philip Holzman, Deborah Levy, Mark Lenzenweger, and Patricia Goldman-Rakic for the invaluable collaborative projects. Finally, we are deeply indebted to Brendan Maher for his unfailing encouragement, support, and literary guidance over the years.

inhibit irrelevant responses, may be understood in terms of the inability to use internal representations or working memory to guide behavior (Goldman-Rakic, 1987, 1991). Working memory is mediated by a circuitry involving the dorsolateral prefrontal system, and it has been argued that some of the most profound cognitive symptoms of schizophrenia can be attributed to a deficit in working memory (e.g., Goldman-Rakic, 1991). To investigate the nature of prefrontal deficits in schizophrenia, our laboratory adopted a theoretical framework of working memory (e.g., Baddeley, 1986; Roitblat, 1987) and developed cognitive methods comparable to those tasks used in lesion studies as tools for analyzing the functions of the frontal cortex.

The main question was whether patients with schizophrenia show deficits in behaviors that are guided by internal representations while sensory–motor functions involved in such behaviors remain intact. A series of studies was launched to address this question. In the following sections, we sketch a brief review of the *frontal-lobe hypothesis* of schizophrenia, followed by a review of cognitive and neuroanatomical models of working memory, before we present a summary of the spatial working memory studies in patients with schizophrenia, their first-degree relatives, and schizotypal individuals.

Frontal-Lobe Dysfunction in Schizophrenia

> A 23 year old male with acute onset of blunted affect, looseness of associations and auditory hallucinations presented to a tertiary care hospital. . . . The patient received a diagnosis of schizophreniform disorder and treatment with haloperidol was started. . . . Examination led to detection of a ruptured cerebral aneurysm in the left frontal lobe. (Hall & Young, 1992, p. 1207)

Schizophrenia may be characterized by delusion and hallucinations, thought disorders, anergia, apathy, and flat or inappropriate affect, as well as more cognitive impairments, including concrete thinking, attentional deficit, and recall memory impairment. Neuropsychological testing of patients with schizophrenia typically yields symptom profiles that are similar to frontal- and temporal-lobe dysfunction but dissimilar to parietal-lobe disorders (e.g., Gur, Saykin, & Gur, 1991; Kolb & Wishaw, 1983; Pantelis et al., 1997). Conversely, patients with lesions in the frontal lobes tend to display anergia, inappropriate affect, and attentional and recall problems (Stuss & Benson, 1984) similar to those observed in a large proportion of patients with chronic schizophrenia.

Frontal-lobe lesions cause a disturbance of mnestic activity, which often leads to inefficient recall (Stuss & Benson, 1984, 1985). Recognition memory is believed to be dependent on a neural circuitry that includes the hippocampus, amygdala, medial thalamus, and nucleus basalis, whereas effortful recall may involve the prefrontal cortex in addition to other cortical and subcortical systems (Bachevalier & Mishkin, 1986; Kowalska, Bachevalier, & Mishkin, 1991; Mishkin, 1957; Taylor, Saint-Cyr, & Lang, 1986). Patients with schizophrenia show relatively intact recognition memory coupled with impaired recall (e.g., Calev, 1984; Koh & Petersen, 1978). In addition, anergia in patients with schizophrenia is correlated with recall but not with recognition memory (Goldberg, Weinberger, Pliskin, Berman, & Podd, 1989).

Demonstrations of frontal-lobe deficits in schizophrenia have also been obtained from functional imaging studies. Medicated patients with schizophrenia do not show hyperfrontal regional cerebral blood flow (rCBF), typically manifested by control participants, which suggests that the frontal system in patients with schizophrenia may be hypoactive at resting state. In addition, hypofrontality seems to be specifically related to negative symptoms (Andreasen et al., 1992; Wolkin et al., 1992). Hypofrontality and specific cognitive deficits are often associated. During the Wisconsin Card Sorting Test (WCST; Heaton, Chelune, Talley, Kay, & Curtis, 1993), the rCBF to the dorsolateral prefrontal cortex (DLPFC) was significantly increased in normal controls but not in patients with schizophrenia (Sagawa et al., 1990; Weinberger, Berman, & Illowsky, 1988; Weinberger, Berman, & Zec, 1986). However, during a number matching task, which requires cognitive effort but is not mediated by the prefrontal cortex, there was no difference in rCBF pattern between normal controls and patients (Weinberger et al., 1988; Wenberger et al., 1986). During the Tower of Hanoi task (Lezak, 1995), which is also widely used to assess frontal functions, schizophrenic patients with negative symptoms (both drug-naive and chronic, medicated patients) failed to show activation in the left medial frontal region, the same area that is specifically and significantly active in normal control participants performing the same task (Andreasen et al., 1992). These results substantiate the claim that the abnormal metabolic activity of the prefrontal cortex during a frontal-lobe-dependent task correlates with impaired performance (Berman, Illowsky, & Weinberger, 1988).

Structural abnormalities in the frontal cortex of patients with schizophrenia have also been observed (e.g., Benes, McSparren, Bird, SanGiovanni, & Vincent, 1991; Breier et al., 1992; Breier, Davis, Buchanan, Moricle, & Munson, 1993; Selemon, Rajkowska, & Goldman-Rakic, 1995), but the details of how these structural abnormalities affect behavior are only beginning to be expressed. Significant volume reduction in prefrontal and limbic white matter was observed in patients with schizophrenia (Breier et al., 1992), and prefrontal volume was associated with abnormal regulation of dopamine (Breier et al., 1993). Volume is a useful index, especially because it can be assessed *in vivo*, but microstructural factors—such as spatial arrangements of neurons, the proportion of different types of cells in the layers of the cortex, or the extent of myelination in different regions—are much more informative. In a postmortem study, Benes and her colleagues (1991) reported that the density of the small interneurons in Layer II is reduced in the prefrontal and the cingulate cortices of patients with schizophrenia, whereas the density of pyramidal cells in Layer V of the prefrontal cortex is increased in these patients. The density of the glial cells was not different from that of normal controls. Benes et al. suggested that a reduction of interneurons in Layer II may result in a partial loss of inhibitory processing within the particular neural circuits that are crucial for schizophrenia. In addition, recent morphometric studies of the DLPFC reveal a pathologic condition in the schizophrenic brain that is characterized by an abnormal neuronal connectivity (Rajkowska, Selemon, & Goldman-Rakic, 1998; Selemon, Rajkowska, & Goldman-Rakic, 1995, 1998). With application of the direct three-dimensional counting technique, neuronal density in Area 9 was calculated to be 17% higher in brains of patients with schizophrenia as compared with healthy controls, yet the cortical thickness was not significantly reduced (Selemon et al., 1995). Measurements made in Area 46 revealed a 21% increase in density of schizophrenic brains (Selemon et al., 1998). Such observations, coupled with longitudinal neurodevelopmental studies, could shed much light on the emergence of schizophrenic symptoms during adolescence when the changes in the corticolimbic relays and synaptic pruning are the most dramatic.

Frontal-lobe deficit in patients with schizophrenia also has been demonstrated by a variety of cognitive experiments, especially those involving oculomotor control. Patients with lesions in the frontal lobes are unable to inhibit automatic but inappropriate saccades in an antisaccade task, in which participants are required to look away from the cue (Guitton, Buchtel, & Douglas, 1985). Patients with schizophrenia show the same pattern of deficit in the antisaccade task (Clementz, McDowell, & Zisook, 1994; Fukushima et al., 1988). One of the reasons for their failure may be abnormal activity of the frontal cortex. Electrophysiological studies (Evdokimidis, Liakopoulos, Constantinidis, & Papageorgiou, 1996) as well as clinical studies (Guitton et al., 1985; Pierrot-Deseilligny, Rivaud, Gaymard, & Agid, 1991) have suggested that efficient antisaccade task performance requires intact DLPFC function. A positron emission tomography (PET) study conducted by Nakashima and his colleagues (1993, 1994) demonstrated that the left DLPFC is hypoactive in patients with schizophrenia during tasks that require memory-guided or volitional saccades. McDowell and Clementz (1997) suggested that the observed antisaccade deficit in patients with schizophrenia is related to a neuropathologic disturbance in the corticostriatal circuitry, particularly the DLPFC. In general, patients with schizophrenia seem unable to control initiation or production of saccades in a variety of eye-movement studies in the absence of simple motor deficit in the saccadic system (e.g., Clementz et al., 1994; Hommer, Clem, Litman, & Pickar, 1991; Mialat & Pichot, 1981; Pivik, 1979; Stark, 1983), and their performance on the saccade task is correlated with impaired performance in several attention tasks (Ross et al., 1998) and on the WCST (Karoumi, Ventre-Dominey, Vighetto, Dalery, & d'Amato, 1998; Park, 1997).

To summarize, the frontal system is important when novel, context-relevant responses are required to override existing, automatic motor schemas, and patients with schizophrenia may show impairments under such circumstances.

Models of Human Working Memory

Working memory may be conceptualized as a system for temporary maintenance of information so that the information can be used to guide behavior or be transferred to a knowledge storage system (Baddeley, 1986, 1992a, 1992b; Roitblat, 1987). Thus, working memory is "a system for the temporary holding and manipulation of information during the performance of a range of cognitive tasks such as comprehension, learning and reasoning" (Baddeley, 1986, p. 34). In Baddeley's (1986) model of working memory, temporary maintenance of information is achieved by an active attention control system termed the *central executive*, aided by modality-specific subsystems: the phonological loop and the visuospatial sketchpad. The *phonological loop* can hold auditory, phonological information by means of rehearsal processes. The phonological loop works together with the central executive to maintain auditory information in working memory by means of subvocal rehearsal in real time. It has been typically investigated with a variety of repetition tasks such as the digit span, although nonword repetition may be a better task for assessing the phonological loop than the digit span (Gathercole & Baddeley, 1989). The *visuospatial sketchpad* maintains and manipulates visuospatial images. Thus, working memory is not a single, unitary system but has separable, functional components that can be systematically probed. Deployment of attentional resources, selection of control processes or strategies, and coordination of information flow from the subsystems are thought to be mediated by the central executive system.

The concept of the central executive is similar to Shallice's (1982, 1988) model of the *supervisory attentional system*, which accounts for deficits shown by patients with bilateral frontal lesions. The supervisory attentional system operates when controlled processing is required to override habitual, automatic, routine processes or motor programs. A good example is the antisaccade task, which requires the suppression of one's automatic tendency to look toward a target and instead to look away from it (Guitton et al., 1985). *Automatic* processes arise as the result of extended practice on a task, but once a skill has been mastered (or a motor program formed), they do not make demands on the central processing capacity and hence they can be carried out in parallel (Shiffrin & Schneider, 1977). In contrast, *controlled* processing makes heavy demands on the central processing capacity. The supervisory attentional system monitors the internal and external context and controls the outputs of independent, schema-like action modules that oversee routine responses (automatic processes). Such a system is flexible and can respond efficiently to changing environmental demands.

Frontal-lobe damage leads to behaviors that are characterized by excessive distractibility, perseveration, and a severe lack of planning. Without the central executive or the supervisory attentional system, behaviors tend to become stereotypic, perseverative, and insensitive to the context; this is observed in a large proportion of patients with bilateral frontal lesions. Patients with frontal-lobe lesions, whether left, right, or bilateral, show deficits in tasks that require working memory (e.g., Freedman & Oscar-Berman, 1986; Lewinsohn, Zieler, Libet, Eyeberg, & Nielson, 1972). Although the extensive connectivity and the heterogeneity of the frontal system pose challenges to empirical study of the central executive, the question of capacity limit has been investigated with fruitful results, especially in relation to reading processes (see Just & Carpenter, 1992). Otherwise, most investigators have focused on either visuospatial or verbal working memory, thereby avoiding the issue of executive control to some extent. It may well be that what is thought of as the central executive is a manifestation of the general property of the neural network system that mediates working memory rather than a separate functional system within a sequential hierarchy of information processing.

Neuroanatomical correlates of working memory in healthy humans have been observed by means of PET and functional magnetic resonance imaging (fMRI), using a variety of tasks. Overall, the results point to the important role of the prefrontal cortex in working memory but, depending on the exact task (e.g., verbal or spatial), different areas within the prefrontal region are activated. Therefore, it may be useful to parse different functional components within the visuospatial working memory.

A spatial working memory task (deciding whether a probe circle marks the location of a previously presented target after a delay period) increased the activity of the right hemisphere inferior frontal (Area 47), posterior parietal, occipital, and premotor areas in a PET study (Jonides et al., 1993). However, during a different spatial working memory task that required participants to note whether any stimuli presented in a sequence occupied the same location, the right middle frontal gyrus (including Brodmann's Area 46) was strongly activated (McCarthy et al., 1994). The disparity between the two results may be due to the different cognitive components required to perform these tasks. Jonides et al.'s (1993) task did not have intervening stimuli between the target presentation and response stage, whereas McCarthy et al.'s (1994) did. Therefore, depending on the exact structure of the task, the prefrontal system plus other cortical and subcortical areas are implicated in working memory.

Verbal or auditory working memory also increases activation of the prefrontal cortex. The mid-DLPFC (including Brodmann's Areas 9 and 46) was also bilaterally activated during a nonspatial working memory task that required participants to maintain a sequence of numbers, whether self-ordered or externally generated (Petrides, Alivisatos, Meyer, & Evans, 1993). A very different verbal working memory task, which heavily taps the verbal articulatory loop, activated more posterior areas, including the supramarginal gyrus and Broca's area (Paulesu, Frith, & Frackowiak, 1993). In addition, a recent study showed a pronounced activation in the left inferior frontal gyrus (Brodmann's Areas 4, 44, and 45) when a tone serial position task was used (Stevens, Goldman-Rakic, Gore, Fulbright, & Wexler, 1998).

The tasks used to probe spatial working memory are most often visual rather than auditory or haptic. Analogous to visual information processing, there is a dissociation between pattern-based, visual working memory and spatial working memory, both in humans (Baddeley & Lieberman, 1980; Farah, 1988) and in monkeys (Bachevalier & Mishkin, 1986; Kowalska et al., 1991; Wilson, Scalaidhe, & Goldman-Rakic, 1993). Ungerleider, Courtney, and Haxby (1998) showed that visual working memory, as assessed by a face-matching task, activated a region in the right inferior frontal cortex, whereas spatial working memory, as assessed by a location-matching task, activated the superior frontal region.

Maintenance of visuospatial information in working memory can be disrupted by either spatial or visual distractors and probably involves a complex network of cortical and subcortical areas (e.g., Jonides et al., 1993). Patients with schizophrenia are able to perform well in tasks involving the visuospatial sketchpad, but they show deficits if the task requires processing of semantics in addition to visuospatial imagery (David & Cutting, 1992).

Pharmacological investigations have shown that the dopamine system plays an important role in working memory. Also, it is important to note that there is a high density of D1 receptors compared with D2 receptors in the prefrontal cortex, and this density is altered in patients with schizophrenia (Goldman-Rakic, 1999). In rhesus monkeys, local injections of dopamine D1 antagonists can either disrupt working memory performance at high doses (Sawaguchi & Goldman-Rakic, 1991) or selectively facilitate the "memory fields" of prefrontal neurons at low levels (Williams & Goldman-Rakic, 1995). Castner, Williams, and Goldman-Rakic (2000) found that chronic haloperidol treatment can induce working memory impairment and that these impairments can be reversed by short-term D1 stimulation in monkeys. The effects of dopamine agonists on working memory in humans are still not clearly understood, but there have been reports of enhanced working memory following dopamine agonist intake. Bromocriptin, a dopamine agonist, improved working memory performance in healthy human participants (Luciana, Depue, Arbisi, & Leon, 1992). Kirrane and her colleagues (2000) showed that amphetamine, which releases monoamines—particularly dopamine and norepinephrine—and blocks their reuptake, improved the performance on visuospatial working memory tasks as well as negative symptoms of patients with schizophrenia spectrum disorders. Further characterization of dopamine receptors in the prefrontal cortex and pharmacotherapy research should lead to additional insights on the neuropharmacology of cognition as well as the development of new antipsychotic drugs with fewer side effects (Rupniak & Iversen, 1993).

The studies just discussed identify the prefrontal cortex, especially the DLPFC, as a critical element in a neural system that uses working memory to hold specific items of spatial or verbal information on-line. However, it is important to note that the neural system that supports working memory capacity does not reside within the prefrontal cortex but extends beyond it to involve and require interactions with other cortical and subcortical areas (Collette et al., 1999). Among these are the posterior parietal cortex, the inferotemporal cortex, the cingulate gyrus, and the hippocampal formation, which are connected with the DLPFC (Cavada & Goldman-Rakic, 1989a, 1989b; Petrides & Pandya, 1984; Selemon & Goldman-Rakic, 1985; Stanton, Bruce, & Goldberg, 1995). Using fMRI, Zarahn, Aguirre, and D'Esposito (1999) showed that functional changes attributable to the retention delay of a spatial working memory task were detected in the DLPFC as well as in the right frontal eye field and in the superior parietal lobule. An fMRI study of a verbal working memory task revealed significant activations in a number of cerebral regions, including the mid-dorsolateral frontal cortex, inferior frontal gyrus, supramarginal gyrus, and cerebellum (de Zubicaray et al., 1998).

Many neuroimaging studies of patients with schizophrenia performing working memory tasks have demonstrated *task-related hypofrontality* (e.g., Callicott et al., 1998; Weinberger & Berman, 1996). Compared with normal controls, patients with schizophrenia show a relative physiological hypoactivity of the prefrontal cortex. Ganguli et al. (1997) reported that patients performed worse than normal controls on the verbal working memory tasks and that they had smaller increases in rCBF than controls in frontal and superior temporal cortical regions bilaterally. However, a simple hypofrontality hypothesis cannot account for more recent imaging data. In two recent studies of working memory, the activation of the right DLPFC in patients with schizophrenia was as robust as that in normal participants, and the activation in the left DLPFC was greater in patients with schizophrenia. In addition, the basal ganglia activity during working memory performance in patients with schizophrenia was greater than in controls (Manoach et al., 1999, 2000; see also chap. 13, this volume).

These contrasting results suggest that several additional factors, such as the task demand and the manipulation of task parameters, must be considered in evaluating the activation patterns in the prefrontal cortices of patients with schizophrenia versus normal controls. For example, reward or reinforcement might enhance DLPFC activation. DLPFC neurons involved in a spatial delayed-response task in monkeys show enhanced activity during delay periods when a preferred reward is anticipated than when it is not (Watanabe, 1996). To understand in depth the neuroanatomical correlates of working memory and the pathophysiology of schizophrenia, one must consider the neural network properties as well as the specific brain systems.

Neural Correlates of Working Memory in Animals

In animals, spatial working memory has been studied most often with the delayed-response paradigm. A prototypical delayed-response task involves presentation of a stimulus, followed by a short delay period and the subsequent presentation of a set of alternative choices. Much is known about the role of the DLPFC in working memory function and its regulation of higher cognitive function in rhesus monkeys (see Goldman-Rakic, 1987, 1991). The ability to perform delayed-response tasks is destroyed by lesions in the DLPFC (e.g., Blum, 1952; Funahashi, Bruce, & Goldman-Rakic, 1989, 1990, 1993; Jacobsen, 1935; Mishkin, 1957). Specifically, the principal sulcus (Area 46) is thought to mediate spatial working memory, because neurons in this area are involved in maintenance of spatial information over time (Funahashi et al., 1989, 1990, 1993; Goldman-Rakic, 1987). For example, when a saccade to a target is delayed, the neurons in the principal sulcus increase and maintain firing during the delay period, but as soon as the response is made, the firing decreases rapidly. The spatial property of the principal sulcus neurons extends to more than one sensory modality. Lesions in principal sulcus neurons impair memory-guided manual and eye movements (Funahashi et al., 1989, 1990, 1993), in contrast to frontal eye field lesions, which impair delayed eye movements but not hand movements (Deng et al., 1984). Both the principal sulcus and the frontal eye field receive parallel projections from the posterior parietal areas (Cavada & Goldman-Rakic, 1985, 1989a, 1989b), but the frontal eye field projects to areas involved in producing eye movements, whereas the principal sulcus projects less restrictively, influencing manual responses as well as eye movements. In addition, the principal sulcus neurons are involved in the shifting of visual attention (Suzuki & Azuma, 1983), which is also an important function of the central executive.

Spatial information and nonspatial, object information seem to be processed by separate neuroanatomical systems within the frontal cortex of monkeys. Dissociation of spatial and object delayed-response performances has been observed in rhesus monkeys (Oscar-Berman, 1975) and in humans (Freedman & Oscar-Berman, 1986). Spatial delayed-response performance is disrupted by lesions in the DLPFC, but object delayed response may be mediated by the orbitofrontal system. Wilson et al. (1993) demonstrated that spatial working memory is mediated by the principal sulcus region, whereas object working memory is mediated by the inferior convexity, ventrolateral to the principal sulcus. However, recordings made in monkeys during a task that required maintenance of both "what" and "where" information revealed that more than half of the neurons with delay activity showed both "what" and "where" tuning (Rao, Rainer, & Miller, 1997). This suggests that object and spatial domains of processing within the prefrontal cortex may not be strictly segregated.

To summarize, a review of the discoveries in neuropsychology, neuroanatomy, neurophysiology, and psychopathology yields a recurrent theme: The prefrontal cortex is crucial when representationally guided behavior is required. Some of the cardinal symptoms of schizophrenia have been attributed to dysfunctional frontal systems.

Spatial Working Memory Studies in Patients With Schizophrenia

The knowledge that prefrontal lesions in humans and primates lead to behavioral deficits that closely resemble some cognitive deficits of people with schizophrenia motivated a series of experiments that are comparable to the animal lesion studies and human neuropsychological studies of prefrontal functions. If patients with schizophrenia display behavioral deficits similar to those shown by lesioned animals and humans, then one might be able to postulate possible prefrontal areas or systems that may be dysfunctional in schizophrenia. Therefore, Park and colleagues tested the hypothesis that patients with schizophrenia are impaired on spatial working memory tasks. The specific questions addressed were as follows:

1. Is there a genuine working memory deficit that is clearly not due to any motor problems? If the problem is a basic motor deficit, then the role of the prefrontal cortex is minimized.
2. If a working memory deficit is present, how general is it? Is it confined to only one sensory modality (e.g., the oculomotor system), or is it a general spatial problem?
3. What is the relationship between the prefrontal dysfunctions and the smooth-pursuit eye tracking deficit, which has been suggested to be a possible biological marker for schizophrenia (e.g., see Holzman, 1987)?
4. Do individuals at risk for schizophrenia also show similar behavioral patterns?

Spatial Working Memory Deficits in Patients With Schizophrenia

In a study of inpatients with schizophrenia, spatial working memory function was assessed by an oculomotor delayed-response paradigm used in neurophysiological studies (Park & Holzman, 1992, 1993). The basic task consisted of flashing a target briefly in the periphery of the participant's visual field, followed by a delay period, after which participants were required to move their eyes to the remembered position of the target (see Figure 5.1 for an illustration of the procedure). To control for the possibility that patients with schizophrenia might have problems in making any eye movements, Park and Holzman also included a sensory-control task was. The sensory task required participants to move their eyes to the target itself. Through a comparison of the two tasks, the motor component may be separated from the working memory component.

Park and Holzman (1992) found that patients with schizophrenia were impaired on the working memory task but not on the sensory-control task, indicating that the patients were able to move their eyes to a visible target but not to a remembered target. Patients with schizophrenia made more errors, and their reaction times were slower, compared with bipolar patients and normal controls. Patients with schizophrenia also made more perseverative errors and hemifield errors. Matched bipolar inpatients and normal control participants were unimpaired. These results have been replicated by many groups since 1992 (e.g., Carter et al., 1996; Fleming et al., 1997; Gooding & Tallent, 2002; Karatekin & Asarnow, 1998; Keefe et al., 1995, 1997; Spindler et al., 1997; Spitzer, 1993).

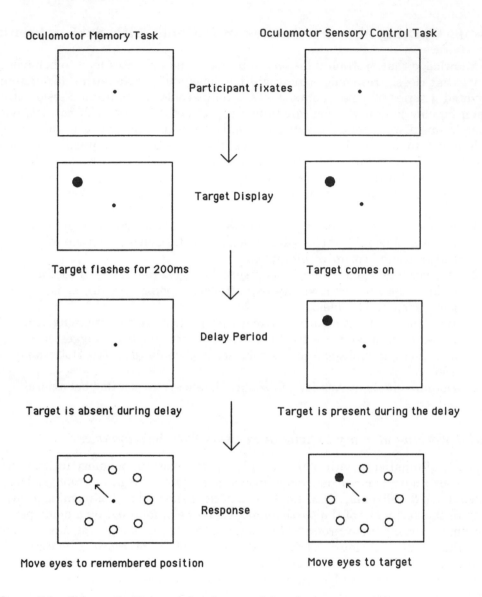

Figure 5.1.   Schematic diagram of oculomotor delayed-response tasks.

One important question is whether the deficit shown on the oculomotor delayed-response task by patients with schizophrenia is a problem of working memory or if it is a deficit confined to the oculomotor system itself. If it is a genuine working memory deficit, then one should be able to detect it independent of the sensory modality of the task. To address this question, Park and Holzman (1992) conducted a haptic delayed-response task with the same participants. The haptic delayed-response task was essentially identical to the oculomotor delayed-response task in design and procedure, but in this case spatial working memory was tested in a nonvisual domain (see Figure 5.2). Blindfolded participants were required move their hands to the remembered position of the target they had touched. In the haptic delayed-response task, all participants were accurate when no memory was required (i.e.,

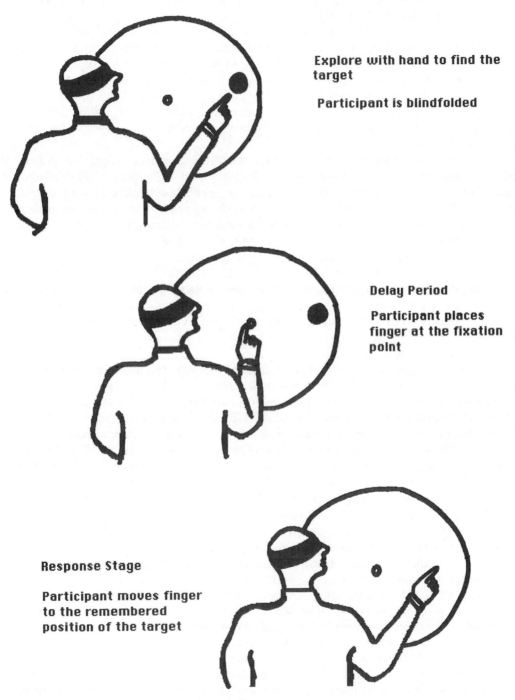

Explore with hand to find the target

Participant is blindfolded

Delay Period

Participant places finger at the fixation point

Response Stage

Participant moves finger to the remembered position of the target

Figure 5.2.   Haptic delayed-response task.

they were able to move their fingers to the target position with or without vision), but patients with schizophrenia were severely impaired when they were required to make memory-guided hand movements. Patients with schizophrenia also made more perseverative errors. Bipolar and normal participants performed accurately on the haptic working memory task.

Whether the delayed-response task was conducted in the oculomotor domain or in the haptic domain, the sensory-control task and the memory task were identical, except for one component: the guidance of response by internal representation. The addition of the working memory component severely affected the patients with schizophrenia but did not significantly affect the performance of the control groups. Therefore, the deficits observed in the oculomotor and the haptic delayed-response tasks are likely to be due to a working memory deficit rather than to a simple motor problem of the eye or the hand.

Is this working memory deficit a reflection of generalized cognitive deficit in all domains? It seems unlikely, because in Park and Holzman's (1992) study all participants were matched on IQ and education level. In addition, the three groups performed equally on the digit span task, which suggests that the verbal articulatory loop was intact in these schizophrenia patients. Although the digit span task is not equivalent to the oculomotor memory task in complexity and difficulty, it is commonly used to assess simple verbal working memory (Villa, Gainotti, De Bonis, & Marra, 1990). Patients with schizophrenia did not differ from bipolar patients and normal controls on the digit span task. They were able to repeat seven digits forward and five digits backward. In this study, patients with schizophrenia were able to attend to a task, and they were able to maintain simple verbal information. Thus, it is unlikely that the spatial working memory deficit in patients with schizophrenia is due to a global, generalized deficit.

There was also some evidence of frontal-lobe dysfunction in patients with schizophrenia (Park, 1999). In this study, patients with schizophrenia were impaired on the WCST, which is widely used to assess prefrontal function, and the correlation between working memory and WCST performance was significant (Park, 1999). However, they were not impaired on all neuropsychological test of frontal function. These patients performed within the normal range on the Verbal Fluency Task (see Lezak, 1995), which taps another aspect of frontal function (Park, 1991). The Verbal Fluency Task is associated with medial frontal function and is suggested to involve more left-hemispheric function. These results are consistent with the results of a recent study (Snitz, Curtis, Zald, Karsanis, & Iacono, 1999) in which spatial working memory impairment was related to fewer categories on the WCST but not to the measures of general cognitive functioning.

In a subsequent study, outpatients in partial remission were tested on the same oculomotor delayed-response tasks, and their smooth-pursuit eye tracking was also assessed (Park & Holzman, 1993). Smooth-pursuit eye tracking performance of patients with schizophrenia has been studied extensively in the past 30 years. A majority of patients with schizophrenia, and about half of their first-degree relatives, are unable to track a smoothly moving target, such as a pendulum, with their eyes (Holzman, 1987; Holzman, Proctor, & Hughes, 1973; Holzman et al., 1974; Keefe et al., 1997; Levy et al., 1983). Normal participants can match their eye velocity to the target velocity almost instantaneously and continue to pursuit smoothly. Schizophrenic patients tend to have poor gain (ratio of eye velocity to target velocity) and generate numerous saccades during smooth-pursuit tracking. This deficit has been suggested to stem from the dysfunction of the frontal system (Levin, 1984a, 1984b) and is hypothesized to be a possible biological marker for schizophrenia (see Holzman, 1987; Holzman & Matthysse, 1990).

Outpatients with schizophrenia showed deficits in working memory, but outpatients with bipolar disorder, and normal control participants, were unimpaired (Park & Holzman, 1993). Thus, working memory deficits seem to be present in patients with schizophrenia regardless of illness state, whereas bipolar patients preserve intact working memory. In a recent study of spatial working memory in floridly psychotic schizophrenia inpatients, Park, Püschel, Sauter, Rentsch, and Hell (1999) tracked the same patients for 4 months until they were in partial remission and functioning relatively well in the outside world. Spatial working memory deficits were present during the acute, psychotic state and at the follow-up when they were outpatients. These results suggest that clinical symptoms may come and go but that the spatial working memory deficit, like the eye tracking deficit, might always be present.

Spatial working memory deficit and smooth-pursuit eye-movement dysfunction were associated in patients with schizophrenia (Park & Holzman, 1993; Snitz et al., 1999). Both tasks are suggested to be mediated by the prefrontal system, and eye tracking dysfunction is present in about half of the first-degree relatives of patients with schizophrenia.

Relatives of Patients With Schizophrenia

Park, Holzman, and Goldman-Rakic (1995) examined whether working memory is impaired in a sample of first-degree relatives of patients with schizophrenia. They predicted that, as a group, relatives would perform better on a working memory task than the patients with schizophrenia but worse than the normal controls, inasmuch as the relatives as a group presumably include not only individuals who are free of any psychiatric dysfunctions but also a subgroup of those who do show psychological and biological dysfunctions, as was found for eye tracking.

Park, Holzman, and Goldman-Rakic (1995) conducted two experiments to test this hypothesis. In Experiment 1, participants completed the oculomotor delayed-response task. For Experiment 2, the authors recruited a new group of participants, who completed a visual–manual delayed-response task (see Figure 5.3). If the working memory deficit is present in some of the first-degree relatives of patients with schizophrenia, then it should be able to be detected, regardless of the response modality of the delayed response.

Relatives of patients with schizophrenia showed significant deficits in working memory in both the oculomotor and visual–manual delayed-response tasks compared with the normal control participants (Park, Holzman, & Goldman-Rakic, 1995). The relatives of patients with schizophrenia were not ill, and they were medication free, yet about half of them showed a working memory deficit. The results suggest that some relatives of patients with schizophrenia are impaired on tasks that implicate the prefrontal system and that the delayed-response paradigm, regardless of modality, may prove to be useful in broadening the schizophrenic phenotype. This finding has been replicated by Myles-Worsley and Park (in press) in the

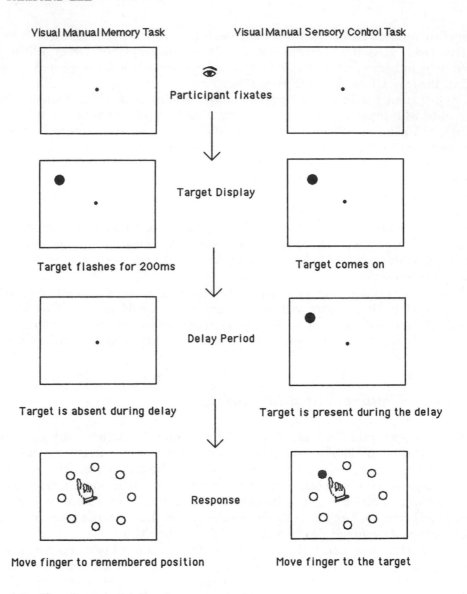

Figure 5.3. Visual manual delayed-response tasks.

first-degree relatives in Palau Micronesia, where the prevalence of schizophrenia is double the worldwide rate.

The association of eye tracking dysfunction and working memory deficit observed in patients with schizophrenia were also present in the first-degree relatives of patients with schizophrenia. Relatives with normal eye tracking tended to be unimpaired on the delayed-response tasks, whereas relatives with abnormal eye tracking showed deficits in working memory (Park, Holzman, & Levy, 1993).

Working memory abnormalities in relatives of patients with schizophrenia reach beyond the spatial domain. Faraone et al. (1999) showed that the nonpsychotic relatives of patients with schizophrenia have deficits in object working memory as well as spatial working memory. Verbal working memory dysfunction has also been reported in the relatives of patients with schizophrenia (Conklin, Curtis, Katsanis, & Iacono, 2000). These results from the first-degree relatives of patients with schizophrenia suggest that spatial and other working memory dysfunction may turn out to be another behavioral marker, as an aid not only in demonstrating the pathophysiology of schizophrenia but also in characterizing the multidimensional aspects of the schizophrenic phenotype.

Spatial Working Memory in Relation to Schizotypy

Hypothetically, "psychosis-prone" individuals (Chapman & Chapman, 1985) within general population may carry a latent liability for schizophrenia, although they may never become ill (Lenzenweger & Loranger, 1989a, 1989b; Meehl, 1990). Schizotypic individuals identified by various personality inventories show subtle deficits in sustained attention (Lenzenweger, Cornblatt, & Putnick, 1991); cognitive inhibition (Beech & Claridge, 1987; Park, Lenzenweger, Puschel, & Holzman, 1996); the WCST (Gooding, Kwapil, & Tallent, 1999; Lenzenweger & Korfine, 1994); and oculomotor tasks, including antisaccadic and smooth-pursuit tasks (O'Driscoll, Lenzenweger, & Holzman, 1998), in the absence of any psychiatric illness. Thus, some features of schizophrenia seem to be present, albeit in a very diluted form, in the general population, and these traits may indicate a predisposition to the illness.

Park, Holzman, and Lenzenweger (1995) examined the working memory function of undergraduate students at Cornell University. The students were assessed with a personality inventory that tapped experiences of perceptual aberrations. The question was whether normally functioning young adults who score high on the Perceptual Aberration Scale (Chapman, Chapman, & Raulin, 1978) show working memory deficits. The WCST was also administered to assess perseverative tendencies and the ability to maintain conceptual set. On the WCST, the authors focused on the Failure to Maintain Set subscale, which has been shown to differentiate schizotypic individuals from normal controls (Lenzenweger & Korfine, 1994; Lyons, Merla, Young, & Kremen, 1991).

Schizotypic participants performed less accurately compared with the normal controls on the working memory task, and schizotypic participants were seven times more likely than normal controls to be impaired. There were no group differences in the number of perseverative errors or the number of categories achieved on the WCST, but schizotypic participants were less able to maintain set than were the control participants. The Failure to Maintain Set score was significantly correlated with the accuracy of working memory; participants who made more errors on the working memory task were less able to maintain set during the WCST.

However, one could argue that these schizotypic participants were recruited on the basis of perceptual aberration and that therefore they may not represent the whole range of schizotypal personality. In a later study, Park and McTigue (1997) recruited healthy schizotypic participants on the basis of their scores on the Schizotypal Personality Questionnaire (Raine, 1991), which taps the nine syndromes of schizotypal personality disorder as described in the *Diagnostic and Statistical Manual of Mental Disorders* (3rd ed., rev.; American Psychiatric Association, 1987). Schizotypic participants showed deficits in spatial working memory; moreover, the subscale that tapped an absence of close social relationships correlated significantly with reduced working memory performance. Tallent and Gooding (1999) also showed that psychosis-prone individuals with social–interpersonal abnormalities as well as with cognitive–perceptual distortions display subtle spatial working memory impairments and that these impairments are associated with poor performance on the WCST.

These results suggest that there may be subtle abnormalities in the functioning of the frontal system in a subgroup of schizotypic individuals who may carry a latent liability for schizophrenia (see Holzman et al., 1995). One important future direction lies in neurodevelopmental studies of working memory during adolescence, in relation to psychopathology in high-risk groups.

Components of Spatial Working Memory Deficit

Patients with schizophrenia perform less accurately than normal control participants on delayed-response tasks, regardless of the sensorimotor modality, but it is not clear why they fail on such a simple task. A componential analysis of the delayed-response performance in patients with schizophrenia indicates that there are many processes that are responsible for their poor performance (Park, Holzman, & Goldman-Rakic, 1995; Park, Holzman, & Lenzenweger, 1995; Park & O'Driscoll, 1996). Successful performance on the delayed-response task depends partly on being able to maintain target representation during the delay period as well as inhibition of irrelevant stimuli and initiation of appropriate motor responses. Failure to facilitate any of these hypothetical components may lead to an overall deficit. In monkeys, maintenance of the target position during the delay period may be disrupted by electrocortical stimulation (Stamm, 1985). If the cell activity is interrupted or discontinued in the principal sulcus, monkeys forget the target position in the oculomotor delayed-response task (Funahashi et al., 1989, 1990, 1993). In patients with schizophrenia or their relatives, it is not known what neurophysiological processes are responsible for maintaining the target representation during the delay.

Do patients with schizophrenia have problems maintaining mental representation during the delay period? Does "hypofrontality" of patients with schizophrenia (e.g., Andreasen et al., 1992; Ingvar, 1980; Ingvar & Franzen, 1974; Nakashima et al., 1994) imply inefficient or decreased activity of the frontal area? What might cause decreased activity of the neurons in the prefrontal cortex during the delay? Experimental manipulations with dopamine show that, at high concentrations, a dopamine D1 antagonist injected into the prefrontal cortex disrupts the oculomotor delayed-response performance in rhesus monkeys (Sawaguchi & Goldman-Rakic, 1991); on the other hand, however, at low concentrations D1 antagonists facilitate working memory performance (Willams & Goldman-Rakic, 1995). Neural network simulation of the frontal cortex also indicates that context-relevant processing may depend on dopamine (Cohen & Servan-Schreiber, 1992). However, the interactions of dopamine with other neurotransmitter systems (e.g., GABA, 5-HT, glutamate, acetylcholine, and norepinephrine) and hormones (e.g., estradiol, cortisol) must also be specified.

Careful examination of errors elicited during the delayed-response task shows that maintenance of representation is not the only reason for making a mistake.

What if the representation were maintained during the delay, but at the response stage one made a wrong eye movement or a hand movement? Such an error can be corrected. All errors were examined to see whether subsequent attempts to correct the mistakes were successful (Park, 1999; Park & O'Driscoll, 1996). The majority of errors made by normal and bipolar participants are such corrected errors. Patients with schizophrenia also correct more than half of their errors. Krappmann and Everling (1998) have also reported that patients with schizophrenia generate corrective saccades in the memory-guided delayed-response task. On the other hand, patients with schizophrenia also make a significant number of errors that are never corrected, which is extremely rare in normal and bipolar participants (see Figure 5.4). If the participants lost the representation of the target during the delay, and that was why they made an error, then any subsequent attempts to correct errors would result in random choices. Hence, patients with schizophrenia do seem to have problems with maintenance of representation during the delay as well as with initiating correct movements and inhibiting incorrect ones at the response stage.

Park and Holzman (1993) found an association of eye tracking performance and working memory in patients with schizophrenia. Closer examination of the patients' errors revealed that eye tracking is associated with the errors that are never corrected (Park & O'Driscoll, 1996). Patients with good eye tracking ability tend to correct their errors, whereas those with impaired eye tracking tend to make never-corrected errors. On the other hand, the number of errors that were corrected after one unsuccessful guess was not associated with eye tracking. Therefore, what may differentiate patients with schizophrenia from bipolar and normal participants, apart from the sheer number of errors, is how these errors arise. All participants

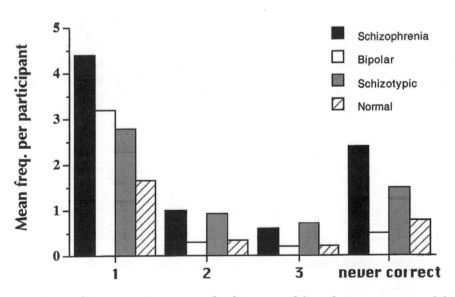

Figure 5.4. Frequency (freq.) of corrected errors per participant.

seem susceptible to making errors due to competing response tendencies at the response stage, but only patients with schizophrenia seem to lose the spatial representation. This tendency is also seen in schizotypic individuals, although the effect is small (see Figure 5.4).

Examination of the never-corrected errors also revealed a hemispheric asymmetry in the spatial working memory deficit, which is not apparent with the total number of errors. Patients with schizophrenia and schizotypic participants make a greater number of never-corrected errors when the target is presented to the right visual field (i.e., left hemisphere) than when the target is presented to the left visual field. Normal controls do not show such asymmetry (Park, 1999).

The question still remains as to why patients with schizophrenia are impaired in maintenance of representation during the delay period of the spatial working memory task, in the absence of generalized, global memory deficit. One exciting possibility for future research lies in functional-imaging techniques. Using the event-related fMRI design, it will be possible to observe activity of the network of cortical areas that are involved in mediating the maintenance of representation during the delay period of the working memory task in patients with schizophrenia. In addition to neuroimaging studies, we are currently examining the effects of spatial and temporal distractors on working memory errors to determine when patients with schizophrenia are most vulnerable to disruptions in working memory processes.

It is likely that some of the major cognitive symptoms of patients with schizophrenia reflect a prefrontal dysfunction that manifests itself as a problem in the integrity of the working memory, but ultimately the results from working memory studies must be interpreted in relation to the actual clinical symptoms of schizophrenia. Carter et al. (1996) reported that spatial working memory deficit and negative symptoms are significantly correlated. Although our data also suggest an association of negative symptoms and working memory deficit at certain times during illness (Park et al., 1999), these results are likely to represent the very tip of the iceberg. To move beyond the realm of correlations one must also begin to specify mediating processes and mechanisms. The potential power of simple, cognitive tools, such as the delayed-response paradigm, in concert with advances in neuroimaging and neurophysiological techniques, will enable us to systematically investigate the pathophysiology of the phenotype of schizophrenia.

References

American Psychiatric Association. (1987). *Diagnostic and statistical manual of mental disorders* (3rd ed., rev.). Washington, DC: Author.

Andreasen, N. C., Rezai, K., Alliger, R., Swayze, V. W., Flaum, M., Kirchner, P., et al. (1992). Hypofrontality in neuroleptic-naive patients and in patients with chronic schizophrenia. *Archives of General Psychiatry, 49*, 943–958.

Bachevalier, J., & Mishkin, M. (1986). Visual recognition impairment follows ventromedial but not dorsolateral prefrontal lesions in monkeys. *Behavioural Brain Research, 20*, 249–261.

Baddeley, A. D. (1986). *Working memory*. New York: Oxford University Press.

Baddeley, A. D. (1992a). Working memory. *Science, 255*, 556–559.

Baddeley, A. D. (1992b). Working memory: The interface between memory and cognition. *Journal of Cognitive Neuroscience, 4*, 281–288.

Baddeley, A. D., & Lieberman, K. (1980). Spatial working memory. In R. S. Nickerson (Ed.), *Attention and performance* (pp. 521–539). Hillsdale, NJ: Erlbaum.

Beech, A., & Claridge, G. (1987). Individual differences in negative priming: Relations with schizotypal personality traits. *British Journal of Psychology, 78*, 349–356.

Benes, F. M., McSparren, J., Bird, E. D., SanGiovanni, J. P., & Vincent, S. L. (1991). Deficits in small interneurons in prefrontal and cingulate cortices of schizophrenic and schizoaffective patients. *Archives of General Psychiatry, 48*, 996–1001.

Berman, K. F., Illowsky, B. P., & Weinberger, D. R. (1988). Physiologic dysfunction of dorsolateral prefrontal cortex in schizophrenia: IV. Further evidence for regional and behavioral specificity. *Archives of General Psychiatry, 45*, 616–623.

Blum, R. A. (1952). Effects of subtotal lesions of frontal granular cortex on delayed reaction in monkeys. *American Medical Association Archives of Neurology and Psychiatry, 67*, 375–386.

Breier, A., Buchanan, R. W., Elkashef, A., Munson, R. C., Kirkpatrick, B., & Gellad, F. (1992). Brain morphology and schizophrenia: An MRI study of limbic, prefrontal cortex and caudate structures. *Archives of General Psychiatry, 49*, 921–926.

Breier, A., Davis, O. R., Buchanan, R. W., Moricle, L. A., & Munson, R. C. (1993). Effects of metabolic perturbation on plasma homovanillic acid in schizophrenia. *Archives of General Psychiatry, 50*, 541–550.

Calev, A. (1984). Recall and recognition in mildly disturbed schizophrenics: Use of matched tests. *Psychological Medicine, 14*, 425–429.

Callicott, J. H., Ramsey, J. H., Tallent, K., Bertolino, A., Knable, M. B., Coppola, R., et al. (1998). Functional magnetic resonance imaging brain mapping in psychiatry: Methodological issues illustrated in a study of working memory in schizophrenia. *Neuropsychopharmacology, 18*, 186–196.

Carter, C. S., Robertson, L. C., Nordahl, T., Chadderjian, M., Kraft, L., & O'Shora-Celaya, L. (1996). Spatial working memory deficits and their relationship to negative symptoms in unmedicated schizophrenia patients. *Biological Psychiatry, 40*, 930–932.

Castner, S. A., Williams, G. V., & Goldman-Rakic, P. S. (2000). Reversal of antipsychotic-induced working memory deficits by short-term dopamine D1 receptor stimulation. *Science, 287*, 2020–2022.

Cavada, C., & Goldman-Rakic, P. S. (1985). Parieto–prefrontal connections in the monkey: Topographical distribution within the prefrontal cortex of sectors connected with the lateral and medial posterior parietal cortex. *Society of Neuroscience Abstracts, 11*, 323.

Cavada, C., & Goldman-Rakic, P. S. (1989a). Posterior parietal cortex in rhesus monkeys: I. Parcellation of areas based on distinctive limbic and sensory cortico–cortical connections. *Journal of Comparative Neurology, 287*, 393–421.

Cavada, C., & Goldman-Rakic, P. S. (1989b). Posterior parietal cortex in rhesus monkeys: II. Evidence for segregated corticocortical networks linking sensory and limbic areas with the frontal lobe. *Journal of Comparative Neurology, 287*, 422–445.

Chapman, L. J., & Chapman, J. P. (1985). Psychosis proneness. In M. Alpert (Ed.), *Controversies in schizophrenia: Changes and constancies* (pp. 157–172). New York: Guilford Press.

Chapman, L. J., Chapman, J. P., & Raulin, M. L. (1978). Body-image aberration in schizophrenia. *Journal of Abnormal Psychology, 87*, 399–407.

Clementz, B. A., McDowell, J. E., & Zisook, S. (1994). Saccadic system functioning among schizophrenia patients and their first degree relatives. *Journal of Abnormal Psychology, 103*, 277–287.

Cohen, J. D., & Servan-Schreiber, D. (1992). Context, cortex and dopamine: A connectionist approach to behavior and biology in schizophrenia. *Psychological Review, 99*, 45–77.

Collette, F., Salmon, E., Van der Linden, M., Chicherio, C., Belleville, S., Degueldre, C., et al. (1999). Regional brain activity during tasks devoted to the central executive of working memory. *Cognitive Brain Research, 7*, 411–417.

Conklin, H. M., Curtis, C. E., Katsanis, J., & Iacono, W. G. (2000). Verbal working memory impairment in schizophrenia patients and their first-degree relatives: Evidence from the digit span task. *American Journal of Psychiatry, 157*, 275–277.

David, A. S., & Cutting, J. C. (1992). Visual imagery and visual semantics in the cerebral hemispheres in schizophrenia. *Schizophrenia Research, 8*, 263–271.

Deng, S.-Y., Segraves, M. A., Ungerleider, L. G., Mishkin, M., & Goldberg, M. E. (1984). Unilateral frontal eye field lesions degrade saccadic performance in the rhesus monkey. *Society of Neuroscience Abstracts, 10*, 59.

de Zubicaray, G. I., Williams, S. C. R., Wilson, S. J., Rose, S. E., Brammer, M. J., Bullmore, E. T., et al. (1998). Prefrontal cortex involvement in selective letter generation: A functional magnetic resonance imaging study. *Cortex, 34*, 389–401.

Evdokimidis, I., Liakopoulos, D., Constantinidis, T. S., & Papageorgiou, C. (1996). Cortical potentials with antisaccades. *Electron Clinical Neurophysiology, 98*, 377–384.

Farah, M. J. (1988). Is visual imagery really visual? *Psychological Review, 95*, 307–317.

Faraone, S. V., Seidman, L. J., Kerene, W. S., Toomey, R., Pepple, J. R., & Tsuang, M. T. (1999). Neuropsychological functioning among the nonpsychotic relatives of schizophrenic patients: A 4-year follow-up study. *Journal of Abnormal Psychology, 108*, 176–187.

Fleming, K., Goldberg, T. E., Binks, S., Randolph, C., Gold, J. M., & Weinberger, D. R. (1997). Visuospatial working memory in patients with schizophrenia. *Biological Psychiatry, 41*, 43–49.

Freedman, M., & Oscar-Berman, M. (1986). Bilateral frontal lobe disease and selective delayed-response deficits in humans. *Behavioral Neuroscience, 100*, 337–342.

Fukushima, J., Fukushima, K., Chiba, T., Tanaka, S., Yamashita, I., & Masamichi, K. (1988). Disturbances of voluntary control of saccadic eye movements in schizophrenic patients. *Biological Psychiatry, 23*, 670–677.

Funahashi, S., Bruce, C. J., & Goldman-Rakic, P. S. (1989). Mnemonic coding of visual cortex in the monkey's dorsolateral prefrontal cortex. *Journal of Neurophysiology, 61*, 331–348.

Funahashi, S., Bruce, C. J., & Goldman-Rakic, P. S. (1990). Visuospatial coding in primate prefrontal neurons revealed by oculomotor paradigms. *Journal of Neurophysiology, 63*, 814–831.

Funahashi, S., Bruce, C. J., & Goldman-Rakic, P. S. (1993). Dorsolateral prefrontal lesion and oculomotor delayed response performance: Evidence for mnemonic "scotomas." *Journal of Neuroscience, 13*, 1479–1497.

Ganguli, R., Carter, C., Mintun, M., Brar, J., Becker, J., Sarma, R., et al. (1997). PET brain mapping study of auditory verbal supraspan memory versus visual fixation in schizophrenia. *Biological Psychiatry, 41*, 33–42.

Gathercole, S., & Baddeley, A. D. (1989). Evaluation of the role of phonological STM in the development of vocabulary in children: A longitudinal study. *Journal of Memory and Language, 28*, 200–213.

Goldberg, T. E., Weinberger, D. R., Pliskin, N. H., Berman, K. F., & Podd, M. H. (1989). Recall memory deficit in schizophrenia: A possible manifestation of prefrontal dysfunction. *Schizophrenia Research, 2*, 251–257.

Goldman-Rakic, P. S. (1987). Circuitry of primate prefrontal cortex and regulation of behavior by representational knowledge. In F. Plum & V. Mountcastle (Eds.), *Handbook of physiology—The nervous system V* (pp. 373–417). Bethesda, MD: American Physiological Society.

Goldman-Rakic, P. S. (1991). Prefrontal cortical dysfunction in schizophrenia: The relevance of working memory. In B. Carroll (Ed.), *Psychopathology and the brain* (pp. 1–22). New York: Raven Press.

Goldman-Rakic, P. S. (1999). The relevance of the Dopamine-D1 receptor in the cognitive symptoms of schizophrenia. *Neuropsychopharmacology, 21*, S170–S180.

Gooding, D. C., Kwapil, T. R., & Tallent, K. A. (1999). Wisconsin Card Sorting Test deficits in schizotypic individuals. *Schizophrenia Research, 40*, 201–209.

Gooding, D. C., & Tallent, K. A. (2002). Spatial working memory performance in patients with schizoaffective psychosis versus schizophrenia: A tale of two disorders? *Schizophrenia Research, 53*, 209–218.

Guitton, D., Buchtel, H. A., & Douglas, R. M. (1985). Frontal lobe lesions in man cause difficulties in suppressing reflexive glances and in generating goal-directed saccades. *Experimental Brain Research, 58*, 455–472.

Gur, R. C., Saykin, A. J., & Gur, R. E. (1991). Neuropsychological study of schizophrenia. In C. A. Tamminga & S. C. Schultz (Eds.), *Advances in neuropsychiatry and psychopharmacology: Vol. 1. Schizophrenia research* (pp. 153–162). New York: Raven Press.

Hall, D. P., & Young, S. A. (1992). Frontal lobe aneurysm rupture presenting as psychosis. *Journal of Neurology, Neurosurgery and Psychiatry, 55*, 1207–1208.

Heaton, R. K., Chelune, G. J., Talley, J. L., Kay, G. G., & Curtis, G. (1993). *Wisconsin Card Sorting Test manual: Revised and expanded*. Odessa, FL: Psychological Assessment Resources.

Holzman, P. S. (1987). Recent studies of psychophysiology in schizophrenia. *Schizophrenia Bulletin, 13*, 49–75.

Holzman, P. S., Coleman, M., Lenzenweger, M. F., Levy, D. L., Matthysse, S., O'Driscoll, G. A., et al. (1995). Working memory, anti-saccade and thought disorder in relation to schizotypy. In A. Raine, T. Lencz, & S. Mednick (Eds.), *Schizotypal personality* (pp. 353–381). Cambridge, England: Cambridge University Press.

Holzman, P. S., & Matthysse, S. (1990). The genetics of schizophrenia: A review. *Psychological Science*, *1*, 279–286.

Holzman, P. S., Proctor, L. R., & Hughes, D. W. (1973). Eye tracking patterns in schizophrenia. *Science*, *181*, 179–181.

Holzman, P. S., Proctor, L. R., Levy, D. L., Yasillo, N. J., Meltzer, H. Y., & Hurt, S.W. (1974). Eye tracking dysfunctions in schizophrenic patients and their relatives. *Archives of General Psychiatry*, *31*, 143–151.

Hommer, D. W., Clem, T., Litman, R., & Pickar, D. (1991). Maladaptive anticipatory saccades in schizophrenia. *Biological Psychiatry*, *30*, 779–794.

Ingvar, D. H. (1980). Abnormal distribution of cerebral activity in chronic schizophrenia: A neurophysiological interpretation. In C. Baxter & T. Melnechuk (Eds.), *Perspectives in schizophrenia* (pp. 107–125). New York: Raven Press.

Ingvar, D. H., & Franzen, I. (1974). Abnormalities of cerebral blood flow distribution in patients with chronic schizophrenia. *Acta Psychiatrica Scandinavica*, *50*, 425–462.

Jacobsen, C. F. (1935). Studies of cerebral functions in primates: I. The functions of the frontal association areas in monkeys. *Comparative Psychology Monographs*, *13*, 3–60.

Jonides, J., Smith, E. E., Koeppe, R. A., Awh, E., Minoshima, S., & Mintun, M. (1993). Spatial working memory in humans as revealed by PET. *Nature*, *363*, 623–625.

Just, M. A., & Carpenter, P. A. (1992). A capacity theory of comprehension: Individual differences in working memory. *Psychological Review*, *99*, 122–149.

Karatekin, C., & Asarnow, R. F. (1998). Working memory in childhood-onset schizophrenia and attention-deficit/hyperactivity disorder. *Psychiatry Research*, *80*, 165–176.

Karoumi, B., Ventre-Dominey, J., Vighetto, A., Dalery, J., & d'Amato, T. (1998). Saccadic eye movements in schizophrenic patients. *Psychiatry Research*, *17*, 9–19.

Keefe, R. S. E., Roitman, S. E. L., Harvey, P. D., Blum, C. S., DuPre, R. L., Davidson, M., & Davis, K. L. (1995). A pen-and-paper human analogue of a monkey prefrontal cortex activation task: spatial working memory in patients with schizophrenia. *Schizophrenia Research*, *17*, 25–33.

Keefe, R. S. E., Silverman, J. M., Mohs, R. C., Siever, L. J., Harvey, P. D., Friedman, L., et al. (1997). Eye tracking, attention, and schizotypal symptoms in nonpsychotic relatives of patients with schizophrenia. *Archives of General Psychiatry*, *54*, 169–176.

Kirrane, R. M., Mitropoulou, V., Nunn, M., New, A. S., Harvey, P. D., Schopick, F., et al. (2000). Effects of amphetamine on visuospatial working memory performance in schizophrenia spectrum personality disorder. *Neuropsychopharmacology*, *22*, 14–18.

Koh, C., & Petersen, A. R. (1978). Recognition memory of schizophrenic patients. *Journal of Abnormal Psychology*, *87*, 303–313.

Kolb, B., & Wishaw, I. Q. (1983). Performances of schizophrenic patients on tests sensitive to left or right frontal, temporal, or parietal function in neurological patients. *Journal of Nervous and Mental Disease*, *171*, 435–443.

Kowalska, D. M., Bachevalier, J., & Mishkin, M. (1991). The role of the inferior prefrontal convexity in performance of delayed nonmatching-to-sample. *Neuropsychologia*, *29*, 583–600.

Krappmann, P., & Everling, S. (1998). Spatial accuracy of primary and secondary memory-guided saccades in schizophrenic patients. *Schizophrenia Research*, *30*, 183–185.

Lenzenweger, M. F., Cornblatt, B. A., & Putnick, M. (1991). Schizotypy and sustained attention. *Journal of Abnormal Psychology*, *100*, 84–89.

Lenzenweger, M. F., & Korfine, L. (1994). Perceptual aberrations, schizotypy, and Wisconsin Card Sorting Test performance. *Schizophrenia Bulletin*, *20*, 345–357.

Lenzenweger, M. F., & Loranger, A. W. (1989a). Detection of familial schizophrenia using a psychometric measure of schizotypy. *Archives of General Psychiatry*, *46*, 902–907.

Lenzenweger, M. F., & Loranger, A. W. (1989b). Psychosis-proneness and clinical psychopathology: Examination of the correlates of schizotypy. *Journal of Abnormal Psychology*, *98*, 3–8.

Levin, S. (1984a). Frontal lobe dysfunctions in schizophrenia: I. Eye movement impairments. *Journal of Psychiatric Research*, *18*, 27–55.

Levin, S. (1984b). Frontal lobe dysfunctions in schizophrenia: II. Impairments of psychological brain functions. *Journal of Psychiatric Research*, *18*, 57–72.

Levy, D. L., Yasillo, N. J., Dorus, E., Shaughnessy, R., Gibbons, R. D., Peterson, J., et al. (1983). Relatives of unipolar and bipolar patients have normal pursuit. *Psychiatry Research*, *10*, 285–293.

Lewinsohn, P. M., Zieler, J. L., Libet, L., Eyeberg, S., & Nielson, G. (1972). Short-term memory: A comparison between frontal and non-frontal right and left hemisphere brain-damaged patients. *Journal of Comparative Physiological Psychology, 81*, 248–255.

Lezak, M. D. (1995). *Neuropsychological assessment* (3rd ed.). New York: Oxford University Press.

Luciana, M., Depue, R. A., Arbisi, P., & Leon, A. (1992). Facilitation of working memory in humans by a D2 dopamine receptor agonist. *Journal of Cognitive Neuroscience, 4*, 58–68.

Lyons, M. J., Merla, M. E., Young, L., & Kremen, W. S. (1991). Impaired neuropsychological functioning in symptomatic volunteers with schiztotypy: Preliminary findings. *Biological Psychiatry, 30*, 424–426.

Manoach, D. S., Gollub, R. L., Benson, E. S., Searl, M. M., Goff, D. C., Halpern, E., et al. (2000). Schizophrenic subjects show aberrant fMRI activation of dorsolateral prefrontal cortex and basal ganglia during working memory performance. *Biological Psychiatry, 48*, 99–109.

Manoach, D. S., Press, D. Z., Thangaraj, V., Searl, M. M., Goff, D. C., Halpern, E., et al. (1999). Schizophrenic subjects activate dorsolateral prefrontal cortex during a working memory task, as measured by fMRI. *Biological Psychiatry, 45*, 1128–1137.

McCarthy, G., Blamire, A. M., Puce, A., Nobre, A. C., Bloch, G., Hyder, F., et al. (1994). Functional magnetic resonance imaging of the human prefrontal cortex activation during a spatial working memory task. *Proceedings of the National Academy of Sciences, USA, 91*, 8690–8694.

McDowell, J. E., & Clementz, B. A. (1997). The effect of fixation condition manipulations on antisaccade performance in schizophrenia: Studies of diagnostic specificity. *Experimental Brain Research, 115*, 333–344.

Meehl, P. E. (1990). Towards an integrated theory of schizotaxia, schizotypy and schizophrenia. *Journal of Personality Disorders, 4*, 1–99.

Mialat, J. P, & Pichot, P. (1981). Eye tracking patterns in schizophrenia: An analysis based on the incidence of saccades. *Archives of General Psychiatry, 38*, 183–186.

Mishkin, M. (1957). Effects of small frontal lesions on delayed alternation in monkeys. *Journal of Neurophysiology, 20*, 615–622.

Myles-Worsley, M., & Park, S. (in press). Working memory deficits in schizophrenia patients and their first-degree relatives in Palau, Micronesia. *American Journal of Medical Genetics.*

Nakashima, Y., Momose, T., Sano, I., Katayama, S., Niwa, S., & Matsushita, M. (1993). Left dorsolateral prefrontal cortex role in the control of saccade and its dysfunction in schizophrenia. *Journal of Cerebral Blood Flow and Metabolism, 13*(Suppl. 1), 507.

Nakashima, Y., Momose, T., Sano, I., Katayama, S., Niwa, S., & Matsushita, M. (1994). Cortical control of saccade in normal and schizophrenic subjects: A PET study using task-evoked rCBF paradigm. *Schizophrenia Research, 12*, 259–264.

O'Driscoll, G. A., Lenzenweger, M. F., & Holzman, P. S. (1998). Antisaccades and smooth pursuit eye tracking and schizotypy. *Archives of General Psychiatry, 55*, 837–843.

Oscar-Berman, M. (1975). The effects of dorsolateral–frontal and ventrolateral–orbitofrontal lesions on spatial discrimination learning and delayed response in two modalities. *Neuropsychologia, 13*, 237–246.

Pantelis, C., Barnes, T. R. E., Nelson, H. E., Tanner, S., Weatherley, L., Owen, D. R., & Ronnins, T. W. (1997). Frontal–striatal cognitive deficits in patients with chronic schizophrenia. *Brain, 120*, 1823–1843.

Park, S. (1991). *The role of prefrontal cortex in spatial working memory deficits of schizophrenic patients.* Unpublished doctoral dissertation, Harvard University.

Park, S. (1997). Association of an oculomotor delayed response task and the Wisconsin Card Sort Test in schizophrenic patients. *International Journal of Psychophysiology, 27*, 147–151.

Park, S. (1999). Hemispheric asymmetry of spatial working memory deficit in schizophrenia. *International Journal of Psychophysiology, 34*, 313–322.

Park, S., & Holzman, P. S. (1992). Schizophrenics show working memory deficits. *Archives of General Psychiatry, 49*, 975–982.

Park, S., & Holzman, P. S. (1993). Association of working memory deficit and eye tracking dysfunction in schizophrenia. *Schizophrenia Research, 11*, 55–61.

Park, S., Holzman, P. S., & Goldman-Rakic, P. S. (1995). Spatial working memory deficits in the relatives of schizophrenic patients. *Archives of General Psychiatry, 52*, 821–828.

Park, S., Holzman, P. S., & Lenzenweger, M. F. (1995). Individual difference in spatial working memory in relation to schizotypy. *Journal of Abnormal Psychology, 105*, 355–364.

Park, S., Holzman, P. S., & Levy, D. L. (1993). Spatial working memory deficit in the relatives of schizo-phrenic patients is associated with their smooth pursuit eye tracking performance. *Schizophrenia Research, 9*, 184.

Park, S., Lenzenweger, M. F., Puschel, J., & Holzman, P. S. (1996). Attentional inhibition in schizophrenia and schizotypy: A spatial negative priming study. *Cognitive Neuropsychiatry, 1*, 125–149.

Park, S., & McTigue, K. (1997). Spatial working memory and the syndrome of schizotypal personality. *Schizophrenia Research, 26*, 213–220.

Park, S., & O'Driscoll, G. A. (1996). Components of working memory deficit in schizophrenia. In S. Mat-thysse, D. L. Levy, J. Kagan, & F. Benes (Eds.), *Psychopathology: The evolving science of mental disorder* (pp. 34–50). Cambridge, England: Cambridge University Press.

Park, S., Püschel, J., Sauter, B., Rentsch, M., & Hell, D. (1999). Spatial working memory deficits and clini-cal symptoms in schizophrenia: A 4-month follow-up study. *Biological Psychiatry, 46*, 392–400.

Paulesu, E., Frith, C. D., & Frackowiak, R. S. J. (1993). The neural components of the verbal working memory. *Nature, 362*, 342–345.

Petrides, M., Alivisatos, B., Evans, A. C., & Meyer, E. (1993). Dissociation of human mid-dorsolateral from posterior dorsolateral frontal cortex in memory processing. *Proceedings of the National Acad-emy of Sciences, 90*, 873–877.

Petrides, M., Alivisatos, B., Meyer, E., & Evans, A. C. (1993). Functional activation of the human frontal cortex during the performance of verbal working memory tasks. *Proceedings of the National Academy of Sciences, 90*, 878–882.

Petrides, M., & Pandya, D. N. (1984). Projections to the frontal cortex from the posterior parietal region in the rhesus monkey. *Journal of Comparative Neurology, 228*, 105–116.

Pierrot-Deseilligny, C., Rivaud, S., Gaymard, B., & Agid, Y. (1991). Cortical control of memory-guided saccades in man. *Experimental Brain Research, 83*, 607–617.

Pivik, R. T. (1979). Smooth pursuit eye movements and attention in psychiatric patients. *Biological Psy-chiatry, 14*, 859–879.

Raine, A. (1991). The SPQ: A scale for the assessment of schizotypal personality based on *DSM–III–R* criteria. *Schizophrenia Bulletin, 17*, 555–564.

Rajkowska, G., Selemon, L. D., & Goldman-Rakic, P. S. (1998). Neuronal and glial somal size in the pre-frontal cortex: A postmortem study of schizophrenia and Huntington's disease. *Archives of General Psychiatry, 55*, 215–224.

Rao, S. C., Rainer, G., & Miller, E. K. (1997). Integration of what and where in the primate prefrontal cortex. *Science, 276*, 821–824.

Roitblat, H. L. (1987). *Introduction to comparative cognition*. New York: Freeman.

Ross, R. G., Harris, J. G., Olincy, A., Radant, A., Adler, L. E., & Freedman, R. (1998). Familial trans-mission of two independent saccadic abnormalities in schizophrenia. *Schizophrenia Research, 30*, 59–70.

Rupniak, N. M. J., & Iversen, S. D. (1993). Cognitive impairment in schizophrenia: How experimental models using non-human primates may assist improved drug therapy for negative symptoms. *Neu-ropsychologia, 31*, 1133–1146.

Sagawa, K., Kawakatsu, S., Shibuya, I., Arata, O., Morinobu, S., Komatani, A., et al. (1990). Correla-tion of regional cerebral blood flow with performance on neuropsychological tests in schizophrenic patients. *Schizophrenia Research, 3*, 241–246.

Sawaguchi, T., & Goldman-Rakic, P. S. (1991). D1 dopamine receptors in prefrontal cortex: Involvement in working memory. *Science, 251*, 947–950.

Selemon, L. D., & Goldman-Rakic, P. S. (1985). Longitudinal topography and interdigitation of corticos-triatal projections in the rhesus monkey. *Journal of Neuroscience, 5*, 776–794.

Selemon, L. D., Rajkowska, G., & Goldman-Rakic, P. S. (1995). Abnormally high neuronal density in the schizophrenic cortex: A morphometric analysis of prefrontal area 9 and occipital area 17. *Archives of General Psychiatry, 52*, 805–818.

Selemon, L. D., Rajkowska, G., & Goldman-Rakic, P. S. (1998). Elevated neuronal density in prefrontal area 46 in brains from schizophrenic patients: Application of a three dimensional, stereologic count-ing method. *Journal of Comparative Neurology, 392*, 402–412.

Shallice, T. (1982). Specific impairments of planning. *Philosophical Transactions of the Royal Society of London, B*, 199–209.

Shallice, T. (1988). *From neuropsychology to mental structures*. Cambridge, England: Cambridge Univer-sity Press.

Shiffrin, R. M., & Schneider, W. (1977). Controlled and automatic human information processing II. *Psychological Review, 84*, 127–190.

Snitz, B. E., Curtis, C. E., Zald, D. H., Karsanis, J., & Iacono, W. G. (1999). Neuropsychological and oculomotor correlates of spatial working memory performance in schizophrenia patients and controls. *Schizophrenia Research, 38*, 37–50.

Spindler, K. A., Sullivan, E. V., Menon, V., Lim, K. O., & Pfefferbaum, A. (1997). Deficits in multiple systems of working memory in schizophrenia. *Schizophrenia Research, 27*, 1–10.

Spitzer, M. (1993). The psychopathology, neuropsychology and neurobiology of associative and working memory in schizophrenia. *European Archives of Psychiatry and Clinical Neuroscience, 243*, 57–70.

Stamm, J. S. (1985). The riddle of the monkey's delayed response deficit has been solved. In E. Perecman (Ed.), *The frontal lobes revisited* (pp. 73–90). Hillsdale, NJ: Erlbaum.

Stanton, G. B., Bruce, C. J., & Goldberg, M. E. (1995). Topography of projections to posterior cortical areas from the macaque frontal eye fields. *Journal of Comparative Neurology, 353*, 291–305.

Stark, L. (1983). Abnormal patterns of normal eye movements in schizophrenia. *Schizophrenia Bulletin, 9*, 55–72.

Stevens, A. A., Goldman-Rakic, P. S., Gore, J. C., Fulbright, R. K., & Wexler, B. E. (1998). Cortical dysfunction in schizophrenia during auditory word and tone working memory demonstrated by functional magnetic resonance imaging. *Archives of General Psychiatry, 55*, 1097–1103.

Stuss, D. T., & Benson, D. F. (1984). Neuropsychological studies of the frontal lobes. *Psychological Bulletin, 95*, 3–28.

Stuss, D. T., & Benson, D. F. (1985). The frontal lobes and control of cognition and memory. In E. Perecman (Ed.), *The frontal lobes revisited* (pp. 141–158). Hillsdale, NJ: Erlbaum.

Suzuki, H., & Azuma, M. (1983). Topographic studies on visual neurons in the dorsolateral prefrontal cortex of the monkey. *Experimental Brain Research, 53*, 47–58.

Tallent, K. A., & Gooding, D. C. (1999). Working memory and Wisconsin Card Sorting Test performance in schizotypic individuals: A replication and extension. *Psychiatry Research, 89*, 161–170.

Taylor, A. E., Saint-Cyr, J. A., & Lang, A. E. (1986). Parkinson's disease: Cognitive changes in response to treatment response. *Brain, 110*, 35–51.

Ungerleider, L. G., Courtney, S. M., & Haxby, J. V. (1998). A neural system for human visual working memory. *Proceedings of the National Academy of Sciences USA, 95*, 883–890.

Villa, G., Gainotti, G., De Bonis, C., & Marra, C. (1990). Double dissociation between temporal and spatial pattern processing in patients with frontal and parietal damage. *Cortex, 26*, 399–407.

Watanabe, M. (1996). Reward expectancy in primate prefrontal neurons. *Nature, 382*, 629–632.

Weinberger, D. R., & Berman, K. F. (1996). Prefrontal function in schizophrenia: Confounds and controversies. *Philosophical Transactions of the Royal Society in London, 351*, 1495–1503.

Weinberger, D. R., Berman, K. F., & Illowsky, B. P. (1988). Physiologic dysfunction of dorsolateral prefrontal cortex in schizophrenia: III. A new cohort and evidence for monoaminergic mechanism. *Archives of General Psychiatry, 45*, 609–615.

Weinberger, D. R., Berman, K. F., & Zec, R. F. (1986). Physiologic dysfunction of dorsolateral prefrontal cortex in schizophrenia: I. Regional cerebral blood flow evidence. *Archives of General Psychiatry, 43*, 114–124.

Williams, G. V., & Goldman-Rakic, P. S. (1995). Modulation of memory fields by dopamine D1 receptor in prefrontal cortex. *Nature, 376*, 572–575.

Wilson, F. A. W., Scalaidhe, S. P. O., & Goldman-Rakic, P. S. (1993). Dissociation of object and spatial processing domains in primate prefrontal cortex. *Science, 260*, 1955–1957.

Wolkin, A., Sanfilipo, M., Wolf, A. P., Angrist, B., Brodie, J. D., & Rotrosen, J. (1992). Negative symptoms and hypofrontality in chronic schizophrenia. *Archives of General Psychiatry, 49*, 959–966.

Zarahn, E., Aguirre, G. K., & D'Esposito, M. (1999). Temporal isolation of the neural correlates of spatial mnemonic processing with fMRI. *Cognitive Brain Research, 7*, 255–268.

6

Understanding the Employment Rate of People With Schizophrenia: Different Approaches Lead to Different Implications for Policy

Crystal R. Blyler

One of the tragedies of modern academic psychology is that the pressure to publish and the need to prove that psychology is, in fact, a real science can lead to the objectification of human beings, including both the "subjects" one is studying as well as the students and colleagues with whom one works. As a student of history, Brendan Maher is confident in the well-established scientific roots of experimental psychopathology. This allows him to convey the importance of objective, quantifiable measurement, even while respecting the validity of internal subjective experience. Thus, in his research studies, he never loses sight of how the participants are experiencing the symptoms that he is so carefully measuring and analyzing. In his teaching, he does not allow his desire to convey specific information to dominate over the humor and storytelling that are so important to motivate students to learn. In his mentorship, he does not confuse his own research interests with those of his student. And in his administrative role, he manages to convey compassion and warmth simultaneously with clarity of purpose and ethical integrity. Although I have learned much from the direct teaching and writing of Professor Maher, the greatest lesson comes from observing him as a role model. The making of a great scientist, I have learned, requires not only the ability to generate creative ideas of one's own but also an inherent respect for the ideas and subjective experiences of others.

I was a graduate student of Maher's from 1988 to 1994. While I was at Harvard, I worked with him on developing a simple method of assessing motor disorder in

The Employment Intervention Demonstration Program (EIDP) is a multisite collaboration among eight research demonstration sites, a coordinating center, and the Substance Abuse and Mental Health Services Administration (SAMHSA) Center for Mental Health Services (CMHS), which funds the initiative (Public Health Service Cooperative Agreement SM51820). The data are from analyses conducted by the Coordinating Center at the University of Illinois at Chicago using preliminary multisite data sets. The publication policy of EIDP does not allow inclusion of final cross-site data in the chapter at this time; all data presented are strictly preliminary. Updated information on the study can be found at the EIDP website: http://www.psych.uic.edu/eidp. This article was written in a personal capacity and does not necessarily represent the opinions of CMHS, SAMHSA, the U.S. Department of Health and Human Services, the federal government, or EIDP collaborating partners.

schizophrenia (Blyler, Maher, Manschreck, & Fenton, 1997), and I wrote my dissertation on the origins of auditory hallucinations (Blyler, 1995). These projects clearly
fell into the category of experimental psychopathology, as taught by Maher, in which
one seeks to better understand the fundamental cognitive, emotional, behavioral,
and biological processes underlying schizophrenia.

I currently work for the Center for Mental Health Services (CMHS) of the
Substance Abuse and Mental Health Services Administration (SAMHSA). Although
less well known among experimental psychopathologists than the National Institute
of Mental Health (NIMH), SAMHSA is also a federal agency that operates at the
same level as, and independently of, the National Institutes of Health, under the
U.S. Department of Health and Human Services. SAMHSA was established in 1992
(ADAMHA Reorganization Act, 1992) and serves a somewhat different purpose than
NIMH. Whereas NIMH focuses primarily on funding independent research, the mis-
sion of the CMHS is directed at assisting states with the funding and improvement
of services in the public mental health system.

Although my current career path represents something of a change from the
basic schizophrenia research in which Maher mentored me, his influence continues
to guide me. The wealth of knowledge that I gained from him about schizophrenia
and research methodology is certainly applicable to my work at SAMHSA. Equally
important, however, are more general skills that he modeled, such as diplomacy,
encouragement of other people's interests and skills, and use of humor in teaching
and carrying out administrative functions.

An important aspect of how Maher studies schizophrenia is that he constantly
seeks to understand the *experience* of the disorder. In thinking about delusional
beliefs, for example, he theorized that delusions do not arise out of a fundamental
illogicality of thought but rather that they may arise as rational explanations for
unusual experiences (Maher, 1988). Such a desire to understand the disorder from
the perspective of the person experiencing it also drives much of the work that I, and
others, do at CMHS.

Within CMHS, I work in the Division of Knowledge Development and Systems
Change. This division serves as a kind of quality-improvement team for the public
mental health system. As such, the staff spends considerable time thinking about
how to most effectively translate research into practice and how to use research
to influence policy. One of the types of activities in which the division engages is
knowledge development. Knowledge development is similar to research but with
some notable differences. Perhaps the most important of these is that, unlike more
basic research, knowledge development is more policy oriented from the start.

One topic area that I have previously studied within a more basic schizophrenia research context and that I am now examining within the CMHS knowledge
development framework is the employment of people with serious mental illness.
Estimates from clinical samples suggest that fewer than 15% of people with the most
serious and persistent mental illnesses, including schizophrenia, are competitively
employed (Anthony & Blanch, 1987; Milazzo-Sayre, Henderson, & Manderscheid,
1997; Mulkern & Manderscheid, 1989). In this chapter, I illustrate how the two
cultures of basic schizophrenia research and knowledge development have tried to
understand this statistic. Readers will see that these two approaches have rather
different implications for policy and practice. I begin by describing the basic schizophrenia research approach.

Basic Schizophrenia Research Approach

Basic schizophrenia research is typically based on the understanding of schizophrenia as a categorical disorder. Basic researchers build on prior research experiences by using the literature to generate new ideas for research. Psychologists studying schizophrenia base their work on examination of the behavioral, cognitive, and emotional manifestations of the disorder: that is, the symptoms.

The symptoms that one most often associates with schizophrenia are the psychotic symptoms, such as delusions and hallucinations. In the past two decades, a new conceptualization has emerged in which, in addition to the older psychotic symptoms, now called *positive symptoms*, a new category of *negative symptoms* has been recognized (American Psychiatric Association, 1994). Part of the reason for this new distinction is that although older antipsychotic medications had a marked effect on symptoms such as delusions and hallucinations, treated patients were not fully recovering. The negative-symptom category describes the types of lingering deficits that people with schizophrenia who are medicated continue to experience, such as a lack of meaningful social relationships, a lack of physical and verbal expressiveness, and decreased interest and activity levels (Andreasen, 1982).

In recent years, investigators have examined the effects of new atypical antipsychotic medications, such as clozapine, on the negative, as well as the positive, symptoms of schizophrenia; effects on cognitive correlates of the disorder have also been examined. Despite equivocal evidence for such effects (Bond & Meyer, 1999; Buckley & Schulz, 1996), people have become hopeful that broader effects of the new medications might lead to improved functioning in areas such as independent living and employment. If medications could alleviate negative symptoms such as lack of persistence at work or school, then one might intuitively expect that they would allow more people with schizophrenia to work.

Recent research regarding employment of people with schizophrenia growing out of the basic research tradition has, therefore, focused on the effects of symptoms (Anthony, Rogers, Cohen, & Davies, 1995; Bell & Lysaker, 1995; Breier, Schreiber, Dyer, & Pickar, 1991; Charisiou et al., 1989; Massel et al., 1990) and cognitive functioning (Brekke, Raine, Ansel, Lencz, & Bird, 1997; Bryson, Bell, Kaplan, & Greig, 1998; Lysaker, Bell, & Beam-Goulet, 1995; Silverstein, Fogg, & Harrow, 1991) on the ability of people with schizophrenia to work. A primary assumption underlying such investigations is that the reason for the extraordinarily low employment rate of people with serious mental illness is that the disorders themselves interfere with the ability of such individuals to work. The primary research question is which symptoms and cognitive dysfunctions most affect employment outcomes and how.

Some studies have found that symptoms and cognition may be related to lower ratings of work skills, performance, and functioning (Anthony et al., 1995; Bell & Lysaker, 1995; Breier et al., 1991; Brekke et al., 1997; Bryson et al., 1998; Charisiou et al., 1989; Lysaker et al., 1995; Massel et al., 1990; Silverstein et al., 1991). These studies, however, are riddled with imprecise definitions and measurements of employment outcomes, such as considering homemakers and students to be employed and relying on clinician ratings of skills in controlled settings rather than soliciting ratings by employers in competitive work environments. In addition, many of these studies have examined relationships among a large array of independent and dependent variables without adequately compensating for the multiple comparisons statistically. Overall, research has not yet clearly linked features of serious mental illness with decreased rates of participation in the competitive labor force (Anthony & Jansen, 1984). Moreover, the effect of treatment with the atypical antipsychotics on competitive employment remains largely unexamined (Bond & Meyer, 1999).

The implications for mental health policy and practice of findings that result from the basic schizophrenia research approach are, therefore, limited. Nevertheless, one might argue, on the basis of this line of thinking and research, that (a) for the most part, people with serious and persistent mental illness cannot work because of their illnesses, and (b) the atypical antipsychotics should be made more widely available to allow people with schizophrenia to work. In addition, one might conclude that better treatments that affect a wider range of symptoms and associated features, while producing fewer side effects, must be developed in order to improve work outcomes.

CMHS Knowledge Development Approach

As stated earlier, CMHS knowledge development activities are more policy focused than basic research activities from the moment of conception. In addition to examining the literature to generate ideas, CMHS solicits extensive input from all of the key stakeholders—including mental health consumers, family members, service providers, administrators, and policymakers—early in the planning process. One of the compelling reasons that CMHS developed the Employment Intervention Demonstration Program, described later, was that when mental health consumers were asked in surveys what their most pressing needs were, they consistently responded that meaningful work was among their top priorities (Campbell & Schraiber, 1989; Rogers, Walsh, Massotta, & Danley, 1991). In meetings with consumer advocates, CMHS heard repeatedly that consumers did not want just any jobs, which might include jobs in sheltered workshops or volunteer jobs; they wanted competitive jobs at real wages.

Despite the stated desire of consumers to work, the statistics showing the low percentage who were working on their own suggested that consumers would need some assistance in achieving their employment goals. The U.S. Department of Education Rehabilitative Services Administration oversees vocational rehabilitation programs, commonly known as the *VR system*, in every state. These programs are available to people with all types of disabilities. Although they are open to people with psychiatric disabilities, the feeling among mental health consumers, providers, and family members was—and continues to be—that despite good intentions, the VR system, for a variety of reasons, was not very effective for people with psychiatric disabilities (Noble, 1998; Noble, Honberg, Hall, & Flynn, 1999; U.S. General Accounting Office, 1993). The feeling was that specialized services that specifically focused on helping people with mental illness to find and maintain competitive employment had to be developed. The literature described some vocational program models that held promise for helping mental health consumers to find competitive work (Bond, 1992; Bond & Boyer, 1988; Bond, Drake, Becker, & Mueser, 1999), but such services were not widely available when the CMHS employment program began in 1995, and it was felt that a rigorous evaluation was needed to determine which models were most effective for helping different types of clients under various circumstances. Out of these considerations grew the CMHS Employment Intervention Demonstration Program (EIDP; 59 Fed. Reg. Doc. 94-21290).

EIDP

The EIDP is a multisite evaluation of the effectiveness of various models of vocational support programs for helping people with serious mental illnesses to find and maintain competitive employment. EIDP includes project sites in eight states: Arizona, Connecticut, Maine, Maryland, Massachusetts, Pennsylvania, South Carolina, and Texas. It also includes a coordinating center, which is headed by Judith Cook at the University of Illinois at Chicago in partnership with the Human Services Research Institute in Cambridge, Massachusetts.

CMHS selected a multisite methodology because it was felt that multisite studies could have a greater influence on policy than studies initiated by single investigators. Some of the reasons for this are that (a) an increased number of participants from multiple sites may be viewed by policymakers as more representative of the country; (b) states and communities that want to implement such programs would have a larger variety of options from which to choose; (c) having multiple sites with a large number of participants might give CMHS a place at the table where policy discussions about employment issues take place; and (d) using common measures of outcomes allows one to compare, contrast, and combine data across sites for a more finely grained analysis of the types of programs that work for different types of consumers under different circumstances.

Method. In all sites except one, participants were not working when they entered the program. In each site, participants were randomly assigned to one of at least two intervention conditions. Participants were followed for 2 years while in the vocational program and underwent a 1- to 2-hr interview every 6 months. Job status was assessed every week for the full 2 years, and both vocational and nonvocational service utilization data were collected for the participants' entire tenure. In addition to the primary outcome assessments of job status, the sites gathered data using a common protocol that included information on demographics, residential status, income sources and entitlements, physical and cognitive impairments, clinical symptoms and medications, quality of life, self-esteem, work motivation, and costs of the vocational programs.

Although the research design elements were similar across sites, the study was not equivalent to a clinical trial in that the interventions being examined differed from site to site. Altogether, 17 intervention conditions were evaluated across the eight sites. Some of these were control conditions, such as *services as usual*. Among the model interventions hypothesized to be best practices were variations on three general types of vocational service models: (a) In assertive community treatment, an integrated clinical team provides services out in the community, rather than in an office, and includes one or more vocational support specialists in frequent, regular team meetings, (b) psychosocial rehabilitation and clubhouse model programs provide a variety of prevocational, vocational, and nonvocational services within the context of a supportive community, and (c) supported employment model programs focus on quick placement of consumers into competitive jobs, in lieu of extensive prevocational training, and then provide ongoing support while the person is working.

Results. At the time of publication, data collection for EIDP had been completed, with more than 1,600 participants enrolled. The EIDP publication policy, however, prohibits publication of final cross-site data until the core papers, which will answer the primary questions of EIDP, have been completed. These papers are scheduled to be completed in 2002. The results presented here, therefore, are very preliminary: (a) They are based on incomplete data from the first 3 years of data collection only; (b) they represent grouped data, whereas the final results are likely to vary among sites; (c) outcomes are based on all of the conditions, both best practices and standard services, combined; and (d) analyses are descriptive, rather than statistical, in nature. Despite the preliminary nature of the results, my purpose is simply to illustrate the myriad ways in which such data can be used to influence policy.

Examination of the characteristics of the participant sample reveals that the goal of enrolling people with serious and persistent mental illness was met. Roughly 50% of participants were diagnosed with schizophrenia, schizoaffective disorder, or other psychotic disorders; all but 12% of the sample had multiple Axis I diagnoses. Participants had a mean of six lifetime hospitalizations, and 77% were taking more than one psychiatric medication. Only 7% of the participants had achieved a 4-year college education, which presented a challenge for finding meaningful and interesting employment. As a final indication of the severity of illness, 72% of participants were receiving federal disability benefits from the Social Security Administration. Only 3% of participants were homeless.

Preliminary analyses showed that roughly 50% of participants who received services for 12 or more months were employed during the study. This percentage is substantially higher than one might expect for this population. The analyses also revealed that the longer people received vocational services, the more likely they were to become employed. During the first 3 years of the study, participants held more than 2,000 jobs, worked almost 800,000 hours, and earned over $4 million, thereby demonstrating that people with serious and persistent mental illness are capable of considerable economic productivity. Although 84% of jobs held paid above minimum wage, the jobs tended to be low paying and part time. Although people with schizophrenia had slightly lower employment rates than people with other diagnoses at all assessment points, the employment rate for people with schizophrenia remained substantially higher than one might expect for this population.

Policy Implications

EIDP was designed to determine which types of interventions are the most effective for helping which consumers to find and maintain competitive employment. At the time of publication, the analyses that would answer these primary questions had not been completed. Nevertheless, because the study was designed to address a topic of utmost importance to consumers and their family members, and because mental health service providers and policymakers provided input at all stages to the design of the study, even preliminary descriptive data such as these can be put to a variety of policy-related ends; for example, the following conclusions might be drawn from these and other findings of EIDP.

1. Even people with the most serious and persistent forms of mental illness *can* work with the appropriate support services.
2. The longer people receive services, the more likely they will be to obtain employment. This suggests that services should be provided over a longer time period than may be common practice.
3. Accompanying substance abuse may account for significant variation in employment outcomes. Substance abuse services, therefore, should be integrated into vocational programs that support people with mental illness.
4. Fear of loss of federal entitlement benefits, such as those from the Social Security Administration, acts as a significant deterrent for people with psychiatric disabilities to work (MacDonald-Wilson, 1999). The Ticket to Work and Work Incentives Improvement Act was signed by former President Clinton on December 17, 1999, to address these concerns, which are similar to those of people with physical disabilities who want to work. CMHS has provided data from EIDP to the Social Security Administration and the Centers for Medicare and Medicaid Services to help these agencies plan the implementation of this legislation in a way that will be most beneficial to people with serious mental illness who want to work.
5. In addition to working directly with consumers, mental health vocational specialists should involve other stakeholders—such as friends and family members, clinical treatment providers, the Department of Education's VR system, and local businesses—in their attempts to find and maintain employment for individual clients.

In addition to the above policy implications, several needs have become apparent through EIDP: (a) Even the best vocational models are not effectively reaching the population of people with mental illness who are homeless (Ducq, Guesdon, & Roelandt, 1997), suggesting that specific efforts will have to be made to engage the homeless population in vocational programs; (b) the jobs that consumers get tend to be low paying, suggesting a need for a greater focus on career development; (c) consumers often lack the education needed to obtain higher paying jobs, suggesting a need for the development of supported education programs; and (d) issues of how to pay for employment support services must be addressed.

Conclusion

In addition to its policy implications, this CMHS knowledge development activity has important implications for the way more basic research is conducted and interpreted. The experience of schizophrenia clearly involves much more than the symptoms of the disorder and the effects of the medications used to treat them. Along with schizophrenia often comes a downward spiral into poverty that is difficult to counter. Dependence on public assistance to pay for food, shelter, and psychiatric care comes with powerful disincentives to future work. Stigma leads to discouragement from family, friends, and mental health care providers who believe that people with serious mental illness are not capable of working. Disruptions of one's education, housing, early work experience, and social development all present barriers that must be overcome in order for people with psychiatric disabilities to return to work later in life. Each of these important variables must be considered when trying to understand the dismal employment rates of people with schizophrenia.

Experimental psychopathology requires, by its nature, a mixture of experimental and quasi-experimental research designs. People cannot be randomly assigned to a schizophrenia versus nonschizophrenia condition. Therefore, to fully understand any fact about schizophrenia, such as its association with a low employment rate, one must fully examine the multiple correlates of the disorder that are pertinent to that fact. If one focuses narrowly on schizophrenia as a disease, rather than more broadly on the lives of the people who experience the disorder, then important correlates that may best explain the association may be overlooked. Only by studying schizophrenia in the fuller context of the lives of the people who experience it can researchers hope to identify all of the factors that might be changed in order to improve the employment rate of this population. By looking beyond aspects of the disorder that reside within the individual, researchers have discovered that hope for recovery lies not just in the ability of therapies and medications to improve symptoms in individuals but also in creating meaningful changes to political and service systems that can positively affect the employment rate of the group as a whole. In sum, improving the employment rate of people with schizophrenia requires much more than just better control over the disorder. It also requires systems change.

References

ADAMHA Reorganization Act, Pub. L. No. 102-321, 42 U.S.C. 290aa (1992).

American Psychiatric Association. (1994). *Diagnostic and statistical manual of mental disorders* (4th ed.). Washington, DC: Author.

Andreasen, N. C. (1982). Negative symptoms in schizophrenia. *Archives of General Psychiatry, 39,* 784–788.

Anthony, W. A., & Blanch, A. (1987). Supported employment for persons who are psychiatrically disabled: An historical and conceptual perspective. *Psychosocial Rehabilitation Journal, 11*(2), 5–23.

Anthony, W. A., & Jansen, M. A. (1984). Predicting the vocational capacity of the chronically mentally ill: Research and policy implications. *American Psychologist, 39,* 537–544.

Anthony, W. A., Rogers, E. S., Cohen, M., & Davies, R. R. (1995). Relationships between psychiatric symptomatology, work skills, and future vocational performance. *Psychiatric Services, 46,* 353–358.

Bell, M. D., & Lysaker, P. H. (1995). Psychiatric symptoms and work performance among persons with severe mental illness. *Psychiatric Services, 46,* 508–510.

Blyler, C. R. (1995). The origins of auditory hallucinations in schizophrenia. *Dissertation Abstracts International, 55* (08), 3614B.

Blyler, C. R., Maher, B. A., Manschreck, T. C., & Fenton, W. S. (1997). Line drawing as a possible measure of lateralized motor performance in schizophrenia. *Schizophrenia Research, 26,* 15–23.

Bond, G. R. (1992). Vocational rehabilitation. In R. P. Liberman (Ed.), *Handbook of psychiatric rehabilitation* (pp. 244–275). New York: Macmillan.

Bond, G. R., & Boyer, S. L. (1988). Rehabilitation programs and outcomes. In J. A. Ciardiello & M. D. Bell (Eds.), *Vocational rehabilitation of persons with prolonged psychiatric disorders* (pp. 231–263). Baltimore: Johns Hopkins University Press.

Bond, G. R., Drake, R. E., Becker, D. R., & Mueser, K. T. (1999). Effectiveness of psychiatric rehabilitation approaches for employment of people with severe mental illness. *Journal of Disability Policy Studies, 10,* 18–52.

Bond, G. R., & Meyer, P. S. (1999). Role of medications in the employment of people with schizophrenia. *Journal of Rehabilitation, 65,* 9–16.

Breier, A., Schreiber, J. L., Dyer, J., & Pickar, D. (1991). National Institute of Mental Health longitudinal study of chronic schizophrenia: Prognosis and predictors of outcome. *Archives of General Psychiatry*, *48*, 239–246.

Brekke, J. S., Raine, A., Ansel, M., Lencz, T., & Bird, L. (1997). Neuropsychological and psychophysiological correlates of psychosocial functioning in schizophrenia. *Schizophrenia Bulletin*, *23*, 19–28.

Bryson, G., Bell, M. D., Kaplan, E., & Greig, T. (1998). Functional consequences of memory impairments on initial work performance in people with schizophrenia. *Journal of Nervous and Mental Disease*, *186*, 610–615.

Buckley, P. F., & Schulz, S. C. (1996). Clozapine and Risperidone: Refining and extending their use. *Harvard Review of Psychiatry*, *4*, 184–199.

Campbell, J., & Schraiber, R. (1989, Summer). *The Well-Being Project: Mental health clients speak for themselves.* (A report of a survey conducted for the California Department of Mental Health, Office of Prevention. Available from the California Network of Mental Health Clients, 1722 J Street, Suite 324, Sacramento, California 95814.)

Charisiou, J., Jackson, H. J., Boyle, G. J., Burgess, P., Minas, I. H., & Joshua, S. D. (1989). Are employment-interview skills a correlate of subtypes of schizophrenia? *Psychological Reports*, *65*, 951–960.

Ducq, H., Guesdon, I., & Roelandt, J. L. (1997). Psychiatric morbidity of homeless persons: A critical review of Anglo–Saxon literature [Electronic version]. *Encephale*, *23*, 420–430.

Lysaker, P., Bell, M., & Beam-Goulet, J. (1995). Wisconsin Card Sorting Test and work performance in schizophrenia. *Psychiatry Research*, *56*, 45–51.

MacDonald-Wilson, K. (1999, November). Navigating the Social Security work incentives: A primer for mental health administrators. In L. L. Mancuso & J. D. Kotler (Eds.), *Technical assistance tool kit on employment for people with psychiatric disabilities* (pp. 135–166). (Available from the National Technical Assistance Center for State Mental Health Planning, National Association of State Mental Health Program Directors, 66 Canal Center Plaza, Suite 302, Alexandria, Virginia.)

Maher, B. A. (1988). Anomalous experience and delusional thinking: The logic of explanations. In T. F. Oltmanns & B. A. Maher (Eds.), *Delusional beliefs* (pp. 15–33). New York: Wiley.

Massel, H. K., Liberman, R. P., Mintz, J., Jacobs, H. E., Rush, T. V., Giannini, C. A., & Zarate, R. (1990). Evaluating the capacity to work of the mentally ill. *Psychiatry*, *53*, 31–43.

Milazzo-Sayre, L. J., Henderson, M. J., & Manderscheid, R. W. (1997). Serious and severe mental illness and work: What do we know? In R. J. Bonnie & J. Monahan (Eds.), *Mental disorder, work disability, and the law* (pp. 13–24). Chicago: University of Chicago Press.

Mulkern, V. M., & Manderscheid, R. W. (1989). Characteristics of community support program clients in 1980 and 1984. *Hospital and Community Psychiatry*, *40*, 165–172.

Noble, J. H., Jr. (1998). Policy reform dilemmas in promoting employment of persons with severe mental illnesses. *Psychiatric Services*, *49*, 775–781.

Noble, J. H., Honberg, R. S., Hall, L. L., & Flynn, L. M. (1999). NAMI executive summary. *Journal of Disability Policy Studies*, *10*, 10–17.

Rogers, E. S., Walsh, D., Massotta, L., & Danley, D. (1991). *Massachusetts Survey of Client Preferences for Community Support Services* (Final report). Boston: Center for Psychiatric Rehabilitation.

Silverstein, M. L., Fogg, L., & Harrow, M. (1991). Prognostic significance of cerebral status: Dimensions of clinical outcome. *Journal of Nervous and Mental Disease*, *179*, 534–539.

Ticket to Work and Work Incentives Improvement Act of 1999, Pub. L. No. 106–170, 113 Stat. 1860 (1999).

U.S. General Accounting Office. (1993, August). *Vocational rehabilitation: Evidence for federal program's effectiveness is mixed* (GAO/PEMD-93-19). Washington, DC: U.S. Government Printing Office.

Part III

Methodological Challenges in Probing Schizophrenia

7

The Neuropsychological Study of Schizophrenia: A Methodological Perspective

Milton E. Strauss and Ann Summerfelt

When I first met Brendan Maher it was as an applicant for admission to graduate school, and I wondered then why a clinical psychologist would have a microscope in his office. The answer came in the one course I had with Professor Maher in graduate school, the proseminar in experimental psychopathology for clinical psychology students. The themes from the start were that the biology of behavior needs to be taken seriously by psychologists, that experimentation is a proper means of studying abnormal behavior, and that the study of psychopathology should proceed from basic psychological theory and research. For some of us in that course, myself included then, ideas such as that schizophrenia is a biologically rooted disorder or that "rat studies" can illuminate clinically relevant concepts just didn't seem reasonable. But that was the early '60s, and most of us weren't where Brendan Maher had already arrived.

Professor Maher was resolute in that class, insisting, along with his colleague Irving Gottesman, that as behavioral scientists, our beliefs need emerge from careful reasoning based on empirical research—ideally experimentation—and explicitly linked theoretical constructs (construct validity was then still a somewhat controversial idea). This was very different from the modal abnormal and clinical psychology of that time.

That message was elegantly developed and elaborated in his textbook, *Principles of Psychopathology: An Experimental Approach* (Maher, 1966), which appeared late in my time in graduate school. *Principles* became for me a handbook early in my career. Professor Maher's elegant studies of conflict summarized therein were a model of careful empirical analysis. That book represented for me a paradigm for the application of the concepts and methods of experimental psychology to the study of psychopathology. We hope that our contribution to this tribute volume justly reflects his influence on me, which, although it took several

Preparation of this chapter was supported by the Louis Stokes Cleveland Department of Veterans Affairs Medical Center and by National Institutes of Health Grants MH43775 and NHLBI SCOR HL 42215. We thank the principal investigators, Godfrey Pearlson and Susan Redline, for making the data available and Terry Goldberg for the data presented in Figure 7.2. We also thank Zeeshan A. Butt, Thomas W. Frazier, and Todd Watson for their contributions to the tasks of compiling and analyzing data presented in this chapter.

years to develop, has become a lasting one that informs the analysis of the neuro-psychology of schizophrenia that is the concern of this chapter.

—Milton E. Strauss

Although they differed greatly in their thinking about much in psychopathology, Kraepelin, Bleuler, and Freud each believed schizophrenia was a brain disease (Zec & Weinberger, 1986). However, schizophrenia remains a clinically defined psychological disorder, and the scientific challenge to develop an understanding of the disturbances of mentation and behavior in schizophrenia at the psychological level, the neurobiological level, and in terms of the relations of these levels of analysis, continues (Frith, 1994; Heinrichs, 1993).

There are many hypotheses about the nature of cognitive and neurological abnormalities in schizophrenia now, as there were at the time that Brendan Maher's (1966) *Principles of Psychopathology* was published. Maher (1966) commented,

> The vast array of data accumulated thus far on the behavior of persons described as schizophrenic fill the reader with puzzled dismay. Hypothesis struggles with hypothesis in a conflict in which new contenders enter the field but the defeated never retire. (p. 433)

Although there is perhaps some hyperbole in the latter sentiment, and by now some hypotheses have disappeared from the field, there remains no shortage of hypotheses about the psychology, neurology, or neuropsychology of schizophrenia.

The subtitle of Maher's (1966) text was *An Experimental Approach*. The application of the experimental methods of psychology has contributed significantly to the development of important contemporary hypotheses about the mechanisms of the perceptual (Knight & Silverstein, 1998), attentional (Weickert et al., 2000), and short-term/working memory (Barch & Carter, 1998) deficits in schizophrenia as well as about symptom characteristics in the disorder (Frith, 1994; Maher, 1988). In addition, neuropsychology has become an increasingly important approach to the analysis of behavior, symptoms, and neurobiological substrates in schizophrenia. Neuropsychology is the study of brain–behavior relationships, that is, the psychological study of cognitive performance in relationship to brain injury, disease, or, more recently, normal brain function.

Clinical neuropsychological tests have been part of the study of schizophrenia for many years (see Goldstein, 1978, for an early review). In clinical neuropsychological studies, measures that are sensitive to specific brain injuries or diseases, including standardized psychological tests, are administered to patients with schizophrenia to develop hypotheses about the structural and functional brain impairments of the disorder. Until the advent of modern brain imaging techniques, neuropsychological studies were among the principal means of studying schizophrenia from a biopsychological perspective (see Levin, Yurgelun-Todd, & Craft, 1989; Randolph, Goldberg, & Weinberger, 1993).

Neuropsychological research in schizophrenia is a very active field. Panel A of Figure 7.1 displays the number of neuropsychological studies in schizophrenia published annually over the past 30 years. The data were derived from searches of PsycLIT and Index Medicus and contain overlapping citations, but it is clear that the number of publications each year has been growing for some time.

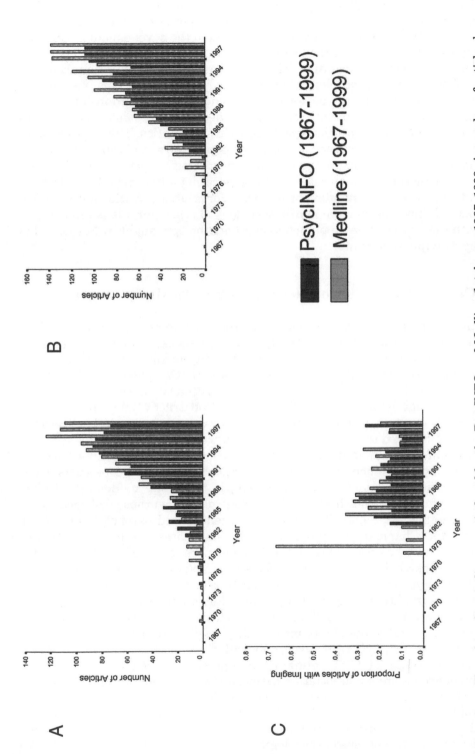

Figure 7.1. The schizophrenia literature indexed by the PsycINFO and Medline databases, 1967–1999. A: number of articles by year that contain the search terms *schizophrenia* and *neuropsychology*. B: number of articles with the search terms *schizophrenia, brain scans, tomography, imaging*, or *neuroimaging*. C: proportion of articles with schizophrenia and neuropsychology search terms that have an imaging component.

Implicit in Maher's (1966) wry observation quoted earlier is the idea that progress comes from rejecting as well as developing hypotheses. In this chapter we discuss several methodological issues that have limited the development of the neuropsychology of schizophrenia by the pruning of less probable hypotheses. There are three major points in our presentation. First, the construct representation (Embretson, 1983) of clinical neuropsychological tests is poorly understood. This is a problem of construct validity. Second, the pattern of differences between groups of patients with schizophrenia and comparison groups may reflect measurement artifacts rather than group differences in psychological processes or abilities. Third, progress in understanding the neuropsychology of schizophrenia requires the conjoint study of brain–behavior relations from an experimental psychological perspective. We suggest that psychological tests may be useful for generating initial hypotheses but are not a sound means for understanding brain–behavior relations in schizophrenia. We propose instead that experimental neuropsychology of schizophrenia is required, in keeping with the experimental approach to psychopathology taught by Maher in his text and by example as a mentor.

Construct Validity of Neuropsychological Measures

It is a truism in psychology that no test measures a single process or ability. This idea is at the heart of concepts of construct validity (Messick, 1995) that emphasize the need for both convergent and discriminant validity to support the proposition that a test measures a specific psychological construct (Campbell & Fiske, 1959). *Convergent validity* is indicated by a relationship between two measures thought to assess the same underlying construct. This aspect of construct validation is common in schizophrenia research, where it is often shown that patients do poorly on several tasks that are purported to measure the same construct.

Discriminant validity is indicated by the absence of relationships between measures that are presumed to measure theoretically unrelated constructs. Consideration of discriminant validity, we believe, is much less evident in studies that compare patients with schizophrenia to controls on neuropsychological tests (Strauss & Summerfelt, 1994). The presence of generalized psychological deficits in schizophrenia (Chapman & Chapman, 1973) complicates the demonstration of discriminant validity, as we discuss later. Furthermore, as Keefe (1995) recently discussed, neuropsychological tests are affected by motivational processes as well as by multiple cognitive constructs. Consequently, scores on a test administered to patients with schizophrenia may be theoretically ambiguous (Keefe, 1995).

The Wisconsin Card Sorting Test (WCST; Heaton, Chelune, Talley, Kay, & Curtis, 1993) is arguably the single most widely used neuropsychological test in schizophrenia research, and it has been particularly important in light of Weinberger, Berman, and Zec's (1986) seminal study reporting lowered prefrontal activation in schizophrenia and an association between low activation and perseverative errors (PE) in the patient group (for reviews of findings in schizophrenia with this test see Goldstein, 1978; Levin et al., 1989; and Randolph et al., 1993). Because of its central place in neuropsychology research, this test is used to illustrate issues about construct validity of neuropsychological tests in schizophrenia research. We underscore, however, in agreement with Keefe's (1995) excellent review of the role of neuropsychology in schizophrenia from a more clinical perspective, that there has generally been insufficient consideration of the question of what neuropsychological tasks measure in schizophrenia much more generally.

The WCST is unusual in that the respondent is given very little information about what to do. She or he is shown four cards that vary in the number, color, and shape of symbols that they contain and is instructed to place each of a series of cards below the one of the four sample cards with which it belongs. These are the only instructions given; the only feedback after each response is whether the placement was correct or incorrect according to one of three principles known by the examiner. The principle is first matching by color, then by form, and last by number. The sorting principle is changed without comment after 10 correct responses in succession.

Although many scores may be derived from the test (Heaton, Chelune, Talley, Kay, & Curtis, 1993), the most important in contemporary schizophrenia research is the PE, which is repeating responses based on the same incorrect concept. Substantial differences between patients with schizophrenia and controls in PEs have been reported in many studies. These differences have been interpreted as evidence of frontal-lobe dysfunction resulting in executive-function deficits, particularly in working memory (Glahn, Cannon, Gur, Ragland, & Gur, 2000). The hypothesis that deficient executive functioning, especially working memory, is a core neuropsychological deficit in schizophrenia has been supported by the deficient performance on other tests interpreted as measures of executive functions (e.g., Bustini et al., 1999; Glahn et al., 2000; Randolph et al., 1993) and on tests of working memory (Goldman-Rakic & Selemon, 1997). Several studies have attempted to remediate the WCST PE error level through instruction or reward. These efforts have been generally unsuccessful, supporting the idea that cognitive processes involved in the WCST PE identify a core dysfunction in schizophrenia (Goldberg, Weinberger, Berman, Pliskin, & Podd, 1987; Green, Satz, Ganzell, & Vaclav, 1992; Hellman, Kern, Neilson, & Green, 1998).

The persistence of this executive-function deficit is not invariant in training studies, however. Summerfelt, Alphs, Funderburk, and Strauss (1991) compared the effects of conventional social reinforcement (right vs. wrong) with social reinforcement plus both positive reinforcement and negative punishment. The reinforcers were monetary incentives: 5 cents for each correct response and the loss of 10 cents for each incorrect response, from an initial stake of $7.50. A repeated measures crossover design was used in which half the patients ($n = 7$) were first tested under typical social reinforcement conditions and half ($n = 7$) with monetary supplementation first. The groups were crossed over 2 weeks later to the other condition.

There are two particularly noteworthy features in the results, shown in Figure 7.2. First, there was a substantial effect of monetary contingencies on PEs as well as total correct responses, both of which were subject to reinforcement. Other scores that were not directly reinforced, such as number of categories achieved, were not affected by the monetary feedback. Second, there was a substantial carryover effect from the first session with monetary reinforcement to the social reinforcement alone testing about 2 weeks later, suggesting some enduring learning. Participants who received monetary reinforcement in the second session also learned. Neither group of participants had scores in the normal range after training, according to the published norms. However, the suitability of these norms for patients with average or lower IQ, such as patients with schizophrenia, has been questioned (Keefe, 1995).

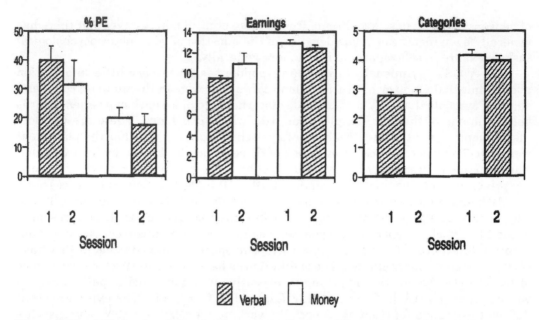

Figure 7.2.   Effects of verbal and monetary feedback on Wisconsin Card Sorting Test performance (data from Summerfelt et al., 1991). PE = perseverative errors.

Of course, variations in participant sampling and design may account for the differences between Summerfelt et al.'s (1991) findings and those of other investigators, but the results suggest that WCST performance reflects motivational as well as cognitive deficits in schizophrenia.

The question of what construct WSCT PEs measure was also the focus of a preliminary study reported by Strauss, Jaskiw, Smith, and Rizzuto (1997). They studied the differential associations of two spatial working memory measures (Keefe, Lees-Roitman, & Dupre, 1997; Park & Holzman, 1992), an auditory test of letter–number sequencing developed by Gold (see Wechsler, 1997, Letter–Number Sequencing subtest), and the WCST PE score with two declarative memory tests and general ability. Declarative memory was assessed by three recall trails on the Hopkins Verbal Learning Test (Brandt, 1991) and by the number of Wechsler Adult Intelligence Scale—Revised (WAIS–R) Digit–Symbol Substitution test (Wechsler, 1991) symbols recalled after completion of this subtest. This was an incidental-learning measure, as participants had not been informed that their memory for these symbols would be tested. IQ was estimated by the Information and Picture Completion subtests of the WAIS–R (Wechsler, 1991), the preferred two-subtest estimate of full-scale IQ (Kaufman, 1990). The correlations among these measures for the 27 patients studied thus far are presented in Table 7.1.

As can be seen in this table, measures of working memory, other than WCST PE, were significantly correlated with each other, suggesting that they measure a common construct. On the other hand, the evidence of discriminant validity vis-à-vis declarative memory and general ability is not clear-cut; there were several significant correlations between working memory tasks and measures of declarative

Table 7.1. Intercorrelations Among Purported Working Memory (WM) and Other Tests in Schizophrenia

Test	Dot	L-N	WCST	HVLT	DSST	IQ
Spatial WM	.54**	.41**	−.08	.34*	.44**	.10
Dot	—	.43**	.26	.36*	.25	.25
L-N		—	.33*	.42**	.46***	.49***
WCST			—	.06	.22	.36

Note: N = 27. Intercorrelations are shown in boldface. Dot = dot location; L-N = Letter–Number Sequencing subtest of Wechsler Adult Intelligence Scale—III; WCST = Wisconsin Card Sorting Test; HVLT = Hopkins Verbal Learning Test; DSST = Digit–Symbol Substitution Test.
*p < .10, one-tailed.   **p < .05, one-tailed.   ***p < .01, one-tailed.

memory and general ability. The relationship between letter–number sequencing and PEs was mediated by IQ; the correlation dropped substantially (from .33 to .17) when IQ was controlled. Gold and his colleagues (Gold, Carpenter, Randolph, Goldberg, & Weinberger, 1997) also found that verbal working memory, assessed by letter–number sequencing span, did not correlate with WCST PEs in schizophrenia patients. They also reported that differences between the patient and comparison groups on the WCST were eliminated when letter–number span was statistically controlled. The association between IQ and PEs suggested in Strauss et al.'s (1997) study (Table 7.1) raises the possibility that the differences between patients with schizophrenia and controls in Gold et al.'s (1997) results may reflect a generalized deficit, as indexed by current IQ.

Neuropsychological researchers are, of course, aware of the confounding effects of IQ on comparisons between patients and psychiatrically normal control groups. The unintended consequences of matching groups on current IQ, first extensively discussed by Chapman and Chapman (1973), have led to the alternatives of matching on parental socioeconomic status as an IQ surrogate or on premorbid intelligence, estimated by one of several methods (see Lezak, 1995). Such matching is concerned only with between-group differences; it does not address the problem of how to interpret patterns of group differences. Matching on estimated premorbid ability does not eliminate group differences in current general ability, and the covariance between general ability and the neuropsychological tests used to assess more specific cognitive processes or abilities is not affected by the matching process. This confound may overshadow the specific variance in neuropsychological tests of interest to investigators.

The confounding effects of generalized deficit, as assessed by current IQ, is illustrated in the analysis of a set of neuropsychological measures obtained from 83 patients with either schizophrenia or bipolar disorder participating in neuroimaging protocols at the Johns Hopkins Hospital (see Table 7.2). Six measures had been selected to represent frontal–executive functions (WCST PE, relationship between Trails B and Trails A [Heaton, Grant, & Matthews, 1991], and letter fluency), temporal–hippocampal/memory functions (word list learning and visuospatial memory span), and parietal–visuospatial functions (Mooney Closure Test; see Lansdell, 1970). The last was a control or reference region–function in the originally planned

Table 7.2. First Principal Component of Neuropsychological Tests

Patients with schizophrenia and bipolar disorder[a]		Sleep study participants[b]	
Measure	Loading	Measure	Loading
Trails B/A	−.45	Trails B/A	−.42
WCST PE	.68	WCST PE	−.55
Letter Fluency	.64	WCST set breaks	−.27
Calev correct	.70	Digits backward	.45
Moss average span	.65	Verbal Fluency	.45
Mooney correct	.27	Letter Cancellation	−.37
		CVLT Immediate Recall	.57
		Complex Figure Recall	.52
		CPT d'	.74
		CPT c'	.28
		Choice decision time	.57
		Information Processing	.75
Eigenvalue	2.08	Eigenvalue	3.21
% Variance	34.6	% Variance	27.3
Correlation with estimated IQ	.66	Correlation with estimated IQ	.60

Note. WCST PE = Wisconsin Card Sorting Test perseverative errors; CVLT = California Verbal Learning Test (Delis et al., 1987); CPT = Continuous Performance Test (Cornblatt et al., 1988).
[a]n = 83.   [b]n = 165.

studies, which were concerned with frontal and temporal–hippocampal structural brain abnormalities in schizophrenia.

We planned to use principal-factor analysis to evaluate the discriminant validity of the constructs guiding test selection and first conducted a principal-components analysis to estimate the number of reliable factors in the data matrix. Two quantitative indices—Horn's parallel analysis and the minimum average partial method (Zwick & Velicer, 1986)—each indicated that a single factor was sufficient to account for the common variance in these data. The first principal component in this analysis (see Table 7.2) accounted for more than one third of the common variance and correlated .66 with IQ, estimated by the Shipley Institute of Living Scale (Zachary, 1986). Only one test, the Mooney Closure, did not have at least a moderate loading (≥.35).

The number of tests and of participants in this analysis is relatively small, but one can find a substantially similar result in the evaluation of a larger battery of neuropsychological tests from a group of 165 persons without evidence of neurologic or psychiatric illness (Adams, Strauss, Schluchter, & Redline, 2001). In this study, 12 neuropsychological measures were selected to tap executive functions. They included Trails A and B; the WCST; Digits Backwards (Wechsler, 1991); Verbal Fluency (Spreen & Strauss, 1991); and Letter Cancellation (Diller, Ben-Yishaay, & Gerstman, 1974). Declarative memory was assessed with list learning and complex figure recall. Attention was measured by the Continuous Performance Test d' and c' (Cornblatt, Risch, Faris, Friedman, & Erlenmeyer-Kimling, 1988), an index of response caution, and decision time in a choice reaction time task. General information processing speed also was recorded. Descriptions of these measures can be found in Strauss, Thompson, Adams, Redline, and Burant (2000) and Redline et al. (1997). The Horn–Cattell and minimum average partial analyses again suggested that only one factor was necessary to account for the covariance structure. The first principal component accounted for 27% of the variance in the matrix (see Table 7.2). All variables other than WCST Set Breaks, which is the frequency of an error after six successive correct responses, and Continuous Performance Test c' loaded on this factor above the conventional threshold of .35. The factor scores for the participants correlated .60 with an estimate of IQ based on the Arithmetic, Similarities, Picture Completion, and Digit Symbol Substitution subtests of the WAIS–R.

In a recent discussion of the contribution of neuropsychology to psychiatry, particularly clinical psychiatry, Keefe (1995) proposed that the assumptions that (a) neuropsychological tests measure specific functions and (b) poor performance on a single test indicates a specific neuropsychological impairment are faulty. Dodrill (1997, p. 3) suggested that the notion that "we have good knowledge of the constructs that our tests measure is a myth." To illustrate this, he compared the correlations among tests believed to measure a construct with the correlations between the summary score for that construct and summary scores representing other neuropsychological functions. The median correlation for tests within groupings was .42 for neurologically normal participants and .52 for neurological patients. The median correlations across constructs were .34 and .44 for normal and patient groups, respectively. This is not comforting evidence of convergent or discriminant validity.

Psychological measures are componentially complex. Their construct representation (Embretson, 1983) is not well understood. The practice of inferring specific deficits from a pattern of performance across many tests may be flawed in schizophrenia research because of the limited construct validity of the measures. Often this issue is not apparent, because the covariances among measures within and across constructs are not included in data analytic models. It may be more fruitful if future studies were developed within the framework of structural equation modeling, which would focus both design and analysis on the latent constructs of theoretical interest instead of the manifest variables through which researchers attempt to measure the role of the psychological constructs in schizophrenia. Bilder et al. (2000) provided a very useful example of such an approach. In their study of first-episode schizophrenia, these investigators derived neuropsychological scale scores from a confirmatory factor analysis of manifest variables. Variables were dropped from inclusion if they did not demonstrate high internal consistency reliability with other scores measuring the same construct. This approach yielded a set of rationally based, internally consistent measures of the latent constructs identified. Structural equation modeling also offers a means of evaluating the role of general ability or deficit in accounting for patterns of observation, because this construct should be part of any research on the neuropsychology of schizophrenia.

The confounding effects of IQ may have been less an issue in classical neuropsychology, where patients with clearly defined lesions were the focus of study. Indeed, the classic cases of H. M., Korsakov amnesia, and frontal lobe injuries were characterized by marked, discrete cognitive deficits in the context of preserved IQ (Kolb & Wishaw, 1996). However, this is clearly not the case in schizophrenia. Structural equation modeling may be an aid in understanding the structure of the measured variables, but in and of itself it does not solve the problem of identifying the specific cognitive deficits that are most pronounced in schizophrenia so that their relations to brain dysfunction can be identified.

Identifying Specific Neuropsychological Deficits in Schizophrenia

Because the cognitive deficits of schizophrenia occur not in isolation but in the context of generalized deficits, identifying a specific or differential deficit that might be taken to implicate a particular brain region requires comparing the magnitude of group differences on theoretically relevant measures with those on control tasks measuring other abilities. Typically, in psychological studies of schizophrenia patients do worse than controls on several (or even all) tasks but are significantly more impaired on some tasks than on others. Although this can give rise to a statistically significant interaction, it does not necessarily mean that there is a differential pattern of deficits on the constructs presumably measured by the tests. The true metric of psychological measures is unknown, so there is no theoretical reason to prefer a raw score to any transformed score to summarize test performance. Statistical transformation can eliminate such ordinal interactions; ordinal interactions are not invariant over measurement scales and consequently are not clear evidence of differential group differences. The only unambiguous interaction is one in which the two groups perform differently from each other on both tasks, but on one task the patients do significantly better than the controls, whereas on the other they do significantly worse. Such *double dissociations* or *disordinal interactions* are rare in schizophrenia research (see Strauss, 2001).

Investigators have also approached the problem of demonstrating specific neuropsychological deficits in schizophrenia using analysis of covariance (ANCOVA). In this approach, variance associated with theoretically irrelevant specific abilities or general ability (IQ) is covaried from the scores on the measure of interest. A specific deficit is said to be demonstrated if the residual group means (adjusted scores) are significantly different. This is generally not a valid inference, however, because the normal ANCOVA model assumes that the groups do not differ on covariates. When groups differ on covariates, statistical adjustment can overcorrect, undercorrect, or correct appropriately, but one cannot tell which has occurred (see Strauss, 2001, for a recent discussion of these issues). At best, the application of ANCOVA to deal with the problem of ordinal interactions is problematic, if not most often incorrect (G. A. Miller & Chapman, 2001). Group matching on potentially confounding variables also is a questionable practice because of regression to the mean, the creation of unrepresentative groups, and potential sample biases (see Strauss, 2001).

Group × Task interactions in neuropsychological studies may also be due to the psychometric properties of the tasks. Differences between test score distributions resulting in ceiling or floor effects can produce patterns of mean differences that would suggest differential or specific deficits in one group where none exist. Although inspection of the shapes of score distributions may reveal such potential artifacts, there are more subtle statistical contributions to artifactual differences between groups (Chapman & Chapman 1973, 1989; M. B. Miller, Chapman, Chapman, & Collins, 1995).

Although the issue of psychometric artifact in identifying specific deficits has been acknowledged from time to time in the schizophrenia literature (Keefe, 1995;

Saykin et al., 1991), researchers do not generally consider the psychometrics of tasks in interpreting results (see Strauss, 1994, for a discussion of one example). In our experience as readers of this literature, we rarely encounter displays of data that permit evaluation of floor or ceiling effects or oddly shaped distributions; the reliability of measurements in study samples is reported infrequently. It is difficult to find the blind alleys without attention to basic issues in measurement.

There have been criticisms of the Chapmans' (1973, 1989) prescriptions for the remediation of psychometric artifact in studies of psychological deficit, which were recently reviewed (Strauss, 2001). In general, these critiques emphasize that manipulation of psychological tasks for psychometric purposes may compromise their construct validity. Knight and Silverstein (2001) offered the most recent statement of this position and a different approach to the issue that relies heavily on an expanded definition of construct validity explicated by Embretson (1983).

Embretson (1983) differentiated between two aspects of construct validity: *nomothetic span* and *construct representation*. The former refers to the network of relations of a test with other measures; this is the classic idea of construct validity considered earlier in this chapter in terms of convergent and discriminant validity. *Construct representation* refers to the model of theoretical mechanisms underlying task performance. Knight and Silverstein (2001) proposed that a strong theoretical model conjoined with experiments that manipulate the implicated process or mechanism, as well as theoretically irrelevant processes across procedurally different but theoretically linked paradigms, can be used to identify specific, differential deficits in schizophrenia. We agree with Knight and Silverstein's position that experimental psychological approaches are likely to have a more profound payoff in the study of schizophrenia than the typically test-based approach of neuropsychological studies (Strauss & Summerfelt, 1994).

The psychometric issues of task matching, however, seem not to be obviated in Knight and Silverstein's (2001) approach. In both the classical test approach to studying cognition and a more experimental psychology–cognitive science model of research, the investigator is comparing assays or probes of psychological processes. It seems to us that psychometric artifact cannot be ruled out as an explanation of Group × Manipulated Variable interactions unless the assays are of comparable sensitivity. Indeed, if the manipulated variables do not produce effects with comparable psychometric properties, neither finding an interaction between groups nor failing to find an interaction is easily interpreted. The interaction may not have emerged because the assay of the mechanism that is more impaired had less discriminating power.

Studying Brain–Behavior Relations in Schizophrenia

Neuropsychological studies are about brain–behavior relations. This field was classically concerned with identifying the psychological sequelae of brain injury or disease in individuals with normal development (Kolb & Wishaw, 1996). The contribution of psychological studies to the characterization of the behavioral effects of brain lesions or disease should not be minimized; however, issues of construct validity aside, psychological studies are a risky basis for inferring specific brain abnormalities in schizophrenia.

The assumption of normal neurological development and specific localization in schizophrenia is likely to be the wrong model. Schizophrenia is increasingly seen as a neurodevelopmental disorder involving improper development of complex brain systems (Hollister & Cannon, 1998; McGlashan & Hoffman, 2000; Walker, Diforio, & Baum, 1999). Second, the sensitivity and specificity of neuropsychological tests to the effects of focal brain abnormalities appear to be less robust than is often assumed (Anderson, Damasio, Jones, & Tranel, 1991; Dodrill, 1997; Keefe, 1995).

In addition, there is a reversal of the independent and dependent variables in the application of cognitive tests or tasks to make inferences about possible brain abnormalities in schizophrenia. In classical neuropsychological research the brain injury is the predictor or independent variable, and the behavioral measure is the criterion or dependent variable. In schizophrenia research there seems to be a tacit assumption that the probability of specific brain damage given psychological test results is symmetrical with the probability of specific test results given a specific brain abnormality. However, sensitivity and specificity are not the same for y on x as for x on y unless the correlation between x and y is 1.0 (Strauss & Summerfelt, 1994).

The difficulty of making inferences about brain dysfunction on the basis of neuropsychological tests is amply illustrated by a study conducted by Goldberg, Berman, Mohr, and Weinberger (1990). These investigators evaluated regional cerebral blood flow during performance of the WCST by patients with schizophrenia or with Huntington's disease. Figure 7.3 is a recasting of their data to emphasize the dif-

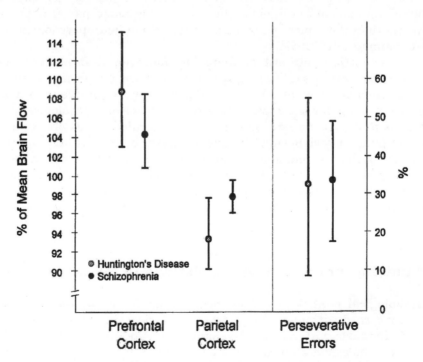

Figure 7.3. Regional cerebral blood flow ($M\pm SD$) during Wisconsin Card Sorting Test performance of patients with schizophrenia and with Huntington's disease (data from Goldberg et al., 1990).

ferent associations between brain and behavior in the two illnesses. Patients with schizophrenia and with Huntington's disease had the same level of PEs (see Figure 7.3, right side); however, the patients with Huntington's disease had the same level of PEs (see Figure 7.3, right side). However, the brain regions with which regional cerebral blood flow was associated during task performance were not the same. In schizophrenia, the regional metabolic abnormality was in the dorsolateral prefrontal cortex; in Huntington's disease, it was in the parietal cortex.

Data such as these advance theoretical knowledge about brain systems and make clear that researchers' understanding of the fundamental neuropsychology of schizophrenia cannot advance though the neuropsychological study of behavior alone. The clinical neuropsychogical approach has useful roles in diagnosis, prognosis, and treatment evaluation at a psychological level (Heaton et al., 1993; Keefe, 1995). For the reasons we have reviewed, however, it is not a useful method for advancing theoretical knowledge about brain dysfunction in relation to psychological deficits in schizophrenia (Keefe, 1995; Strauss & Summerfelt, 1994).

The development of modern brain imaging techniques opened a new and fundamental approach to studying the brain and schizophrenia. Over the past 30 years, the application of increasingly sensitive imaging methodologies and models to the measurement of brain structure and activity to schizophrenia has been a very active area of research. As Panel B in Figure 7.1 shows, after a slow beginning in the 1970s, there was a very rapid rise in publications, through the 1990s, but relatively few investigators used imaging methods in conjunction with neuropsychological assessments. On average, over the past 20 years, 12%–15% of neuropsychology studies reported relations with measures of brain structure or activity (see Figure 7.1, Panel C).

The studies comprising the counts in Figure 7.1 are virtually all reports of brain–behavior correlations at one point in time. The studies describe parallels between neuropsychological differences between groups and structural brain differences or correlations between individual differences in structural or physiological measurements and in neuropsychological variables in schizophrenia (Strauss & Summerfelt, 1994). Studies of associations are useful for generating hypotheses about what structural or physiological characteristics of the brain in schizophrenia might underlie neuropsychological deficits and for eliminating hypotheses about possible associations; however, they are not very useful for developing or testing models of the functional relationships between cognitive and brain processes.

Performance differences and physiological differences are confounded both within groups and between groups in correlational studies (Holcomb et al., 2000; Strauss & Summerfelt, 1994). From a reductionist perspective, or from interacting-levels models (Mortimer & McKenna, 1994), one would ideally like to manipulate brain processes and evaluate the effects of psychological measures. In the absence of that, one must rely on using behavioral probes of brain processes in schizophrenia, and this requires attention to task design and implementation so that both psychometric and substantive confounds can be taken into account (Gur, Erwin, & Gur, 1992). We believe that physiological processes should be studied from an experimental perspective in which either task performance levels are matched or the influences of theoretically based manipulations of an experimental parameter produce comparable changes in behavior. This permits one to address the important question of how similarly or differently the brains of persons with and without schizophrenia function while they are performing a theoretically interpretable task at the same level of competence, in either accuracy or speed (see Holcomb et al., 2000, for an interesting example).

This is an aspirational goal. Neuropsychological tests are generally too complex for theoretically driven research on brain–behavior relations in schizophrenia. Furthermore, the classic methods of construct validation applied to tests may be inadequate for the identification of specific cognitive processes or mechanisms. The classic model of convergent and discriminant validity establishes the nomothetic span of a test, its relationship with other measures (Embretson, 1983). However, such studies do not assist in the decomposition of a task into underlying mechanisms. Process decomposition requires experimentation to provide evidence of the construct representation of a task (Embretson, 1983; Knight & Silverstein, 2001). Process identification research in basic psychology identifies for investigators of schizophrenia the specific parameter(s) that should be manipulated to affect a particular underlying process. An experimental psychology of cognitive processes, mindful of the psychometric principles of discriminating power, applied conjointly with studies of the working brain, may foster a neuropsychology of schizophrenia that generates new hypotheses and facilitates the retirement from the field of others.

References

Adams, N., Strauss, M. E., Schluchter, M., & Redline, S. (2001). Relation of measures of sleep disordered breathing to neuropsychological function. *American Journal of Respiratory and Critical Care Medicine, 163*, 1626–1631.

Anderson, S.W., Damasio, H., Jones, R. D., & Tranel, D. (1991). Wisconsin Card Sorting Test performance as a measure of frontal lobe damage. *Journal of Clinical and Experimental Neuropsychology, 13*, 909–922.

Barch, D. M., & Carter, C. (1998). Selective attention in schizophrenia: Relationship to verbal working memory. *Schizophrenia Research, 33*, 53–61.

Bilder, R. M., Goldman, R. S., Robinson, D., Reiter, G., Bell, L., Bates, J. A., et al. (2000). Neuropsychology of first-episode schizophrenia: Initial characterization and clinical correlates. *American Journal of Psychiatry, 157*, 549–559.

Brandt, J. (1991). The Hopkins Verbal Learning Test: Development of a new verbal memory test with six equivalent forms. *The Clinical Neuropsychologist, 5*, 125–142.

Bustini, M., Stratta, P., Daneluzzo, E., Pollice, R., Prosperini, P., & Rossi, A. (1999). Tower of Hanoi and WCST performance in schizophrenia: Problem-solving capacity and clinical correlates. *Journal of Psychiatric Research, 33*, 285–290.

Campbell, D. T., & Fiske, D. W. (1959). Convergent and discriminant validity with the multitrait–multimethod matrix. *Psychological Bulletin, 56*, 81–105.

Chapman, L. J., & Chapman, J. P. (1973). *Disordered thought in schizophrenia.* New York: Appleton, Century, Crofts.

Chapman, L. J., & Chapman, J. P. (1989). Strategies for resolving the heterogeneity of schizophrenics and their relatives using cognitive measures. *Journal of Abnormal Psychology, 98*, 357–366.

Cornblatt, B. A., Risch, N. J., Faris, G., Friedman, D., & Erlenmeyer-Kimling, L. (1988). The Continuous Performance Test, Identical Pairs Version (CPT-IP): I. New findings about sustained attention in normal families. *Psychiatry Research, 26*, 223–238.

Delis, D. C., Kramer, J. H., Kaplan, E., & Ober, B. A. (1987). *California Verbal Learning Test: Adult Version.* San Antonio, TX: Psychological Corporation.

Diller, L. Ben-Yishaay, Y., & Gerstman, L. J. (1974). *Studies in cognition and rehabilitation in hemiplegia* (Rehabilitation Monograph No. 50). New York: New York University Institute of Rehabilitation Medicine.

Dodrill, C. B. (1997). Myths of neuropsychology. *The Clinical Neuropsychologist, 11*, 1–17.

Embretson, S. (1983). Construct validity: Construct representation vs. nomothetic span. *Psychological Bulletin, 93*, 179–197.

Frith, C. D. (1994). *The cognitive neuropsychology of schizophrenia.* Hillsdale, NJ: Erlbaum.

Glahn, D. C., Cannon, T. D., Gur, R. E., Ragland, J. D., & Gur, R. C. (2000). Working memory constrains abstraction in schizophrenia. *Biological Psychiatry, 47*, 34–42.

Gold, J. M., Carpenter, C., Randolph, C., Goldberg, T. E., & Weinberger, D. R. (1997). Auditory working memory and Wisconsin Card Sorting Test performance in schizophrenia. *Archives of General Psychiatry, 54*, 159–165.

Goldberg, T. E., Berman, K. F., Mohr, E., & Weinberger, D. R. (1990). Regional cerebral blood flow and cognitive function in Huntington's disease and schizophrenia: A comparison of patients matched for performance on a prefrontal-type task. *Archives of Neurology, 47*, 418–422.

Goldberg, T. E., Weinberger, D. R., Berman, K. F., Pliskin, N. H., & Podd, M. H. (1987). Further evidence for dementia of the prefrontal type in schizophrenia? A controlled study of teaching the Wisconsin Card Sorting Test. *Archives of General Psychiatry, 44*, 1008–1014.

Goldman-Rakic, P., & Selemon, L. D. (1997). Working memory in schizophrenia. *Journal of Neuropsychiatry and Clinical Neuroscience, 6*, 348–357.

Goldstein, G. (1978). Cognitive and perceptual differences between schizophrenics and organics. *Schizophrenia Bulletin, 4*, 161–185.

Green, M. F., Satz, P., Ganzell, S., & Vaclav, J. F. (1992). Wisconsin Card Sorting Test performance in schizophrenia: Remediation of a stubborn deficit. *American Journal of Psychiatry, 149*, 62–67.

Gur, R. C., Erwin, R. J., & Gur, R. E. (1992). Neurobehavioral probes for physiological neuroimaging studies. *Archives of General Psychiatry, 49*, 409–414.

Heaton, R. K., Chelune, G. J., Talley, J. L., Kay, G. G., & Curtis, G. (1993). *Wisconsin Card Sorting Test manual: Revised and expanded.* Odessa, FL: Psychological Assessment Resources.

Heaton, R. K., Grant, I., & Matthews, C. G. (1991). *Comprehensive norms for an expanded Halstead-Reitan battery: Demographic corrections, research findings, and clinical applications.* Odessa, FL: Psychological Assessment Resources.

Heinrichs, R. W. (1993). Schizophrenia and the brain: Conditions for a neuropsychology of madness. *American Psychologist, 48*, 221–233.

Hellman, S. G., Kern, R. S., Neilson, L. M., & Green, M. F. (1998). Monetary reinforcement and Wisconsin Card Sorting performance in schizophrenia: Why show me the money? *Schizophrenia Research, 34*, 67–75.

Holcomb, H. H., Lahti, A. C., Medoff, D. R., Weiler, M., Dannals, R. F., & Tamminga, C. A. (2000). Brain activation patterns in schizophrenic and comparison volunteers during a matched-performance auditory recognition task. *American Journal of Psychiatry, 157*, 1634–1645.

Hollister, J. M., & Cannon, T. D. (1998). Neurodevelopmental disturbances in the aetiology of schizophrenia. In M. A. Ron & A. S. David (Eds.), *Disorders of brain and mind* (pp. 280–302). New York: Cambridge University Press.

Kaufman, A. S. (1990). *Assessing adolescent and adult intelligence.* Boston: Allyn & Bacon.

Keefe, R. S. E. (1995). The contribution of neuropsychology to psychiatry. *American Journal of Psychiatry, 52*, 6–15.

Keefe, R. S. E., Lees-Roitman, S. E., & Dupre, R. L. (1997). Performance of patients with schizophrenia on a pen and paper visuospatial working memory task with short delay. *Schizophrenia Research, 11*, 55–61.

Knight, R. A., & Silverstein, S. M. (1998). The role of cognitive psychology in guiding research on cognitive deficits in schizophrenia: A process-oriented approach. In M. F. Lenzenweger & R. H. Dworkin (Eds.), *Origins and development of schizophrenia: Advances in experimental psychopathology* (pp. 247–295). Washington, DC: American Psychological Association.

Knight, R. A., & Silverstein, S. S. (2001). A process-oriented approach for averting confounds resulting from general performance deficiencies in schizophrenia. *Journal of Abnormal Psychology, 110*, 15–30.

Kolb, B., & Wishaw, I. (1996). *Fundamentals of human neuropsychology* (4th ed.). New York: Freeman.

Lansdell, H. (1970). Relation of extent of temporal removals to closure and visuomotor factors. *Perceptual and Motor Skills, 31*, 491–498.

Levin, S., Yurgelun-Todd, D., & Craft, S. (1989). Contributions of clinical neuropsychology to the study of schizophrenia. *Journal of Abnormal Psychology, 98*, 341–356.

Lezak, M. (1995). *Neuropsychological assessment* (3rd ed.). New York: Oxford University Press.

Maher, B. A. (1966). *Principles of psychopathology: An experimental approach.* New York: McGraw-Hill.

Maher, B. A. (1988). Anomalous experience and delusional thinking: The logic of delusions. In T. F. Oltmanns & B. A. Maher (Eds.), *Delusional beliefs* (pp. 15–33). New York: Wiley.

McGlashan, T. H., & Hoffman, R. E. (2000). Schizophrenia as a disorder of developmentally reduced synaptic connectivity. *Archives of General Psychiatry, 57*, 637–648.

Messick, S. (1995). Validity of psychological assessment: Validation of inferences from persons' responses and performances as scientific inquiry into score meaning. *American Psychologist, 50*, 741–749.

Miller, G. A., & Chapman, J. P. (2001). Misunderstanding analysis of covariance. *Journal of Abnormal Psychology, 110*, 40–48.

Miller, M. B., Chapman, J. P., Chapman, L. H., & Collins, J. (1995). Task difficulty and cognitive deficits in schizophrenia. *Journal of Abnormal Psychology, 104*, 251–258.

Mortimer, A. M., & McKenna, P. J. (1994). Levels of explanation: Symptoms, neuropsychological deficit and morphological abnormalities in schizophrenia. *Psychological Medicine, 24*, 541–545.

Park, S., & Holzman, P. S. (1992). Schizophrenics show working memory deficits. *Archives of General Psychiatry, 49*, 975–982.

Randolph, C., Goldberg, T. E., & Weinberger, D. R. (1993). The neuropsychology of schizophrenia. In K. M. Heilman & E. Valenstein (Eds.), *Clinical neuropsychology* (3rd ed., pp. 499–522). New York: Oxford University Press.

Redline, S., Strauss, M. E., Adams, N., Winters, M., Roebuck, T., Spry, K., et al. (1997). Neuropsychological functions in mild sleep apnea. *Sleep, 20*, 160–167.

Saykin, A. J., Gur, R. C., Gur, R. E., Mozley, M. D., Mozley, L. H., Resnick, S. M., et al. (1991). Neuropsychological function in schizophrenia: Selective impairment in memory and learning. *Archives of General Psychiatry, 48*, 618–624.

Spreen, O., & Strauss, E. (1991). *A compendium of neuropsychological tests.* New York: Oxford University Press.

Strauss, M. E. (1994). Olfactory memory deficits in schizophrenia: Differential deficit or psychometric artifact? *Schizophrenia Research, 12*, 89–90.

Strauss, M. E. (2001). Demonstrating specific cognitive deficits: A psychometric perspective. *Journal of Abnormal Psychology, 110*, 6–14.

Strauss, M. E., Jaskiw, G. E., Smith, R. W., & Rizzuto, L. (1997). The working memory construct: Convergent and discriminant validity. *Schizophrenia Research, 24*, 137.

Strauss, M. E., & Summerfelt, A. (1994). Response to Serper and Harvey. *Schizophrenia Bulletin, 20*, 13–21.

Strauss, M. E., Thompson, P. T., Adams, N. L., Redline, S., & Burant, C. (2000). Evaluation of a model of attention with confirmatory factor analysis. *Neuropsychology, 14*, 201–208.

Summerfelt, A. T., Alphs, L. D., Funderburk, F. R., & Strauss, M. E. (1991). Monetary reinforcement reduces perseverative errors in patients with schizophrenia. *Journal of Abnormal Psychology, 100*, 613–616.

Walker, E. F., Diforio, D., & Baum, K. (1999). Developmental neuropathology and the precursors of schizophrenia. *Acta Psychiatrica Scandinavica Supplementum, 99*(Suppl. 395), 12–19.

Wechsler, D. (1991). *Manual for the Wechsler Intelligence Scale—Revised.* San Antonio, TX: Psychological Corporation.

Wechsler, D. (1997). *WAIS–III administration and scoring manual.* San Antonio, TX: Psychological Corporation.

Weickert, T. W., Goldberg T. E., Gold, J. M., Bigelow, L. B., Egan, M. F., & Weinberger, D. R. (2000). Cognitive impairments in patients with schizophrenia displaying preserved and compromised intellect. *Archives of General Psychiatry, 57*, 907–913.

Weinberger, D. R., Berman, K. F., & Zec, R. F. (1986). Physiological dysfunction of the dorsolateral prefrontal cortex in schizophrenia. I: Regional cerebral blood flow (rCBF) evidence. *Archives of General Psychiatry, 43*, 114–125.

Zachary, R. A. (1986). *Shipley Institute of Living Scale: Revised manual.* Los Angeles: Western Psychological Services.

Zec, R., & Weinberger, D. R. (1986). Brain sites implicated in schizophrenia: A selective overview. In H. A. Nasrallah & D. R. Weinberger (Eds.), *Handbook of schizophrenia* (pp. 175–206). Amsterdam: Elsevier.

Zwick, W. R., & Velicer, W. F. (1986). Comparison of five rules for determining the number of components to retain. *Psychological Bulletin, 99*, 432–442.

8

Methodological Excursions in Pursuit of a Somatosensory Dysfunction in Schizotypy and Schizophrenia

*Mark F. Lenzenweger, Ken Nakayama,
and Bernard P. Chang*

I first came into contact with the thinking of Brendan A. Maher when I, as an undergraduate student at Cornell University, was assigned his now-classic article on language in schizophrenia, which appeared in the *British Journal of Psychiatry* in 1972. In a very real sense, I was introduced to experimental psychopathology through that particular article, and I now regard it as having been one of a handful that moved me in the direction of a research career. In graduate school, Maher's (1966) *Principles of Psychopathology: An Experimental Approach* became one of the primary pillars of my research training, and it remains required reading for my students to this day. Simply put, there is no finer encapsulation of what is meant by the spirit and approach of experimental psychopathology than that found in *Principles*. Over time, I developed a collaborative research program with Professor Maher in which we are studying the relationships between schizotypy and fine motor performance (Lenzenweger & Maher, in press).

—Mark F. Lenzenweger

Brendan A. Maher's lasting and powerful influence on the methodological approach of experimental psychopathology has been to encourage close inspection of the processes of interest; use of the methods of the experimental psychology laboratory; and, if possible, the study of simple processes, which should not be conflated with unimportant processes (Maher, 1966). The latter element of this observation is particularly salient, as a considerable amount of effort has been expended, for example, in schizophrenia research that has focused on any number of complex

We thank Robert H. Dworkin, Lauren Korfine, Stephen M. Kosslyn, Brendan A. Maher, Paul E. Meehl, and Michael L. Raulin for useful comments on this research. We also thank Jennifer Ballard, Heather Bergida, Margaret Costello, Andrea Drummond, Judith Leone, Margo McKenna, Sharmila Sandhu, Laurie Scott, and Marni Sholiton for their assistance with the data collection.

neurocognitive processes, such as sustained attention deficits (Cornblatt & Keilp, 1994), smooth-pursuit eye movement dysfunction (Levy, Holzman, Matthysse, & Mendell, 1993), and spatial working memory impairment (e.g., Park & Holzman, 1992), and rightfully so as each of these processes has been shown to have a reasonably robust connection to schizophrenia liability. However, it must be noted that in each instance the process in question delivers up a relatively complex phenomenon that represents the interaction of multiple operations in a nearly simultaneous manner. This complexity, for example, was described well by Levy (1996), who used the antisaccade task, which is currently a focus of attention in a number of schizophrenia research laboratories, to illustrate the considerable complexity of this deceptively simple task (i.e., inhibit a saccade toward a target, make a saccade in the opposite direction). Levy parsed this task into no fewer than six discrete, yet interacting, operations—clearly not a simple task. The point here is straightforward: Even neurocognitive processes that appear simple are usually not so simply understood on closer inspection. From the standpoint of experimental psychopathology, which seeks to pinpoint the precise nature of the pathology of interest or the causal factors underpinning a pathology, this complexity can readily frustrate the efforts of even the most intensive research efforts. This reality is particularly glaring in the case of schizophrenia, where heterogeneity of symptom presentation and cognitive impairment are the rule, not the exception. To profitably take on the rigorous study of illnesses such as schizophrenia, Maher has urged his students to keep it clear, keep it simple, and use the methods of experimental psychology as the powerful tools they are in the quest to unravel thorny matters in psychopathology. We describe in this chapter our approach to the issue of somatosensory functioning in schizotypy and schizophrenia.

On the Origin of Our Explorations in Somatosensory Functioning in Schizotypy

The collection of studies we describe in this chapter grew out of some anecdotal empirical observations by Mark F. Lenzenweger. In the process of conducting research on schizotypic individuals one very cold winter at Cornell University in Ithaca, New York, it was rather remarkable to note that several of the research participants reported for their appointments with a relatively light amount of clothing (e.g., t-shirt and jogging shorts) given the outside temperatures, which hovered well below freezing. After completion of the research, it was found, on breaking the diagnostic blind, that all of the individuals whose attire seemed ill suited to the frigid weather were among the putatively schizotypic individuals. At other times, Lenzenweger has noted that persons who would be best characterized as odd or eccentric in their behavior were dressed in excessively heavy (warm) clothing, given ambient temperatures in the 90°–95° range. In short, it seemed that wearing goosedown parkas and wool caps on hot summer days was both atypical and fascinating. These observations, anecdotal as they were, suggested that perhaps individuals who would be designated as schizotypic might be somewhat less sensitive to exteroceptive stimuli (in this case, heat or cold). Although one might consider other possibilities in explaining these observations, the hypothesis regarding exteroceptive sensitivity led to a review of the classic descriptions of somatosensory (or body sense) functions in schizophrenia.

Classic Descriptive Observations and Theoretical Speculations Regarding Somatosensory Processes in Functioning in Schizophrenia

The somatosensory system processes multiple types of sensation from the body—light touch, pain, pressure, temperature, and joint and muscle position sense. *Exteroceptive somatosensation* refers to the perception of stimuli touching the skin from external sources (e.g., a light touch on the palm of the hand). The somatosensation system or process that detects and integrates muscle and body position is known as *proprioception* and reflects kinesthetic awareness. That a somatosensory dysfunction might be an important component of the schizophrenia disease process has long been suggested by psychopathologists. Bleuler (1911/1950) noted that "very often it is assumed that the sensations derived from the body organs are altered in these patients" (p. 57) and that "even in well oriented patients one may often observe the presence of complete analgesia which includes deeper parts of the body as well as the skin" (p. 57). Others have conjectured, more specifically, that a proprioceptive somatosensory dysfunction is an important feature of the schizotype, that is, the person who carries a liability for schizophrenia regardless of whether it is expressed clinically. Rado (1960) observed that among schizotypes "the individual's awareness of his own body is, or tends to become distorted . . . precipitated by what we provisionally call a proprioceptive (kinesthetic) diathesis" (p. 88). Meehl (1964), in his classic *Manual for Use With Checklist of Schizotypic Signs*, noted a proprioceptive diathesis described as a "spatial–motoric–kinesthetic defect" as important diagnostic signs for schizotypy, his putative schizophrenia liability construct. Meehl (1990) later described this as a fundamental dysfunction in a "spatial–kinesthetic–vestibular" system representing central nervous subsystems "that must be hierarchically integrated for a human being to locomote, stand straight, orient in space and have 'normal' perception of his own body (and, psychodynamically, his ego boundaries)" (p. 19). The overall impression of these views suggests an enduring and fundamental dysfunction in the perception and integration of both exteroceptive and proprioceptive stimuli (i.e., two domains of the somatosensory system) in clinical schizophrenia and, presumably, individuals who carry a liability for schizophrenia (cf. Holzman, 1969).

The proprioceptive component of the somatosensory system provides information about both the position of the body in space as well as the relation of the body segments to one another (Kolb & Whishaw, 1996). This system involves integration of body position information through both kinesthetic or static stimuli arising from the body. Therefore, it is not surprising that theoretical conjectures regarding a proprioceptive dysfunction in schizophrenia have derived in part from the frequent occurrence of body image and perceptual distortions in the illness. For example, Rado (1960) was impressed by the body image distortions and perceptual anomalies that characterized the psychological experience of the schizotype. Meehl denoted body image aberrations as a schizotypic sign in his 1964 manual, providing rich descriptions of the clinical manifestations of such phenomena (pp. 24–27), and he (Meehl, 1990) referred to body image distortions several times in his revised theory of schizotypy (see Meehl, 1990, pp. 9, 19, & 23). Perceptual and body image distortions as phenomenologic manifestations of a liability for (or expression of) schizophrenia have a long history in descriptive psychopathology (L. J. Chapman, Chapman, & Raulin, 1978; Erwin & Rosenbaum, 1979; see also Fisher, 1964). Finally, a growing body of evidence has shown that nonpsychotic individuals who score high on a measure of body image and perceptual distortions—so-called psychometric schizotypes—demonstrate a multitude of deficits on laboratory tasks and other correlated features comparable in quality to those seen in schizophrenia (Lenzenweger, 1998).

Neuropsychological and Neurophysiological Bases of Proprioceptive and Exteroceptive Functioning

What might be the basis for a somatosensory dysfunction involving both proprioceptive and exteroceptive components? The neuropsychological literature suggests that disturbances in body image (or body schema) require parietal-lobe involvement (Benton & Sivan, 1993; Hecaen & Albert, 1978; Kolb & Whishaw, 1996). Kolb and Whishaw (1996) suggested that Area PE (Brodmann's Area 5) of the posterior parietal lobe is especially relevant to body image disturbances. However, in order not to localize the central nervous system site subserving body image awareness with undue certainty, we note that lesions to the thalamus can create the impression of body part loss (see Hecaen & Albert, 1978). Nonetheless, parietal involvement is strongly suggested in the area of body image disturbance as well as the detection of proprioceptive sensory information (Kolb & Whishaw, 1996). Indeed, recent evidence from a primate study clearly supports the importance of Area 5 neurons in the integration of visual and somatosensory information in the monitoring of limb position (Graziano, Cooke, & Taylor, 2000).

Is there evidence to suggest parietal involvement underlying actual deficits in the detection of external (i.e., exteroceptive) sensory information? Disturbances in the somatosensory system, typically in the form of increased somatosensory thresholds, have long been associated with parietal-lobe damage (Kolb & Whishaw, 1996). Damage to the anterior parietal areas (Areas 1, 2, and 3; i.e., postcentral gyrus) has been closely associated with disorders of tactile function, most typically assessed using a two-point discrimination threshold procedure, such that discrimination thresholds are increased significantly (Corkin, Milner, & Rasmussen, 1970; Pause, Kunesch, Binkofski, & Freund, 1989; Salanova, Andermann, Rasmussen, Olivier, & Quesney, 1995; Semmes, Weinstein, Ghent, & Teuber, 1960; see also Forss, Hietanen, Salonen, & Hari, 1999; Martin, 1996). Moreover, it has been shown that two-point discrimination task performance is associated ($r = .83$) with the N20 component in psychophysiologic analysis, which is generated by the S1 area of the postcentral gyrus (most likely Areas 3b and 1 of the anterior parietal lobe; Knecht, Kunesch, & Schnitzler, 1996; see also Wikström et al., 1999). Damage to other brain areas does not notably affect the two-point discrimination threshold (Corkin et al., 1970; Semmes et al., 1960). Thus, anterior parietal damage is associated with deficits in the perception of exteroceptive stimuli in the general somatosensory system. Taken together, it appears that parietal-lobe damage can result in somatosensory dysfunction involving both exteroceptive stimuli (anterior parietal), in the form of tactile sensation, and proprioceptive stimuli (posterior parietal), in the form of body schema disturbances.

Prior Empirical Research on the Somatosensory System in Relation to Schizophrenia

Despite the importance attached to the notion of somatosensory deficits in schizophrenia, little prior research has been done in the area. For example, only two studies have previously examined exteroceptive deficits using two-point discrimination thresholds in schizophrenia patients (Broekma & Rosenbaum, 1975; Malamud & Nygard, 1931), and both used definitions of schizophrenia according to the second edition of the *Diagnostic and Statistical Manual of Mental Disorders* (American Psychiatric Association, 1968) or earlier criteria. Malamud and Nygard (1931) qualitatively contrasted the detection of touch versus noxious (pain) stimuli within four patients with schizophrenia but did not compare their schizophrenia results with those obtained from both normal participants and neurotic patients. A secondary analysis of their published data revealed that patients with schizophrenia had higher, although not statistically significant, two-point discrimination thresholds than normal participants. Broekma and Rosenbaum (1975) found that patients with schizophrenia ($n = 20$) displayed higher two-point discrimination thresholds relative to 20 normal control participants. Others have used weight discrimination (kinesthetic) tasks to assess proprioceptive functioning in schizophrenia and other psychiatric patients (Leventhal, Schuck, Clemons, & Cox, 1982; Ritzler, 1977; Ritzler & Rosenbaum, 1974), and these studies have suggested that a proprioceptive deficit exists in, but is not specific to, schizophrenia. Javitt, Liederman, Cienfuegos, and Shelley (1999) found evidence of proprioception deficits in schizophrenia using a weight discrimination task; however, the specificity issue was not addressed, because they did not have a psychiatric control group for comparison. These data, such as they exist are, of course, limited both in terms of generalizability due to sample sizes as well as the well-known third-variable confounds attending the study of expressed schizophrenia (i.e., deterioration, institutionalization, medication, and motivation effects; cf. Lenzenweger, 1998).

Regarding pain perception, Dworkin (1994) cogently argued that pain insensitivity can be observed in schizophrenia, and he noted that research conducted to date "provides neither a satisfactory characterization nor an adequate explanation of pain insensitivity in schizophrenia" (p. 235). Dworkin et al. (1993) provided some of the first empirical evidence for such insensitivity using a signal detection paradigm with thermal stimuli (Dworkin et al., 1993). More recently, Hooley and Delgado (2001) reported an increased pain insensitivity to be associated with schizotypic features in nonpsychotic participants. Given that pain and touch stimuli are gated through different networks in the somatosensory system (see Kolb & Whishaw, 1996), it is interesting to ponder the possible relations between exteroceptive and proprioceptive functions on the one hand, and pain insensitivity on the other hand, in schizophrenia. Our work in this area has taken as its initial focus exteroceptive sensitivity, specifically, tactile perception of light non-noxious touch.

On the Need for a Modern Study of Exteroceptive Functioning in Schizophrenia: Using the Leverage of the Schizotypy Construct

This pattern of empirical relationships regarding somatosensory phenomena, as well as the theoretical perspectives mentioned earlier, suggested a question for further study in research on schizotypy (i.e., the liability for schizophrenia): Would individuals with somatosensory deficits also reveal high levels of schizotypic features as assessed by well-established measures of schizotypy? It is well known that schizotypic psychopathology is especially useful for schizophrenia liability related investigations given the relative absence of the third-variable confounds noted earlier.

Before we describe our empirical studies, it is useful to review the nature of schizotypy and how one can define the construct in operational terms. In short, schizotypy itself cannot be observed directly; rather, it is a latent construct that expresses itself at the manifest level in different forms, ranging from frank schizophrenic psychosis to a near complete absence of any clinical indications (cf. Lenzenweger, 1998; Meehl, 1990). Thus, schizotypy can manifest itself in alternative forms, and as a result, one must be open to different methods of defining schizotypy that are less reliant on just clinical phenomenology. The notion that schizotypy can be conceptualized as an alternative expression of schizophrenia liability has its basis in a growing empirical database (Lenzenweger, 1998).

Three methods are used in the definition and detection of schizotypy, which are not mutually exclusive in terms of implementation: (a) clinical, (b) familial–biologic, and (c) psychometric–laboratory index approaches. The clinical approach implied in psychiatric diagnostic schemes involves, quite obviously, the use of explicit diagnostic criteria to identify either schizotypal personality disorder or paranoid personality disorder (e.g., *DSM–IV*; American Psychiatric Association, 1994). Limitations of the clinical approach include the reality that most schizotypes probably never present at clinics, and the *DSM* constructs of schizotypal and paranoid personality disorders may miss important aspects of schizotypy.

Second, one can be concerned with the biologic relatives of patients with schizophrenia and speak of "genotypic" schizotypes. Although many first-degree relatives of patients with schizophrenia will not evidence their underlying genetic predisposition to the illness through schizotypic symptomatology (and fewer still will have schizophrenia), they are, as a group, at increased statistical risk for schizophrenia and can be spoken of as schizotypes. Some relatives of patients with schizophrenia will indeed display schizotypic symptomatology (e.g., Kendler et al., 1993). It is essential to note that not all biologic relatives of patients with schizophrenia will carry the liability for the illness (Hanson, Gottesman, & Meehl, 1977); therefore this approach to defining schizotypes will yield an admixture of at-risk individuals versus individuals who are not at risk.

Finally, the psychometric–laboratory index approach involves the use of reliable and valid psychometric (or laboratory) measures of schizotypy to detect schizotypic psychopathology as defined by quantitative deviance on such measures. In the psychometric variant, scales designed to assess various schizotypic manifestations define and measure the schizotypy construct; schizotypic status may be defined by deviance on one or more of such measures. The psychometric approach has been discussed and reviewed (J. P. Chapman, Chapman, & Kwapil, 1995; Lenzenweger, 1998). A limitation of both psychometrically assessed schizotypy and clinically identified conditions (e.g., schizotypal personality disorder) is that neither is likely to be perfectly related to an underlying schizotypy construct and, therefore, they should both be considered fallible approaches to the measurement of true schizotypy. In short, the empirical research literature concerned with schizotypy is based on a variety of studies that use one of these three general approaches, and we suggest that it is essential to always note which approach is being used in any given study to maintain clarity among the findings as effectively as possible.

Empirical Studies of Somatosensory Functioning in Relation to Schizotypy and the Development of Laboratory Methods

Study 1: Two-Point Discrimination Thresholds and Schizotypy

Consistent with the data reviewed above regarding somatosensory abnormalities in schizophrenia as well as the clinical and theoretical observations of Bleuler, Rado, and Meehl, in the first investigation we undertook we sought to determine whether, in a series of randomly ascertained individuals with no prior history of psychosis, people who display relatively high two-point discrimination thresholds would be characterized by elevated levels of schizotypic features. In this particular study (Lenzenweger, 2000), 100 young adults drawn randomly from a university population were evaluated for their two-point discrimination thresholds as well as their levels of psychometrically identified schizotypic features, using four prominent reliable and valid psychometric measures of schizotypy. The schizotypy measures used in this study were the Perceptual Aberration Scale (PAS; L. J. Chapman et al., 1978), the Magical Ideation Scale (MIS; Eckblad & Chapman, 1983), the Referential Thinking Scale (REF; Lenzenweger, Bennett, & Lilenfeld, 1997), and the Rosen Paranoid Schizophrenia Scale (Pz; Rosen 1952, 1962; see Lenzenweger, 2000, for details).

For the purposes of this study, two-point discrimination thresholds were determined using a standard two-point anesthesiometer. Two-point discrimination thresholds were determined for each participant on both the right and left palms, along the lateral medial transverse axis, in both an ascending and descending series. Both ascending and descending series were used given that both approaches have been used in the determination of two-point thresholds in the neurological literature (Kolb & Whishaw, 1996). Each participant was told that his or her palm would be lightly touched and that his or her task would be to respond as to whether he or she felt one point or two points touching his or her skin. Assessments were done on each of the participant's hands with the test hand occluded by a screen that prevented him or her from seeing the procedure. Extensive detail on this procedure is given in Lenzenweger's (2000) article. The two-point discrimination threshold was determined for each hand of each participant for the ascending and descending series of stimulations; thus each participant received 4 two-point discrimination values. For the purposes of this study, the smallest interval at which the participant could discern two points touching his or her skin was recorded as the two-point discrimination threshold for a given series.

In this context we should note that there are at least three approaches to the assessment of two-point discrimination thresholds. The first, and traditional, approach derives from neurology–neuropsychology, and it involves the determination of thresholds in the same manner as in this study. The second approach is in the tradition of psychophysics in experimental psychology and involves approaches such as the method of limits or, preferably, *adaptive assessment* (e.g., the staircase method or the method of constant stimuli). The third approach involves adaptation of the two-point discrimination task for signal detection analysis. The three methods are complementary but allow for different inferences regarding the phenomenon under study.

As described by Lenzenweger (2000), the primary findings from this study concerned the two-point thresholds derived from the ascending stimulation series in association with schizotypy, whereas the descending series data were less strongly associated with schizotypy. For the ascending series-based two-point discrimination thresholds, it was found that elevated scores on the MIS and Pz scales were significantly correlated with higher two-point discrimination thresholds. For the MIS, scale scores correlated .27 ($p < .005$) with the mean two-point threshold (i.e., average of right- and left-hand values), .20 ($p < .05$) for the left hand and .26 ($p < .005$) for the right hand. For the Rosen Pz scale, scale scores correlated .29 ($p < .005$) with the mean two-point threshold (i.e., average of right- and left-hand values), .21 ($p < .05$) for the left hand and .27 ($p < .005$) for the right hand. The REF was associated with the mean ($r = .16, p < .10$) and left-hand ($r = .16, p < .10$) two-point thresholds at the trend level. Scores on the PAS were not strongly related to the two-point discrimination threshold values for the ascending series.

An alternative way to examine these data was to parse the participants into two groups defined by their two-point threshold value based on the mean threshold obtained for the ascending series. Such an analysis can be thought of in probability terms as having the structure "given deviance on the two-point threshold, what is the probability of deviance on the schizotypy scales?" Therefore, using the average ascending two-point threshold values, the participant pool was divided into participants representing the highest 10% of the distribution, those falling at or below a cutoff score equal to 0.50 *SD* above the group mean, and participants who fell between these two points. For the purposes of this analysis, the highest 10% group was contrasted with the group consisting of those scoring no higher than 0.50 *SD* above the mean, holding aside the middle group. Group means on the schizotypy measures were compared using the *t* test, and the results of this analysis were very clear-cut. The participant group defined by the most deviant (i.e., highest 10%) two-point thresholds was significantly elevated on all four schizotypy scales relative to the contrast group. The test statistics for these contrasts are summarized as follows: MIS ($p < .001, d = 1.16$, effect size $r = .36$), Pz ($p < .001, d = 1.14$, effect size $r = .38$), REF ($p < .03, d = 0.59$, effect size $r = .23$), and PAS ($p < .03, d = 0.63$, effect size $r = .23$). Finally, as described by Lenzenweger (2000), mental state factors (anxiety, depression) and intellectual functioning (e.g., SAT scores, Digit Symbol performance on the Wechsler Adult Intelligence Scale) were unrelated to the two-point discrimination threshold values. Moreover, statistical removal of their effect from the associations between the schizotypy measures and the ascending series two-point discrimination values had no effect on the strength of the latter.

These results were interpreted as providing some preliminary evidence of an association between an exteroceptive somatosensory process and schizotypy, such that higher levels of schizotypy were associated with less exteroceptive sensitivity, as indexed by the traditional determination of two-point discrimination thresholds. At the same time, these results helped to raise some important substantive and methodological issues, which were pursued in subsequent studies. At the substantive level, these data seemed consistent with some of the earlier clinical observations (e.g., Bleuler, 1911/1950) and theoretical speculations (Meehl, 1962, 1964, 1990; Rado, 1960) regarding somatosensory abnormalities in relation to schizophrenia; that is, they linked reliably assessed schizotypic deviance with increased thresholds. Moreover, the results suggested the possibility of a link between schizotypic deviance and, perhaps, a subtle, parietally mediated somatosensory deficit, given the well developed relations between anterior parietal lobe functions (particularly Areas 1, 2, and 3) and the two-point measure (see Lenzenweger, 2000, for an extended discussion).

These results also raised some important methodological questions for consideration. One important issue concerned the stability of the estimate of the two-point threshold, as determined through use of the anesthesiometer using single ascending and descending series of stimulations. In short, was this the best way to derive a stable threshold estimate? Could a method be used to arrive at a more stable estimate of the threshold? Second, although it was appealing to consider that the elevated two-point thresholds observed in relation to elevated schizotypic signs indicated a decreased tactile sensitivity in the presence of increased schizotypy, there existed the possibility that the process driving the correlations between the ascending series thresholds and schizotypy was one concerned with response bias (or response criterion) rather than sensitivity. Therefore, it seemed optimal to consider adapting the two-point threshold task to a signal detection format in which sensitivity (i.e., discriminability) could be effectively separated from response bias. Third, this initial study constrained itself to psychometrically assessed schizotypy, and it would be important to determine if the relations between schizophrenia-related liability and poor performance on the two-point discrimination task would also be found among individuals defined as schizotypic using one of the other strategies noted earlier (e.g., first-degree biological relatives of patients with schizophrenia). A fourth issue concerned the extent to which the observed relations among the schizotypy measures and the two-point thresholds were indicative of a schizophrenia-specific association. Although features of anxiety and depression in these participants did not account for the observed associations, this issue raised the need for additional study that included the equivalent of a psychiatric control group. We subsequently undertook the research suggested by these issues.

Study 2: Estimation of Thresholds Using the Method of Constant Stimuli

A primary concern arising from Study 1 concerned the stability of the discrimination threshold estimate obtained by means of the traditional anesthesiometer approach to the assessment of two-point thresholds. Specifically, the value retained as an individual's two-point threshold really reflected a single stimulus interval that appeared in either an ascending or descending stimuli series. Thus, it would not be unreasonable to think that such an estimate may be less robust than one obtained through multiple trials. The anesthesiometer approach to the determination of two-point thresholds has been the standard approach in applied disciplines, such as clinical neuropsychology and neurology; however, the methods of experimental psychology could also be brought to bear on this issue of threshold estimation.

There is, in fact, a historical precedent for using experimental psychology methodology in the determination of two-point thresholds. For example, the two-point limen (or *liminal stimulus difference*, also known as the *just noticeable difference*) was the focus of discussion in many early experimental psychology texts (e.g., Boring, Langfeld, & Weld, 1935; Titchener, 1910), and these discussions usually arose within the context of a discussion of methods for the determination of either the *absolute limen* (or threshold) or the *differential limen* (or threshold; DL). The absolute limen concerns, typically, the "minimum value of a physical stimulus that will evoke a sensation," whereas the DL has been defined as "the minimum amount of stimulus change required to produce a sensation difference" (D'Amato, 1970, p 118). The two-point threshold can be thought of as an exemplar of the DL, that is, the stimulus interval required to allow a person to determine that two points rather than a single point are touching a cutaneous surface.

In Study 1 an approach to the determination of the two-point threshold was used that essentially represented determination by the *method of limits* (also known as the *method of serial exploration* or the *method of minimal changes*). In the method-of-limits approach, stimuli are presented to the participant in an increasing or decreasing order, starting from a point that is either well above or well below his or her possible threshold. A participant's DL is thought to lie, as determined by this method, somewhere between the two stimuli values that bracket perception of the stimulus intervals as two points versus one point. It is important to note that even though the two-point threshold concerns a DL, the participant is not actually presented with two stimuli on every trial; rather, he or she is required to mentally determine whether two points or one point is touching the skin. The method of limits is known to have some major shortcomings that would be especially salient in this context. For example, some participants might continue to describe two points touching his or her skin even after the point at which two points cannot be effectively resolved; this would be termed an *error of habituation*. Other participants might realize that sooner or later his or her perception of the stimuli must change and therefore might anticipate the change; this is known as an *error of anticipation*. Either of these two types of errors, known as *constant errors*, could bias the determination of the two-point threshold.

In an effort to improve the estimation of the two-point threshold, we turned our attention to the method of constant stimuli, which involves the presentation of stimuli to a participant, not in serial order but in a random or quasi-random fashion. This feature of the method of constant stimuli eliminates the errors of anticipation and habituation known to characterize the method-of-limits approach. Moreover, the method of constant stimuli yields more informative psychometric functions that provide data that cannot be easily discerned from functions that derive from the method-of-limits approach (see D'Amato, 1970, for an illustration). It is interesting that through our work we discovered that the use of the method of constant stimuli had been advocated for the determination of two-point thresholds some time ago (Gates, 1915; Titchener, 1905).

The first step in our development of a protocol for the determination of two-point thresholds using the method of constant stimuli was to select a range of stimuli values that bracketed the probable value of the two-point threshold. This range of values was informed by Study 1 (Lenzenweger, 2000) and yielded a range of stimuli covering values that would be rather difficult to detect as two points (e.g., 4 mm) through those that should be fairly easy to detect as two points (e.g., 15 mm). For the purposes of this experiment, we chose the following stimulus values: 4 mm, 6 mm, 8 mm, 10 mm, 12 mm, 14 mm, and 15 mm. The next step in the method of constant stimuli was the development of stimuli sequences in which each participant was presented with each individual stimulus value a relatively large number of times. Therefore, we developed 10 stimuli sequences, assembled in a quasi-random fashion, that included each of the seven selected stimulus values ranging from 4 mm through 15 mm, and therefore, each participant judged 70 stimulus presentations as being either one point or two points touching their skin (lateral medial axis of the palm) on each hand. One of the disadvantages of the method-of-constant-stimuli approach is that the procedure can become rather tedious for both the participant and the experimenter; therefore, we restricted the number of stimulus repetitions for each stimulus value to 10. On balance, we sought to achieve a better threshold estimate while preserving the participants' engagement in the experiment.

We recruited 20 undergraduate participants from the student body of Harvard College. Each participant was administered the stimuli sequences, on both the right and left hands, with their hand obscured from view by a screen. To administer the stimuli we used the *Disk-Criminator* device from Sensory Management Service (Lutherville, MD). It consists of a set of plastic disks, each containing a series of metal rods fixed at varying intervals from 1 mm to 15 mm apart. The participants' task was to report whether one point or two points were touching their skin. The order of administration of the stimuli sequences was randomized across participants; so was the initial hand used for the task administration (10 participants started with their right hand, and 10 started with their left hand).

The data were reduced for each participant by hand and represented the proportion of correct identifications (i.e., two points identified as two points) for each stimulus value. We then plotted for each participant the proportion of correct identifications across the entire range of the stimuli, beginning at 4 mm through 15 mm. Then, using a logistic function, we estimated the psychometric function for each hand of each participant. We also estimated the psychometric function for an average curve based on all 20 participants, separately for the right and left hands. The logistic function we used generated both a slope and an intercept value. In this model, the intercept was defined as the inflection point of the function and represented the point of 50% accuracy in performance. On could consider the intercept as the threshold, difficulty level, or point of subjective equality for the participant. The slope of the function was also estimated and could be taken to indicate the discriminability of the participant. In other words, "the slope indicates how rapidly the perceptual effect grows with stimulus value, that is, how sensitive the observer is to systematic stimulus changes" (Macmillan & Creelman, 1991, p. 213).

The psychometric functions for the averaged data of the 20 participants, one each for the right and left hands, are presented in Figure 8.1. Inspection of the two

(a)

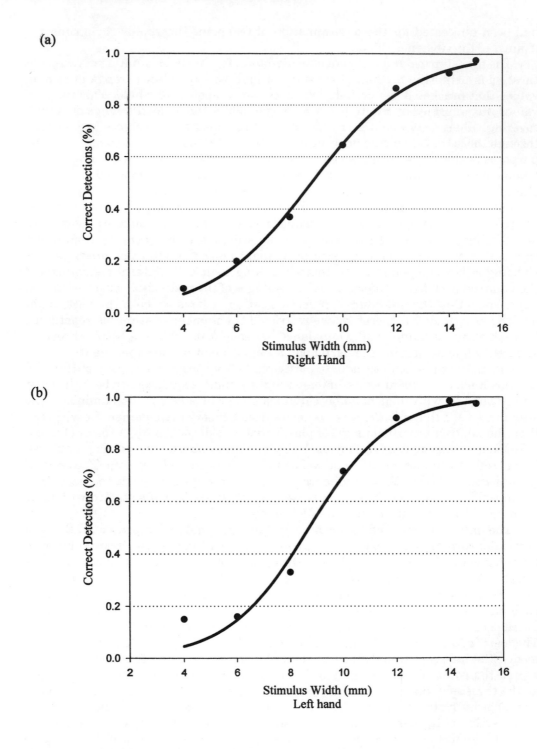

Figure 8.1. Psychometric functions for (a) right-hand and (b) left-hand data derived from the method-of-constant-stimuli two-point discrimination task. These are grouped data, averaged across 20 participants.

functions reveals that the averaged curves conform well to traditional psychometric functions, as described in the psychophysics and experimental psychology literature (cf. D'Amato, 1970; Nunnally & Bernstein, 1994). The stimulus values we chose to bracket the likely two-point discrimination threshold seem to have performed well in that the mean threshold values across the participants were 8.76 mm (SD = 1.78; right hand) and 8.86 mm (SD = 1.10; left hand), with no evidence of outlier or extreme values on boxplot analysis. A paired t-test analysis revealed that the thresholds across right and left hands did not differ significantly, $t(18)= 0.37$, $p = .72$. One feature of the data was particularly interesting, namely, the right- and left-hand threshold values were not strongly correlated within participants ($r = .10$, $p = .68$). The threshold values for the average group curve were 8.82 mm (right hand) and 8.72 mm (left hand). The slope values (i.e., discriminability) varied considerably across participants, ranging from 0.31 to 1.75 for the right hand and from 0.38 to 11.87 for the left hand. The wide range of slope values for the left-hand data reflected three individuals whose performance function closely resembled a step function, and these three individuals were identified as extreme values with boxplot analysis of the left-hand data.

The results of this study suggested to us that a threshold for two-point discrimination on the palm could be located within a 4- to 14-mm bracket of stimuli and that the performance of the individuals, and for the group as a whole, appeared to be well characterized by a logistic function. Furthermore, the range of stimuli values suggested to us that stimuli below 8 mm would be relatively difficult for many people to detect, whereas stimuli at or above 8 mm would be somewhat easier to detect. One issue that these data did not address, however, was the issue of discriminability versus response bias. This was because the threshold values we obtained were based entirely on the correct detections (hits) data (i.e., not on the false-alarm rate) and were, therefore, bias contaminated. One could estimate the degree of bias operating for each individual through the use of the psychometric function data by defining *bias* as arbitrarily measured from the mean of an endpoint stimulus distribution (i.e., select the extreme point as the starting point for calculations; see Macmillan & Creelman, 1991, p. 213). An index of sensitivity, namely a cumulative d', could also be estimated from these data. However, given that the participants were never actually presented with a single-point stimulus, which could serve as a genuine basis for false-alarm detections, we took a conservative approach to these data and did not estimate d' and bias measures from them. We used the 50% accuracy point on the psychometric functions to serve as an index of the two-point discrimination threshold following the traditional approach to such functions in psychophysics. In sum, the results of this study provided us with encouraging data suggesting directions for further development of the two-point discrimination task for work in schizotypy and schizophrenia.

Study 3: A Signal Detection Approach: Separating Sensitivity From Bias

The results from Study 2, in which we used the method of constant stimuli, revealed that a stable estimate of the two-point discrimination threshold could be found for our particular task. The next step in the development of the method for our purposes involved adaptation of the task to a signal detection framework, which would allow us to actually disentangle sensitivity (or discriminability) from response bias (or criterion). For this aspect of our work we sought to use the well-known and well-established measures of d' (sensitivity) and $ln\beta$ (response bias; Green & Swets, 1966; Macmillan & Creelman, 1991; Swets & Pickett, 1982). On the basis of the results we obtained in Study 2, we selected two stimulus values to represent those that would be used within a signal detection oriented protocol, namely 6-mm and 10-mm stimulus values. We selected these values because 6 mm appeared to represent a challenging stimulus to detect in Study 2, whereas 10 mm appeared to be considerably easier to detect. We used the 10-mm stimulus value to facilitate active engagement of the participants with our task by not making the task extremely frustrating.

These two stimulus values were then embedded into 10 stimuli sequences; each sequence contained 10 stimuli. Each sequence contained, on the basis of a quasi-random ordering, two 10-mm stimuli, two 6-mm stimuli, and 6 single-point stimuli. Therefore, there were 100 stimuli in total: twenty 6-mm, twenty 10-mm, and 60 single-point stimuli; thus, each two-point stimulus class had a 20% signal probability. The single-point stimuli offered participants the opportunity to actually commit false-alarm errors (i.e., report a two-point perception in the presence of a single-point stimulus), thus creating what is termed an *objective* two-point discrimination task (Craig & Johnson, 2000). We note that two-point discrimination tasks that do not actually present a single-point stimulus during the procedure are known as *subjective* tasks (Craig & Johnson, 2000). Thus, for the purposes of calculating two sets (separately for 6-mm and 10-mm stimuli) of d' and $ln\beta$ values (Green & Swets, 1966; Macmillan & Creelman, 1991), there were 20 possible hits for each stimulus (i.e., target 6-mm or target 10-mm stimuli) and 60 nontargets (i.e., single-point stimuli). Thus, we calculated two sets of d' and $ln\beta$: one for the 6-mm data and one for the 10-mm data. We calculated the signal detection indexes directly using the maximum likelihood based *Signal* program (Stenson, 1988); the indexes were not estimated from tables.

The primary objective of this study was to determine that false-alarm errors would be made to the single-point stimulations and that the 6-mm stimuli were indeed significantly more difficult to detect than the 10-mm stimuli in terms of d'. We were also interested in determining whether statistically reliable differences in response criterion ($ln\beta$) would emerge across the 6-mm and 10-mm trials. Finally, we also administered the same method-of-constant-stimuli version of the two-point discrimination task to the participants who completed the signal detection version of the two-point discrimination task. For this particular administration of the method-of-constant-stimuli version of the two-point task the 15-mm stimulus was deleted; thus, the stimuli range was 4 mm–14 mm. We readministered the constant stimuli version of the task to ensure that the thresholds estimated in this sample would be comparable to those in Study 2. Finally, we sought to explore the relations between the slope (discrimination) and intercept (threshold) indexes from the method-of-constant-stimuli variant and the d' and $ln\beta$ indexes from the signal detection variant of the two-point discrimination tasks.

These two tasks were again administered, counterbalanced for order, to a new sample of 20 Harvard College undergraduate students in a manner similar to that described in Study 2. Because of the absence of significant laterality effects in both Study 1 and Study 2, we decided to administer the experimental procedures only to the dominant hand of each participant.

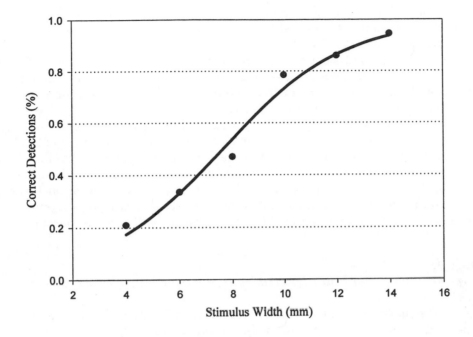

Figure 8.2.   Psychometric function for method-of-constant-stimuli data from Study 3. These are grouped data, averaged across 20 participants.

For these 20 participants the psychometric function for the data grouped across the participants for the method-of-constant-stimuli task are presented in Figure 8.2. The mean threshold value for the group was 7.57 (SD = 1.38), and the mean slope was 1.02 (SD =1.46). The slope estimate from the averaged group curve was 7.65, and the slope was 0.43. These values were broadly consistent with those obtained in Study 2. For the 6-mm stimulus the mean d' was 0.93 (SD = 0.76) and the mean $ln\beta$ was 0.62 (SD = 0.93), and for the 10-mm stimulus the mean d' was 2.30 (SD = 0.78) and the mean $ln\beta$ was –0.01 (SD = 1.27). For the d' indexes the 6-mm stimuli were considerably harder to detect than the 10-mm stimuli, paired $t(19)$ = 8.789, $p < .001$. The 6-mm and 10-mm d' indexes were substantially correlated within individuals (r = .59, $p < .006$). The $ln\beta$ indexes for the 6-mm and 10-mm stimuli also differed significantly, paired $t(19)$ = 4.151, $p < .001$, with a more conservative criterion found for the 6-mm stimuli. The 6-mm and 10-mm $ln\beta$ indexes were highly correlated within individuals (r = .85, $p < .001$). In evaluating the relations across the two tasks, we found that the 6-mm d' was correlated –.22 (*ns*) with the slope measure from the constant-stimuli task, whereas the 10-mm d' was correlated .53 ($p < .02$) with the slope measure. We view these correlational relationships with some degree of caution, however, given the relatively small sample size in the study (i.e., n = 20).

The results from Study 3 indicated to us that the signal detection version of the two-point discrimination task that we had developed functioned well, with the 6-mm task indeed being harder than the 10-mm task. Moreover, the two tasks differed significantly on both d' and $ln\beta$; this indicated to us the value in teasing these two performance components apart in future work. The method-of-constant-stimuli version of the two-point task seemed to generate performance among the participants that was consistent with that observed in Study 2, providing us with some evidence that the threshold and slope parameters derived from the psychometric functions were reasonably stable. We did observe a substantial correlation between the 10-mm d' index and the slope parameter from the method-of-constant-stimuli task, as one would expect. However, we viewed the latter finding merely as suggestive given the small sample size of the study. At this juncture of our work, we were now ready to once again turn our attention away from methodological development of the task to an experimental protocol with a substantive focus on schizophrenia liability. Finally, we note that with the adaptation of the two-point discrimination task to the signal detection framework, we moved away from two-point discrimination thresholds per se and adopted a focus that emphasized detection of two-point stimuli that is relevant to a threshold but not directly indicative of the threshold concept.

Study 4:
Examination of Two-Point Discrimination Performance in the Relatives

Having developed the two-point discrimination task for use within a signal detection framework, we then proceeded to conduct a fourth study of the two-point discrimination task in a population of relevance to schizophrenia (Chang & Lenzenweger, 2001). We chose to focus on the first-degree biological relatives of individuals with schizophrenia for this study, and in doing so we extended the exploration of exteroceptive sensitivity to another of the classic approaches for the study of individuals at increased risk for schizophrenia (see above). This study was also undertaken, in part, to further investigate exteroceptive sensitivity using standardized two-point stimulation in an effort to separate the issues of sensitivity and response bias. We hypothesized, guided by the results of Study 1 (Lenzenweger, 2000), and using our adaptation of the two-point discrimination technique that was amenable to the methods of signal detection theory, that the biological relatives of patients with schizophrenia would display deficits in the discrimination of two-point stimulation relative to normal control participants, whereas the relatives and controls should not differ with respect to response bias. We again emphasize here that in this study we were less concerned with two-point discrimination thresholds per se but rather with the capacity to detect two-point stimulation.

As detailed by Chang and Lenzenweger (2001), we examined the two-point discrimination performance in 39 participants who were the first-degree biological relatives of individuals with schizophrenia, who themselves had no history of psychosis, and 30 normal adult control participants recruited from the community. The participants completed the objective two-point discrimination task that we adapted for use with a signal detection approach detailed in Study 3.

We again used the 6-mm and 10-mm stimuli for use in this task. We continued to view the 6-mm interval as a challenging stimulus to detect, but not one that was unduly difficult, and it constituted our experimental task. Given the fact that the 10-mm task was considerably easier to complete with high levels of accuracy, we viewed it as our control condition to help to ensure that participants would remain engaged with the task and not become easily frustrated during the protocol. As in Study 3, the 100 stimulations were organized into 10 sequences, each containing 10 stimulations (two 6 mm, two 10 mm, and 6 single-point stimulations). Each sequence was randomly ordered, and the administration order of the 10 sequences was randomized across participants. We again calculated the signal detection indexes directly using the *Signal* program (Stenson, 1988).

As predicted, the relatives of patients with schizophrenia performed more poorly ($M = 2.10$, $SD = 0.39$) on the 6-mm d' index compared with the controls ($M = 2.29$, $SD = 0.40$), $t(67) = 2.06$, $p < .05$, d (effect size) = .50, and the two groups did not differ on $ln\beta$ (relatives: $M = 1.94$, $SD = 0.52$, controls: $M = 1.90$, $SD = 0.60$), $t(67) = -0.25$, $p < .80$, Cohen's (1988) d (effect size) = .06, which suggested a genuine difference in sensitivity and not response bias. The deficit in sensitivity (i.e., d') was driven principally by a lower hit rate on the two-point 6-mm trials and not an elevated false-alarm rate on the single-point stimuli. The relatives and control participants did not differ significantly on either d' or $ln\beta$ for the 10-mm control task (see Chang & Lenzenweger, 2001, for details). It is also important to note that we found that relatives of patients with schizophrenia, as contrasted with the normal control participants, were not deficient in their performance on several neuropsychological tasks that were also computed (e.g., Rey Complex Figures Test; Meyers & Meyers, 1995), which argues against a generalized-deficit explanation of these findings. Finally, the poor performance on the 6-mm d' index of the biological relatives was most closely associated with two schizotypic features that were measured in all the participants, namely, "odd beliefs and magical thinking."

In this study we found, as predicted, that the first-degree biological relatives of patients with schizophrenia performed significantly worse on the two-point discrimination task, and the deficit was found in the discriminability (i.e., sensitivity) aspect of performance (not in response bias). The results of this study were largely consistent with those observed initially in Study 1 (Lenzenweger, 2000). We have continued to conceptualize these findings within a framework that emphasizes a parietally mediated somatosensory deficit in schizophrenia and schizotypy. However, as noted by both Lenzenweger (2000) and by Chang and Lenzenweger (2001), we caution against an undue rush to localization to the anterior parietal cortex (Areas 1, 2, and 3) and instead prefer more of a network-oriented conceptualization that takes into account the rich complexity of the exteroceptive somatosensory system and related processes (e.g., proprioception). A brief review of recent neuropsychological and neuroimaging data that establish the relevance of parietal-area dysfunction in relation to schizophrenia can be found in Lenzenweger's (2000) and Chang and Lenzenweger's (2001) articles.

Summary and Future Directions

In exploring a possible somatosensory processing deficit in schizophrenia and schizotypy, our work proceeded from anecdotal clinical observations; to classic descriptions by Bleuler (1911/1950), Rado (1960), and Meehl (1964, 1990); through an exploration of neuropsychological methods and refinement of our methods using the tools of experimental psychology. In short, we have attempted to bring this phenomenon into the experimental psychology laboratory. In doing so, we have encountered any number of methodological challenges and have attempted to address them using methods from psychophysics and signal detection frameworks.

What has been particularly exciting to learn is that, quite apart from the work involving the two-point discrimination threshold in psychopathology, there has been substantial interest in this phenomenon for nearly 100 years in applied disciplines (e.g., neuropsychology and neurology) as well as in experimental psychology itself (e.g., Gates, 1915; Loomis & Lederman, 1986; Titchener, 1916). Although the two-point discrimination task has been criticized for one shortcoming or another, it is reasonable to assert that it is viewed as a task that does tap the exteroceptive somatosensory function in a systematic fashion (Loomis & Lederman, 1986; Vallbo & Johansson, 1978). Johnson and his colleagues have devoted a considerable amount of effort in the study of the two-point discrimination threshold (Craig & Johnson, 2000; Johnson & Phillips, 1981). An interesting question they have raised concerns the precise nature of the process that is involved in two-point discrimination performance. In a sense, just what is being measured? It has long been suggested that the two-point discrimination threshold provides a measure of spatial resolution; however, that view is not shared by all workers in this area (e.g., Craig & Johnson, 2000). According to Johnson and his colleagues, because of the nature of two-point stimulation, performance on the task may represent either decreased spatial acuity, impaired intensity cue processing of tactile stimuli, or both, and alternative methods have been proposed for studies directed at spatial resolution (e.g., gap detection, grating resolution, letter recognition; Johnson & Phillips, 1981). For our purposes in psychopathology, we deem either possibility (i.e., spatial resolution vs. intensity processing deficits) worthy of further investigation.

In the experimental psychopathology of schizophrenia, workers have long realized that one must not necessarily expect that the disease will reveal itself clearly and consistently across affected people, and there is no compelling reason to expect schizophrenia liability to reveal itself in an unambiguous fashion either. We hope to pursue our empirical work on the apparent exteroceptive deficits observed in both nonpsychotic but schizotypic individuals as well as in the first-degree biological relatives of patients with schizophrenia. This work will continue to take guidance from the laboratory methods of experimental psychology in our efforts to further dissect this interesting phenomenon.

References

American Psychiatric Association. (1968). *Diagnostic and statistical manual of mental disorders* (2nd ed.). Washington, DC: Author.

American Psychiatric Association. (1994). *Diagnostic and statistical manual of mental disorders* (4th ed.). Washington, DC: Author.

Benton, A., & Sivan, A. B. (1993). Disturbances of body schema. In K. M. Heilman & E. Valenstein (Eds.), *Clinical neuropsychology* (pp. 123–140). New York: Oxford University Press.

Bleuler, E. (1950). *Dementia praecox or the group of schizophrenias* (J. Zinkin, Trans.). New York: International Universities Press. (Original work published 1911)

Boring, E. G., Langfeld, H. S., & Weld, H. P. (1935). *Psychology: A factual textbook.* New York: Wiley.

Broekma, V., & Rosenbaum, G. (1975). Cutaneous sensitivity in schizophrenics and normals under two levels of proprioception arousal. *Journal of Abnormal Psychology, 84,* 30–35.

Chang, B. P., & Lenzenweger, M. F. (2001). Somatosensory processing in the biological relatives of schizophrenia patients: A signal detection analysis of two-point discrimination thresholds. *Journal of Abnormal Psychology, 110,* 433–442.

Chapman, J. P., Chapman, L. J., & Kwapil, T. R. (1995). Scales for the measurement of schizotypy. In A. Raine, T. Lencz, & S. Mednick (Eds.), *Schizotypal personality* (pp. 79–106). New York: Cambridge University Press.

Chapman, L. J., Chapman, J. P., & Raulin, M. L. (1978). Body-image aberration in schizophrenia. *Journal of Abnormal Psychology, 87,* 399–407.

Cohen, J. (1988). *Statistical power analysis for the behavioral sciences* (2nd ed.). Hillsdale, NJ: Erlbaum.

Corkin, S., Milner, B., & Rasmussen, T. (1970). Somatosensory thresholds: Contrasting effects of postcentral-gyrus and posterior parietal-lobe excisions. *Archives of Neurology, 23,* 41–58.

Cornblatt, B. A., & Keilp, J. G. (1994). Impaired attention, genetics, and the pathophysiology of schizophrenia. *Schizophrenia Bulletin, 20,* 31–46.

Craig, J. C., & Johnson, K. O. (2000). The two-point threshold: Not a measure of tactile spatial resolution. *Current Directions in Psychological Science, 9,* 29–32.

D'Amato, M. R. (1970). *Experimental psychology: Methodology, psychophysics, and learning.* New York: McGraw-Hill.

Dworkin, R. H. (1994). Pain insensitivity in schizophrenia: A neglected phenomenon and some implications. *Schizophrenia Bulletin, 20,* 235–248.

Dworkin, R. H., Clark, S. C., Lipsitz, J. D., Amador, X. F., Kaufmann, C. A., Opler, L.A., et al. (1993). Affective deficits and pain insensitivity in schizophrenia. *Motivation and Emotion, 17,* 245–276.

Eckblad, M., & Chapman, L. J. (1983). Magical ideation as an indicator of schizotypy. *Journal of Consulting and Clinical Psychology, 51,* 215–225.

Erwin, B. J., & Rosenbaum, G. (1979). Parietal lobe syndrome and schizophrenia: Comparison of neuropsychological deficits. *Journal of Abnormal Psychology, 88,* 234–241.

Fisher, S. (1964). Body image and psychopathology. *Archives of General Psychiatry, 10,* 519–529.

Forss, N., Hietanen, M., Salonen, O., & Hari, R. (1999). Modified activation of somatosensory cortical network in patients with right hemisphere stroke. *Brain, 122,* 1889–1899.

Gates, E. J. (1915). The determination of the limens of single and dual impression by the method of constant stimuli. *American Journal of Psychology, 26,* 152–157.

Graziano, M. S. A., Cooke, D. F., & Taylor, C. S. R. (2000). Coding the location of the arm by sight. *Science, 290,* 1782–1786.

Green, D. M., & Swets, J. A. (1966). *Signal detection theory and psychophysics.* New York: Wiley.

Hanson, D. R., Gottesman, I. I., & Meehl, P. E. (1977). Genetic theories and the validation of psychiatric diagnosis: Implications for the study of children of schizophrenics. *Journal of Abnormal Psychology, 86,* 575–588.

Hecaen, H., & Albert, M. L. (1978). *Human neuropsychology.* New York: Wiley.

Holzman, P. S. (1969). Perceptual aspects of schizophrenia. In J. Zubin & C. Shagass (Eds.), *Neurobiological aspects of psychopathology* (pp. 144–178). New York: Grune & Stratton.

Hooley, J. M., & Delgado, M. L. (2001). Pain insensitivity in the relatives of schizophrenia patients. *Schizophrenia Research, 47,* 265–273.

Javitt, D. C., Liederman, E., Cienfuegos, A., & Shelley, A. (1999). Panmodal processing imprecision as a basis for dysfunction of transient memory storage systems in schizophrenia. *Schizophrenia Bulletin, 25,* 763–775.

Johnson, K. O., & Phillips, J. R. (1981). Tactile spatial resolution: I. Two-point discrimination, gap detection, grating resolution, and letter recognition. *Journal of Neurophysiology, 46,* 1177–1191.

Kendler, K. S., McGuire, M., Gruenberg, A. M., O'Hare, A., Spellman, M., & Walsh, D. (1993). The Roscommon Family Study: III. Schizophrenia-related personality disorders in relatives. *Archives of General Psychiatry, 50,* 781–788.

Knecht, S., Kunesch, E., & Schnitzler, A. (1996). Parallel and serial processing of haptic information in man: Effects of parietal lesions on sensorimotor hand function. *Neuropsychologia, 34,* 669–687.

Kolb, B., & Whishaw, I. Q. (1996). *Fundamentals of human neuropsychology* (4th ed.). New York: Freeman.

Lenzenweger, M. F. (1998). Schizotypy and schizotypic psychopathology: Mapping an alternative expression of schizophrenia liability. In M. F. Lenzenweger & R. H. Dworkin (Eds.), *Origins and development of schizophrenia: Advances in experimental psychopathology* (pp. 93–121). Washington, DC: American Psychological Association.

Lenzenweger, M. F. (2000). Two-point discrimination thresholds and schizotypy: Illuminating a somatosensory dysfunction. *Schizophrenia Research, 42,* 111–124.

Lenzenweger, M. F., Bennett, M. E., & Lilenfeld, L. R. (1997). The referential thinking scale as a measure of schizotypy: Scale development and initial construct validation. *Psychological Assessment, 9,* 452–463.

Lenzenweger, M. F., & Maher, B. A. (in press). Psychometric schizotypy and motor performance. *Journal of Abnormal Psychology.*

Leventhal, D. B., Schuck, J. R., Clemons, T., & Cox, M. (1982). Proprioception in schizophrenia. *Journal of Nervous and Mental Disease, 170,* 21–26.

Levy, D. L. (1996). Location, location, location: The pathway from behavior to brain locus in schizophrenia. In S. Matthysse, D. L. Levy, J. Kagan, & F. M. Benes (Eds.), *Psychopathology the evolving science of mental disorder* (pp. 100–126). New York: Cambridge University Press.

Levy, D. L., Holzman, P. S., Matthysse, S., & Mendell, R. (1993). Eye tracking dysfunction and schizophrenia: A critical perspective. *Schizophrenia Bulletin, 19,* 461–536.

Loomis, J. M., & Lederman, S. J. (1986). Tactual perception. In K. R. Boff, L. Kaufman, & J. P. Thomas (Eds.), *Handbook of perception and human performance: Vol. II. Cognitive processes and performance* (chap. 31, pp. 1–41). New York: Wiley.

Macmillan, N. A., & Creelman, C. D. (1991). *Detection theory: A user's guide.* New York: Cambridge University Press.

Maher, B. A. (1966). *Principles of psychopathology: An experimental approach.* New York: McGraw-Hill.

Maher, B. A. (1972). The language of schizophrenia: A review and interpretation. *British Journal of Psychiatry, 120,* 3–17.

Malamud, W., & Nygard, W. J. (1931). The role played by the cutaneous senses in spatial perceptions: II. Investigations with mental diseases. *Journal of Nervous and Mental Disease, 73,* 465–477.

Martin, S. P. (1996). *Neuroanatomy: Text and atlas* (2nd ed.). New York: Appleton & Lange.

Meehl, P. E. (1962). Schizotaxia, schizotypy, schizophrenia. *American Psychologist, 17,* 827–838.

Meehl, P. E. (1964). *Manual for use with Checklist of Schizotypic Signs.* Minneapolis: University of Minnesota Press.

Meehl, P. E. (1990). Toward an integrated theory of schizotaxia, schizotypy, and schizophrenia. *Journal of Personality Disorders, 4,* 1–99.

Meyers, J. E., & Meyers, K. R. (1995). *Rey Complex Figure Test and Recognition Trial: Professional manual.* Odessa, FL: Psychological Assessment Resources.

Nunnally, J. C., & Bernstein, I. H. (1994). *Psychometric theory* (3rd ed.). New York: McGraw-Hill.

Park, S., & Holzman, P. S. (1992). Schizophrenics show working memory deficits. *Archives of General Psychiatry, 49,* 975–982.

Pause, M., Kunesch, E., Binkofski, F., & Freund, H.-J. (1989). Sensorimotor disturbances in patients with lesions of the parietal cortex. *Brain, 112,* 1599–1625.

Rado, S. (1960). Theory and therapy: The theory of schizotypal organization and its application to the treatment of decompensated schizotypal behavior. In S. C. Scher & H. R. Davis (Eds.), *The outpatient treatment of schizophrenia* (pp. 87–101). New York: Grune & Stratton.

Ritzler, B. (1977). Proprioception and schizophrenia: A replication study with nonschizophrenic patient controls. *Journal of Abnormal Psychology, 86,* 501–509.

Ritzler, B., & Rosenbaum, G. (1974). Proprioception in schizophrenia and normals: Effects of stimulus intensity and interstimulus interval. *Journal of Abnormal Psychology, 83,* 106–111.

Rosen, A. (1952). Development of some new MMPI scales for differentiation of psychiatric syndromes within an abnormal population. *Dissertation Abstracts, 12,* 785A.

Rosen, A. (1962). Development of the MMPI scales based on a reference group of psychiatric patients. *Psychological Monographs, 76*(8, Whole No. 527).

Salanova, V., Andermann, F., Rasmussen, T., Olivier, A., & Quesney, L. F. (1995). Tumoural parietal lobe epilepsy: Clinical manifestations and outcome in 34 patients treated between 1934 and 1988. *Brain, 118,* 1289–1304.

Semmes J., Weinstein, L., Ghent, L., & Tueber, H. L. (1960). *Somatosensory changes after penetrating brain wounds in man.* Cambridge, MA: Harvard University Press.

Stenson, H. (1988). *Manual for the Signal program: A supplementary module for SYSTAT.* Evanston, IL: Systat.

Swets, J. A., & Pickett, R. M. (1982). *Evaluation of diagnostic systems: Methods from signal detection theory.* New York: Academic Press.

Titchener, E. B. (1905). *Experimental psychology: A manual of laboratory practice.* New York: Macmillan.

Titchener, E. B. (1910). *A textbook of psychology.* New York: Macmillan.

Titchener, E. B. (1916). On ethnological tests of sensation and perception with special reference to the tests of color vision and tactile discrimination described in the reports of the Cambridge Anthropological Expedition to Torres Straits. *Proceedings of the American Philosophical Society, 55,* 204–236.

Vallbo, A. B., & Johansson, R. S. (1978). The tactile sensory innervation of the glabrous skin of the human hand. In G. Gordon (Ed.), *Active touch—The mechanism of recognition of objects by manipulation: A multi-disciplinary approach* (pp. 29–51). Oxford, England: Pergamon Press.

Wikström, H., Roine, R. O., Salonen, O., Lund, K. B., Salli, E., Ilmoniemi, R. J., et al. (1999). Somatosensory evoked magnetic fields from the primary somatosensory cortex (SI) in acute stroke. *Clinical Neurophysiology, 110,* 916–923.

9

Pain Insensitivity in Relatives of Patients With Schizophrenia and Bipolar Disorder

Jill M. Hooley and Richard J. Chung

I have had the privilege of being Brendan Maher's colleague at Harvard University for the past 17 years. During this time I have observed the ways (at times direct and explicit, at other times beautifully subtle) that Brendan's clarity of thinking and his emphasis on methodology and careful experimentation have inspired those who have had the good fortune to know him. His methodological sophistication and his ability to instantly get to the essence of a research problem have made him an invaluable colleague to me. More important, his intellectual generosity, his kindness, and his unfailing sense of humor have made him a treasured friend. One recollection I have about Brendan concerns his lack of tolerance for theorizing in the absence of empirical data. A student in Denmark once told Brendan that he wanted to understand why elderly people always sat at the back of buses when they traveled around the town. Brendan's first comment was to ask whether this was, in fact, what the senior citizens of Copenhagen actually did. The poor student, quite taken aback, said he did not know. Brendan dispatched him to get on some buses and collect some data. In this manner was a PhD thesis idea no doubt abandoned. The data showed that the good citizens of Copenhagen sat at the front, middle, and back of the bus, regardless of age. There were thus no data to justify any attempts at theory. In this chapter, however, quite the converse is true: We report an apparently reliable finding concerning pain insensitivity and risk for psychopathology. At present, however, these are very much data in search of an explanation. We hope Brendan will approve.

—Jill M. Hooley

Pain insensitivity in schizophrenia has been an acknowledged clinical phenomenon for some time. Noted by both Bleuler (1924/1988) and Kraepelin (1919/1989), accounts of patients with schizophrenia showing markedly diminished responses to painful stimuli are scattered throughout the medical literature. For example,

We extend thanks to Heather Barnett, Minu Avgheli, Lia Delgado, Jessica Cohen, Devon Quasha, Bernie Chang, and Maya Bourdeau for their assistance with data collection. We also thank Jordan Peterson for providing us with the pressure algometer, and we gratefully acknowledge the financial support of the Harvard College Research Fund.

Arieti (1945) observed that patients with schizophrenia seldom complained when their wounds were being sutured, and Goldfarb (1958) reported that the majority of a sample of 31 children diagnosed with schizophrenia showed markedly aberrant reactions to painful physical trauma. By way of example, he described a child who gashed the palm of his hand with a knife and yet showed no evidence of any pain.

Surprisingly, pain insensitivity in schizophrenia has remained a relatively neglected and unexplored topic for many years, and we must thank Robert H. Dworkin, a former student of Brendan Maher's, for drawing our own attention to it (Dworkin, 1994). However, it is clearly more than a phenomenon of minor historical interest. More recent clinical accounts paint a picture similar to those reported a century ago. For example, Rosenthal and his colleagues described a male patient with schizophrenia who reported only occasional mild discomfort and who showed very little abdominal tenderness during a physical examination, despite having a perforated bowel (Rosenthal, Porter, & Coffey, 1990). Still other anecdotal accounts document conditions, such as a perforated and gangrenous gallbladder (Bickerstaff, Harris, Leggett, & Cheah, 1988), a perforated ulcer, and a broken ankle (Fishbain, 1982), in schizophrenic patients who appeared to experience very little of the pain commonly associated with these conditions.

This is not to say that patients with schizophrenia never report pain (see Delaplaine, Ifabumuyi, Merskey, & Zarfas, 1978; Torrey, 1989; Watson, Chandarana, & Merskey, 1981). Indeed, it would be surprising if pain insensitivity were characteristic of all patients with this disorder. However, taken together, the clinical data suggest that pain insensitivity in schizophrenia may be a very real phenomenon that has the potential to lead to serious health risks and even death from misdiagnosis or failure to receive appropriate medical attention (Bickerstaff et al., 1988).

It is also interesting to note that some of the more recent anecdotal reports of pain insensitivity concern patients with mania (e.g., Fishbain, 1982). This suggests that pain insensitivity may characterize psychotic patients more broadly and may not be limited to patients with schizophrenia. Moreover, given the unreliability of the diagnosis of schizophrenia in the United States before the publication of the third edition of the *Diagnostic and Statistical Manual of Mental Disorders* (*DSM–III*; American Psychiatric Association, 1980), it is reasonable to expect that some of the patients described as schizophrenic in early clinical reports were actually suffering from affective psychosis. The extent to which the pain-insensitivity phenomenon is specific to schizophrenia is thus an interesting issue.

As Dworkin (1994) noted, the empirical literature on pain insensitivity is difficult to review for many reasons. Many of the studies were conducted before *DSM–III* was published and are therefore open to concerns about diagnostic reliability. Sample sizes are also typically quite small, in some cases being as few as 13 or 14 participants. Comparison of results across studies is further complicated by the variation in pain induction methods used (e.g., thermal pain, electrical pain) and the site of application of the painful stimulus (e.g., left forearm, right hand, forehead). However, several empirical investigations have found limited support for pain insensitivity in schizophrenia (e.g., Davis, Buchsbaum, Van Kammen, & Bunney, 1979; Dworkin et al., 1993; Hall & Stride, 1954), although this is not invariably the case (see Collins & Stone, 1966). There are also reasons to believe that the pain-insensitivity phenomenon might characterize some patients with mood disorders (e.g., Davis et al., 1982; Dworkin, Clark, & Lipsitz, 1995; Hall & Stride, 1954). Mood can certainly influence pain sensitivity. Using cold pressor pain with normal participants, Zelman, Howland, Nichols, and Cleeland (1991) found that an induced depressed mood decreased pain tolerance, whereas induced elevations of mood increased pain tolerance. However, Davis, Buchsbaum, and Bunney (1979) reported that patients with bipolar disorder exhibited pain insensitivity independent of affective phase. Mood state may thus not be the whole story. As with schizophrenia, however, the literature concerning pain sensitivity and depression is difficult to review for a variety of clinical and methodological reasons (see Lautenbacher & Krieg, 1994).

What makes the current empirical and clinical literature even more problematic to interpret is that, to date, all studies on pain insensitivity and psychopathology have included psychiatric patients as participants. Although the reasons for this are obvious, it is difficult to know the extent to which current severe psychopathology affects patients' abilities to detect and respond to pain. Medication status is also a problem. Although many of the clinical observations of pain insensitivity predate antipsychotic medications, the extent to which more recent data might be confounded by medications is another source of concern.

We have tried recently to circumvent some of these problems by studying healthy individuals who, by virtue of their relation to a patient with schizophrenia, are at genetic high risk for schizophrenia. In a previous study, Hooley and Delgado (2001) explored pain insensitivity in a group of participants with a family history of schizophrenia and compared their pain thresholds and pain tolerances with those of controls with no family history of psychopathology. Participants with a family history of schizophrenia showed elevated pain thresholds and pain tolerances relative to the controls. Moreover, a small subsample of the family history positive (FHP) participants were particularly deviant with respect to their pain tolerances.

In this chapter we describe a recent replication and extension of Hooley and Delgado's (2001) work. We examined the reliability of their finding of elevated pain threshold and tolerance in the healthy biological relatives of patients with schizophrenia by studying a second sample of FHP participants. We also explored the association between pain insensitivity and a family history of bipolar disorder in an effort to learn whether pain sensitivity is a phenomenon associated only with schizophrenia or whether it characterizes psychotic patients more broadly. On the basis of the reports from the clinical literature and from the few empirical studies, we hypothesized that both the bipolar and schizophrenia relative groups would exhibit greater pain insensitivity relative to controls. Finally, we conducted a preliminary investigation into some of the psychological correlates of pain insensitivity. More than 20 years ago, Davis and his colleagues speculated that pain insensitivity in schizophrenia and mood disorders might be mediated by different mechanisms (Davis, Buchsbaum, & Bunney, 1979, 1980). In this study we aimed to see whether this might indeed be the case.

Method

Participants

We present data on 123 participants. Hooley and Delgado (2001) examined pain sensitivity in 32 healthy relatives of patients with schizophrenia and 21 controls with no family history of psychopathology. The data from these participants are included here. In addition, we present data on a small replication sample of 15 new participants with a family history of schizophrenia and 35 participants with a family history of bipolar disorder. Finally, limited data from a second sample of family history negative (FHN) controls ($n = 20$) are also added.

Participants were recruited through posted advertisements and e-mail notices soliciting people for a study exploring physical and psychological sensitivity. The majority of participants were students attending colleges in and around the Boston area. Prospective participants were excluded if they had an excessively complex family history of several different forms of psychopathology, a personal history of mental illness, or if they themselves were suffering from a serious physical ailment. A history of chronic pain or significant use of pain medications were also used as exclusion criteria. The relatedness of the participants in the FHP groups ranged from first-degree (e.g., full sibling, parent) to third-degree (e.g., cousin) relatives. Descriptive information for participants in each group is summarized in Table 9.1.

Pain Induction

We assessed pain threshold and tolerance using a finger pressure algometer (Forgione & Barber, 1971). This instrument, which is based on a hinge and weight system, involves a weighted metal lever (35 cm) that is attached to a 75 cm × 2 cm × 4 cm block of wood. A contact point, 1.5 cm long and 1 mm wide, is placed between the first and second knuckles of a finger. The pressure at the contact point is fixed and does not change during or across trials; however, when the contact point is lowered onto the finger it results in a growing sensation of pressure that builds to become "aching" pain. A dial ranging from 1 to 10 allows the participant to indicate how he or she subjectively evaluates the pressure and pain elicited by the algometer at different points during each trial. Throughout each assessment, participants are in complete control of the procedure and can terminate the trial at any time.

Pressure algometry was chosen over other experimental pain models, such as cold pressor and tourniquet pain, because it is less vulnerable to complications from heart rate, blood pressure, and other physiological variables (Forgione & Barber, 1971). It is also very simple and quick to use. Finally, because the edge of the lever

Table 9.1.   Descriptive Information for Participants in Each Group

Characteristic	Group				
	Control 1 ($n = 21$)	Control 2 ($n = 20$)	Schiz 1 ($n = 32$)	Schiz 2 ($n = 15$)	Bipolar ($n = 35$)
Men (n/%)	6/29	4/20	10/31	4/27	12/34
Women (n/%)	15/71	16/80	22/69	11/73	23/66
Age (years; M/SD)	20.2/1.2	18.6/0.9	22.6/3.8	22.0/5.1	23.1/6.9
Weight (lbs; M/SD)	133.3/23.3	133.3/17.8	152.6/32.3	134.9/21.6	153.9/35.2
Weight (kg; M/SD)	60.5/10.6	60.5/8.1	69.2/14.7	61.2/9.8	69.8/16.0

Note. Schiz = schizophrenia.

is dull (similar to a butter knife), there is no risk of tissue damage or injury to the participant.

Psychological Measures

The Schizotypal Personality Questionnaire (SPQ; Raine, 1991) comprises 74 true–false questions designed to assess *Diagnostic and Statistical Manual of Mental Disorders* (*DSM–III–R*; American Psychiatric Association, 1987) schizotypal personality disorder criteria. There are nine subscales within the 74 items. These measure ideas of reference (e.g., "Do you sometimes feel that things you see on the TV or read in the newspaper have a special meaning for you?"), unusual perceptual experiences (e.g., "Does your sense of smell sometimes become unusually strong?"), odd beliefs or magical thinking (e.g., "Are you sometimes sure that other people can tell what you are thinking?"), excessive social anxiety (e.g., "I sometimes avoid going to places where there will be many people because I will get anxious"), odd or eccentric behavior (e.g., "People sometimes comment on my unusual mannerisms and habits"), odd speech (e.g., "I often ramble on too much when speaking"), lack of close friends (e.g., "Do you feel that you cannot get 'close' to people?"), constricted affect (e.g., "I am not good at expressing my true feelings by the way I talk and look"), and suspiciousness (e.g., "I am sure I am being talked about behind my back"). The items from each of the nine different subscales are interspersed throughout the assessment. The psychometric properties of the instrument are generally good, and Raine (1991) demonstrated the validity of this self-report measure in discriminating cases of clinically diagnosed schizotypal personality disorder.

Procedure

All participants were guided through the same procedure by experimenters who were thoroughly trained in the specifics of the protocol. On arrival in the testing room, participants were given details about what their participation entailed and signed a written consent form. A family mental history questionnaire was then administered. This questionnaire probed both the individual's own mental history as well as the mental history of his or her immediate and extended families. Instances of counseling, hospitalizations, official diagnoses, and medications taken were all covered.

This questionnaire was followed by a detailed explanation of the pressure algometry apparatus and procedure. In addition to the explanation provided by the experimenter, written instructions with illustrations were given to participants to ensure their complete understanding. During each pressure algometry assessment the participant lowered the contact point of the algometer onto the index finger of his or her left hand, between the first and second knuckles. The participant then turned the subjective report dial to 1, signaling that the lever was making contact with his or her finger. The participant was instructed to turn the dial to 5 when the pressure on the finger changed into a sensation that he or she subjectively called pain (pain threshold). As this sensation of pain increased in intensity, the participant turned the dial up still farther, with a rating of 10 indicating when his or her pain tolerance had been reached. At this point, the participant removed the contact point from his or her finger and ended the trial. The times taken to reach 5, indicating pain threshold, and to terminate the trial (pain tolerance) were recorded with a stopwatch. After a brief period of rest, the participant repeated the procedure using the middle finger of the same hand, and then after another rest period, repeated the procedure with the index finger once again.

An 8-min (480-s) ceiling was used for each individual trial. If, after 8 min, the participant still had not turned the dial to 10 and ended the trial, the experimenter reentered the testing room and asked the participant to end the current trial and begin the next trial. Such trials were denoted as "time outs." Throughout the pain-sensitivity trials, the participant was alone in the testing room while the experimenter viewed him or her through a one-way mirror.

After the pressure algometry trials, participants provided additional personal information and completed other questionnaires, including the SPQ.

Results

Reliability of the Pain-Sensitivity Measures

In all testing sessions, three separate pain-sensitivity assessments were administered in which participants alternated between the index and middle finger of the left hand. As noted earlier, pain threshold (time to report the onset of pain) and tolerance (time to end each trial) were recorded for all three trials. We also used the longest pain tolerance time on any single trial as a measure of maximum pain tolerance. Because of large and significant within-subject correlations across the three trials, we used mean scores for pain threshold and pain tolerance to increase reliability and simplify data analysis.

There was a high positive correlation between pain threshold and pain tolerance, $r(103) = .65$, $p < .001$. Participants who were slow to report the onset of pain also tended to have higher pain tolerance. It was not surprising that participants who had high pain tolerance also tended to have a high maximum pain tolerance, $r(103) = .96$, $p < .001$.

Weight and Pain Sensitivity

Weight and pain sensitivity were highly related. Across all participants, weight was significantly correlated with pain threshold, $r(97) = .44$, $p < .001$; pain tolerance, $r(117) = .31$, $p < .001$; and maximum pain tolerance, $r(97) = .31$, $p = .002$. The heavier participants were, the less sensitive they were to finger pressure pain. This makes intuitive sense and is probably linked to overall body size and build. However, it was also the case that participants with a family history of schizophrenia or bipolar disorder were significantly heavier than were the control participants, $F(2, 114) = 4.79$, $p = .01$. Whereas the mean weight of the control participants was 133.3 lbs (60.5 kg), the average weight of the participants with a relative with schizophrenia was 146.5 lbs (66.5 kg). Participants with a relative with bipolar disorder were even heavier, with a mean weight of 154.0 lbs (69.9 kg). Post hoc least significant difference tests revealed that participants in both FHP groups were significantly heavier than the control participants. This significant weight difference was not explained by differences in the distribution of men and women across the three groups.

To remove the confound of weight, we used regression analysis to compute standardized residuals. These reflected weight-corrected pain threshold, pain tolerance, and maximum pain tolerance. We used these standardized residuals in place of the raw pain-sensitivity measures in all subsequent analyses; however, for ease of interpretation, all tables and figures present non-weight-corrected raw scores measured in seconds.

Pain Sensitivity in Relatives of Patients With Schizophrenia

Table 9.2 presents data showing the mean time to reach pain threshold, mean pain tolerance, and mean maximum pain tolerance in two separately recruited groups of control participants and two separately recruited groups of participants with a family history of schizophrenia. Control Sample 1 is the sample of FHN negatives described in Hooley and Delgado's (2001) article. Schizophrenia Sample 1 is the sample of healthy young adults with a family history of schizophrenia also described in the same investigation. Control Sample 2 is a new sample of 20 young adult participants with no family history of psychopathology for whom pain tolerance data were collected as part of another investigation. Schizophrenia Sample 2 is an independently ascertained new replication sample.

Hooley and Delgado (2001) found that participants who had a biological relative with schizophrenia were less sensitive to experimental pain than were FHN controls. The same was also true in our replication sample. Planned contrasts using the weight-corrected pain measures revealed that, compared with the original sample of control participants, the replication sample ($n = 15$) of FHP participants was also characterized by significantly higher pain thresholds, $t(31) = 2.71, p = .01$; pain tolerances, $t(31) = 3.13, p = .007$; and maximum pain tolerances, $t(31) = 3.51, p = .003$.

It is important to note that there were no significant differences between the two samples of FHP participants (original sample and replication sample) for any of

Table 9.2. Mean Pain Sensitivity in Control Participants and Relatives of Patients With Schizophrenia

Pain sensitivity measure	Control 1 ($n = 21$)	Control 2 ($n = 20$)	Schiz 1 ($n = 32$)	Schiz 2 ($n = 15$)
		Group		
Threshold (M/SD)	24.3/17.5		44.7/34.6	43.4/19.8
Tolerance (M/SD)	66.9/48.2	46.2/26.1	159.0/145.1	215.1/174.4
Maximum tolerance (M/SD)	86.0/57.6		200.2/165.6	265.4/187.3
Timed out (%)	0.0	0.0	18.8	40.0

Note. Pain sensitivity scores are raw scores (i.e., not weight corrected) and are measured in seconds. Control Group 1 and Schizophrenia (Schiz) Group 1 are the participants from Holley and Delgado's (2001) study. Schizophrenia Group 2 is a new replication sample, and Control Group 2 is also a new sample. Pain threshold data and maximum tolerance data were not available for Control Group 2.

the pain variables examined. In other words, regardless of whether they had been recruited into the original sample or the replication sample, the two study groups of biological relatives of patients with schizophrenia were remarkably similar with regard to pain sensitivity.

Our replication sample of relatives of patients with schizophrenia also demonstrated significantly higher pain tolerance compared with the second sample (n = 20) of healthy controls with no family history of psychopathology. As noted above, no measure of pain threshold was available for these participants, and we had only a single (one-trial) measure of pain tolerance. However, replicating the findings reported by Hooley and Delgado (2001), FHP participants in the replication sample took significantly longer to remove their fingers from the pressure algometer than did control participants from Sample 2, $t(33) = 3.69, p = .002$.

Taken together, these findings provide further support for the previously reported association between a family history of schizophrenia and diminished sensitivity to experimental pressure pain. They also justify our combining of the data from the two FHP samples and the two control samples to provide the most reliable estimates of effect sizes. When combined, weight-corrected pain sensitivity data show that participants who had a biological relative with schizophrenia had elevated pain thresholds, $t(60) = 2.01, p = .049, r = .25$; pain tolerances, $t(80) = 4.28, p < .001, r = .43$; and higher maximum pain tolerances, $t(60) = 4.12, p < .00, r = .47$, than did control participants with no family history of psychopathology.

Pain Sensitivity in Relatives of Patients With Bipolar Disorder

To what extent is elevated pain insensitivity found only in the relatives of patients with schizophrenia? To explore this issue we examined pain thresholds, pain tolerances, and maximum pain tolerances in 35 participants who had a family history of bipolar disorder but no family history of schizophrenia.

Mean scores for the non-weight-corrected pain variables are provided in Table 9.3. Although the raw means for pain threshold appear very different (56.01 s vs.

Table 9.3.   Mean Pain Sensitivity in Control Participants, Relatives of Patients With Schizophrenia, and Relatives of Patients With Bipolar Disorder

Pain sensitivity measure	Group		
	Controls ($n = 41$)	Schizophrenia ($n = 47$)	Bipolar ($n = 35$)
Threshold (M/SD)	24.3/17.5	44.3/30.5	56.01/65.0
Tolerance (M/SD)	56.8/39.9	177.0/155.3	179.9/173.3
Maximum tolerance (M/SD)	86.0/57.6	221.0/173.5	207.7/179.3
Timed out (%)	0.0	25.5	28.6

Note. Pain sensitivity scores are raw scores (i.e., not weight corrected) and are measured in seconds. The control group combines data from Control Samples 1 and 2. The schizophrenia group combines data from Schizophrenia Groups 1 and 2. Pain threshold data and maximum tolerance data were not available for Control Group 2; these means are therefore based on a sample size of 21, not 41.

24.3 s), participants with a family history of bipolar disorder did not differ significantly from Control Group 1 when weight was accounted for, $t(51) = 1.21$, $p > .1$, $r = .17$. However, the relatives of patients with bipolar disorder did show significantly higher weight-corrected pain tolerance, $t(71) = 3.22$, $p = .003$, $r = .37$, and a higher weight-adjusted maximum pain tolerance, $t(51) = 2.68$, $p = .01$, $r = .35$, relative to the FHN controls. In other words, unlike their counterparts with a family history of schizophrenia, participants with a family history of bipolar disorder did not take longer to report the onset of pain relative to the control participants. However, with regard to pain tolerance and maximum pain tolerance, participants with family history of major psychiatric illness were more pain insensitive than the controls. This was the case regardless of whether the relative had schizophrenia or bipolar disorder. Weight-adjusted maximum pain tolerance scores for relatives of patients with schizophrenia, relatives of patients with bipolar disorder, and control participants are shown in Figure 9.1.

One of the most striking aspects of our pain data concerned the number of participants in each group who failed to remove their finger from the pressure algometer at all. As we noted earlier, in cases where a participant failed to end a trial after 8 min of pressure pain, the trial was terminated by the experimenter, and the participant was considered to have timed out. Participants were not informed of this fact in advance to avoid revealing any information about how long a "typical"

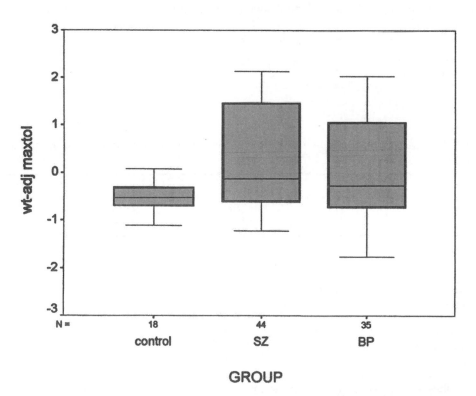

Figure 9.1. Weight-adjusted maximum pain tolerances (wt-adj maxtol) in control participants and relatives of patients with schizophrenia (SZ) and bipolar disorder (BP).

participant might keep his or her finger in the algometer. As noted in Table 9.3, not 1 of our 41 control participants was timed out of any trial. However, 12 of 47 (25.5%) participants with a family history of schizophrenia and 10 of 35 (28.6%) participants with a family history of bipolar disorder were timed out. These are highly significant differences relative to the controls: $\chi^2(1, N = 88) = 12.12$, $p < .001$, for control participants versus participants FHP for schizophrenia, and $\chi^2(1, N = 76) = 13.49$, $p < .001$, for control participants versus participants FHP for bipolar disorder. A significant minority of the relatives of patients with schizophrenia and bipolar disorder can thus be regarded as highly deviant compared with both control participants and their peers in their responses to pain.

Psychological Correlates of Pain Insensitivity

The SPQ was administered to all participants in Hooley and Delgado's (2001) study and to all the participants with a family history of schizophrenia in the replication sample. Participants with a family history of bipolar disorder also completed the SPQ.

Table 9.4 shows the correlations between weight-corrected maximum pain tolerance and the nine SPQ scales for participants with family histories of schizophrenia or bipolar illness. Hooley and Delgado (2001) found that maximum pain tolerance was significantly associated with the SPQ subscales Ideas of Reference, Odd Perceptual Experiences, Odd Speech, and Suspiciousness. These correlations, now corrected for weight, are shown in Table 9.4. Table 9.4 also shows the same correlations for the replication sample and for the two samples combined. It should be noted that, because of a clerical error, two subscales of the SPQ were inadvertently omitted in Hooley and Delgado's study.

Table 9.4. Maximum Pain Tolerance and Schizotypal Personality Questionnaire (SPQ) Subscales

	Group			
SPQ scale	Schiz 1 ($n = 32$)	Schiz 2 ($n = 15$)	Schiz 1 + 2 ($n = 47$)	Bipolar ($n = 35$)
Ideas of Reference	.39*	.52*	.33*	−.10
Social Anxiety	−.23	.32	.02	−.28
Odd Beliefs	—	−.07	—	−.08
Odd Perceptions	.37*	.54*	.36*	−.00
Odd Behavior	—	.44	—	−.06
No Close Friends	−.06	−.19	−.13	−.23
Odd Speech	.50*	.34	.41**	−.27
Constricted Affect	.10	−.01	−.06	−.23
Suspiciousness	.37*	.13	.23	−.01

Note. Dashes indicate the scale was not administered, owing to a clerical error. Schiz = schizophrenia.
*$p < .05$.   **$p < .005$.

As can be seen in the table, the same subscales that were positively associated with pain insensitivity in Hooley and Delgado's (2001) study also appear to be correlated with pain insensitivity in the replication sample. Although low power in the replication sample renders it necessary to focus more on effect sizes than on significance levels, it is clear that both samples show a very similar association between pain insensitivity and elevated scores on the Ideas of Reference and Odd Perceptual Experiences subscales. When the two samples are combined, Ideas of Reference, Odd Perceptual Experiences, and Odd Speech all emerge as highly significant correlates of pain insensitivity. In other words, those family members of patients with schizophrenia who show high levels of maximum pain tolerance are more likely to report certain types of unusual thoughts and perceptions as well as problems with the clarity of their communication. It is important to note, however, that pain insensitivity does not seem to be associated with the SPQ subscales that measure constricted affect or social isolation.

In participants with a family history of bipolar disorder, however, these associations are conspicuous by their absence. Contrary to what was found for the participants with a family history of schizophrenia, none of the SPQ subscales was significantly associated with pain insensitivity. The correlation between maximum pain tolerance and odd perceptual experiences was .00; moreover, the associations between maximum pain tolerance and both ideas of reference and odd speech were both negative and nonsignificant rather than positive and significant. In summary, what these data appear to show is that the correlates of pain insensitivity in relatives of patients with schizophrenia and bipolar disorder are quite different.

Discussion

In this study we examined pain sensitivity in young adult and healthy biological relatives of patients with schizophrenia or bipolar disorder, in comparison with two groups of control participants with no family history of psychopathology. We hypothesized that both the relatives of patients with schizophrenia and the relatives of patients with bipolar disorder would exhibit pain insensitivity relative to controls. After controlling for the contribution of weight to pain insensitivity, we found that the schizophrenia relatives in the replication sample performed very similarly on the pain sensitivity assessment compared with the original group of schizophrenia relatives reported by Hooley and Delgado (2001). Our findings suggest that the well relatives of patients with schizophrenia have elevated pain thresholds and pain tolerances compared with controls with no family history of psychopathology. It is also the case that a small subset of these FHP participants are particularly pain insensitive, both relative to controls and relative to other participants with a family history of schizophrenia.

Findings from the participants with a family history of bipolar disorder were both similar to and different from the findings obtained from the schizophrenia relatives sample. Unlike participants who were FHP for schizophrenia, participants with a family history of bipolar disorder did not show elevated pain thresholds compared with the controls. However, like their counterparts with a family history of schizophrenia, participants with a family history of bipolar disorder did show greater pain tolerance and maximum pain tolerance than did the control participants. Again, a significant minority of them were also highly deviant with respect to their peers and to the controls, as reflected in their being timed out during a pain induction trial.

Perhaps the most striking difference between the relatives of the patients with schizophrenia and the relatives of the patients with bipolar disorder concerned the correlates of their higher pain tolerances. In the FHP schizophrenia sample, greater pain insensitivity was highly correlated with self-reported psychotic-like symptoms, especially the Perceptual Aberrations and Ideas of Reference subscales of the SPQ. In the relatives of the patients with bipolar disorder, however, no such associations were apparent. Although much more remains to be learned about the psychological correlates of pain insensitivity in these groups, these preliminary findings suggest that the variables that predict pain insensitivity in participants with a family history of schizophrenia may not be the same as the variables that predict pain insensitivity in the relatives of patients with bipolar disorder. As Davis, Buchsbaum, and Bunney (1979) noted, pain insensitivity in different forms of psychopathology may indeed be mediated by different mechanisms.

The findings we report are especially interesting in light of the fact that we specifically excluded both participants who had personal histories of mental problems and participants taking medications. However, our research design also had its limitations. Because we did not conduct personal interviews with participants' family members, we cannot say for certain that they suffered from the psychiatric problems reported by their relatives. We certainly did our best to include only cases for which there had been formal contact with psychiatric services (e.g., hospitalization) and for which a diagnosis had been given to the family by a psychiatrist or other medical professional. However, our inability to verify this information directly clearly introduces a potential source of error.

Another problem concerned our choice of a pressure algometer to induce pain. The pressure algometer used in this investigation applied a constant and nonvarying weight to the finger. Consequently, we were unable to use signal detection approaches to explore whether our findings reflect differences in participants' sensitivities to physical pain or response biases in the reporting of pain. Our finding of only pain tolerance differences in the relatives of patients with bipolar disorder but pain threshold and pain tolerance differences in the relatives of patients with schizophrenia clearly warrants further exploration using more sophisticated signal detection approaches.

From a research perspective, the way forward now seems clear. First, signal detection approaches need to be used to study pain insensitivity in reliably diagnosed samples of patients with schizophrenia and bipolar disorder and their biological relatives. Second, a much larger array of potential correlates of pain insensitivity also needs to be explored. Although our study failed to support any link between pain insensitivity and anhedonia (see Dworkin et al., 1993), a more detailed examination of this issue would be valuable. We also recommend that future studies include experimental measures of attentional functioning. Pain and attention are undoubtedly linked (Arntz, Dreessen, & Merckelbach, 1991; Eccleston & Crombez, 1999). Moreover, attentional problems have been shown to characterize children at high genetic risk for schizophrenia (Cornblatt, Lenzenweger, Dworkin, & Erlenmeyer-Kimling, 1992) as well as individuals who score high on scales of psychosis proneness (Fernandes & Miller, 1995; Lenzenweger, Cornblatt, & Putnick, 1991).

Given our findings of a link between perceptual aberrations and greater pain insensitivity, it seems reasonable to suggest that highly pain insensitive participants might well be those who also show poorer sustained attention on tasks such as the Continuous Performance Test (Rosvold, Mirsky, Sarason, Bransome, & Beck, 1956). Finally, researchers need to know if statistically deviant pain sensitivity places FHP participants at greater risk of developing major psychopathology in the future. Subsequent investigations should explore the potential long-term outcomes of participants at various points on the pain sensitivity–insensitivity continuum. Approaches of this sort hold the potential not only to contribute to a theoretical understanding of the etiology of major mental illness but also to possibly help identify individuals who might be especially vulnerable to psychopathology in the longer term.

In addition to the above-mentioned avenues for further empirical inquiry, researchers would do well to give serious thought to the issue of why pain insensitivity and some forms of major psychopathology might be linked at all. The answers are unlikely to come easily. Pain perception is a complex phenomenon that requires the integration of sensory information with emotional and affective responses as well as with cognitive evaluations and control. Although space does not permit a detailed discussion of the neurobiology of pain (see Martin, 1996; Price, 1988), what is striking is that several of the brain areas involved in pain perception are also areas of the brain that are receiving attention with respect to schizophrenia. These include the thalamus (Ettinger et al., 2001) and the anterior cingulate (Benes & Bird, 1987). The neurotransmitter glutamate, which is currently receiving a great deal of attention from schizophrenia researchers (Olney & Farber, 1995), is also involved in the transmission of noxious stimuli, as are other neurotransmitters of interest to psychopathologists, such as serotonin and norepinephrine.

Yet another possibility is that individual differences in pain sensitivity are mediated by endorphins (see Davis & Buchsbaum, 1981; Davis et al., 1982). Uhl, Sora, and Wang (1999) used positron emission tomography to show that the number of a certain type of opioid receptor varies greatly in humans, with some people having twice as many receptors than others. These receptors are thought to bind to endogenous opiates and therefore mediate pain sensitivity. Moreover, there is some evidence that opioid receptor density may be genetically regulated (Uhl et al., 1999). The possible genetic foundation of pain sensitivity is currently an exciting and dynamic area of research that has particular relevance to studies involving biological relatives of clinical populations. The possibility that some of the most important genes determining opioid receptor density simply happen to be close to some of the genes that might confer liability to psychosis is an intriguing and as-yet-unexplored idea.

Of course, at present all of this is nothing more than unchecked speculation. Although it has a long and rich clinical history, the systematic study of pain insensitivity and psychopathology is still in its infancy. Moreover, just because some of the same brain areas or neurotransmitters are both involved in pain perception and implicated in some forms of major psychopathology does not necessarily mean that they are linked in any functional way. In short, researchers are still a long way from understanding why certain forms of psychopathology might be linked to higher levels of pain insensitivity. However, we are willing to venture that the programmatic study of this issue will provide rich rewards to those who seek answers to the nature and origins of some important major mental disorders.

References

American Psychiatric Association. (1980). *Diagnostic and statistical manual of mental disorders* (3rd ed.). Washington, DC: Author.

American Psychiatric Association. (1987). *Diagnostic and statistical manual of mental disorders* (3rd ed., rev.). Washington, DC: Author.

Arieti, S. (1945). Primitive habits and perceptual alterations in the terminal stage of schizophrenia. *Archives of Neurology and Psychiatry, 53*, 378–384.

Arntz, A., Dreessen, L., & Merckelbach, H. (1991). Attention, not anxiety, influences pain. *Behavior Research and Therapy, 29*, 41–50.

Benes, F. M., & Bird, E. D. (1987). An analysis of the arrangement of neurons in the cingulate cortex of schizophrenic patients. *Archives of General Psychiatry, 44*, 608–616.

Bickerstaff, L. K., Harris, S. C., Leggett, R. S., & Cheah, K. C. (1988). Pain insensitivity in schizophrenic patients: A surgical dilemma. *Archives of Surgery, 123*, 49–51.

Bleuler, E. (1988). *Textbook of psychiatry* (A. A. Brill, Trans.). New York: Classics of Psychiatry and Behavioral Sciences Library. (Original work published 1924)

Collins, L. G., & Stone, L. A. (1966). Pain sensitivity, age and activity level in chronic schizophrenics and normals. *British Journal of Psychiatry, 112*, 33–35.

Cornblatt, B. A., Lenzenweger, M. F., Dworkin, R. H., & Erlenmeyer-Kimling, L. (1992). Childhood attentional dysfunction predicts social deficits in unaffected adults at risk for schizophrenia. *British Journal of Psychiatry, 161*(Suppl. 18), 59–64.

Davis, G. C., & Buchsbaum, M. S. (1981). Pain sensitivity and endorphins in functional psychosis. *Modern Problems in Pharmacopsychiatry, 112*, 33–35.

Davis, G. C., Buchsbaum, M. S., & Bunney, W. E. (1979). Analgesia to painful stimuli in affective illness. *American Journal of Psychiatry, 136*, 1148–1151.

Davis, G. C., Buchsbaum, M. S., & Bunney, W. E. (1980). Pain and psychiatric illness. In L. K. Y. Ng & J. J. Bonica (Eds.), Pain, discomfort, and humanitarian care (pp. 221–231). New York: Elsevier–North Holland.

Davis, G. C., Buchsbaum, M. S., Naber, D., Pickar, D., Post, R., Van Kammen, D., & Bunney, W. E. (1982). Altered pain perception and cerebrospinal endorphins in psychiatric illness. *Annals of the New York Academy of Sciences, 398*, 366–373.

Davis, G. C., Buchsbaum, M. S., Van Kammen, D. P., & Bunney, W. E. (1979). Analgesia to pain stimuli in schizophrenics and its reversal by naltrexone. *Psychiatry Research, 1*, 61–69.

Delaplaine, R., Ifabumuyi, O. I., Merskey, H., & Zarfas, J. (1978). Significance of pain in psychiatric hospital patients. *Pain, 4*, 361–366.

Dworkin, R. H. (1994). Pain insensitivity in schizophrenia: A neglected phenomenon and some implications. *Schizophrenia Bulletin, 20*, 235–248.

Dworkin, R. H., Clark, W. C., & Lipsitz, J. D. (1995). Pain responsivity in major depression and bipolar disorder. *Psychiatry Research, 56*, 173–181.

Dworkin, R. H., Clark, W. C., Lipsitz, J. D., Amador, X. F., Kaufman, C. A., Opler, L. A., et al. (1993). Affective deficits and pain insensitivity in schizophrenia. *Motivation and Emotion, 3*, 245–276.

Eccleston, C., & Crombez, G. (1999). Pain demands attention: A cognitive–affective model of the interruptive function of pain. *Psychological Bulletin, 125*, 356–366.

Ettinger, U., Chitnis, X. A., Kumari, V., Fannon, D. G., Sumich, A. L., O'Ceallaigh, S., et al. (2001). Magnetic-resonance imaging of the thalamus in first-episode psychosis. *American Journal of Psychiatry, 158*, 116–118.

Fernandes, L. O. L., & Miller, G. A. (1995). Compromised performance and abnormal psychophysiology associated with the Wisconsin Scales of Psychosis Proneness. In G. A. Miller (Ed.), *The behavioral high-risk paradigm in psychopathology* (pp. 47–87). Springer: New York.

Fishbain, D. A. (1982). Pain insensitivity in psychosis. *Annals of Emergency Medicine, 11*, 630–632.

Forgione, A. G., & Barber, T. X. (1971). A strain gauge pain simulator. *Psychophysiology, 8*, 102–106.

Goldfarb, W. (1958). Pain reactions in a group of institutionalized children. *American Journal of Orthopsychiatry, 28*, 777–785.

Hall, K. R. L., & Stride, E. (1954). The varying response to pain in psychiatric disorders: A study in abnormal psychology. *British Journal of Medical Psychology, 27*, 48–60.

Hooley, J. M., & Delgado, M. L. (2001). Pain insensitivity in the relatives of schizophrenia patients. *Schizophrenia Research, 47*, 265–273.

Kraepelin, E. (1989). *Dementia praecox and paraphrenia.* New York: Classics of Psychiatry and Behavioral Sciences Library. (Original work published 1919)

Lautenbacher, S., & Krieg, J.-C. (1994). Pain perception in psychiatric disorders: A review of the literature. *Journal of Psychiatric Research, 26,* 109–122.

Lenzenweger, M. F., Cornblatt, B. A., & Putnick, M. (1991). Schizotypy and sustained attention. *Journal of Abnormal Psychology, 100,* 84–89.

Martin, J. H. (1996). *Neuroanatomy: Text and atlas* (2nd ed.). Stamford, CT: Appleton and Lange.

Olney, J. W., & Farber, N. B. (1995). Glutamate receptor dysfunction and schizophrenia. *Archives of General Psychiatry, 52,* 998–1007.

Price, D. D. (1988). *Psychological and neural mechanisms of pain.* New York: Raven Press.

Raine, A. (1991). The SPQ: A scale for the assessment of schizotypal personality based on *DSM–III–R* criteria. *Schizophrenia Bulletin, 17,* 555–564.

Rosenthal, S. H., Porter, K. A., & Coffey, B. (1990). Pain insensitivity and schizophrenia: Case report and review of the literature. *General Hospital Psychiatry, 12,* 319–322.

Rosvold, H. E., Mirsky, A. F., Sarason, I., Bransome, E. D., & Beck, L. H. (1956). A continuance performance test of brain damage. *Journal of Consulting Psychology, 20,* 343–350.

Torrey, E. F. (1989). Headache in schizophrenia and seasonality of births. *Biological Psychiatry, 26,* 852–853.

Uhl, G. R., Sora, I., & Wang, Z. (1999). The Mu opiate receptor as a candidate gene for pain: Polymorphisms, variations in expression, nociception, and opiate responses. *Proceedings of the National Academy of Sciences, 96,* 7752–7755.

Watson, G. D., Chandarana, P. C., & Merskey, H. (1981). Relationships between pain and schizophrenia. *British Journal of Psychiatry, 138,* 33–36.

Zelman, D. C., Howland, E. W., Nichols, S. M., & Cleeland, C. S. (1991). The effects of induced mood on laboratory pain. *Pain, 46,* 105–111.

Part IV

Methodological Advances in the Study of Psychopathology

10

Less Is Truly More: Psychopathology Research in the 21st Century

Philip S. Holzman

In the preface to the monograph series he founded in 1964, called *Progress in Experimental Personality Research*, Brendan Maher wrote,

> Personality psychology has changed during the past two or three decades. The change has been marked by a move away from theorizing on a grand scale and toward a greater concern with obtaining empirical answers to questions of manageable and modest proportions. By the same token, research in personality has turned increasingly to the methods and concepts of other areas of behavioral science: the shift from the study of the single case to the use of the controlled experiment is perhaps the most striking instance of this. (Maher, 1964, p. vii)

His monograph series also underwent a metamorphosis, shifting from presenting studies of personality—with its emphasis on broad issues of inter- and intrapersonal dynamics—to experimental psychopathology, which boasts of its emphasis on finding specific pathological structures and functions. Maher discerned that in this newer effort lay the psychological counterpart to the sciences of physiology and anatomy, where human psychology could truly be carved at its joints, and the study of abnormal functioning promised to open a special window of privilege on human behavior.

However, the single case was not to be totally abandoned. In the shift to psychopathology, the single case yielded its place as the principal tool for demonstrating personality dynamics to take up its role as one starting point for an investigation. The single case will always call scientists' attention to an anomaly, a discrepancy, or a puzzle that compels one to notice it and then to think about it and to study it. It remains the heuristic irritant that disturbs complacency and thus claims a place as a powerful generator of hypotheses.

The experimental work discussed in this chapter was supported in part by United States Public Health Service Grants MH 31154, MH 31340, MH49487, MH 44876, MH 61824, and MH 01021 and a grant from the Roy Hunt Foundation, and it is the result of the collaborative efforts of Yue Chen, Deborah L. Levy, Steven Matthysse, and Ken Nakayama, with the active participation of the Psychology Research Laboratory of McLean Hospital, Harvard Medical School. I appreciate Deborah L. Levy's helpful comments on a draft of this chapter.

The Issue of Reductivism

This shift edged the study of psychopathology from a concern with grand theories toward an empiricism that emphasized a profitable simplification, which the empirical sciences demand. Rather than dealing with formal systems that rarely yielded empirical predictions—and, in Popperian terms, were difficult to falsify—the new empiricism seemed to shun broad theoretical efforts, as exemplified in the *Diagnostic and Statistical Manuals* (*DSMs*) of the American Psychiatric Association (e.g., American Psychiatric Association, 1987), which specifically eschewed any theoretical position on both the etiology and dynamics of psychopathological disorders. The prescription in these diagnostic manuals requires descriptions of the various psychiatric disorders, relying on committees of psychiatrists to form a consensus about inclusion and exclusion criteria. The current diagnostic manuals all take an explicitly agnostic view about theories to explain disorders.

This shift has had a salutary effect on research activity, because it implicitly encourages empirical study to find the methods in the various forms of madness. The shift, however, brings with it a certain danger: Agnosticism with respect to grand theories can result in a perilous circularity in which the same disorders, like a single deck of cards that is constantly being reshuffled, are constantly being recategorized. Note, for example, the minor differences among *DSM–III* (American Psychiatric Association, 1980), *DSM–III–R* (American Psychiatric Association, 1987), and *DSM–IV* (American Psychiatric Association, 1994). Without a vigorous empirical thrust to accompany the new diagnostic classification schemas, and without some overarching theoretical template to guide that research, very little new information will be generated from mere recategorization efforts.

The new climate of empiricism, however, challenges psychopathologists to launch ever more finely grained searches for the basic elements that make up the larger behaviors that cry out to be explained. The directive now is to dive below the surface to discover why some behaviors have gone awry. John Dryden (1678/1975) expressed this idea poetically in *All for Love*: "Errors, like straws, upon the surface flow;/ He who would search for pearls must dive below." A reductive effort characterizes the more productive research enterprises.

Research studies today, for the most part, have freed themselves from the Cartesian divide between the mind and the body. It is commonplace now for scientists who study psychiatric disorders to regard Descartes's separation of mind and body as an interesting historical, philosophical, and theological development rather than as a reliable guide to scientific undertakings. The cognitive neurosciences provide one example of this trend. Here, mind, brain, behavior, and consciousness ignore the Cartesian boundary between mind and body. It is remarkable that, in the history of psychopathology, each time an understanding of the etiology of a serious mental disorder was gained, that disorder disappeared from the catalogue of "mental" disorders and returned as a "physical" disorder. Pellagra and tertiary syphilis are examples of this trend. The former was discovered to be due to a deficiency of niacin, a B vitamin, the latter to infection by a specific spirochete. These severe metal disorders were thus reduced to cellular activities implicated in their etiology.

Although this procedure has been followed in the investigation of other human diseases (such as brain disorders of various types), it has only recently come into prominence in the study of psychopathology. The prescription calls for progressive simplification: from madness to the chemistry of a vitamin deficiency or the invasion of brain cells by a microorganism. I have more to say about this reductive effort later, but I want first to illustrate this progressive reductivism by describing some recent work done in my laboratory—the laboratory of psychology at McLean Hospital—on the psychophysiology of schizophrenia.

The Family as the Unit

My colleagues and I have focused on cognitive and physiological traits that are found not only in people who suffer from a schizophrenic illness but also in people who are biological relatives of persons with schizophrenia, although they, themselves, have no clinical symptoms of this disorder. Examples of these traits are a disorder in smooth eye tracking of a target (Holzman, Proctor, & Hughes, 1973; Holzman et al., 1974), spatial working memory impairments (Park & Holzman, 1992; Park, Holzman, & Goldman-Rakic, 1995), mild thought disorders (Shenton, Holzman, & Solovay, 1989), and certain dysmorphic facial features. We have adopted this strategy because it has been known since the early systematic descriptions of schizophrenia (Bleuler, 1924) that the disorder tends to run in families. Of course, it could be prevalent in certain families for many reasons. Like silverware and poverty, it can be passed from one generation to another by social mechanisms of inheritance; and like measles, it can be transmitted horizontally by infection, a biological mechanism that is not genetic—or, like hair color, the shape of one's face, and the white eyes of some *drosophila melanogaster*, it can be transmitted vertically from one generation to another and implicate specific molecular genetic mechanisms. We study selected cofamilial traits in our laboratory because we believe that in this frankly reductive project we are probably studying genetically transmitted traits and that a careful dissection of their physiology will ultimately lead to underlying cellular and genetic processes that form relevant conditions, if not the necessary one, for developing clinical schizophrenia. These reductive steps are short, and they tend to be taken without dramatic conceptual leaps. They rely heavily on the efforts of many neuroscientists who penetrate the boundaries of disciplines such as psychology, neurology, physiology, neuroanatomy, and genetics.

Smooth-Pursuit Eye Movements and Schizophrenia

Following the path of a moving target with one's eyes is not a difficult task. Because many neurological abnormalities can disrupt smooth-pursuit eye movement (SPEM), neurologists and ophthalmologists routinely examine the oculomotor system. We have found that about 50% to over 80% of patients with schizophrenia perform this task poorly, although they have no other recognizable central nervous system disease. In our first experiments, in the early 1970s, we asked patients to follow a pendulum that we made from a fishing sinker suspended from a string. We made it swing back and forth across about 20 degrees of arc. In later studies we controlled the stimulus more precisely by electronically generating a small spot of light that moved sinusoidally back and forth across a computer screen at 0.4 Hz. Using instruments that record the millisecond-to-millisecond position of the eye, we were able to observe that almost all normal people (about 95%) follow the target smoothly. Schizophrenia patients, however, showed very irregular pursuit movements; their eye movements were jerky, with irregular shifts in direction (Holzman et al., 1973, 1974). Figure 10.1 illustrates the pattern. In subsequent studies, we were able to determine that these bumpy patterns showed that the eye was moving more slowly than the target, thus falling behind it. To compensate for the eye's slower relative movement, the visual system generated repeated rapid, ballistic movements to place the fovea back on the target (Levin, Jones, Stark, Merrin, & Holzman, 1982a). Many independent investigators quickly confirmed our observations, and to this day there has been no reported failure to find this pattern of SPEM disruptions in most patients with schizophrenia (for a comprehensive review, see Levy, Holzman, Matthysse, & Mendell, 1993).

Because most patients with schizophrenia perform many tasks poorly, it is not unreasonable to suppose that this same "general deficit" (Chapman & Chapman, 1973) produces the poor SPEM, even though the task is motorically and cognitively very simple and does not seem to tax the cognitive resources of patients. Support for the view that this poor performance in generating pursuit eye movements is specific and not general comes from the observation that these same patients show normal

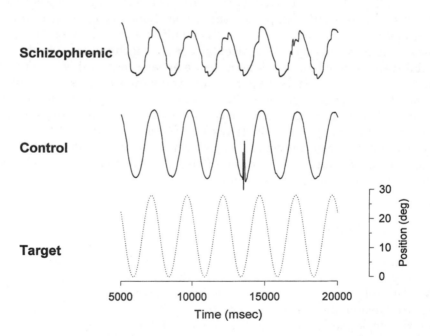

Figure 10.1. Examples of smooth-pursuit eye movement tracings in response to a sinusoidal target (lowest panel, dotted line) moving at 0.4 Hz. The top panel shows a portion of the record of a patient with schizophrenia. Note that the patient's tracing is very irregular, indicating low gain pursuit accompanied by numerous saccades. The middle panel is that of a normal participant's pursuit eye movements; it is smooth, with one interruption that indicates a blink.

performance on other eye movement tasks that are somewhat more demanding than the pursuit task, such as making rapid and accurate saccadic movements to targets that jump from one location to another (Iacono, Tuason, & Johnson, 1981; Levin, Holzman, Rothenberg, & Lipton, 1981; Levin, Jones, Stark, Merrin, & Holzman, 1982b). We were also able to rule out any role that antipsychotic medications, which are usually prescribed for patients with schizophrenia, might play in producing these pursuit abnormalities (Holzman, Levy, Uhlenhuth, Proctor, & Freedman, 1975; Levy, Holzman, et al., 1993).

Most startling was our discovery that 25% to 45% of first-degree relatives of patients with schizophrenia showed the same eye tracking abnormalities, in contrast to only about 5% to 8% of the normal population (Holzman et al., 1974). After eliminating the obvious sources of artifact, such as drug effects, motivation, and measurement errors, we embarked on a systematic effort of simplification and reduction to more basic processes that could explain the presence of smooth-pursuit abnormalities.

First, however, we searched for obvious reasons why schizophrenia and abnormal SPEM should go together. We could find none. Researchers in neurology and genetics frequently confront the curious co-occurrence of unexpected characteristics. In these disciplines, disparate symptoms within a patient, or between a patient and family members, can actually yield clues about the mechanism of a particular disease. For example, in phenylketonuria, mental retardation and light pigmentation of the hair, skin, and eyes co-occur. This conjunction was not appreciated until the role of tyrosine hydroxylase, which affects both traits, was detected in this autosomal recessive disorder. The co-occurrence of schizophrenia and abnormal eye tracking, therefore, is a puzzle, the solution to which may lead to the basic processes involved in schizophrenia. The search for the solution traverses the route of progressive simplification, which involves reducing the larger phenomenon—in this instance, poor eye tracking—to basic physiological processes, and perhaps beyond. First, however, we explored the cofamilial occurrence of abnormal smooth pursuit to learn whether this trait was genetically transmitted.

The Genetic Strategy

The familial distribution of the eye tracking dysfunction (ETD) suggested that an autosomal dominant mode of familial transmission was a reasonable hypothesis, because in almost every family we had studied, a person with ETD had at least one parent with ETD (Holzman et al., 1974; Holzman, Solomon, Levin, & Waternaux, 1984). Establishing a genetic cause for this distribution required a carefully controlled twin study, in which the concordance of ETD among monozygotic (MZ) twins (who share 100% of their genes) would be compared with that among dizygotic (DZ) twins (who share about 50% of their genes). We selected samples of twins, who had been previously studied by the Norwegian psychiatrist Einar Kringlen, with respect to their concordance for clinical schizophrenia. Kringlen (1967) found that the concordance for clinical schizophrenia in his sample of MZ twins ranged from 25% to 38%, and averaged about 9% in his DZ twins, depending on how restrictive the diagnosis was. Kringlen's sample was particularly important for our work, because between 68% and 75% of his sample were discordant for clinical schizophrenia, and we selected only the discordant twins for our study. Clinically discordant twins were critical for the task of distinguishing between ETD secondary to being ill and ETD due to a shared genotype. We predicted that if ETD were a genetically transmitted trait, then the concordance for ETD in this sample of discordant twins should be about 100% in the MZ pairs and about 50% in the DZ pairs. Indeed, in two separate studies we found that ETD was twice as concordant in the MZ pairs as in the DZ pairs, with concordances approximating those we had predicted (Holzman, Kringlen, Levy, & Haberman, 1980; Holzman et al., 1977). Specifically, among the clinically discordant twins, 80% of the MZ twins and 40% of the DZ twins were concordant for ETD.

The distribution of ETD among the DZ twins, however, puzzled us, because it contained a curious feature. Of the 30 sets of DZ twins in the two studies, there were 5 sets in which the twin with schizophrenia, the proband, had normal eye tracking, but the healthy cotwin had ETD. We had noted the same pattern in a previous study: An occasional patient with schizophrenia who had normal eye tracking had a clinically normal first-degree relative with ETD (Holzman et al., 1984). This unexpected distribution suggested that ETD is not an outcome of having a schizophrenic psychosis, because many healthy relatives show poor pursuit. It also rules out a multiple-threshold model in which ETD has a lower threshold than schizophrenia, because many patients with schizophrenia have normal eye tracking.

Using those data, my colleague Steven Matthysse constructed a model that encompassed these occurrences, which he called the "modified Mendelian latent trait hypothesis" (Matthysse, Holzman, & Lange, 1986). The model proposes the existence of a latent trait, that is, a trait that is not yet measurable, or even apparent. The trait can be expressed either as clinical schizophrenia, ETD, or both. What is genetically transmitted is the latent trait, in a pattern that is closer to a dominant gene than either schizophrenia or ETD alone. The model thus suggests that schizophrenia is the rare form of a more prevalent phenotype that includes schizophrenia, ETD, and perhaps other phenotypes that could be studied and parsed more easily than the broad diagnostic class called *schizophrenia*. Probabilities of the occurrence of either schizophrenia or ETD can be computed in family members of a proband. This model fit our previously gathered data and now could now be tested in a new study. Figure 10.2 presents a schematic representation of the latent trait hypothesis.

When seen as a new formulation about the nature of schizophrenia, the model possesses a generative power. Research on the disease process now focuses not on schizophrenia as the principal entity that is transmitted but on the *latent trait*, which can be thought of as a process that can invade one brain region or another and give rise to different symptoms, depending on the region that is invaded. First-degree relatives, too, will be at risk for having the same disease process, but that process will cause ETD with a high probability and schizophrenia with a much lower probability. The latent trait model fit the data for schizophrenia, but in bipolar affective psychoses ETD was seen as the result of the disease or treatment for the disease, inasmuch as lithium salts induce ETD (Holzman, O'Brian, & Waternaux, 1991; Levy et al., 1985).

Support for the model required an independent test on new data, because the crucial test of any hypothesis is the degree to which it can predict the outcome in new experiments. We therefore tested the latent trait model in a study of the offspring of the MZ and DZ discordant twins we had previously tested. This experiment

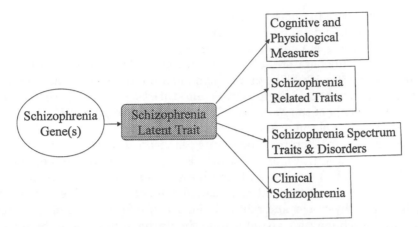

Figure 10.2. Schematic illustration of the modified Mendelian latent trait model. The causal chain in this model is roughly as follows: The gene or genes give rise to a schizophrenia disposition, which Matthysse et al. (1986) called a *latent* trait (shaded to indicate it is not [yet] an observable entity) and which Meehl (1990) referred to as *schizotaxia* or *hypokrisia*. The predisposition can independently give rise to clinical schizophrenia, schizophrenia-related traits (such as interpersonal aversiveness), diagnosable schizotypy or other schizophrenia spectrum disorders, or deviant performance on the several laboratory tests associated with schizophrenia (such as eye tracking dysfunction). These outcomes are independent of each other but are conditioned on the presence of the schizophrenia predisposition.

was based on the fact that the offspring of the clinically normal MZ cotwins of the schizophrenic probands are legally nieces and nephews of the ill twin, but because they were reared in a family with no schizophrenic parent, the study is in effect a cross-fostering or adoption study. The offspring of the unaffected DZ cotwins are biologically second-degree relatives of the affected twin and present an interesting comparison group for the offspring of the MZ cotwins. The prevalence of both schizophrenia and ETD in the offspring of the MZ probands should be the same as in the offspring of the MZ cotwins. However, the prevalence in the offspring of the DZ cotwins should be much less than in the offspring of the DZ probands. The latent trait model predicted the number of offspring with either schizophrenia or ETD, and indeed, there were no significant differences between the predictions and the obtained frequencies. This study of 120 offspring of MZ and DZ twins discordant for schizophrenia and 42 offspring of MZ twins discordant for other psychotic conditions (e.g., mania and schizophreniform psychosis) supported the formulation that when schizophrenia and ETD are considered together as alternate, independent expressions of the latent trait, the distribution of these two traits fit a pattern predicted by a dominant autosomal gene (Holzman et al., 1988).

In studying the genetics of schizophrenia using chromosomal linkage analysis, we were emboldened by these data to adopt the strategy of using ETD as a more prevalent phenotype than schizophrenia, which we regard now as the rarer form of the phenotype. We began a collaborative study with Josef Parnas, of the Institute for Preventive Medicine in Copenhagen, to collect data on five large families in Denmark. The data include detailed psychiatric interviews, SPEM records, samples of thought disorder, and DNA samples. These records are currently being analyzed. Thus far, we have full data on 385 people, which include 34 with a diagnosis of schizophrenia and 139 with ETD, giving us a fourfold increase in the number of affected individuals and thus adding significant statistical power to the search for a linkage. James Gusella of the Molecular Neurogenetics Section of Harvard Medical School is leading the molecular analysis of these data.

Researchers at our laboratory have thus partitioned schizophrenia into two related but independent entities, one of which, ETD, can itself be further refined and progressively reduced to smaller and smaller entities that will yield their secrets more easily than has the broad category called schizophrenia. The parsing of ETD begins with psychophysiology and requires the use of several psychological research tools, including psychophysics, to determine the pathophysiology of the pursuit eye movement abnormality that, putatively, is an independent expression of schizophrenia.

The Pathophysiology of ETD

SPEM can be generated either voluntarily or involuntarily. The latter may occur, for example, when one wants to read one's watch or a sign while one is walking or running. These eye movements help us keep our surrounding visual world stable while our retinal images are in constant flux as we move about. In this instance, our eyes are moved reflexively to keep the object on the fovea despite our head and body movements. These involuntary, reflexive SPEMs, which are generated by the brain stem and the vestibular system, function normally in patients with schizophrenia (Levy, Holzman, & Proctor, 1978). It is the voluntarily generated SPEMs that are abnormal in schizophrenia. As I mentioned earlier, voluntary SPEM is easy to generate. All one needs to do is attend to a moving object, such as a car rolling along a highway, a tennis ball being returned across the net, or a bird in flight. Often one must make an effort *not* to follow the object in order to stop the eyes' voluntary pursuit movements. Furthermore, in the absence of a moving target, smooth pursuit cannot be effectively generated.

Simple as they appear to be, however, these voluntary SPEMs involve complex activities, and they must be broken down into their components. SPEM consists of two basic processes: one that initiates the pursuit movement and one that maintains it. Both of these, in turn, depend on the brain's ability to transmit the presence of motion signals from a visual stimulus to specific centers in the brain and on intact pathways in the brain for processing these motion signals once they have arrived there. Of course, SPEM requires an intact motor apparatus for executing the pursuit movements: the extra-ocular musculature that generates eye movements. Impairment in any of these will disrupt SPEM. A systematic inventory of these requirements indicates that in patients with schizophrenia, visual sensitivity and the capacity to detect a change in the visual surround are unimpaired. Patients with schizophrenia recognize when a target jumps from one location to another. The latencies and accuracies of their saccadic eye movements are also unimpaired (Iacono et al., 1981; Levin et al., 1981, 1982b). They also recognize when a target is being moved smoothly across a screen. The motor pathways also function normally, because they are able to make smooth eye movements when their eyes are stimulated by the vestibular system, as in the phenomena of nystagmus, the optokinetic reflex, or the oculocephalic reflex (Latham, Holzman, Manschreck, & Tole, 1981; Levin et al., 1981, 1982b; Levy et al., 1978; Lipton, Levin, & Holzman, 1980). It appears that only SPEM to a moving target is impaired.

The Role of Motion Discrimination

Following a target accurately requires that the eye track the speed of the target accurately. The ratio of eye velocity to target velocity provides a measure of the efficiency of SPEM during target pursuit. This ratio is commonly referred to as pursuit *gain*. Normal gain is usually unity, indicating that eye speed accurately matches target speed. Impairments of SPEM are recognized when gain is reduced. Most studies have found that gain scores tend to be low in patients with schizophrenia, although there is considerable variability among these patients, with gain scores ranging from about .65 to 1.0 and the average being about .85 (Levy, Holzman, et al., 1993).

In seeking to understand the nature of ETD, the reductivist strategy requires that one ask why gain is reduced in schizophrenia. A defect in motion perception suggests itself as a likely reason. We were attracted to this hypothesis because previous research had shown that of the more than 20 distinct areas in the extrastriate cortex of macaque and owl monkeys that have been identified, the middle temporal area (MT) and the medial–superior–temporal area (MST) play an important role in the processing of motion information and in the control of pursuit eye movements (Maunsell & Newsome, 1987; Van Essen & Maunsell, 1983). Extensive physiological studies indicate that Area MT, lying deep within the posterior bank of the superior temporal sulcus, at the junction of the temporal, occipital, and parietal lobes, is mainly activated by motion signals and is referred to as the visual motion center of the brain (Zeki, 1974). Cells in this area respond selectively to the direction of motion and are tuned to the velocity of a moving target as well as to apparent motion (Albright, 1984; Allman, Miezin, & McGuinness, 1985; Mikami, Newsome, & Wurtz, 1986). Moreover, both the MT and MST areas contain cells that respond vigorously during SPEM. Lesions of Area MT result in motion detection deficits and produce abnormal SPEM (Newsome, Wurtz, Dursteler, & Mikami, 1985), but contrast sensitivity remains intact (Newsome & Pare, 1988).

Lesions of Area MT produce eye movement patterns like those we found in ETD in schizophrenia. These include compensatory saccades and dysmetric saccades (underestimating the amplitude required for an accurate saccade) only to moving targets (but not to stationary targets). This suggests that information about the position of a target is preserved after these lesions but that velocity discrimination is not. In studies with humans, Plant, Laxer, Barbaro, Schiffman, and Nakayama (1993) and Plant and Nakayama (1993) have reported strikingly similar patterns of spared abilities for the perception of motion in patients with unilateral occipito–parietal lesions. They found that in several visual tasks, only the patients' sensitivity to relatively small differences in the velocity of a moving grating was seriously compromised. There thus seemed to us to be a close connection between motion sensitivity and SPEM.

We therefore began a set of studies to examine the connection between ETD and motion perception. One way to assess motion perception is to measure how much contrast is needed to perform a specific motion task. From physiological, psychophysical, and computational studies, we know that motion perception requires contrast perception, which is necessary for other visual perceptual acts as well (Adelson & Bergen, 1985; Nakayama, 1985; Watson, Barlow, & Robson, 1983). When the mechanisms for analyzing motion signals (as well as other visual signals) are impaired, the corresponding motion perception either requires much higher contrast from stimuli or becomes impossible (e.g., Pasternak, 1987; Pasternak & Merrigan, 1994). Thus, contrast sensitivity measurements provide a common metric for assessing the functional integrity of the motion system as well as of other types of visual processing.

German Palafox and Yue Chen, of our laboratory, showed that patients with schizophrenia showed higher contrast thresholds than normal control participants for detecting small differences in the velocity of two gratings (Chen, Palafox, et al., 1999). That is, velocity differences smaller than 20% between stimuli showed significantly raised contrast, but larger differences in speeds were detected normally. The thresholds for detecting differences in contrast, however, were the same as those of the normal group, even for very small differences, when judging other visual tasks that did not involve motion, such as the slant, orientation, or the contrast itself of a series of gratings (see Figure 10.3). Using a different method for measuring velocity sensitivity, Stuve et al. (1997) found in an independent study that the percentage coherence of random dots yielded a similar result. It is also noteworthy that a significant proportion of the patients' first-degree relatives also showed raised contrast thresholds to moving gratings. We also determined that these thresholds, whether normal or raised, remained rather stable over time and therefore are characteristic of the person.

We further narrowed the phenomenon of impaired motion discrimination by testing whether impaired velocity sensitivity in schizophrenia occurred over a wide or narrow range of speeds. This study, conducted by Yue Chen and his colleagues, measured the Weber fraction. The Weber fraction is a time-honored constant in psychology: It indicates the just-noticeable-difference that a person can discriminate between any two intensities, such as heat, brightness, contrast, size, or, in this instance, velocity (Chen, Nakayama, Levy, Matthysse, & Holzman, 1999). Participants viewed two sequentially moving gratings that differed in velocity, and their task was to decide which target moved faster. The two-alternative forced-choice method, a standard method in psychophysics, was used to determine the velocity discrimination threshold. It is a simple task, and no participant experiences failure, because there is no way that a person can tell whether he or she is doing better or worse than anyone else. Our dependent measure was the smallest difference between two velocities that a person can discriminate at different base velocities ($\Delta V/V$). The base velocities we used ranged from a rather slow speed of 3.8°/s to a fast one of almost 30°/s. Most people are best at discriminating velocities in the moderate range of about 10°/s to about 20°/s. We found, as expected from many previous studies of normal participants (Woodworth, 1938), that the velocity detection thresholds ($\Delta V/V$) for normal controls showed a U-shaped curve, with the lowest thresholds—that is, the best discrimination—occurring at intermediate velocities and higher thresholds occurring at the slowest and fastest velocities. This pattern

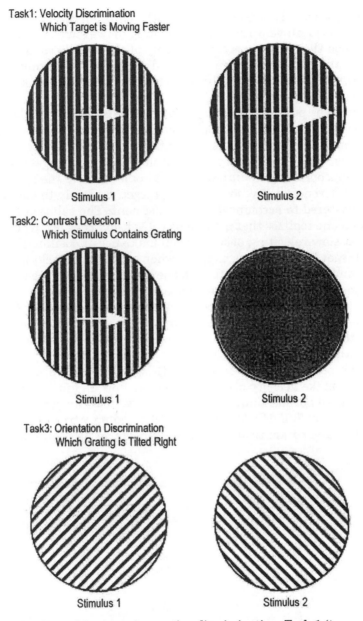

Figure 10.3. Stimuli used in assessing motion discrimination. Task 1 (top panel) presents two gratings successively, separated by 500 ms. One grating moves faster than the other, and the participant is requested to indicate whether the first or the second moves faster. As the observer judges the speeds correctly, the two gratings are made more similar in speed, until the observer cannot discriminate between the two velocities. Task 2 (middle panel) presents two stimuli, one of which contains a grating. The participant is requested to indicate which one contains the grating. The contrast of the grating is varied from trial to trial until the contrast threshold is determined. Task 3 (bottom panel) presents two gratings with tilted bars that vary in their orientation and degree of tilt. The participant is requested to decide which one is tilted to the right. A procedure similar to that used for velocity and contrast sensitivity is used to determine the orientation threshold.

is illustrated in Figure 10.4. The patients with schizophrenia, however, showed elevated thresholds at all velocities. It was striking, however, that the significant differences between the two groups occurred only at the middle range of velocities. At higher speeds, the differences were small and statistically insignificant, and at the slowest speed, the patients with schizophrenia performed at the same level as did the normal control participants.

This result was puzzling. A deficit in motion sensitivity at midrange might explain a problem patients with schizophrenia have in initiating eye movements in a pursuit task; but normal-velocity discrimination at slow speeds does not square with their difficulties in maintaining of pursuit of slowly moving targets. That is because maintaining appropriate pursuit requires that one regulate the speed of the eye to cancel small differences between it and the target, and only the slowest velocities need to be registered to accomplish this adjustment. The solution to this puzzle is apparent when one realizes that making use of velocity cues is only one way of judging velocity. At slow velocities, observers can make use of position changes to determine that a target has moved, as happens when one looks at a clock and judges that the minute hand has moved, even though one has not actually seen it move. Indeed, for a fixed time of presentation, people judge that the targets that move the fastest are those that have moved the greatest distance (see, e.g., McKee, 1981). At higher velocities, the blurring of a target tends to give one cues about the relative speeds of objects, with the faster moving targets creating less contrast because of blurring (see, e.g., Pantle, 1978).

To test the possibility that patients with schizophrenia use these subtle non-velocity cues to make velocity discriminations at slow and fast speeds, thereby appearing to be more normal than they really are, we used a psychophysical strategy often used in the testing of color vision, in which simply by randomly varying the luminance of a target from trial to trial one can cancel its contaminating influence

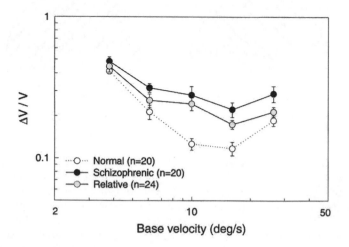

Figure 10.4. Velocity discrimination thresholds of patients with schizophrenia, relatives of the patients, and normal participants. The abscissa is a logarithmic scale of the range of velocities used in this experiment (from 3.8°/s to 26.2°/s). The ordinate, also a logarithmic scale, is the velocity discrimination threshold ($\Delta V/V$) of the three groups. Error bars denote ± 1 *SE*.

on judgments of, say, saturation. With this strategy we attempted to eliminate the influence of position and contrast cues by randomly varying them between comparison targets to see whether this manipulation raised the thresholds of patients with schizophrenia in relation to normal participants. We thus randomly varied the position and contrast from trial to trial. These unpredictable changes in the duration of a target at slow speeds, and the contrast of the targets at high speeds, effectively prevented participants from using nonvelocity cues to judge the target speed. This manipulation effectively minimized the use of displacement as a cue for inferring velocity, because it is not easy to judge how far a target has traveled compared with another target presented for a different time duration. To minimize the use of contrast as a cue about velocity in the high-velocity comparisons, we varied the contrast of the faster target comparisons among .10, .125, .15, .175, and .20.

This manipulation raised the velocity thresholds of all but 1 patient with schizophrenia, whereas the normal control participants showed no changes in their thresholds. Figure 10.5 shows this effect, indicating that when patients with schizophrenia are forced to rely mainly on velocity cues, they show raised Weber thresholds. We concluded that in schizophrenia there is defective velocity discrimination at a wide range of base velocities. Consistent with our previous findings, we noted that similar dysfunctions in velocity discrimination occur in a significant proportion of 20 relatives of patients with schizophrenia (Chen, Nakayama, et al., 1999).

We have parsed the phenomenon of ETD in schizophrenia to discover that defective velocity discrimination occurs in this disorder—but is this defect related to ETD? If it is, how is it implicated in the eye movement disturbance? Can we move back up to the broader phenomenon, perhaps to explain some aspect of ETD?

Recall that smooth pursuit consists, generally speaking, of two processes: the initiation of pursuit and its maintenance. The former is called the *open loop period*.

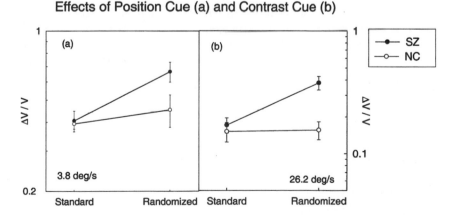

Figure 10.5. Velocity discrimination thresholds before and after randomizing positional (a) and contrast (b) cues. When administered under standard presentations of constant timing and contrasts for both stimuli to be compared, velocity thresholds of patients with schizophrenia (SZ) and normal control participants (NC) are not significantly different from each other. During randomized presentations, which prevent the use of nonvelocity cues, the groups differ at statistically significant levels.

When a person begins a pursuit movement—as, for example, when a fly comes into view and one starts to follow it—the eye accelerates from its resting velocity of 0°/s to match the velocity of the target. Usually other eye movements occur during this time, such as initial saccades that aid in placing the fovea on the target. There is a special target, a variation of a step-ramp, that Rashbass (1961) introduced to eliminate the initial saccade observers tend to make to a target. Using this target permits one to measure the latency and acceleration of the earliest pursuit response to perceived movement, uncorrected by cognitive factors, such as anticipation or prediction of target path or by feedback from one's own eye movement or target position.

When the eye begins its ramp trajectory, it normally has a latency of about 150 ms before it begins to accelerate to place the fovea on the target. This acceleration continues for about 100 ms, after which eye position begins to be corrected on the basis of retinal slip and other cognitive factors. A saccadic corrective movement may then be generated to place the target on the fovea. We measured this early period of smooth pursuit, the open loop acceleration, to three targets that moved to the right or left in a Rashbass-type step-ramp pattern at three velocities: 5°/s, 10°/s, and 20°/s, with the direction and speed made unpredictable. This arrangement produces novel motion signals in every trial. In an earlier study, we found that patients with schizophrenia showed slower latency to the first eye movement and significantly slower initial eye acceleration to the Rashbass target (Levin et al., 1988). In this present study we found the same result, as illustrated in Figure 10.6.

We then examined the relation between the velocity thresholds obtained from our Weber fractions and open-loop acceleration for the targets at 10°/s, where the schizophrenia group showed the greatest deficit. The Pearson correlation between these two variables was −.60 ($p < .01$) for the schizophrenia group but only −.18 (ns) for the normal control group. A similar relationship exists within the group of first-degree relatives (Chen, Nakayama, et al., 1999). Using positron emission tomography in a study of SPEM in relatives of patients with schizophrenia, O'Driscoll et al. (1999) found that the relatives activated an area homologous to Area MT; however, fewer than 40% of relatives with ETD, in contrast with all of the controls and all of the relatives with normal SPEM, activated the frontal eye fields during pursuit. The failure to activate the frontal eye fields was significantly related to steady-state gain, that is, to the maintenance of smooth pursuit. Similar heterogeneity in eye tracking performance is characteristic of patients with schizophrenia as well (Levy et al., 2000).

Reductivism Redux

The reductive effort that we advocate has dissected the broad category of schizophrenia into physiological components that relegate the psychotic form of the disease to a minor manifestation of a larger physiological phenomenon that includes an unexpected phenotype, ETD. ETD, in turn has been parsed into smaller physiological components that reveal their roots in impaired velocity discrimination, which in turn is regulated in the motion-sensitive areas of the parietal lobe—that is, Areas MT and MST—and probably includes an associated network that involves the frontal and prefrontal areas of the brain. We have used this method of successive simplification to probe the essential pathophysiology of schizophrenia.

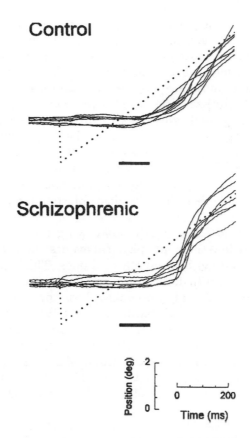

Figure 10.6. Step-ramp pursuit of a normal control participant (top panel) and a patient with schizophrenia (bottom panel). Seven trials are shown for each person. The target, represented in the dotted line, steps abruptly to the left (downward in figure) and then immediately begins a 20°/s ramp trajectory in the opposite direction (to the right). It crosses the midline, its original starting position, 200 ms after the ramp begins. About 300 ms after the ramp begins, the normal record shows a smooth accelerating pursuit eye movement toward the target in all seven trials. The patient with schizophrenia, however, executes an initial saccadic eye movement about 400 ms after the ramp begins. This saccade attempts to correct for eye position. One trial of the seven shows a weak initial acceleration. The thick black bar indicates the time window for computing the open-loop acceleration.

In a similar way, we have been studying working memory (Coleman, Ramagopal, Levy, & Holzman, 1999; Park & Holzman, 1992; Park, Holzman, & Goldman-Rakic, 1995; Park, Holzman, & Lenzenweger, 1995; Park, Lenzenweger, Puschel, & Holzman, 1996) and formal thought disorder (Johnston & Holzman, 1979; Levy, Smith, et al., 1993; Makowski et al., 1997; Shenton et al., 1989, 1992; Shenton, Solovay, & Holzman, 1987; Solovay, Shenton, & Holzman, 1987). In all instances, we have studied phenomena that appear to be stable over time and that occur with significant frequency in the nonpsychotic relatives of patients with schizophrenia.

The temporal stability of these phenomena gives them the characteristics of quasi-stable traits that occur in the absence of any diagnosed central nervous system disease, although they implicate specific brain systems and circuits. Our probes seek to move beyond the physiological arena, perhaps even into cellular areas implicated by neuroanatomy and neuropathology. Our genetic studies, too, move to the molecular level in the search for linkages between the phenomena we have been studying and a gene or genes. The latent trait theory (Matthysse et al., 1986) guides this search. The method is much like the one used at the very dawn of behavior genetics, which began with the studies on *drosophila melanogaster* by Thomas Morgan and his students at Columbia University. We have been using the tools not only of psychology, where we have been psychophysiologists and psychophysicists, but also of many of our scientific neighbors in physiology, biochemistry, neuroanatomy, and genetics.

My colleagues and I do not advocate disavowing the reality of psychological events by rushing to translate them into physical events and thereby to consider the psychological events as nothing but the physical ones. The experimental reductivism we have pursued attempts to discover the smallest number of elements or units that make up a behavior and that can explain how the more complex behaviors work. Such experimental reductivism sparks progress. Watson and Crick's discovery of the double helix structure of DNA was a triumphant example of such reductivism. Here the reductivist assertion is that all living organisms, from the simplest to the most complex, can be explained as the outcome of a simple pattern of four bases arranged as triads. Although they cause the organism, they must not be mistaken for the organism any more than the act of attention should be mistaken for neural firing in a specific brain area.

One may ask whether researchers can reverse the direction of inquiry and move up from genes to brain chemistry to brain physiology to physiology and to behavior. Although it would seem that there could be a two-way exchange, my colleague Steven Matthysse has convinced me that the effort to move from the bottom up has too many problems to be rewarding. One problem lies in the nature of the neuron itself. A neuron or neural network does not lead to only one behavioral consequence. Neural wiring patterns are unlike electrical wiring, because they are modified by experience. That is the nature of learning, and the plasticity of the nervous system accommodates the effects of experience. As for genes, any single gene is likely to have many effects, depending on mutations, allelic variations, simultaneous actions of other genes, and environmental factors.

Schizophrenia is much more complex than most of us realized. Its manifestations are varied and protean. They include not only the mild forms of the psychotic disorder within the *schizophrenic spectrum*, such as schizotypal and schizoid personality disorders, but also behavioral and physiological variations that previously have never come within the purview of this disease, such as ETD, mild thought disorder, impaired spatial working memory, and cranio–facial dysmorphic features. These associated phenotypes are familial, and they seem to have greater recurrence risks as well as relative risks than does schizophrenia itself. The new approach to psychopathology, which values the reductive method, takes researchers to the edge of predictability and holds the promise of bringing them closer to the solution of the puzzle presented to them by these brain–behavior disorders, of which schizophrenia is an exemplar. Nature's code is not unbreakable.

We stand at the beginning of a new era in experimental psychopathology. We are buoyed by the possibilities presented by new knowledge of the nervous system and of behavior and by new methods for probing into how people function, both in sickness and in health.

References

Adelson, E. H., & Bergen, J. R. (1985). Spatiotemporal energy models for the perception of motion. *Journal of the Optical Society of America*, *2*, 284–299.

Albright, T. D. (1984). Direction and orientation selectivity of neurons in visual area MT of the macaque. *Journal of Neurophysiology*, *52*, 1106–1130.

Allman, J., Miezin, F., & McGuinness, E. (1985). Direction- and velocity-specific responses from beyond the classical receptive field in the middle temporal visual area (MT). *Perception*, *14*, 105–126.

American Psychiatric Association. (1980). *Diagnostic and statistical manual of mental disorders* (3rd ed.). Washington, DC: Author.

American Psychiatric Association. (1987). *Diagnostic and statistical manual of mental disorders* (3rd ed., rev.). Washington, DC: Author.

American Psychiatric Association. (1994). *Diagnostic and statistical manual of mental disorders* (4th ed.). Washington, DC: Author.

Bleuler, E. (1924). *Textbook of psychiatry* (A. A. Brill, Trans.). New York: Macmillan.

Chapman, L., & Chapman, J. (1973). *Disordered thought in schizophrenia*. New York: Appleton-Century-Crofts.

Chen, Y., Nakayama, K., Levy, D. L., Matthysse, S., & Holzman, P. S. (1999). Psychophysical isolation of motion processing deficits in schizophrenics and their relatives and its relation to eye tracking deficits. *Proceedings of the National Academy of Sciences*, *96*, 4724–4729.

Chen, Y., Palafox, G., Nakayama, K., Levy, D., Matthysse, S., & Holzman, P. (1999). Motion perception in schizophrenia. *Archives of General Psychiatry*, *56*, 149–154.

Coleman, M. J., Ramagopal, V., Levy, D. L., & Holzman, P. S. (1999). Thought disorder and schizophrenia: Specificity and familial aggregation. *Schizophrenia Research*, *36*, 162.

Dryden, J. (1975). *All for love*. London: BENN. (Original work published 1678)

Holzman, P. S., Kringlen, E., Levy, D. L., & Haberman, S. (1980). Deviant eye tracking in twins discordant for psychosis. *Archives of General Psychiatry*, *37*, 627–631.

Holzman, P. S., Kringlen, E., Levy, D. L., Proctor, L. R., Haberman, S., & Yasillo, N. J. (1977). Abnormal pursuit eye movements in schizophrenia: Evidence for a genetic marker. *Archives of General Psychiatry*, *34*, 802–805.

Holzman, P. S., Kringlen, E., Matthysse, S. W., Flanagan, S., Lipton, R. B., Cramer, G., et al. (1988). A single dominant gene can account for eye tracking dysfunctions and schizophrenia in offspring of discordant twins. *Archives of General Psychiatry*, *45*, 641–647.

Holzman, P. S., Levy, D. L., Uhlenhuth, L. R., Proctor, L. R., & Freedman, D. X. (1975). Smooth-pursuit eye movements and diazepam, CPZ, and secobarbital. *Psychopharmacologia*, *44*, 111–115.

Holzman, P. S., O'Brian, C., & Waternaux, C. (1991). Effects of lithium treatment on eye movements. *Biological Psychiatry*, *29*, 1001–1015.

Holzman, P. S., Proctor, L. R., & Hughes, D. W. (1973). Eye tracking patterns in schizophrenia. *Science*, *181*, 179–181.

Holzman, P. S., Proctor, L. R., Levy, D. L., Yasillo, N. J., Meltzer, H. Y., & Hurt, S. W. (1974). Eye tracking dysfunctions in schizophrenic patients and their relatives. *Archives of General Psychiatry*, *31*, 143–151.

Holzman, P. S., Solomon, C. M., Levin, S., & Waternaux, C. S. (1984). Pursuit eye movement dysfunctions in schizophrenia: Family evidence for specificity. *Archives of General Psychiatry*, *41*, 136–139.

Iacono, W. G., Tuason, V. B., & Johnson, R. A. (1981). Dissociation of smooth pursuit and saccadic eye tracking in remitted schizophrenics: An ocular reaction time task that schizophrenics perform well. *Archives of General Psychiatry*, *38*, 991–996.

Johnston, M. H., & Holzman, P. S. (1979). *Assessing schizophrenic thinking* (Vol. 310). San Francisco: Jossey-Bass.

Kringlen, E. (1967). Heredity and environment in the functional psychoses. *Norwegian Monographs on Medical Science*.

Latham, C., Holzman, P. S., Manschreck, T. C., & Tole, J. (1981). Optokinetic nystagmus and pursuit eye movements in schizophrenia. *Archives of General Psychiatry, 38,* 997–1003.

Levin, S., Holzman, P. S., Rothenberg, S. J., & Lipton, R. B. (1981). Saccadic eye movements in psychotic patients. *Psychiatry Research, 5,* 47–58.

Levin, S., Jones, A., Stark, L., Merrin, E. L., & Holzman, P. S. (1982a). Identification of abnormal patterns in eye movements of schizophrenic patients. *Archives of General Psychiatry, 39,* 1125–1130.

Levin, S., Jones, A., Stark, L., Merrin, E. L., & Holzman, P. S. (1982b). Saccadic eye movements of schizophrenic patients measured by reflected light technique. *Biological Psychiatry, 17,* 1277–1287.

Levin, S., Luebke, A., Zee, D., Hain, T., Robinson, D. R., & Holzman, P. S. (1988). Smooth pursuit eye movements in schizophrenics: Quantitative measurements with the search-coil technique. *Journal of Psychiatric Research, 22,* 195–206.

Levy, D. L., Dorus, E., Shaughnessy, R., Yasillo, N. J., Pandey, G. N., Janicak, P. G., et al. (1985). Pharmacologic evidence for specificity of pursuit dysfunction to schizophrenia: Lithium carbonate associated abnormal pursuit. *Archives of General Psychiatry, 42,* 335–341.

Levy, D. L., Holzman, P. S., Matthysse, S., & Mendell, N. R. (1993). Eye tracking and schizophrenia: A critical perspective. *Schizophrenia Bulletin, 19,* 461–536.

Levy, D. L., Holzman, P. S., & Proctor, L. R. (1978). Vestibular responses in schizophrenia. *Archives of General Psychiatry, 35,* 972–981.

Levy, D. L., Lajonchere, C., Dorogusker, B., Min, D., Lee, S., Tartaglini, A., et al. (2000). Quantitative characterization of eye tracking dysfunction in schizophrenia. *Schizophrenia Research, 42,* 171–185.

Levy, D., Smith, M., Robinson, D., Jody, D., Lerner, G., Alvir, J., et al. (1993). Methylphenidate increases thought disorder in recent onset schizophrenics, but not in normal controls. *Biological Psychiatry, 34,* 507–514.

Lipton, R. B., Levin, S., & Holzman, P. S. (1980). Horizontal and vertical pursuit movements, the oculocephalic reflex, and the functional psychoses. *Psychiatry Research, 3,* 193–203.

Maher, B. A. (Ed.). (1964). *Progress in experimental personality research* (Vol. 1). New York: Academic Press.

Makowski, D., Waternaux, C., Lajonchere, C. M., Dicker, R., Smoke, N., Koblewicz, H., et al. (1997). Thought disorder in adolescent-onset schizophrenia. *Schizophrenia Research, 23,* 147–165.

Matthysse, S., Holzman, P. S., & Lange, K. (1986). The genetic transmission of schizophrenia: Application of Mendelian latent structure analysis to eye tracking dysfunctions in schizophrenia and affective disorder. *Journal of Psychiatric Research, 20,* 57–65.

Maunsell, J. H. R., & Newsome, W. T. (1987). Visual processing in monkey extrastriate cortex. *Annual Review of Neuroscience, 10,* 363–401.

McKee, S. (1981). A local mechanism for differential velocity detection. *Vision Research, 21,* 491–500.

Meehl, P. E. (1990). Toward an integrated theory of schizotaxia, schizotypy, and schizophrenia. *Journal of Personality Disorders, 4,* 1–99.

Mikami, A., Newsome, W. T., & Wurtz, R. H. (1986). Motion selectivity in macaque visual cortex: I. Mechanisms of direction and speed selectivity in extrastriate area MT. *Journal of Neurophysiology, 55,* 1308–1327.

Nakayama, K. (1985). Biological image motion processing: A review. *Vision Research, 25,* 625–660.

Newsome, W. T., & Pare, E. B. (1988). A selective impairment of motion perception following lesions of the middle temporal visual area (MT). *Journal of Neuroscience, 8,* 2201–2211.

Newsome, W. T., Wurtz, R. H., Dursteler, M. R., & Mikami, A. (1985). Deficits in visual motion processing following ibotenic acid lesions of the middle temporal visual area of the macaque monkey. *Journal of Neuroscience, 5,* 825–840.

O'Driscoll, G. A., Benkelfat, C., Florencio, P. S., Wolff, A. V. G., Joober, R., Lal, S., & Evans, A. C. (1999). Neural correlates of eye tracking deficits in first-degree relatives of schizophrenic patients. *Archives of General Psychiatry, 56,* 1127–1134.

Pantle, A. (1978). Temporal frequency response characteristics of motion channels with three different psychophysical techniques. *Perception & Psychophysics, 24,* 285–294.

Park, S., & Holzman, P. S. (1992). Schizophrenics show spatial working memory deficits. *Archives of General Psychiatry, 49,* 975–982.

Park, S., Holzman, P. S., & Goldman-Rakic, P. S. (1995). Spatial working memory deficits in the relatives of schizophrenic patients. *Archives of General Psychiatry, 52,* 821–828.

Park, S., Holzman, P. S., & Lenzenweger, M. F. (1995). Individual differences in spatial working memory in relation to schizotypy. *Journal of Abnormal Psychology, 104*, 355–363.

Park, S., Lenzenweger, M. F., Puschel, J., & Holzman, P. S. (1996). Attentional inhibition in schizophrenia and schizotypy: A spatial negative priming study. *Cognitive Neuropsychiatry, 1*, 125–149.

Pasternak, T. (1987). Discrimination of differences in velocity and flicker rate depends on directionally selective mechanisms. *Vision Research, 30*, 625–660.

Pasternak, T., & Merrigan, W. H. (1994). Motion perception following lesions of the superior temporal sulcus in the monkey. *Cerebral Cortex, 4*, 247–259.

Plant, G. T., Laxer, K. D., Barbaro, N. M., Schiffman, J. S., & Nakayama, K. (1993). Impaired visual motion perception in the contralateral hemifield following unilateral posterior cerebral lesions in humans. *Brain, 116*, 1303–1335.

Plant, G. T., & Nakayama, K. (1993). The characteristics of residual motion perception in the hemifield contralateral to lateral occipital lesions in humans. *Brain, 116*, 1337–1353.

Rashbass, C. (1961). The relationship between saccadic and smooth tracking eye movements. *Journal of Physiology, 159*, 326–338.

Shenton, M. E., Holzman, P. S., & Solovay, M. (1989). Thought disorder in the relatives of psychotic patients. *Archives of General Psychiatry, 46*, 897–901.

Shenton, M. E., Kikinis, R., Jolesz, F. A., Pollak, S., LeMay, M., Wible, C. G., et al. (1992). Abnormalities of the left temporal lobe and thought disorder in schizophrenia. *New England Journal of Medicine, 327*, 604–612.

Shenton, M. E., Solovay, M. R., & Holzman, P. S. (1987). Comparative studies of thought disorder: II. Schizoaffective disorder. *Archives of General Psychiatry, 44*, 21–30.

Solovay, M. R., Shenton, M. E., & Holzman, P. S. (1987). Comparative studies of thought disorder: I. Mania and schizophrenia. *Archives of General Psychiatry, 44*, 13–20.

Stuve, T. A., Friedman, L., Jesberger, J. A., Gilmore, G. C., Strauss, M. E., & Meltzer, H. Y. (1997). The relationship between smooth pursuit performance, motion perception and sustained visual attention in patients with schizophrenia and normal controls. *Psychological Medicine, 27*, 143–152.

Van Essen, D. C., & Maunsell, J. H. R. (1983). Hierarchical organization and the functional streams in the visual cortex. *Trends in Neuroscience, 6*, 370–375.

Watson, A. B., Barlow, H. B., & Robson, J. G. (1983). What does the eye see best? *Nature, 302*, 419–422.

Woodworth, R. S. (1938). *Experimental psychology* (Vol. 889). New York: Holt.

Zeki, S. M. (1974). Functional organization of a visual area in the posterior bank of the superior temporal sulcus of the rhesus monkey. *Journal of Physiology, 236*, 549–573.

11

Event-Related Brain Potential Indices of Memory Biases in Major Depression

Patricia J. Deldin, Avgusta Y. Shestyuk,
and Pearl H. Chiu

As with most psychopathologists, Brendan Maher first influenced my work long before we met through his extensive writing on delusions and language disturbance in schizophrenia. I very often referred to his work throughout graduate school and during my internship. In many meetings as a collaborator and colleague since then, Brendan has influenced my thinking with his insistence on letting the data guide my ideas and theories, instead of the contrary. He gives me reminders about the importance of open-mindedly looking at my data through his tongue-in-cheek comments about psychologists who really seem to want to be philosophers. He often helps interpret data sets that have me stumped by asking shrewd questions that lead to the "right" analysis or the "right" interpretation of the data. In short, Brendan has been a wonderful mentor, in the truest sense of the word.

—Patricia J. Deldin

Both poor memory performance and persistence of negative thoughts and recollections have long been identified as characteristic of depression and, as such, have motivated a rigorous investigation of these phenomena (Beck, 1967; Bower, 1981; Teasdale & Barnard, 1993; Williams, Watts, MacLeod, & Mathews, 1997). Indeed, preferential processing of negative information, which in turn may contribute to negative memory biases, is theorized to play a major role in the onset and maintenance of depression (Beck, 1967; Williams et al., 1997). Thus, elucidating the nature of these information-processing biases is essential to a thorough understanding of depression and its treatment.

In this chapter we briefly review cognitive and biological models of depression as well as empirical findings that support and contradict these models. We then outline several possible factors that may moderate the manifestation of negative biases in depression. Throughout the chapter, we present our own data from a series of event-related brain potential (ERP) studies aimed at identifying biased memory processes.

The ultimate goal of this research program is to understand the relationship among the brain, information processing, and behavior in psychopathology. Understanding this relationship is important, in part because mental illness is not a unitary phenomenon instantiated only at one system level. Therefore, to fully understand and treat depression, mental health professionals need theory and empirical work that crosses different system levels (e.g., self-report, behavioral, and physiological). ERP technology serves as a tool to directly examine the interface of physiology and psychology.

Negative Biases and Positive Illusions: Behavioral Perspectives

In an explication of the etiology and manifestation of major depression, Beck (1967) proposed that depressed individuals hold distorted negative schemas of the self, others, and the future. Once in place, these schemas alter an individual's cognitive style, sending him or her into a downward spiral of dysfunctional negative thoughts and emotion. This spiral leads depressed individuals to focus on negative aspects of the environment, to overgeneralize, and to make hasty and arbitrary inferences based on insufficient evidence. Bargh and Tota (1988) further suggested that the activation of these schemas is automatic, and they reported that reaction time measures for depressed individuals in response to negative stimuli do not vary as a function of cognitive demands of the task. Moreover, both explicit and implicit memory biases for negative information in major depression have been identified, suggesting that a negative self-schema may be activated subconsciously. (For a review, see Mineka & Sutton, 1992; see also Bradley, Mogg, & Williams, 1994; Ruiz-Caballero & Gonzalez, 1997.)

Consistent with cognitive theories of depression, one of the most robust findings of memory research in major depression is that depressed individuals tend to remember less positive and more negative information relative to nondepressed control participants (Blaney, 1986). Specifically, numerous studies have found increased memory for negative information in depressed individuals and increased memory for positive information in control participants, which provides evidence for mood-congruent facilitation of information processing (for a review, see Blaney, 1986, and Matt, Vazquez, & Campbell, 1992; see also Bower, Gilligan, & Monteiro, 1981; Bradley & Mathews, 1983; Gotlib, 1981; Kuiper & Derry, 1982). Moreover, evidence for a negative memory bias in depressed populations has come primarily from behavioral studies of direct tests of memory, including free- and cued-recall tasks (Blaney, 1986; Denny & Hunt, 1992; Martin & Clark, 1986). Nondepressed control participants, on the other hand, typically demonstrate a bias for positive information regardless of memory task or stimulus type (Alloy & Abramson, 1988; Greenberg & Alloy, 1989; Hammen & Zupan, 1984; Isen, 1985; Matt et al., 1992).

Despite the number of studies confirming the existence of preferential memory for negative information in depressed individuals, there is some evidence that Beck's (1967) cognitive model of depression in its original form may lack the precision and depth necessary to account for certain empirical data. For example, although a majority of studies that have investigated the effects of self-schemas on memory processes have been able to identify negative biases in depressed individuals (Bargh & Tota, 1988; Bradley & Mathews, 1983; Breslow, Kocsis, & Belkin, 1981; Gotlib, 1981; Holtgraves & Athanassopoulou, 1991; Kuiper & Derry, 1982; MacDonald & Kuiper, 1985; Nelson & Craighead, 1977), they have failed to find negative biases when depressed individuals are asked to recall non-self-relevant information (Bargh &

Tota, 1988; Bradley & Mathews, 1983; Calev, 1996). Moreover, memory biases have been less pronounced in studies in which shallow levels of encoding and retrieval, such as nonsemantic processing and recognition, were used (Williams et al., 1997). Furthermore, other factors, such as severity of depressive symptoms, stimulus type, and research paradigm, have also been found to influence the manifestation of negative-memory biases.

In the remainder of the chapter we provide an overview of several cognitive and biological factors (i.e., relative activation of specific brain regions, component processing of information, stimulus type, self-relevance, and arousal level of the stimulus) that may influence preferential processing of negative information. We also discuss our own investigation of these issues and provide data from several ERP studies we conducted to examine cognitive processes and neurobiological mechanisms associated with biased information processing.

ERP Methodology and Its Utility in Studying Memory Biases in Depression

ERPs are voltage changes that are time locked to stimulus presentation. The amplitude and latency of these changes are thought to reflect the cognitive processing associated with the presentation, or pending presentation, of discrete events. Indeed, various ERPs have been related to such processes as selective attention, response preparation, stimulus anticipation, and memory (Fabiani, Gratton, & Coles, 2000). Relative immunity to demand characteristics renders ERPs a particularly useful tool for exploring the cognitive and emotional components of memory biases. Moreover, ERPs are considered the "gold standard" among noninvasive imaging methods for measuring the temporal resolution of the physiological manifestation of psychological processes (Fabiani et al., 2000).

This temporal resolution is assessed through the analysis of specific components of an ERP. ERP components reflect peaks and troughs in averaged cortical activity that tend to covary in response to experimental manipulations. These components can be further defined in three different ways, as (a) maximum and minimum voltage points within a given time frame, (b) aspects of cortical activity that are functionally related, or (c) the products of specific neural generators (Fabiani et al., 2000). We and our colleagues in the laboratory are particularly interested in the P300, an ERP component thought to reflect relatively early stimulus encoding and resource allocation during novelty assessment and in memory tasks (Fabiani, Karis, & Donchin, 1986; Kramer, Wickens, & Donchin, 1983), and the slow wave, a composite of ERP components thought to index either elaborative encoding or subsequent retrieval processes of memory (for a review, see Johnson, 1995; see also Ruchkin, Johnson, Grafman, Canoune, & Ritter, 1992; Ruchkin, Johnson, Mahaffey, & Sutton, 1988; Shestyuk, Casas, & Deldin, 2002). Because these components are thought to represent brain activation during cognitive processes and are associated with core aspects of information processing (i.e., encoding and retrieval) that are identified as potential substrates of negative memory biases in major depression, it is of clinical utility to determine the differences in ERP processing of valenced information in depressed and nondepressed populations.

Neurobiological Models of Depression and Regional Brain Activation

Neuropsychological and neuroanatomical correlates of various dimensions of emotion and mood, as they relate to memory, provide a framework within which one may begin to understand biased information processing. Indeed, much positron emission tomography (PET) and electroencephalography (EEG) evidence demonstrates that left and right anterior regions of the brain are specialized, respectively, for experiencing positive (approach) and negative (withdrawal) emotions and motivations (for a review, see Davidson, 1998). Furthermore, these findings have been related to depression in that individuals diagnosed with major depression exhibit resting EEG patterns that reflect decreased left relative to right frontal cortical activation (Davidson, 1989). In addition, the right posterior region of the cortex may be related to the autonomic arousal dimension of emotion and, as such, may influence the manifestation of the symptoms of depression (Bruder et al., 1997; Deldin, Keller, Gergen, & Miller, 2000; Heller, Etienne, & Miller, 1995; Heller, Nitschke, Etienne, & Miller, 1997; Keller et al., 2000). Moreover, a bilateral deactivation of the parietal areas of the cortex has been found to be associated with negative affectivity and depressive symptoms (Liotti et al., 2000; Mayberg, 1997). Although attempts have been made to refine these neuroanatomical and localization models of depression (Mayberg, 1997), how these findings relate to specific information processing in depressed individuals and cognitive theories of depression is still largely unknown. Indeed, what is missing from these fairly broad theories of depression is an explanation of how neurobiological changes in depression influence, and are influenced by, the psychological aspects of the disorder.

We have incorporated these localization models into our work, and in subsequent sections of this chapter we discuss ERP studies in which we and our colleagues have investigated memory processing of valenced stimuli, focusing on the differences in ERP amplitudes over parietal sites. We anticipate a decrease in the cognitive functions that are closely associated with diminished activity of the parietal brain regions in general (i.e., phonological loop of the working memory) and right parietal areas of the cortex more specifically (i.e., nonverbal processing, such as face recognition and encoding). Moreover, because deactivation in parietal areas may be associated with negative emotional states, we suggest that negative-memory biases in depression may be especially prominent during tasks that use these areas (e.g., working memory, long-term memory encoding, and face processing).

Component Processing and Working Memory

Negative biases in depression have been found most reliably in paradigms that require elaborative encoding strategies, such as deep semantic encoding (Teasdale & Barnard, 1993). Thus, using tasks that are less demanding of participants' conscious cognitive resources may consequently be less likely to elicit negative biases in depression (Williams et al., 1997). Furthermore, preferential negative processing of information in depression is more evident in paradigms that use free recall, compared with recognition or facilitated recall, which suggests two possibilities: that (a) given equal encoding of the material, negative biases emerge during the retrieval process and are sensitive to the cognitive demands of the task and (b) both encoding and retrieval processes of stimuli can potentially produce memory biases in depression and are dependent on task characteristics and the depth with which information is processed. Indeed, Williams et al. (1997) proposed that traditional cognitive theories of the relationship between emotion and memory in depression may overlook the role of these various stages and components of information processing. They hypothesized that cognitive deficits found in depression are associated with dysfunctions during the conscious elaborative stages of information processing and reported that depressed individuals exhibit preferential memory for negative information only when they are required to establish or retrieve connections between new and old stimuli and elaborate on the semantic significance of the information. Thus, both encoding and retrieval abnormalities may contribute to the manifestation of the memory biases (Williams et al., 1997).

Although numerous studies that have used behavioral methods and paradigms have successfully elucidated the role of encoding and retrieval in the etiology of memory biases, the interaction between those two stages of information processing remains unclear. Moreover, behavioral studies have limited direct access to the different components of memory processes: Researchers are able to maximize or minimize the role of encoding or retrieval processes by means of various experimental manipulations (e.g., adjusting the depth of encoding or time of exposure to stimuli), but what is ultimately being tested in any memory paradigm is the level of performance on the memory task.

ERPs, on the other hand, can provide an on-line representation of brain activity during earlier memory processes, such as encoding. For example, in an ERP study using a delayed match-to-sample paradigm, Ruchkin et al. (1992) identified a number of slow wave (SW) subcomponents with overlapping but distinct time windows, topographical distributions, and functional significance with respect to working-memory processes. Specifically, they interpreted early SW (0.6–1.5 s) as being related to phonological input operations, middle SW (1–3 s) to longer duration encoding processes, and late SW (3–5 s) to a phonological rehearsal loop in line with Baddeley's (1986) model of working memory.

Deldin, Deveney, Kim, Casas, and Best (2001) adapted the S1–S2 SW paradigm of Ruchkin and his colleagues (Ruchkin et al., 1992; Ruchkin et al., 1988) for use with emotional words. In this paradigm, depressed and control participants were presented with words of positive or negative valence and, 5 s later, were asked to indicate whether a target letter was part of the previously presented word. Deldin et al. (2001) found that the nondepressed group exhibited a larger SW in response to positive than to negative stimuli, whereas the depressed group exhibited larger SW amplitude for negative as compared with positive stimuli at the left parietal electrode site (P3) for the middle SW component (see Figure 11.1). Furthermore, the depressed participants demonstrated a smaller SW amplitude in response to positive stimuli than did the control group, but there was no difference between the groups in SW processing of the negative stimuli (Deldin et al., 2001). These results are consistent with Deldin's (1996) previous finding of a positive processing bias in a nondepressed population and provide evidence for a negative-memory bias in depression. In the context of Graf and Mandler's (1984) model, we further interpret the early SW as corresponding to the activation of perceptual and semantic representations associated with integration, whereas the longer duration encoding processes

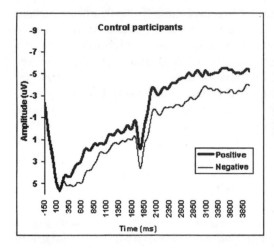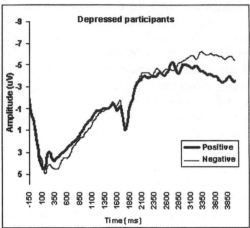

Figure 11.1. Control and depressed participants' slow wave at Site P3 in response to positive and negative words in a working memory paradigm.

of the middle SW may correspond to the strengthening of relations associated with elaboration. Thus, in accord with Deldin et al.'s (2001) predictions, negative biases in participants with depression were prominent during the encoding portion of the SW; however, the positive bias in control participants did not differ across the early, middle, or late components of SW, suggesting that the development of a positive bias spans input operations (integration), longer duration encoding (elaboration), and rehearsal aspects of the task.

Preferential Processing of Negative Facial Expressions: Beyond Stimulus-Specific Deficits

The presence of a negative bias in depressed individuals, as indexed by SW amplitude in response to valenced words, confirms and reinforces similar findings in the memory literature in depression. However, one of the immediate questions stemming from this research is whether memory biases found in depression are stimulus specific or whether they represent greater processing deficits. Consequently, depressed individuals' difficulties in processing, remembering, and evaluating facial expression have long been a focus of research attention (e.g., Mandal & Palchoudhury, 1985; Sweeney, Wetzler, Stokes, & Kocsis, 1989). Difficulties in both recognizing positive facial expressions and in the preferential attentional and memory processing of negative facial expressions have been found in patients with major depression. These deficits are consistent with what would be expected given the literature regarding the neurobiological patterns of cortical activity during face processing. Specifically, face identification and initial processing of facial stimuli are associated with activation of the right parietal and occipital brain regions, whereas working-memory processes for facial stimuli are localized to left parietal areas (Cabeza & Nyberg, 2000; Phillips et al., 1998). Indeed, research reveals that depressed individuals exhibit facial recognition deficits at site P4 as early as 200 ms after stimulus onset, as indexed by the N200 component of ERPs (Deldin et al., 2000). Moreover, in studies of working memory, left parietal areas of the brain have been found to be more active in response to happy than to neutral faces. These regions have also been found to be hypoactive in response to negative relative to neutral facial expressions (Phillips et al., 1998). In conjunction with previously mentioned neurobiological abnormalities in parietal regions in depression, these findings together suggest that memory deficits for facial stimuli found in depression may be associated with aberrant processing of valenced facial expressions in these areas of the brain.

In an extension of Deldin et al.'s (2001) original working memory study, in which verbal stimuli were used, Deveney and Deldin (2002) adapted that paradigm to include emotional facial stimuli. Doing so allowed them to (a) investigate whether SW processing differences between groups may be replicated with nonlinguistic stimuli and (b) evaluate whether SW in response to emotional words and faces is exhibited preferentially in different brain regions. Thus, Deveney and Deldin were able to examine whether SW differences are indicative of general processing biases not specific to stimulus category type and to further evaluate purportedly region-specific dysfunction in depressed individuals. They found that control participants exhibited greater SW amplitude in response to positive than to negative faces, confirming previous findings of positive bias in a nondepressed population. Depressed participants, on the other hand, showed a trend toward preferential processing of negative faces. Furthermore, depressed individuals exhibited increased SW processing of negative faces relative to controls. These effects were localized over the left posterior regions of the brain (P3) associated with the working memory processing of faces (see Figure 11.2; Deveney & Deldin, 2002; Phillips et al., 1998). These findings reinforce the presence of enhanced processing of negative information in depression. Moreover, the pattern of results seems to be quite different from the ones obtained from Deldin

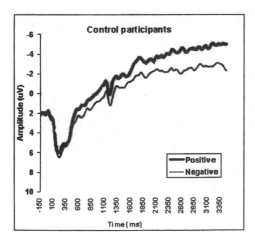 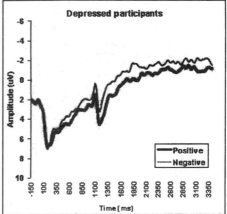

Figure 11.2.   Control and depressed participants' slow wave at Site P3 in response to positive and negative faces in a working memory paradigm.

et al.'s (2001) SW study conducted with verbal stimuli: For words, depressed participants exhibited diminished processing of positive stimuli compared with controls,
whereas in the face study, depressed participants demonstrated enhanced processing of negative stimuli compared with controls. Therefore, it seems reasonable to
suggest that although depressed individuals exhibit preferential memory processing
of negative information, the mechanisms behind this phenomenon may be different
for various types of stimuli.

Self-Schema Activation During Memory Tasks

Evidence suggests that the extent to which memory biases manifest themselves in
depression may depend on the degree to which the stimuli are self-referent (i.e.,
representative of the negative self-schema; Matt et al., 1992). An extensive literature indicates that self-referent information is better remembered and more easily
retrieved than information that is not self-referent (Greenwald & Banaji, 1989;
Ingram, Partridge, Scott, & Bernet, 1994; Klein & Kihlstrom, 1986). The superior
recall of self-referent information has been related to both an advantage in the
encoding of self-congruent information and a greater availability of retrieval cues
(Rogers, Kuiper, & Kirker, 1977). Furthermore, a number of studies have found an
advantage for self-referential negative, but not positive, words among depressed individuals and an advantage for self-referent positive, but not negative, words among
nondepressed control participants (Bradley & Mathews, 1983, 1988; Moretti, Segal,
McCann, & Shaw, 1996; Rude, Krantz, & Rosenhan, 1988). Moreover, an absence
of memory biases in either group has mostly been found in studies that have used
standard non-self-referent stimuli (Breslow et al., 1981; Gotlib & McCann, 1984;
Hammen & Zupan, 1984; Hasher, Rose, Zacks, Sanft, & Doren, 1985).

Self-reference may also facilitate direct encoding of stimuli. Miall (1986) suggested that orientation toward the self influences the depth of processing such that
any information that is encoded with reference to the self is processed more deeply
than other types of information. Thus, given the tendency of individuals with major
depression to ruminate about themselves and events that are relevant to them,
negative self-referent information may be generally more available for them (Hertel,
1998), leading to the increased accessibility and retrievability of such information.
If negative information is more easily accessed and retrieved, then negative biases
in major depression should become evident predominantly in studies that include
a self-referential condition during which a self-schema is purportedly activated.
Indeed, Bargh and Tota (1988) determined that self-referential recall is susceptible
to negative biases only when participants' self-schema is initially activated through
priming.

Given the apparent importance of self-related information for the manifestation
of negative biases in major depression, Deldin, Shestyuk, and Deveney (2002) used
self-relevant stimuli to investigate memory processes in a traditional free-recall
paradigm. The stimuli for this study were individually scripted, on the basis of responses from a questionnaire designed to elicit personal and potent responses from
the participants. Five lists, each composed of 18 proper names, places, events, and
concepts that a participant had identified as being either positive or negative in his
or her life, were created. Participants were asked to remember each word for later

recall, and at the end of each list presentation, they were asked to generate as many words as they could remember. ERPs were recorded during the encoding phase of the study. The authors found that depressed participants exhibited greater SW processing of negative compared with positive stimuli. In contrast, control participants exhibited preferential processing of positive compared with negative words. In addition, for positive stimuli, control participants exhibited greater SW amplitude than did depressed participants. The results were predictably localized over the left parietal regions of the brain (see Figure 11.3). Thus, the overall patterns of activation suggest diminished processing of positive information and increased processing of negative information in depressed participants relative to control participants, specifically in the parietal regions (Deldin, Shestyuk, & Deveney, 2002).

Arousal and Valence: Two Sides of the Same Coin?

Similar to mood-dependent memory, arousal-dependent memory is a well-documented and reliable psychological phenomenon (for a review, see Revelle & Loftus, 1992). Both internal state of arousal and arousing characteristics of stimuli are known to influence memory processes in clinical as well as nonclinical populations. In the domain of major depression, there exist at least two ways in which arousal interacts with valence. First, physiological arousal is characteristic of anxiety—a condition known to be highly comorbid with depression (Barlow, 1991). Indeed, more than half (43%–75%) of patients with major depression also meet the diagnostic criteria for one or more anxiety disorders (Angst, Vollrath, Merikangas, & Ernst, 1984; Murphy, 1984), and nearly every person diagnosed with depression reports some symptoms of anxiety (DiNardo & Barlow, 1990). Second, physiological arousal is thought to be an integral part of any emotional experience (Cacioppo, Klein, Berntson, & Hatfield, 1993), whether the arousal is seen as a dimension orthogonal to valence (Lang,

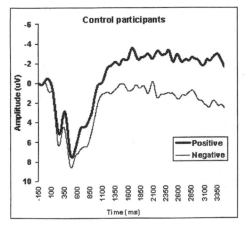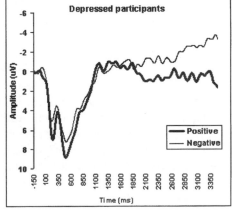

Figure 11.3. Control and depressed participants' slow wave at Site Pz in response to positive and negative self-relevant words in a free-recall paradigm.

Bradley, & Cuthbert, 1992) or as a manifestation of the relative activation of the valence dimension (Cacioppo & Berntson, 1994; Lang, Bradley, & Cuthbert, 1997).

However, although the significance of the arousal–valence interaction has been widely acknowledged, its nature is still being debated. For example, Watson and Clark (1984, 1992) have proposed that the arousal is an intrinsic quality of valence (at least in the framework of personality and psychopathology). They have further suggested that emotional experiences may be arranged along two axes: positive and negative affectivity, with arousal defining the intensity of these dimensions. Depressed individuals, then, can be characterized as being high on the negative affectivity dimension and low on the positive affectivity dimension, whereas control individuals exhibit the reverse patterns of emotional reactivity. Moreover, if arousal represents the intensity of the emotional experience (Lang, Bradley, & Cuthbert, 1990), then the effect of the valence of information on memory processes will be moderated by the arousing characteristics of that information.

A number of psychophysiological and neuroimaging studies support the idea that even though the physiological representations of valence and arousal can be separated and studied individually, one will always influence the other. For example, experiential sadness and anxiety, as well as stimulus-related valence and arousal, are known to activate convergent areas of the brain (Davidson, Abercrombie, Nitschke, & Putnam, 1999; Lane, Chua, & Dolan, 1999; Liotti et al., 2000). Moreover, studies of startle reflex, as measured by eyeblink and skin conductance response, indicate that participants exhibit differential eyeblink amplitude in response to positive and negative stimuli, whereas skin conductance response varies as a function of arousal (for a review, see Lang et al., 1990). Similarly, a significant difference in SW amplitude has been observed during the viewing of emotionally charged pictures between neutral and valenced stimuli; no difference between responses to positive and negative stimuli was observed (Lang et al., 1997). This pattern of results suggests that SW is sensitive to the arousal characteristics of the stimuli and highlights the importance of examining arousal in research of emotion and memory.

Following this rationale, Deldin, Naidu, Shestyuk, and Deveney (2002) adapted Deldin, Shestyuk, and Deveney's (2002) free-recall memory design to investigate encoding of low- and high-arousal negative and positive words in major depression. They compiled a list of 120 words, which were then separated into four distinct categories: positive high arousal (e.g., *excited*), positive low arousal (e.g., *nice*), negative high arousal (e.g., *anguish*), and negative low arousal (e.g., *down*). In the paradigm, identical to Deldin, Shestyuk, and Deveney's free-recall study using self-relevant stimuli, described above, ERPs were recorded as participants viewed and tried to remember each word. As expected, Deldin, Naidu, et al. observed a significant interaction among valence, arousal, and diagnostic group at parietal sites (see Figure 11.4). Specifically, control participants demonstrated greater SW amplitude in response to positive than negative high-arousal words, whereas there was no SW difference in processing of positive and negative low-arousal stimuli. Depressed individuals exhibited a trend toward enhanced SW processing of negative compared with positive high-arousal words. Moreover, depressed participants demonstrated greater SW amplitudes in response to negative high-arousal stimuli than did control participants. Between-group analyses revealed that the observed difference in SW processing between control and depressed participants were restricted to the high-

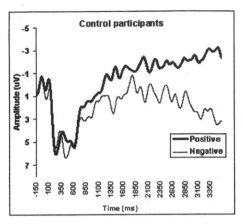
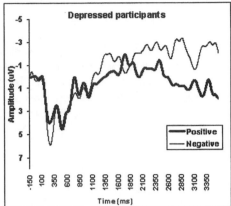

Figure 11.4. Control and depressed participants' slow wave at Site P3 in response to positive and negative high-arousal words in a free-recall paradigm.

arousal stimuli (Deldin, Naidu, et al., 2002). Thus, it seems that the manifestation of memory biases in both groups is likely dependent on the intensity of emotional activation, as indexed by the arousal qualities of the stimuli.

Conclusion and Closing Remarks

Together, the preliminary results of the studies we have described provide strong evidence of a preferential processing of positive information in control participants and suggest the presence of a bias for negative information in individuals with depression. These findings are generalizable across stimulus and paradigm types. Specifically, in each of the four studies, the nondepressed control participants exhibited a preferential processing for positive information at encoding stages of memory. Furthermore, in the free-recall study that used self-relevant information (Deldin, Shestyuk, & Deveney, 2002), and in the working memory study that used standard positive and negative stimuli (Deldin et al., 2001), the depressed group exhibited a significant bias for negative information. Also, in the free-recall study that used high-arousal stimuli (Deldin, Naidu, et al., 2002) and in the working memory study that used faces as stimuli (Deveney & Deldin, 2002), strong between-group differences in processing of negative information were observed despite marginal significance of the within-group negative bias.

A meta-analysis of the patterns of preferential processing elicited by the four studies reveals a combined alpha of $p < .001$ for the positive bias in control participants. In depressed individuals, a combined alpha of $p < .005$ supports preferential processing of negative information. However, a chi-square test investigating the heterogeneity of the negative bias found in depressed participants, $\chi^2(3, N = 4) = 6.62$, $p < .1$, suggests that the four studies may not be homogeneous. It is clearly important to delineate the factors that may contribute to this heterogeneity. Although we are at the beginning stages of understanding processing of emotional information, our data indicate that stages of memory processing; regional cortical activity; and stimulus, paradigm, and population characteristics influence the manifestation of memory biases.

Data from our laboratory provide strong support for the presence of a positive bias in nondepressed control participants and suggest the presence of a bias for negative information in depressed individuals. Moreover, these data demonstrate the influence of self-relevance and arousal on the processing of valenced information and are, to our knowledge, the first to present evidence of a physiological marker of the cognitive biases in major depression.

References

Alloy, L. B., & Abramson, L. Y. (1988). Depressive realism: Four theoretical perspectives. In L. B. Alloy (Ed.), *Cognitive processes in depression* (pp. 223–265). New York: Guilford Press.

Angst, J., Vollrath, M., Merikangas, K., & Ernst, C. (1984). Comorbidity of anxiety and depression in the Zurich cohort study of young adults. In J. Maser & C. R. Cloninger (Eds.), *Comorbidity of mood and anxiety disorders* (pp. 123–138). Washington, DC: American Psychiatric Press.

Baddeley, A. (1986). *Working memory.* New York: Clarendon Press/Oxford University Press.

Bargh, J., & Tota, M. E. (1988). Context-dependent automatic processing in depression: Accessibility of negative constructs with regard to self but not to others. *Journal of Personality and Social Psychology, 54,* 925–939.

Barlow, D. H. (1991). Disorders of emotion. *Psychological Inquiry, 2,* 58–71.

Beck, A. T. (1967). *Depression: Clinical, experimental and theoretical aspects.* New York: Harper & Row.

Blaney, P. H. (1986). Affect and memory: A review. *Psychological Bulletin, 99,* 229–246.

Bower, G. H. (1981). Mood and memory. *American Psychologist, 36,* 129–148.

Bower, G. H., Gilligan, S. G., & Monteiro, K. P. (1981). Selectivity of learning caused by affective states. *Journal of Experimental Psychology: General, 110,* 451–473.

Bradley, B., & Mathews, A. (1983). Negative self-schema in clinical depression. *British Journal of Clinical Psychology, 22,* 173–181.

Bradley, B. P., & Mathews, A. (1988). Memory bias in recovered clinical depressives. *Cognition & Emotion, 2,* 235–245.

Bradley, B., Mogg, K., & Williams, R. (1994). Implicit and explicit memory for emotional information in non-clinical subjects. *Behavioral Research and Therapy, 32,* 65–78.

Breslow, R., Kocsis, J., & Belkin, B. (1981). Contribution of the depressive perspective to memory functioning in depression. *American Journal of Psychiatry, 138,* 227–230.

Bruder, G. E., Fong, R., Tenke, C. E., Leite, P., Towey, J. P., Stewart, J. E., et al. (1997). Regional brain asymmetries in major depression with or without an anxiety disorder: A quantitative electroencephalographic study. *Biological Psychiatry, 41,* 39–48.

Cabeza, R., & Nyberg, L. (2000). Imaging cognition II: An empirical review of 275 PET and fMRI studies. *Journal of Cognitive Neuroscience, 12,* 1–47.

Cacioppo, J. T., & Berntson, G. G. (1994). Relationships between attitudes and evaluative space: A critical review with emphasis on the separability of positive and negative substrates. *Psychological Bulletin, 115,* 401–423.

Cacioppo, J. T., Klein, D. J., Berntson, G. G., & Hatfield, E. (1993). The psychophysiology if emotion. In M. Lewis & J. M. Haviland (Eds.), *Handbook of emotions* (pp. 119–142). New York: Guilford Press.

Calev, A. (1996). Affect and memory in depression: Evidence of better delayed recall of positive than negative affect words. *Psychopathology, 29,* 71–76.

Davidson, R. J. (1989). Affective style and affective disorders: Perspectives from affective neuroscience. *Cognition & Emotion, 12,* 307–330.

Davidson, R. J. (1998). Anterior electrophysiological asymmetries, emotion, and depression: Conceptual and methodological conundrums. *Psychophysiology, 35,* 607–614.

Davidson, R. J., Abercrombie, H., Nitschke, J. B., & Putnam, K. (1999). Regional brain function, emotion and disorders of emotion. *Current Opinion in Neurobiology, 9,* 228–234.

Deldin, P. J. (1996). *Information processing in major depression: The ERP connection.* Unpublished doctoral dissertation, University of Illinois, Urbana.

Deldin, P. J., Deveney, C. M., Kim, A. S., Casas, B. R., & Best, J. L. (2001). A slow wave investigation of working memory biases in mood disorders. *Journal of Abnormal Psychology, 110,* 267–281.

Deldin, P. J., Keller, J., Gergen, J. A., & Miller, G. A. (2000). Right-posterior face processing anomaly in depression. *Journal of Abnormal Psychology, 109,* 116–121.

Deldin, P. J., Naidu, S. K., Shestyuk, A. Y., & Deveney, C. M. (2002). *Differential cognitive processing of valenced and arousing information in depression as measured by ERPs.* Manuscript in preparation.

Deldin, P. J., Shestyuk, A. Y., & Deveney, C. M. (2002). *Slow wave study of memory processing of self-relevant information in depression.* Manuscript in preparation.

Denny, E. B., & Hunt, R. R. (1992). Affective valence and memory in depression: Dissociation of recall and fragment completion. *Journal of Abnormal Psychology, 101,* 575–580.

Deveney, C. M., & Deldin, P. J. (2002). *Processing of emotional faces in depression: A slow wave ERP analysis.* Manuscript in preparation.

DiNardo, P. A., & Barlow, D. H. (1990). Syndrome and symptom co-occurrence in the anxiety disorders. In J. D. Maser & C. R. Cloninger (Eds.), *Comorbidity of mood and anxiety disorders* (pp. 205–230). Washington, DC: American Psychiatric Press.

Fabiani, M., Gratton, G., & Coles, M. G. H. (2000). Event-related brain potentials: Methods, theory. In J. T. Cacioppo, L. G. Tassinary, & G. G. Berntson (Eds.), *Handbook of psychophysiology* (pp. 53–84). Cambridge, England: Cambridge University Press.

Fabiani, M., Karis, D., & Donchin, E. (1986). P300 and recall in an incidental memory paradigm. *Psychophysiology, 23,* 293–308.

Gotlib, I. H. (1981). Self-reinforcement and recall: Differential deficits in depressed and nondepressed psychiatric inpatients. *Journal of Abnormal Psychology, 90,* 521–530.

Gotlib, I. H., & McCann, C. D. (1984). Construct accessibility and depression: An examination of cognitive and affective factors. *Journal of Personality and Social Psychology, 47,* 427–439.

Graf, P., & Mandler, G. (1984). Activation makes words more accessible, but not necessarily more retrievable. *Journal of Verbal Learning and Verbal Behavior, 23,* 553–568.

Greenberg, M. S., & Alloy, L. B. (1989). Depression versus anxiety: Processing of self- and other-referent information. *Cognition & Emotion, 3,* 207–223.

Greenwald, A. G., & Banaji, M. R. (1989). The self as a memory system: Powerful, but ordinary. *Journal of Personality and Social Psychology, 57,* 41–54.

Hammen, C., & Zupan, B. A. (1984). Self-schema, depression, and processing of personal information in children. *Journal of Experimental Child Psychology, 37,* 598–608.

Hasher, L., Rose, K. C., Zacks, R. T., Sanft, H., & Doren, B. (1985). Mood, recall, and selectivity in normal college students. *Journal of Experimental Psychology, 114,* 104–118.

Heller, W., Etienne, M., & Miller, G. A. (1995). Patterns of perceptual asymmetry in depression and anxiety: Implications for neuropsychological models of emotion and psychopathology. *Journal of Abnormal Psychology, 104,* 327–333.

Heller, W., Nitschke, J. B., Etienne, M. A., & Miller, G. A. (1997). Patterns of regional brain activity differentiate types of anxiety. *Journal of Abnormal Psychology, 106,* 376–385.

Hertel, P. T. (1998). Relation between rumination and impaired memory in dysphoric moods. *Journal of Abnormal Psychology, 107,* 166–172.

Holtgraves, T., & Athanassopoulou, M. (1991). Depression and processing information about others. *Journal of Research in Personality, 25,* 445–453.

Ingram, R. E., Partridge, S., Scott, W., & Bernet, C. Z. (1994). Schema specificity in subclinical syndrome depression: Distinctions between automatically versus effortfully encoded state and trait depressive information. *Cognitive Therapy & Research, 18,* 195–209.

Isen, A. M. (1985). Asymmetry of happiness and sadness in effects on memory in normal college students: Comment on Hasher, Rose, Sanft, & Doren. *Journal of Experimental Psychology: General, 114,* 388–391.

Johnson, R. Jr. (1995). Event-related potential insights into the neurobiology of memory systems. In F. Boller & J. Grafman (Eds.), *Handbook of neuropsychology* (Vol. 10, pp. 135–159). New York: Elsevier Science.

Keller, J., Nitschke, J., Bhargava, T., Deldin, P., Gergen, J., Miller, G., & Heller, W. (2000). Neuropsychological differential of depression and anxiety. *Journal of Abnormal Psychology, 109,* 3–10.

Klein, F. B., & Kilhstrom, J. F. (1986). Elaboration organization and the self-reference effect in memory. *Journal of Experimental Psychology: General, 115,* 26–38.

Kramer, A., Wickens, C. D., & Donchin, E. (1983). Analysis of the processing requirements of a complex perceptual–motor task. *Human Factors, 25,* 597–621.

Kuiper, N. A., & Derry, P. A. (1982). Depressed and nondepressed content self-reference in mild depression. *Journal of Personality, 50,* 67–79.

Lane, R. D., Chua, P. M.-L., & Dolan, R. J. (1999). Common effects of emotional valence, arousal and attention on neural activation during visual processing of pictures. *Neuropsychologia, 37,* 989–997.

Lang, P. J., Bradley, M. M., & Cuthbert, B. N. (1990). Emotion, attention, and the startle reflex. *Psychological Review, 97,* 377–395.

Lang, P. J., Bradley, M. M., & Cuthbert, B. N. (1992). A motivational analysis of emotion: Reflex–cortex connections. *Psychological Science, 3,* 44–49.

Lang, P. J., Bradley, M. M., & Cuthbert, B. N. (1997). Motivated attention: Affect, activation, and action. In P. J. Lang, R. F. Simons, & M. T. Balaban (Eds.), *Attention and orienting: Sensory and motivational processes* (pp. 97–135). Mahwah, NJ: Erlbaum.

Liotti, M., Mayberg, H. S., Brannan, S. K., McGinnis, S., Jerabek, P., & Fox, P. T. (2000). Differential limbic–cortical correlates of sadness and anxiety in healthy subjects: Implications for affective disorders. *Biological Psychiatry, 48,* 30–42.

MacDonald, M. R., & Kuiper, N. A. (1985). Efficiency and automaticity of self-schema processing in clinical depressives. *Motivation and Emotion, 9,* 171–184.

Mandal, M. K., & Palchoudhury, S. (1985). Responses to facial expression of emotion in depression. *Psychological Reports, 56,* 653–654.

Martin, M., & Clark, D. M. (1986). On the response bias explanation of selective memory effects in depression. *Cognitive Therapy and Research, 10,* 267–270.

Matt, G. E., Vazquez, C., & Campbell, W. K. (1992). Mood-congruent recall of affectively toned stimuli: A meta-analytic review. *Clinical Psychology Review, 12,* 227–255.

Mayberg, H. S. (1997). Limbic–cortical dysregulation: A proposed model of depression. *Journal of Neuropsychiatry and Clinical Neurosciences, 9,* 471–481.

Miall, D. S. (1986). Emotion and the self: The context of remembering. *British Journal of Psychology, 77,* 389–397.

Mineka, S., & Sutton, S. K. (1992). Cognitive biases and the emotional disorders. *Psychological Science, 3,* 65–69.

Moretti, M. M., Segal, Z. V., McCann, C. D., & Shaw, B. F. (1996). Self-referent versus other-referent information processing in dysphoric, clinically depressed, and remitted depressed subjects. *Personality and Social Psychology Bulletin, 22,* 68–80.

Murphy, J. (1984). Diagnostic comorbidity an symptom co-occurrence: The Stirling County study. In J. Maser & C. R. Cloninger (Eds.), *Comorbidity of mood and anxiety disorders* (pp. 153–176). Washington, DC: American Psychiatric Press.

Nelson, R. E., & Craighead, W. E. (1977). Selective recall of positive and negative feedback, self-control behavior, and depression. *Journal of Abnormal Psychology, 86,* 379–388.

Phillips, M. L., Bullmore, E. T., Howard, R., Woodruff, P. W. R., Wright, I. C., Williams, S. C. R., et al. (1998). Investigation of facial recognition memory and happy and sad facial expression perception: An fMRI study. *Psychiatry Research: Neuroimaging, 83,* 127–138.

Revelle, W., & Loftus, D. (1992). The implications of arousal effects for the study of affect and memory. In S. Christianson (Ed.), *The handbook of emotion and memory: Research and theory* (pp. 153–176). Hillsdale, NJ: Erlbaum.

Rogers, T. B., Kuiper, N. A., & Kirker, W. S. (1977). Self-reference and the encoding of personal information. *Journal of Personality and Social Psychology, 35,* 677–688.

Ruchkin, D. S., Johnson, R., Grafman, J., Canoune, H., & Ritter, W. (1992). Distinctions and similarities among working memory processes: An event-related potential study. *Cognitive Brain Research, 1,* 53–66.

Ruchkin, D. S., Johnson, R., Jr., Mahaffey, D., & Sutton, S. (1988). Toward a functional categorization of slow waves. *Psychophysiology, 25,* 339–353.

Rude, S. S., Krantz, S. E., & Rosenhan, D. L. (1988). Distinguishing the dimensions of valence and belief consistency in depressive and nondepressive information processing. *Cognitive Therapy and Research, 12,* 391–407.

Ruiz-Caballero, J. A., & Gonzalez, P. (1997). Effects of level of processing on implicit and explicit memory in depressed mood. *Motivation & Emotion, 21*, 195–209.

Shestyuk, A. Y., Casas, B. R., & Deldin, P. J. (2002). *Memory-related slow wave processing in a free recall paradigm*. Manuscript submitted for publication.

Sweeney, J. A., Wetzler, S., Stokes, P., & Kocsis, J. (1989). Cognitive functioning in depression. *Journal of Clinical Psychology, 45*, 836–842.

Teasdale, J. D., & Barnard, P. J. (1993). *Affect, cognition, and change: Re-modelling depressive thought.* Hove, England: Erlbaum.

Watson, D., & Clark, L. A. (1984). Negative affectivity: The disposition to experience aversive emotional states. *Psychological Bulletin, 96*, 465–490.

Watson, D., & Clark, L. A. (1992). Affects separable and inseparable: On the hierarchical arrangement of the negative affects. *Journal of Personality and Social Psychology, 62*, 489–505.

Williams, J. M. G., Watts, F. N., MacLeod, C., & Mathews, A. (1997). *Cognitive psychology and emotional disorders* (2nd ed.). Chichester, England: Wiley.

12 _____

Magnetic Resonance Methods for the Study of Psychopathology

Deborah A. Yurgelun-Todd and Staci A. Gruber

As technology continues to advance at an unprecedented rate, it has become increasingly possible to examine the human brain through the application of a range of neuroimaging modalities. In patients with psychiatric disorders, neuroimaging methods provide one of the most exciting strategies for the identification of neurobiological changes associated with both the pathophysiology of the illness and the effects of treatment. Moreover, recent developments in imaging technology have afforded researchers the capability to examine *in vivo* not only brain structure but also neurochemistry and functional architecture through the implementation of magnetic resonance (MR) techniques.

Until recently, the technologies available for the direct assessment of brain structure, chemistry, and function were both costly and potentially hazardous. Although a number of techniques based on methods using X rays or other ionizing radiation have been developed and used for studying the brain in adults with neurological and psychiatric disorders over the past 10 years, these methods are not well suited for repeated studies. In contrast, most MR scanning is noninvasive and free of ionizing radiation, allowing participants to complete multiple experiments or several repetitions of the same experiment without risk. MR techniques also allow investigators the flexibility of imaging in multiple planes without having to physically reposition a participant and have therefore been used to verify and expand initial findings from computerized tomography (CT) studies. Finally, MR techniques offer superior resolution, contrast, and soft-tissue imaging capabilities. For these reasons, magnetic resonance imaging (MRI) has become the preferred modality for anatomical imaging applications.

Neuroimaging studies of patients with psychopathology are generally based on findings from previous research investigations that have identified physiologic, neurologic, or neuropsychological dysfunction in these individuals. The transfer of robust, clearly delineated methods such as those tested and refined in off-line studies provides a strong foundation for the extension of neuroimaging studies. For example, cortical dysfunction in patients with psychopathology has been described for a number of functional areas, including language-based processes such as verbal

This work was supported in part by National Institute of Mental Health Grant PO 1 MH31154 to Deborah A. Yurgelun-Todd and by a National Alliance for Research on Schizophrenia and Depression Young Investigator Award to Deborah A. Yurgelun-Todd.

memory, thought disorder, and semantic processing. Each of these domains may be associated with focal cortical changes that in turn may help clarify the underlying neural processes associated with these disorders. Regional brain changes are readily identifiable through the application of MR methods, making the examination of these functional systems feasible.

In general, MR methods are based on the fact that specified nuclei may align with or against a static magnetic field, at slightly different energy levels. Two events are necessary for the generation and observation of MR signals. Two magnetic fields are needed for a signal to be recorded: (a) a stable field (usually in the range of 1.5 Tesla to 4.0 Tesla), which is characteristic of the magnetic strength of the MR scanner, and (b) a transient magnetic field that is introduced at a specific frequency, causing a transition of some lower energy spins (aligned with the static magnetic field) to the higher energy level (aligned against the static magnetic field). This second field is typically introduced using a radiofrequency coil, or antenna. For each magnetic nucleus in the brain, a given static magnetic field is associated with a particular resonance frequency, often called the *Larmor frequency*. For example, at 1.5 Tesla, the proton resonance frequency is 63.88 MHz. When the second magnetic field is removed, usually by turning off the second radiofrequency magnetic field, energy at the resonance frequency is released from the higher energy spins as they align with the magnetic field and may be detected. This release of energy comprises the MR signal. The process by which the nuclei realign themselves with the static constant field is called *relaxation*, or *recovery* (Time 1 [T1] relaxation is within the longitudinal axis, and Time 2 [T2] is within the transverse axis; Krishnan & Doraiswamy, 1997; Mukherji, 1998).

Frequency and relaxation times of atomic nuclei within tissue are dependent on the specific molecule that contains each nucleus and the surrounding chemical environment of the molecule. Accordingly, the electromagnetic signal can be examined to produce structural (MRI), chemical (magnetic resonance spectroscopy [MRS]), or functional (blood flow, or overall blood volume, or functional MRI [fMRI]) data. Given this fact, studies of the human brain that apply all three of these techniques may be completed with the same magnet or hardware, which has been modified to collect additional MR data types. This provides an opportunity to implement a protocol that uses multiple MR techniques within a single scanning session.

Initial studies that applied MRI to psychiatric populations generally examined high-resolution structural scans. These data provided static, objective, quantitative volume measurements of select brain regions, as well as measures of whole brain volume. In this chapter we focus on the more recently developed dynamic methods for investigating brain integrity, which include MRS and fMRI. It is of note that both of these methods require the acquisition of structural MR data for localization and interpretation; therefore, the importance of this technique should not be minimized.

MRS

The first MR technique to be developed was MRS, a method that exploits the magnetic properties of nuclei with unpaired protons and neutrons. MRS is important for understanding neuropathological processes, because it characterizes the chemical content of the tissue being studied. As the technique provides investigators with data that describe not only the chemistry but also the physical environment of the tissue under study, it is possible to examine and quantify changes in metabolite levels of chemical substances such as N-acetyl-aspartate (NAA), creatine/phospho-creatine (Cre), cytosolic choline compounds (Cho), and others and relate them to changes in structural pathology.

MR visible compounds produce distinct peaks, or resonances, that are proportional to the concentration of molecules that contribute to the resonance. Thus, quantitation of resonance intensities may be used to derive tissue concentration estimates for brain chemicals. In practice, these calculations also require knowledge of the relaxation times (T1 and T2) of the molecule of interest; the data acquisition parameters, repetition time (TR) and time to echo (TE); the tissue volume of interest; and the efficiency of signal detection. The collection of these parameters is very time consuming; therefore, it is a common practice to express MRS data as metabolite ratios or in terms of institutional or standardized units. In addition, the chemical composition of gray matter and white matter are quite different. For many study hypotheses, it is important to assess the tissue content of specific brain regions.

Brain phosphorus-31 (31P), hydrogen-1 (1H), and carbon-13 (13C) spectra give rise to MR lines, all of which are generated by compounds containing 31P, 1H, and 13C nuclei. The difference in resonance frequencies for different compounds arises from interactions within molecules (Bovey, Jelinski, & Mirau, 1988), making it possible to assess the concentrations of a number of different compounds using these methods. Each nucleus has a different MR sensitivity, which in turn limits the spatial resolution of the MR experiment. Sensitivity is an important consideration in MRS studies, in that the metabolites being observed are typically present at concentrations in the millimolar range. In contrast, the concentration of brain water is on the order of 40 molar, which is the primary reason that MR images of brain water have such striking contrast. At the other end of the sensitivity spectrum, radionuclide imaging (e.g., positron emission tomography, single photon emission computed tomography) allows the detection of molecules that are present at nanomolar concentrations and is used to measure, among other applications, brain receptor distributions. Parameters for MRS experiments can be adjusted to maximize the detection of metabolites by increasing their "MRS-visibility." The most common field strength for human MRS studies at the present time is 1.5 Tesla; however, a number of research centers are currently installing scanners at a field strength of 3 or 4 Tesla. These higher field scanners are particularly valuable for MRS studies, as MR signals increase linearly with field strength, which in turn results in increased sensitivity.

Several methods are currently used for the acquisition of spectroscopic data; they include both single-voxel and chemical shift imaging. Spectroscopic data may be obtained from either single, predefined tissue volumes (voxels) or from two- or three-dimensional arrays of tissue (spectroscopic images; see Figure 12.1). It is generally easier to perform single-voxel MRS as opposed to spectroscopic imaging, because it requires less imaging time for the subject. However, when spectroscopic imaging parameters have been optimized, data sets may be obtained without penalty in terms of data acquisition time or spatial resolution. Therefore, it is ordinarily preferable to obtain spectroscopic imaging data when possible. Single-voxel spectroscopy provides information about a specific cube of tissue localized in a particular

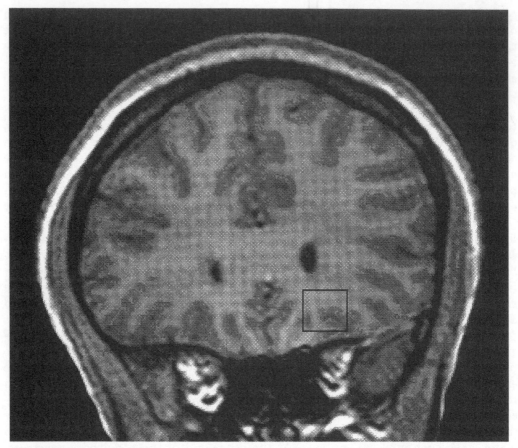

Figure 12.1. Example of a single predefined voxel described for acquisition of magnetic resonance spectroscopy data.

brain region, defined with help from the magnetic field gradients. Chemical shift imaging (CSI) is actually a multivoxel method in which a signal is collected from a wide region of tissue and may include up to an entire brain slice (see Figure 12.2). This array of data is later decoded into individual spectra from each of the voxels. In practice, most single-voxel studies of human participants include anywhere from one to three voxels per imaging session. The resolution of single-voxel spectroscopy is considered superior, as the magnetic field can be optimally homogenized for the volume selected, whereas CSI has the advantage of being able to acquire simultaneously data from multiple regions of the brain. For clinical investigations aimed at the identification of focal pathology, the single-voxel method may be most advantageous.

Quantification of brain metabolites for specific brain regions is accomplished by measurement of the spectrum or spectra after the data collection is complete. The MR signal is displayed as a spectrum with characteristic peaks associated with different elements. The area under individual peaks is measured relative to specified reference compounds, although estimation of the area under each peak is

(a)

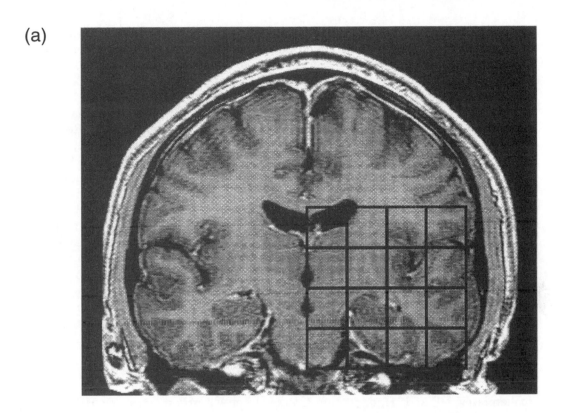

(b)

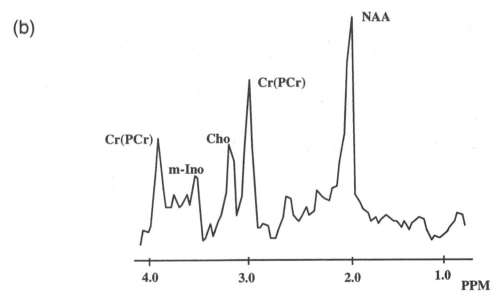

Figure 12.2. Example of chemical shift imaging. In Panel A, the box illustrates predefined tissue voxels from a two-dimensional array of tissue. Panel B shows a sample of proton spectrum from a voxel. Cr = creatine; PCr = phospho-creatine; m-Ino = myo-inositol; Cho = choline; NAA = n-acetyl-aspartate; PPM = parts per million.

often confounded by overlapping peaks. Some investigators report their findings as absolute values, and others report their data as a ratio of one metabolite to another. Interpretation of spectral data requires that saturation and relaxation effects be considered and that the underlying tissue content of the regions of interest is known and examined.

MR-visible compounds that can be measured noninvasively in the human brain include psychotropic medications, such as lithium (Jensen et al., 1996; Renshaw & Wicklund, 1998; Riedl et al., 1997; Sachs et al., 1995; Soares, Krishnan, & Keshavan, 1996), and some fluorinated polycyclic drugs (Komoroski, Newton, Karson, Cardwell, & Sprigg, 1991; Miner et al., 1995; Renshaw et al., 1992; Strauss, Layton, & Dager, 1998; Strauss, Layton, Hayes, & Dager, 1997). Spectra arising from either the lithium-7 (^{7}Li) ion or drugs that contain fluorine-19 (^{19}F) are typically single lines, which may also include signal from active and inactive metabolites. These studies have generally reported whole brain drug concentrations, because of the relatively low brain concentrations of the therapeutic agents (0.1–1.0 mM for lithium and 1–10 mM for fluorinated drugs). The validity of 19F MRS as a means for assessing brain drug levels has been validated using a primate model (Christensen, Babb, Cohen, & Renshaw, 1998). To date, ^{7}Li and ^{19}F MRS have not been widely studied in the human brain. Measurement of resonance intensities is possible for an additional number of nuclei, including phosphorus (^{31}P), proton (^{1}H), and carbon (^{13}C). Thus far, the majority of research in neuropsychiatric disorders has used ^{31}P MRS and ^{1}H MRS techniques.

Two different MRS-visible nuclei have been the focus of most studies of brain biochemistry: ^{31}P and ^{1}H, or proton. Unlike ^{7}Li or ^{19}F MR spectra, ^{31}P MR and ^{1}H spectra give rise to several resonance lines that arise from well-defined metabolite pools. Phosphorus MR spectra provide information on the concentration of high-energy phosphate compounds (e.g., PCr and nucleoside triphosphate, primarily reflecting adenosine triphosphate in the brain), and phospholipid metabolites, which include phosphomonoesters, phosphodiesters, and inorganic phosphate. Information on alterations in brain energy metabolism may be gained by measuring the relative levels of phosphocreatine (~1.4 mM/L), nucleoside triphosphate (2.8 mM/L), and inorganic phosphate (1.4 mM/L; Buschli, Duc, Martin, & Boesiger, 1994). The brain phosphomonoesters' resonance, which arises primarily from the phospholipid precursors phosphoethanolamine and phosphocholine, as well as from sugar phosphates, derives from a total metabolite pool of approximately 3.0 mM (Pettegrew et al., 1991). The *in vivo* phosphodiesters' resonance has a broad component, arising from membrane bilayers, and a narrow component, which is derived from the phospholipid catabolites glycerophosphocholine and glycerophosphoethanolamine. Phosphorous-31 MRS has proven useful in the investigation of phosphorus-containing metabolites that are associated with energy and lipid metabolism.

At 1.5 Tesla, metabolite information can usually be obtained from brain regions as small as 25–50 cm^3. Brain phosphorous-31 MRS data are typically acquired either from single volumes (voxels) using spatial localization (Bottomley, Foster, & Darrow, 1984; Ordidge, Connelly, & Lohman, 1986) or from low-resolution, two- or three-dimensional spectroscopic images (Brown, Kincaid, & Ugurbil, 1982). If desired, one can increase the sensitivity of phosphorus spectroscopy by applying a proton-decoupling technique that requires a special coil for each metabolite of interest (Luyten et al., 1989; Murphy-Boesch et al., 1993). Proton decoupling will produce line-narrowing effects for improved resolution of the phospholipid precursors, phosphocholine and phosphoethanolamine, in the phosphomonoesters' peak and the phospholipid breakdown products, glycerophosphocholine and glycerophospho-ethanolamine in the phosphodiesters' peak.

In vivo proton MRS provides a means of detecting and quantifying a number of additional cerebral metabolites, including NAA, Cre, Cho, and myo-inositol (M-Ino). NAA contributes the largest signal to water-suppressed cerebral spectra and is found primarily in neurons (Birken & Oldendorf, 1989; Tsai & Coyle, 1995). Consequently, the NAA resonance has been viewed as a neuronal marker by a number of investigators; however, the exact role of NAA and other *in vivo* metabolites is not yet known. Phosphocreatine is a high-energy phosphate, and the Cre resonance has been used as a reference standard, reflecting the fact that the total concentration of Cre is similar in many brain regions, although it is slightly higher in the cerebral cortex than in white matter (Petroff, Spencer, Alger, & Prichard, 1989). Most of the choline in the brain is incorporated in the membrane lipid phosphatidylcholine, which undergoes a restricted range of motion and therefore is largely invisible to *in vivo* MRS (Miller, Satz, & Visscher, 1991). The major contributors to the Cho peak are phosphocholine and glycerophosphocholine (Barker et al., 1994). Inositol is involved in phospholipid metabolism as well as in the maintenance of osmotic equilibrium (Moore et al., 1999).

The acquisition of ^{1}H MRS data is complicated by the fact that the signals from most metabolites of interest are five orders of magnitude smaller than the signals arising from tissue water and lipid. However, over the last several years, methods for the routine suppression of water signals (Ogg, Kingsley, & Taylor, 1994) and localized brain spectra do not contain large signals from lipids (Behar, Rothman, Spencer, & Petroff, 1994). Because of differences in the relaxation times of metabolites, spatial localization methods differ for phosphorus and proton MRS studies (Moore & Renshaw, 1997). Several methods are often used to collect proton MRS data (Moonen et al., 1989), and metabolite information can be obtained from brain volumes on the order of 1–10 cm^3. The relatively high spatial resolution of proton MRS makes it possible to distinguish metabolite differences in gray and white matter (Pouwels & Frahm, 1998), although relatively few studies to date have reported segmented imaging data in conjunction with metabolite information (Lim et al., 1998; Renshaw et al., 1997; Yurgelun-Todd, Renshaw, Gruber, Waternaux, & Cohen, 1996).

Although psychiatric investigations have generally been limited to the study of lithium, fluorine, hydrogen, and phosphorus, recent studies of neurologic patients have reported interesting findings with sodium and ^{13}C. Sodium gives rise to a single resonance line, and changes in the sodium MRS resonance have been associated with cerebral ischemia (Tyson, Sutherland, & Peeling, 1996). Carbon-13 is a stable isotope with a low natural abundance, which makes it possible to administer and detect labeled compounds (Mason, Behar, & Lai, 1996). Currently, ^{13}C is very expensive, which limits its experimental use. Over time, it is likely that ^{13}C MRS methods will be developed, which will permit the direct observation of neurotransmitter cycling by introducing a neurotransmitter or its precursor labeled with ^{13}C. Studies of each nucleus are associated with specific advantages and limitations. From a practical perspective, because each nucleus will have a unique resonance frequency at a given field strength, additional radiofrequency coils and amplifiers are usually necessary for each MRS nucleus. Therefore, most clinical studies of patients report findings that are based on a single nucleus.

Initial studies that applied MRS methods to psychiatric populations generally examined a single voxel in the brain. In contrast, recent studies using CSI have provided more extensive, quantitative measurements of metabolite concentrations in multiple brain regions. One exciting example of an extension of the CSI method is seen in Figure 12.3, in which one can see brain metabolite concentrations that have been acquired with an automated quantitative analysis short-echo program and displayed as functional metabolite maps. This procedure generates functional metabolite maps and underscores the dynamic nature of MRS as a functional imaging technique. In studies based on individual voxel acquisition, interpretation of data is dependent on the reliability of voxel placement. Even recent studies, in which high-resolution MR-acquisition techniques have been used, are constrained by the absence of completely objective and reliable anatomical landmarks to demarcate specific brain regions of interest. This difficulty in localization is due in part to an absence of formal agreement as to the cortical landmarks to be used in human MRS studies and the inability to establish isotropic cortical volumes in study subjects. For patient populations that display only small quantitative differences from control participants in brain structure and chemistry, the inability of imaging techniques

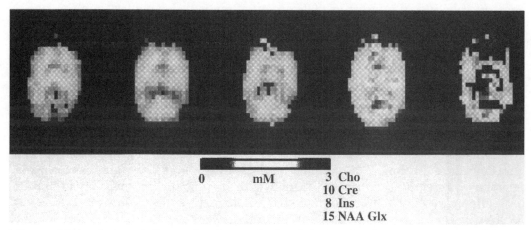

Figure 12.3. Automated quantitative analysis of short-echo (20-ms) proton echo planar spectroscopic imaging (PEPSI) at 1.5 Tesla. Maps of major brain chemicals, reliably measured at 1.5 Tesla, were created using LCModel for spectral fitting, chemical phantoms validated across sites, and software developed as part of an ongoing dual-site project between McLean Hospital of Harvard University and the University of Washington. Spectral fitting of both echoes, metabolite reconstruction, masking by fit confidence, and quantification (using the internal water signal) occur in one automated run. Areas without signal (evidenced in the center of the 20-mm axial slab formyo-inositol [Ins] and within the majority of the glutamate + glutamine [GLX] image) reflect spectra with poor peak resolution. Improvements in signal-to-noise ratio and the ability to observe additional metabolites at high field strength will greatly aid the ability to monitor disease progression. (PEPSI time to echo [TE] = 20 ms/repetition time [TR] = 2,000 ms, 32 × 32, 4-min acquisition.) Cho = choline; Cre = creatine; NAA = n-acetylaspartate. From S. R. Dager (personal communication, September 2001). Copyright 2001 by S. R. Dager. Reprinted with permission of the author.

to precisely characterize cortical regions contributes to the difficulty in reliably detecting group differences. Methodologic limitations also exist both for MR data acquisition and image-analytic techniques. Few investigators, for example, have used the same MRS-acquisition parameters, postimaging data processing techniques, or statistical approaches to data analyses and hypothesis testing.

Although studies that have used MRS have yielded an abundance of information about both the structure and chemical composition of tissue, the clinical application of MR technology is limited by a number of factors. As with any neuroimaging technique, MRS requires that study participants remain completely still for the duration of the examination, which may be difficult for children. In addition, the signal from one nucleus or from a group of nuclei may be dispersed into two or more because of spin coupling. Although it is often used for the identification of specific resonances, this splitting of the signal results in a reduced signal-to-noise ratio, because it complicates the spectra and makes the interpretation of the data more difficult. Perhaps the most significant limitation of MRS is its lack of sensitivity. The signal strength of a particular nuclei is dependent on its inherent magnetogyric ratio and the external applied magnetic field strength. Furthermore, the magnetic field needs to be precisely homogenized to acquire narrow, clear resonance peaks. The sensitivity of MRS can be increased by altering a number of imaging and study design parameters—for example, increasing the applied magnetic field strength.

Echo Planar Imaging (fMRI)

The application of functional neuroimaging to characterize cortical dysfunction in patients with psychiatric disorders provides one of the most exciting *in vivo* techniques for the identification of both pathophysiologic factors and treatment effects. The use of MRI to study changes in brain activity with either a conventional or an echo planar scanner is referred to as *fMRI*. In recent years, the number of techniques that fall into this category has continued to increase, as we mentioned in our earlier discussion of MRS methods. However, *fMRI* typically refers to a noninvasive method to assess cortical activation by measuring changes in oxidation and regional blood flow. The most frequently used fMRI paradigms involve primary sensory stimulation, including visual stimulation and motor sequencing.

Functional brain imaging studies have historically been limited both by the need to use radioactive tracers and by poor temporal resolution. Developments in the area of MRI may largely surmount these limitations. First, the development of high-speed echo planar imaging devices has greatly enhanced the temporal resolution of MRI. With echo planar imaging, single-image planes can be acquired in 50–100 ms, or multiple-image planes can be acquired each second. Functional MRI studies, which may be performed with or without a high-speed MR scanner, selectively detect image parameters that are proportional to cerebral blood flow or blood volume. This strategy capitalizes on the fact that, in general, focal changes in neuronal activity are closely coupled to changes in cerebral blood flow and blood volume.

Functional MRI studies are generally divided into two separate classes. The first includes studies that make use of endogenous physiologic factors to detect changes in cerebral activation, often referred to as the *noncontrast techniques* (Kwong et al., 1992). The second group of studies require the intravenous administration of a paramagnetic agent and comprise the *contrast techniques* (Belliveau et al., 1990). Noncontrast techniques make use of either T1-weighted pulse sequences to detect changes in blood flow or, more commonly, T2-weighted pulse sequences to detect changes in the local concentration of paramagnetic deoxyhemoglobin. The latter method has been referred to as *blood oxygen-level dependent imaging* (BOLD). In a BOLD experiment, regional brain activation is associated with changes in both blood flow and blood volume, generally leading to a washout of paramagnetic deoxyhemoglobin, which results in an increase in local signal intensity.

In human studies of brain function based on the BOLD fMRI technique, the interpretation of activation data is also constrained by the analytic strategy applied. In general, the conventional analytic methods for BOLD fMRI results require the independent application of parametric tests to time series data at each voxel sampled within the brain. Anatomic localization of function is therefore determined by statistical procedures that assess each of these time series separately and then construct a spatial map of the results. To correct for the problem of false positives (identification of spurious signals) in the image as a whole, one is required to use a stringent cutoff for alpha probability. This criterion is typically computed as a Bonferroni correction for the number of voxels analyzed. Although this correction strategy does reduce the number of false positives to an acceptable level, it tends to overcompensate, as it neglects to take into account linear dependencies between different voxels. In addition to the issue of spatial dependencies among observations, there is the assumption, implicit in standard parametric tests, that the observations are drawn from a normal distribution. The use of this stringent correction strategy also eliminates genuinely activated voxels whose signals happen to be weak. This is particularly problematic in studies of higher cortical functions where, as noted earlier, activation is known to be less robust than signal from sensory functions. This raises a conceptual difficulty in that investigators have no definitive guidelines as to where alpha should be set and whether the same cutoffs should be applied to different tasks that are likely to elicit varied ranges of signal. Nevertheless, statistical parametric mapping techniques applied with robust activation paradigms have begun to demonstrate consistent activation patterns in healthy human participants (see Figure 12.4).

The application of fMRI techniques has introduced greater spatial and temporal resolution than has previously been possible (Kwong et al., 1994). However, this increased sensitivity has been compromised by the potential confound of motion artifact. Indeed, previous investigators have found that in some fMRI studies motion artifact often produced changes that appeared to be related to cortical stimulation (Hajnal et al., 1994). With regard to small amounts of in-plane motion, a number of methods for postprocessing of motion artifacts have been developed and successfully implemented (Maas, Frederick, & Renshaw, 1997). It is of note, however, that these techniques can correct only for motion that does not exceed 1–2 mm in translation or 1–2 degrees in rotation; data sets that exceed this level must be excluded from analyses. It is therefore imperative that investigators keep the issue of motion artifact in mind when designing experimental paradigms for use with functional neuroimaging techniques.

Recent work also suggests that the magnitude of BOLD signal intensity changes may vary with participant age and sex. To investigate the effects of age and sex on cortical activation, Ross et al. (1997) measured signal intensity changes during

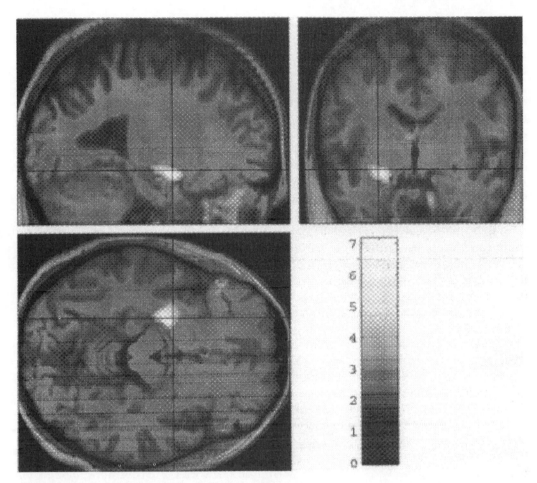

Figure 12.4. A functional magnetic resonance imaging statistical parametric map representing the average activation in 26 healthy individuals while they were viewing photographs of faces expressing happiness. The largest region of activation is located within the left peri-amygdaloid region.

photic stimulation in a group of young adults and in a group of elderly participants. The older participants produced significantly less signal change in response to photic stimulation compared with younger participants. An examination of the younger group revealed that women demonstrated significantly less signal change in response to photic stimulation when compared with men. These findings indicated that men produced greater activation in the right occipital lobe and suggest that both age and sex are important covariates in analyzing fMRI data.

Furthermore, many medications directly alter vascular tone and modify BOLD signal changes, presenting an important confound for studies of participants with psychiatric illness. The importance of this factor will be shown more clearly in the dynamic susceptibility contrast MRI data we present below. Finally, the uncoupling of cerebral blood flow and volume, which occurs acutely after cerebral activation and produces the BOLD effect, appears to resolve with prolonged stimulation. This will alter the ability to detect signal changes if the experimental paradigm does not fall within the physiologic window. In response to these problems, many research groups are developing noncontrast fMRI methods, which have a greater sensitivity to changes in cerebral blood flow.

The progress in fMRI technology is paralleled by the rapidly evolving knowledge base in cognitive neurobiology, which has important implications for study design and interpretation. As the implementation of rapidly evolving sophisticated neuroimaging methods provides researchers with the opportunity to measure brain processes with increased spatial and temporal resolution, they are left with the challenge of relating these imaging findings to meaningful units of human behavior. In general, investigators strive to design experiments that measure levels of brain function, which can be reasonably associated with their neuroimaging methods. However, the modeling of brain–behavior relationships is dependent on the definition of a number of important factors, including the identification of the level of brain function to be studied.

One important consideration in designing and understanding functional imaging studies is the neurobiologic theory on which the study is based. In recent years, the assumption underlying the interpretation of most functional brain imaging data is that human cognition can be parsed into separate components (Wise et al., 1991). The modular approach to human cognition hypothesizes that neuropsychological processing is the result of a sequence of individual cognitive components, each with its own neuroanatomic locus. Within this framework, loss of cognitive function would occur when discrete brain regions are impaired. Regional cerebral blood flow studies of the visual and motor cortex (primary sensory cortex) have supported this view with demonstrations of regional cerebral activation in discrete anatomic regions in response to sensory stimulation paradigms (Fox & Raichle, 1985). The interpretation of functional imaging data for more complex higher cognitive functions has not been as clear. One reason is that higher order functions, such as language processing, are subserved by widely distributed networks. Furthermore, models for language processing are complex and include elements of dynamic interactive activation and parallel processing (Wise et al., 1991). These factors reduce the likelihood of finding unique anatomical correlates for higher cognitive functions and may contribute to the relatively small cortical activation observed during cognitive tasks.

The second fMRI technique is based on the quantitative measurement of cerebral perfusion. Dynamic susceptibility contrast MRI has been helpful in documenting brain changes associated with a number of neurologic and psychiatric disorders. The contrast method is a tracer kinetic technique in which a bolus injection of a paramagnetic contrast agent is used to produce changes in tissue magnetic susceptibility and MR image intensity (Belliveau et al., 1990). During the first pass of the contrast agent, MR signal intensity may decrease by as much as 20%–40%. This method may be used to map the distribution of cerebral blood volume at rest or to measure changes in response to cerebral activation. Resting cerebral blood volume maps have been shown to correlate well with positron emission tomography images of fluorodeoxyglucose uptake and with single positron emission computed tomography images of cerebral blood flow. The development of a multiple-bolus method for performing dynamic susceptibility contrast studies is likely to facilitate the measurement of sensitive changes such as those induced by drug effects on cerebral hemodynamics.

Many fMRI BOLD neuroimaging studies use task activation paradigms that compare changes in resting and activated states to define neurobiologic changes. However, the interpretation of these challenge studies is dependent on the characteristics of resting-state hemodynamics. Quantitative data analysis of resting-state hemodynamics requires that the bolus of contrast material must be rapidly administered. Furthermore, it is assumed that the material remains within the intravascular compartment throughout its first pass through the brain. The mathematical techniques necessary to separate the contributions to the widening of the tissue concentration curve by the tissue itself and the finite width of the bolus are called *deconvolution techniques*. In cerebral blood volume (CBV) studies of clinical participants, the derivation of arterial input function and the selection of an appropriate deconvolution technique present important methodologic challenges for study interpretation. Technical difficulties notwithstanding, the importance of CBV data in the interpretation of BOLD data is seen in Figure 12.5. Patients taking conventional or typical antipsychotics demonstrate significantly lower cerebellar blood volume than patients on atypical antipsychotics or normal control participants.

Summary

MR brain imaging technologies offer exceptional promise for greater clarification and understanding of psychopathology. The clinical utility of MRS and fMRI to patients has thus far been limited, as no findings have been shown to be diagnostically specific for any psychiatric illness or treatment. Although many hospitals and research facilities complete MRI on psychiatric patients, this information cannot

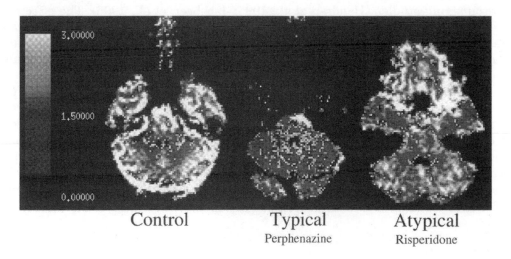

Figure 12.5. Illustration of regional cerebellar blood volume (rCBV) measures of patients with bipolar disorder taking antipsychotic medication. Patients taking conventional antipsychotics demonstrate significantly lower rCBV than patients on atypical antipsychotic medications or healthy control participants.

as yet be used reliably to generate a psychiatric diagnosis; however, scans are often used to rule out the presence of a neurological illness. In addition, the considerable cost associated with neuroimaging techniques reduces the number of referrals from clinicians who may need to protect the limited resources available for the accurate diagnosis and treatment of their patients. However, important new insights into neural changes associated with psychiatric illness have already been gained. For example, metabolite changes have been identified early in the course of illness in patients with schizophrenia and bipolar disorder. These changes are now being examined for their potential to predict treatment outcome. Within the functional domain, studies that use cognitive challenge paradigms before and after treatment have demonstrated differential activation in distinct cortical regions, indicating unique neural responses to pharmacologic intervention. Although these documented findings remain preliminary, they provide a basis from which to develop larger, more robust studies for the investigation of psychiatric disorders.

In general, two major factors contribute to the somewhat inconsistent results from neuroimaging studies. The first factor that restricts the interpretation of neuroimaging studies is the absence of standard study methods. As with any new technique, debate remains as to the optimal parameters and procedures for the application of MRS and fMRI procedures. In addition, investigators currently use a number of data analytic strategies that make assumptions about the data under study. Although several distinct strategies have emerged, new methods are continually being developed. Finally, conceptual approaches regarding how best to define and demonstrate what is abnormal, and what falls within the spectrum of normal brain variance, has remained a point of discussion.

The second factor limiting study interpretation involves the nature and extent of potential biases in the selection of both patient and control participants. Participant selection, sample size, and variables on which patients and controls are matched have all been demonstrated to be important factors for the outcome of neuroimaging studies (Hendren et al., 1995; Jacobsen et al., 1996). The effects of age and sex are potent determinants of regional morphometry, metabolite concentration, and cortical activation (Kreis, Suter, & Ernst, 1985; Witelson, 1985) and may critically affect investigators' ability to identify cortical changes among study participants from different diagnostic groups.

It is clear that the design of neuroimaging experiments requires that study parameters are set to optimize signal to noise from a clearly delineated brain region in as rapid a time course as possible. This broad strategy has allowed MR investigators to develop a number of independent procedures to address their study questions. The flexibility inherent in the development of MR protocols is a tremendous advantage for the study of human brain function; however, without a thorough appreciation of the technical and methodologic limits inherent to MRS and fMRI imaging, investigators may be in danger of producing ambiguous study findings.

References

Barker, P., Breiter, S., Soher, B., Chatham, J., Forder, J., Samphilipo, M., et al. (1994). Quantitative proton spectroscopy of canine brain: *In vivo* and *in vitro* correlations. *Magnetic Resonance in Medicine*, *32*, 157–163.

Behar, K., Rothman, D., Spencer, D., & Petroff, O. (1994). Analysis of macromolecule resonances in 1H NMR spectra of human brain. *Magnetic Resonance in Medicine, 32*, 294–302.

Belliveau, J. W., Rosen, B. R., Kantor, H. L., Rzedzian, R. R., Kennedy, D. N., McKinstry, R. C., et al. (1990). Functional cerebral imaging by susceptibility-contrast NMR. *Magnetic Resonance in Medicine, 14*, 538–546.

Birken, D. L., & Oldendorf, W. H. (1989). N-acetyl-L-aspartic acid: A literature review of a compound prominent in ^{1}H NMR spectroscopic studies of brain. *Neuroscience & Biobehavioral Reviews, 13*, 23–31.

Bottomley, P., Foster, T., & Darrow, R. (1984). Depth-resolved surface coil spectroscopy (DRESS) for in vivo ^{1}H, ^{31}P, and ^{13}C NMR. *Journal of Magnetic Resonance, 59*, 338–343.

Bovey, F., Jelinski, L., & Mirau, P. (1988). *Nuclear magnetic resonance spectroscopy* (2nd ed.). San Diego, CA: Academic Press.

Brown, T., Kincaid, B., & Ugurbil, K. (1982). *NMR chemical shift imaging in three dimensions. Proceedings of the National Academy of Sciences, 79*, 3523–3526.

Buschli, R., Duc, C., Martin, E., & Boesiger, P. (1994). Assessment of absolute metabolite concentrations in human tissue by ^{31}P MRS *in vivo*: Part I. Cerebrum, cerebellum, cerebral gray matter and white matter. *Magnetic Resonance in Medicine, 32*, 447–454.

Christensen, J., Babb, S., Cohen, B., & Renshaw, P. (1998). Quantitation of dexfenfluramine/norfenfluramine in primate brain using ^{19}F NMR spectroscopy. *Magnetic Resonance in Medicine, 39*, 149–154.

Fox, P., & Raichle, M. (1985). Stimulus rate determines regional brain blood flow in striate cortex. *Annals of Neurology, 17*, 303–305.

Hajnal, J. V., Myers, R., Oatridge, A., Schwieso, J. E., Young, I. R., & Bydder, G. M. (1994). Artifacts due to stimulus correlated motion in functional imaging of the brain. *Magnetic Resonance in Medicine, 31*, 283–291.

Hendren, R., Hodde-Vargas, J., Yeo, R., Vargas, L., Brooks, W., & Ford, C. (1995). Neuropsychophysiological study of children at risk for schizophrenia: A preliminary report. *Journal of the American Academy of Child and Adolescent Psychiatry, 34*, 1284–1291.

Jacobsen, L., Hong, W., Hommer, D., Hamburger, S., Castellanos, F., Frazier, J., et al. (1996). Smooth pursuit eye movements in childhood-onset schizophrenia: Comparison with attention-deficit hyperactivity disorder and normal controls. *Biological Psychiatry, 40*, 1144–1154.

Jensen, H., Plenge, P., Stensgaard, A., Mellerup, E., Thomsen, C., Aggernaes, H., & Henriksen, O. (1996). Twelve-hour brain lithium concentration in lithium maintenance treatment of manic–depressive disorder: Daily versus alternate-day dosing schedule. *Psychopharmacology, 124*, 275–278.

Komoroski, R., Newton, J., Karson, C., Cardwell, D., & Sprigg, J. (1991). Detection of psychoactive drugs *in vivo* using 19F NMR spectroscopy. *Biological Psychiatry, 29*, 711–716.

Kreis, R., Suter, D., & Ernst, R. (1985). Time-domain zero-field magnetic resonance with field pulse excitation. *Chemical Physics Letters, 118*, 120–124.

Krishnan, R., & Doraiswamy, P. (Eds.). (1997). *Brain imaging in clinical psychiatry.* New York: Marcel Dekker.

Kwong, K., Belliveau, J., Chesler, D., Goldberg, I., Weisskoff, R., Poncelet, B., et al. (1992). Dynamic magnetic resonance imaging of human brain activity during primary sensory stimulation. *Proceedings of the National Academy of Sciences, 89*, 5675–5679.

Kwong, K., Chesler, D., Boxerman, J., Davis, T., Weisskoff, R., & Rosen, B. (1994, August). *Strategies to reduce macrovascular effects in fMRI* [Abstract]. Paper presented at the 2nd annual meeting Society of Magnetic Resonance, San Francisco.

Lim, K., Adalsteinsson, E., Spielman, D., Sullivan, E., Rosenbloom, M., & Pfefferbaum, A. (1998). Proton magnetic resonance spectroscopic imaging of cortical gray matter and white matter in schizophrenia. *Archives of General Psychiatry, 55*, 346–352.

Luyten, P., Bruntink, G., Sloff, F., Vermeulen, J., Van der Hiejden, J., & den Hollander, J. (1989). Broadband proton decoupling in human ^{31}P NMR spectroscopy. *NMR in Biomedicine, 1*, 177–183.

Maas, L., Frederick, B., & Renshaw, P. (1997). Decoupled automated rotational and translational registration for functional MRI time series data: The DART registration algorithm. *Magnetic Resonance in Medicine, 37*, 131–139.

Mason, G., Behar, K., & Lai, J. (1996). The ^{13}C isotope and nuclear magnetic resonance: Unique tools for the study of brain metabolism. *Metabolic Brain Disorders, 11*, 283–313.

Miller, E., Satz, P., & Visscher, B. (1991). Computerized and conventional neuropsychological assessment of HIV-1-infected homosexual men. *Neurology, 41*, 1608–1616.

Miner, C., Davidson, J., Potts, N., Tupler, L., Charles, H., & Krishnan, K. (1995). Brain fluoxetine measurements using fluorine magnetic resonance spectroscopy in patients with social phobia. *Biological Psychiatry*, *38*, 696–698.

Moonen, C., Von Kienlin, M., Van Zijl, P., Cohen, J., Gillen, J., Daly, P., & Wolf, G. (1989). Comparison of single-shot localization methods (STEAM and PRESS) for *in vivo* proton NMR spectroscopy. *NMR in Biomedicine*, *2*, 101–112.

Moore, C., Breeze, J., Kukes, T., Rose, S., Dager, S., Cohen, B., & Renshaw, P. (1999). Effects of myo-inositol ingestion on human brain myo-inositol levels: A proton magnetic resonance spectroscopic imaging study. *Biological Psychiatry*, *45*, 1197–1202.

Moore, C., & Renshaw, P. (1997). Magnetic resonance spectroscopy studies of affective disorders. In K. Krishnan & P. Doraiswamy (Eds.), *Brain imaging in clinical psychiatry* (pp. 185–214). New York: Marcel Dekker.

Mukherji, S. K. (1998). The American Society of Head and Neck Radiology. Head and neck imaging: The next 10 years. *Radiology*, *209*, 8–14.

Murphy-Boesch, J., Stoyanova, R., Srinivasan, R., Willard, T., Vigneron, D., Nelson, S., et al. (1993). Proton-decoupled 31P chemical shift imaging of the human brain in normal volunteers. *NMR in Biomedicine*, *6*, 173–180.

Ogg, R., Kingsley, P., & Taylor, J. (1994). WET, a T1- and B1-insensitive water suppression method for *in vivo* localized 1H NMR spectroscopy. *Journal of Magnetic Resonance Series B*, *104*, 1–10.

Ordidge, R., Connelly, A., & Lohman, J. (1986). A general approach to selection of multiple cubic volume elements using the ISIS technique. *Journal of Magnetic Resonance*, *66*, 283–294.

Petroff, O., Spencer, D., Alger, J., & Prichard, J. (1989). High-field proton magnetic resonance spectroscopy of human cerebrum obtained during surgery for epilepsy. *Neurology*, *39*, 1197–1202.

Pettegrew, J., Keshavan, M., Panchalingam, K., Strychor, S., Kaplan, D., Tretta, M., & Allen, M. (1991). Alterations in brain high-energy phosphate and membrane phospholipid metabolism in first-episode, drug-naive schizophrenics. *Archives of General Psychiatry*, *48*, 563–568.

Pouwels, P., & Frahm, J. (1998). Regional metabolite concentrations in human brain as determined by quantitative localized proton MRS. *Magnetic Resonance in Medicine*, *39*, 53–60.

Renshaw, P., Guimaraes, A., Fava, M., Rosenbaum, J., Pearlman, J., Flood, J., et al. (1992). Accumulation of fluoxetine and norfluoxetine in human brain during therapeutic administration. *American Journal of Psychiatry*, *149*, 1592–1594.

Renshaw, P., Lafer, B., Babb, S., Fava, M., Stoll, A., Christensen, J., et al. (1997). Basal ganglia choline levels in depression and response to fluoxetine treatment: An *in vivo* proton magnetic resonance spectroscopy study. *Biological Psychiatry*, *41*, 837–843.

Renshaw, P., & Wicklund, S. (1998). *In vivo* measurement of lithium in man by nuclear magnetic resonance spectroscopy. *Biological Psychiatry*, *23*, 465–472.

Riedl, U., Barocka, A., Kolem, H., Demling, J., Kashchka, W., Schelp, R., et al. (1997). Duration of lithium treatment and brain lithium concentration in patients with unipolar and schizoaffective disorder—A study with magnetic resonance spectroscopy. *Biological Psychiatry*, *41*, 844–850.

Ross, M., Yurgelun-Todd, D., Renshaw, P., Maas, L., Mendelson, J., Mello, N., et al. (1997). Age-related reduction in functional MRI response to photic stimulation. *Neurology*, *48*, 173–176.

Sachs, G., Renshaw, P., Lafer, B., Stoll, A., Guimaraes, A., Rosenbaum, J., & Gonzalez, R. (1995). Variability of brain lithium levels during maintenance treatment: A magnetic resonance spectroscopy study. *Biological Psychiatry*, *38*, 422–428.

Soares, J., Krishnan, K., & Keshavan, M. (1996). Nuclear magnetic resonance spectroscopy: New insights into the pathophysiology of mood disorders. *Depression*, *4*, 14–30.

Strauss, W., Layton, M., & Dager, S. (1998). Brain elimination half-life of fluvoxamine measured by ^{19}F magnetic resonance spectroscopy. *American Journal of Psychiatry*, *155*, 380–384.

Strauss, W., Layton, M., Hayes, C., & Dager, S. (1997). [19]F magnetic resonance spectroscopy investigation *in vivo* of acute and steady-state brain fluvoxamine levels in obsessive–compulsive disorder. *American Journal of Psychiatry*, *154*, 516–522.

Tsai, G., & Coyle, J. (1995). N-acetyl aspartate in neuropsychiatric disorders [Review]. *Progress in Neurobiology*, *46*, 531–540.

Tyson, R., Sutherland, G., & Peeling, J. (1996). [23]Na nuclear magnetic resonance spectral changes during and after forebrain ischemia in hypoglycemic, normoglycemic, and hyperglycemic rats. *Stroke*, *27*, 957–964.

Wise, R., Chollet, F., Hadar, U., Friston, K., Hoffner, E., & Frackowiak, R. (1991). Distribution of cortical neural networks involved in word comprehension and word retrieval. *Brain, 114*, 1803–1817.

Witelson, S. (1985). The brain connection: The corpus callosum is larger in left-handers. *Science, 229*, 665–668.

Yurgelun-Todd, D., Renshaw, P., Gruber, S., Waternaux, C., & Cohen, B. (1996). Proton magnetic resonance spectroscopy of the temporal lobes in schizophrenics and normal controls. *Schizophrenia Research, 19*, 55–59.

13

Functional Neuroimaging Investigations of Working Memory Deficits in Schizophrenia: Reconciling Discrepant Findings

Dara S. Manoach

This chapter illustrates the critical importance of carefully considering methodological issues in interpreting group data from neuroimaging studies. This emphasis directly reflects the mentorship of Professor Brendan Maher. Maher takes a particular delight in grappling with thorny issues that many investigators regard as nuisance variables and would prefer to sweep under the rug. In our graduate seminars and individual research meetings, Maher repeatedly emphasized the importance of considering the heterogeneity of individuals with schizophrenia and the variability in their presentation and behavior. In his own words, "the heterogeneity that led Bleuler to refer to 'the group of schizophrenias' (Bleuler, 1911/1950) must be borne in mind if we are to understand the degrees of variability that are found in the manifest symptoms of schizophrenia" (Maher, 1999, p. 547). Because neuroimaging findings (e.g., task-related hypofrontality) form the crux of many theoretical conceptualizations of schizophrenia, a consideration of heterogeneity and variability becomes particularly important in the context of interpreting neuroimaging data. Careful consideration of these issues allows a theoretical reconciliation of apparently contradictory results, captures the complexities of working memory dysfunction in schizophrenia, and furthers an ongoing reconceptualization of the meaning of neuroimaging findings. In this chapter I hope to convince readers, as Maher has convinced me, that variability is not a nuisance variable. It might best be regarded as intrinsic to schizophrenia and as having a neural basis that requires explanation.

Working memory is a cognitive psychological construct that refers to the process of actively holding information on-line in the mind's eye and manipulating it in the service of guiding behavior (Baddeley, 1992). It is hypothesized to be a temporary store the contents of which are continually updated, scanned, and manipulated in response to immediate information-processing demands. It is a critical building

This work was supported by the Mathers Charitable Foundation, the National Alliance for Research on Schizophrenia and Depression, and the Scottish Rite Schizophrenia Research Program. I am very grateful to my collaborators in the work presented herein and to my mentors, particularly Professor Brendan Maher.

block of normal cognition and is essential for higher cognitive functions and goal-directed behavior. In schizophrenia, working memory deficits have been demonstrated in medicated and unmedicated patients (Carter et al., 1996; Park & Holzman, 1992), persist throughout the course of illness (Park, Puschel, Sauter, Rentsch, & Hell, 1999), and are relatively resistant to pharmacotherapy (Goldberg & Weinberger, 1996). They are also seen in healthy relatives of patients with schizophrenia, suggesting that they may be a behavioral marker of genetic liability for schizophrenia (Park, Holzman, & Goldman-Rakic, 1995). Some investigators have hypothesized that many of the cognitive deficits and symptoms of schizophrenia stem from deficient working memory processes that lead to a failure to guide behavior on the basis of internalized representations such as schemas and ideas (Cohen, Braver, & O'Reilly, 1996; Goldman-Rakic, 1991). Thus, the implications of working memory deficits for functional outcome in schizophrenia are profound. Working memory deficits may lead to behaviors that are stimulus bound rather than guided by context. Such behaviors will appear stereotypic and perseverative.

The participation of the dorsolateral prefrontal cortex (DLPFC) in working memory is well established on the basis of evidence from single-unit recordings in nonhuman primates and from neuroimaging studies of humans (Friedman & Goldman-Rakic, 1994; Petrides, Alivisatos, Meyer, & Evans, 1993). Although the neuroanatomic underpinnings of schizophrenia remain controversial, a wealth of data from clinical, neuropsychological, and eye movement studies indirectly implicates prefrontal cortex dysfunction. Neuroimaging studies have provided more direct evidence of prefrontal cortex dysfunction during working memory performance in schizophrenia, usually in the form of decreased prefrontal activity. However, the direction of the difference is inconsistent, and there are also reports of increased prefrontal activity. The primary goal of this chapter is to reconcile these seemingly discrepant findings and, in so doing, to illuminate methodological considerations particular to neuroimaging studies of schizophrenia. The issues of heterogeneity and variability in schizophrenia and their relevance to both the selection of experimental methods and the interpretation of group data are considered.

Is the DLPFC Under- or Overactivated During Working Memory Performance in Schizophrenia?

Neuroimaging studies of patients with schizophrenia performing working memory tasks, with few exceptions (Frith et al., 1995), have demonstrated *task-related hypofrontality* (Andreasen et al., 1992; Callicott et al., 1998; Carter et al., 1998; Weinberger & Berman, 1996; Yurgelun-Todd et al., 1996). Compared with normal individuals, patients with schizophrenia show a relative physiologic hypoactivity of the prefrontal cortex. Hypofrontality is a fairly consistent finding in spite of widely varying methods, patient status, and tasks used. Using functional magnetic resonance imaging (fMRI), several studies recently found that patients with schizophrenia exhibit increased activation of the DLPFC during working memory performance (Callicott et al., 2000; Manoach et al., 2000; Manoach et al., 1999). *Activation* can be defined as significant task-related changes in fMRI signal intensity. This finding of an increased magnitude of DLPFC activation during working memory performance in schizophrenia contrasts with the predominant finding in the literature. Discrepant findings are common in the literature on schizophrenia. Efforts to reconcile them often reveal something of the nature of schizophrenic pathology. Several plausible contributors to these seemingly contradictory findings are considered. These include both factors intrinsic to schizophrenic illness and the methodology of neuroimaging. More specifically, in this section I review the nature of the tasks used, group differences in task performance and motivation, and the use of methodologies that require intersubject averaging.

Different Tasks Emphasize Different Components of Working Memory

Working memory is not a unitary process. It comprises both maintenance and manipulative components, and depending on the task, these components are emphasized to different degrees. My colleagues and I have used the Sternberg Item Recognition Paradigm (SIRP; Sternberg, 1966) as adapted for fMRI (Manoach et al., 1997; see Figure 13.1). The SIRP (Sternberg, 1966) is a continuous-performance, choice reaction time (RT) task that requires working memory. The SIRP differs from many other working memory tasks (e.g., n-back, Tower of London, Wisconsin Card Sorting Test) in that it emphasizes maintenance rather than manipulative processes (e.g., the updating and temporal tagging of the contents of working memory). These processes may be mediated by different neural circuitry. For example, a dorsal–ventral functional subdivision of the lateral prefrontal cortex has been proposed on the

A. High WM Load	B. Low WM Load	C. Baseline
Learn These 8 1 3 9 2	**Learn These** 7 2	Arrows
6 (foil)	7	←
1 (target)	4	→
4	8	→
2	2	←
8	3	←

Figure 13.1. The Sternberg Item Recognition Paradigm as adapted for neuroimaging. In the working memory (WM) conditions (Columns A and B), participants memorize a set of digits (targets). This is followed by trials in which they are presented with a probe (single digit) and respond by indicating whether the probe is a target (a member of the memorized set) or a foil (not a member of the memorized set). The number of targets can be varied to produce high and low WM load conditions. Accurate responding is predicated on the internal representation of the targets in WM. In the baseline condition (Column C), participants respond to the display of arrows pointing right or left by pressing the corresponding trigger. This condition requires a visually guided response rather than a memory-guided response.

basis of the type of processing performed on information held in working memory. Dorsal regions are hypothesized to be preferentially recruited for manipulative processes (D'Esposito, Postle, Ballard, & Lease, 1999). The specific working memory processes that are deficient in schizophrenia have not been clearly delineated. If there are selective rather than generalized impairments of working memory in schizophrenia, differences in the processing requirements of the tasks used may contribute to discrepant findings.

Group Differences in Task Performance: Relation of Task Performance to DLPFC Activation

Findings of hypofrontality have been challenged as a possible artifact of poor task performance (Ebmeier, Lawrie, Blackwood, Johnstone, & Goodwin, 1995). Hypofrontality and poor performance may arise from a failure of the DLPFC to support behavior. Alternatively, poor performance may reflect poor effort or motivation, the use of an inappropriate strategy, or that the task was simply too difficult, and for these reasons result in hypofrontality (Frith et al., 1995). It is not surprising that, given their well-documented deficiency, patients with schizophrenia perform significantly worse than normal participants on working memory tasks during neuroimaging studies. These performance differences are likely to be reflected in regional brain activation. Some evidence that suggests that the direction of difference in brain activation may depend on the level of working memory load. *Working memory load* can be defined as the level of task demand with regard to the amount of information that has to be maintained and the manipulative processes required. In the case of the SIRP, *working memory load* refers to the number of targets that are held on-line.

Recent findings suggest that DLPFC activation increases with working memory load (Braver et al., 1997). However, when working memory load exceeds an individual's capacity to manage this material, DLPFC activation decreases (Callicott et al., 1999; Goldberg et al., 1998). These findings suggest a nonlinear relationship between DLPFC activation and working memory load. This relationship is depicted in Figure 13.2. Increased working memory load leads to increased DLPFC activation, but only up to the point that the task remains manageable. When the task demands exceed capacity, participants may engage cognitive and affective processes that are unrelated to working memory, and DLPFC activation may diminish. These processes may include error monitoring, attempts at compensation, disengaging from the task, feeling overwhelmed, and guessing.

Previous studies that used tasks with high working memory demands may have exceeded the working memory capacity of patients with schizophrenia and consequently found hypofrontality. In recent studies, my colleagues and I have kept the task demands within the capacity of most of the patients with schizophrenia (Manoach et al., 2000; Manoach et al., 1999). As a consequence, with few exceptions, patients with schizophrenia performed significantly above chance in all of the task conditions. Although they performed above chance, patients with schizophrenia performed significantly worse than normal participants. (See Figure 13.2 for a schematic illustration of the main fMRI activation findings as described below). Their increased DLFPC activation and poorer performance may reflect that, given identical task demands, performance was more effortful for them (see points labeled

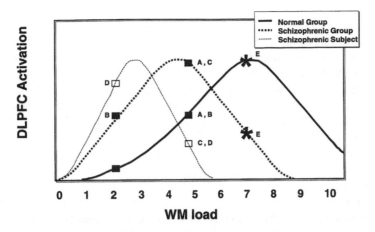

Figure 13.2. The hypothetical relationship of activation of the dorsolateral prefrontal cortex (DLPFC) to working memory (WM) load in the normal and schizophrenia groups and in a hypothetical patient with schizophrenia who was below the group mean with regard to WM capacity. This figure provides a schematic illustration of the findings of Manoach et al. (2000). A = The schizophrenia group showed increased DLPFC activation in the high WM load condition (five targets) relative to the normal group. B = When task performance was matched by comparing the schizophrenia group in the low WM load condition (two targets) with the normal group in the high WM load condition, DLPFC activation did not differ. C = In the schizophrenia group, performance was related to activation. Participants who performed the worst (i.e., had the lowest WM capacity as represented by the curve of the individual schizophrenic patient that is shifted to the left relative to the schizophrenia group mean) showed the least DLPFC activation in the high WM load condition. D = Participants who performed the worst were also more likely to show greater activation in the low versus high WM load condition. E = If WM load were increased, then one would expect relative hypofrontality in the schizophrenia group. (These data points are represented by an asterisk because they were not tested.)

A in Figure 13.2). In other words, their working memory capacity was reduced. As a reflection of this reduced capacity, the curve that describes the schizophrenia group's DLPFC activation as a function of working memory load is shifted to the left. To account for the differential capacity of the normal and schizophrenia groups, and to match for performance, we compared the groups at different levels of working memory load (Manoach et al., 2000). The schizophrenia group's performance in the low working memory load condition matched the normal group's performance in the high working memory load condition for both accuracy and RT. Under conditions of matched performance, as the model would predict, the groups did not differ in DLPFC activation (see points labeled B in Figure 13.2).

This model also suggests an interpretation of the observed relations of activation to performance within the schizophrenia group. Poorer performance was significantly associated with decreased DLPFC activation. For participants who performed the worst, the high working memory load condition may have been too demanding (e.g., their hypothetical curve was shifted further to the left; see points labeled C in Figure 13.2). In these participants, decreased activation and performance, indicative of decreased capacity, may reflect greater DLPFC dysfunction. Greater dysfunction may render the DLPFC less able to subserve working memory. Also consistent with the model was the observation that patients with schizophrenia who performed the worst tended to show greater DLPFC activation in the low versus high working memory load condition (see points labeled *D* in Figure 13.2). In contrast, patients who performed the best showed the greatest differences in the opposite direction (more activation in the high than low working memory load conditions). This finding did not reach significance, possibly because of the small sample size ($n = 9$). For the normal participants, who performed near ceiling levels, there were no relations between task performance and activation. This likely reflects a restriction of range.

The proposed model also leads to a prediction regarding the likely outcome of using higher working memory loads. The increased demand would likely exceed the working memory capacity of the patients with schizophrenia, resulting in a breakdown of their performance and consequent hypofrontality relative to normal participants (see points labeled *E* in Figure 13.2). For the normal participants, the increased demand would make the task more challenging, but not overwhelming. This would result in decreased performance and increased DLPFC activation. This prediction has not been tested. It is clear that the relation of activation to performance and to task demands is complex, especially in the context of pathology. It may involve a number of variables (i.e., the possibility of recruiting compensatory neural circuitry) that were not addressed in this work (Manoach et al., 2000). Although this model is oversimplified, it provides a basis for understanding and reconciling discrepant findings.

Is Hypofrontality an Artifact of Motivational Deficits?

Amotivation is a prominent feature of schizophrenia and represents a possible confound in studies of cognitive performance (Schmand et al., 1994). When a participant performs poorly, it is often difficult to determine whether this reflects a true information-processing deficit or whether the participant was unwilling to exert the effort necessary for optimal performance. In addition, tasks may differ in the amount of effort required, and suboptimal motivation may be more detrimental to some tasks than to others. There are few satisfactory solutions to the possibility of motivational deficits. The approach my colleagues and I have used is to provide a monetary reward for correct responses. Monetary reinforcement has met with only mixed success in ameliorating performance deficits on the Wisconsin Card Sorting Test (Green, Satz, Ganzell, & Vaclav, 1992; Hellman, Kern, Neilson, & Green, 1998; Summerfelt et al., 1991). In our studies, participants were able to perform the SIRP accurately (Manoach et al., 1999, 2000). Although we did not compare rewarded with unrewarded performance, we hypothesized that reward enhanced motivation, task performance, and activation. This is consistent with studies of single-unit recordings from the principal sulcus of nonhuman primates that demonstrate increased firing of working memory neurons during working memory delays in anticipation of a preferred reward (Watanabe, 1996). Because previous neuroimaging studies of working memory did not provide incentives, a potential contribution from motivational deficits cannot be ruled out.

Implications of Using Individual Versus Averaged Group Data in Neuroimaging Studies

Findings of hypofrontality may also be an artifact of methodologies that require group averaging and for this reason mask possible structural and functional heterogeneity of the DLPFC. Group comparisons in neuroimaging studies often rely on data that are averaged across the individuals within each group. Averaging is used to enhance the signal-to-noise properties of the images. Using the averaged group data, images obtained during a control state are statistically compared with those obtained during an experimental or task state to reveal significant differences in regional brain activation attributable to the cognitive process of interest. Groups can then be compared on these analyzed images to determine differences in regional brain activation during task performance.

Positron emission tomography studies often depend on group-averaging techniques for the power to discern significant differences in regional brain activation between conditions and between groups. Functional MRI, in contrast, allows sufficient power to examine significant differences between conditions in individual participants. This allows group comparisons to be made using indices of activation gleaned from both the individual participants and from the group-averaged data.

To average data across individuals it is necessary to transform both the structural and functional brain images into a common space. Transformation requires the stretching and shrinking of the acquired images to fit a particular model and may obscure individual differences in both anatomy and regional brain activation. For this reason, individual versus group-averaging methods may yield contrasting findings. Manoach et al.'s (2000) study illustrates this point. In the group-averaged data, the normal group activated more voxels in the DLPFC than the schizophrenia group. This finding could be considered to be consistent with hypofrontality. In the data derived from individual participants, in contrast, the patients with schizophrenia actually activated more voxels. To understand this discrepancy, Manoach et al. (2000) examined the overlap of clusters of activated voxels in the DLPFC for each individual with those of the averaged group data for each group separately. The individual clusters of the normal participants were almost three times more likely (71% vs. 24%) to overlap with their averaged group clusters than was the case for the patients with schizophrenia. These findings indicate that patients with schizophrenia were more heterogeneous in the spatial distribution of activated voxels within the DLPFC. Similar findings of increased spatial heterogeneity of activation in schizophrenia have been reported in motor regions during performance of a sensorimotor task (Holt et al., 1998) and in the DLPFC during performance of the n-back working memory task (Holt et al., 1999).

There are several possible explanations for both the increased spatial heterogeneity and different location of DLPFC activation in the schizophrenia group. There is substantial structural variability of the DLPFC in normal individuals (Rajkowska & Goldman-Rakic, 1995). In imaging studies, this is compensated for, in part, by spatial normalization and image smoothing. Patients with schizophrenia may be even more variable than normal individuals in the gross morphology, functional organization, or both, of the DLPFC. Our study (Manoach et al., 2000) cannot distinguish between these possibilities. They may also be more variable and less efficient in their use of strategies to accomplish the task. A related concern and possible source of error is that, unlike other primates, the human DLPFC is not bounded by definitive sulcal or gyral landmarks. Because neuroimaging lacks the resolution to discern cytoarchitecture, the anatomic criteria applied to define the DLPFC are necessarily arbitrary and differ between studies.

To summarize, group averaging may mask structural and functional heterogeneity of the DLPFC and, in this way, underestimate DLPFC activation in schizophrenia. In normal participants, general principles of functional brain organization may transcend these transformations. In schizophrenia, however, the increased interindividual variability may make comparisons of averaged group data misleading. It is important to note that several fMRI studies using measures gleaned from individual participants have also demonstrated hypofrontality (Callicott et al., 1998; Yurgelun-Todd et al., 1996). Thus, the use of group-averaging techniques does not provide a full explanation of hypofrontality. However, consideration of several of the factors reviewed here—including differences in task parameters and task performance and methodological issues such as whether individual participant data were examined—may provide a more complete explanation of the discrepant findings.

How Reliable Are Neuroimaging Findings in Schizophrenia?

The study described above demonstrated greater heterogeneity among patients with schizophrenia versus normal participants with regard to the location of activation within the DLPFC during a single scanning session (Manoach et al., 2000). In a follow-up study, Manoach et al. (2001) examined variability in both working memory performance and regional brain activation within subjects over time. In schizophrenia, repeated fMRI studies may allow a determination of brain activity changes over the course of illness and in response to changes in symptomatology and to pharmacologic or other interventions. In particular, they may allow an assessment of interventions that purportedly improve prefrontal function and associated working memory deficits (Honey et al., 1999). To evaluate the findings of repeated studies, however, it is crucial to know the test–retest reliability of the measures used. Manoach et al. (2001) scanned a subset of the original cohort on two occasions separated by at least a month. Rescanning of the patients with schizophrenia was contingent on no changes in medication and no significant changes in clinical status as indicated by rating scale scores. The task and the scanning and analysis methods were identical. They computed intraclass correlation coefficients to quantify the reliability of task performance and activation. The intraclass correlation coefficient represents the proportion of total variability accounted for by the variability between rather than within subjects.

Patients with schizophrenia were reliable with regard to errors. Normal participants performed near ceiling levels during both sessions, and their low intraclass correlation coefficient reflected this restricted range of errors (see Figure 13.3.A.1). Mean RTs across conditions were reliable in both groups (see Figure 13.3.A.2). The plot of the difference in mean RT across sessions for each group illustrates that, although this difference was close to zero and did not differ between groups, the patients with schizophrenia were more variable in the magnitude and direction of RT change across sessions (see Figure 13.3.A.3). Patients with schizophrenia also

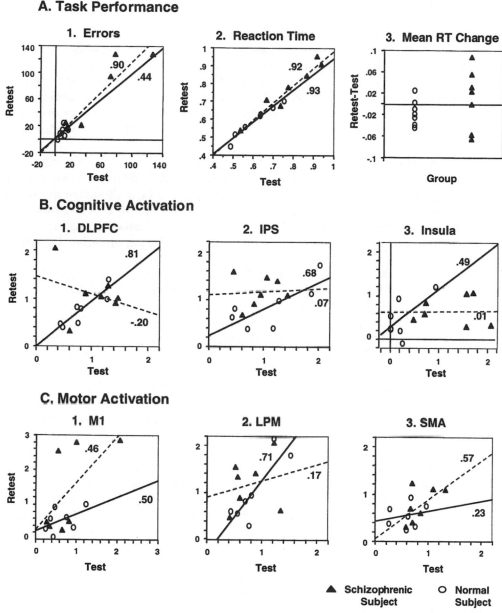

Figure 13.3. Scatter plots of test and retest data with regression lines and intraclass correlation coefficients for each group. Normal participants are represented by open circles and have solid regression lines, and patients with schizophrenia are represented by filled triangles and dashed regression lines. Row A shows task performance as measured by errors and reaction time (RT) and a plot of the differences in mean RT from test to retest for each group separately. Row B shows activation, as measured by an index of the magnitude of activation, in regions associated with cognitive function: the dorsolateral prefrontal cortex (DLPFC), intraparietal sulcus (IPS), and insula. Row C shows activation in regions associated with motor function: the primary motor cortex (M1), lateral premotor areas (LPM), and supplementary motor area (SMA).

showed significantly greater within-subject variability of RT at both time points, as indicated by coefficients of variation.

In group-averaged test and retest data, both groups activated all the a priori regions. However, when activation indices from individual participants were used, patients with schizophrenia consistently showed less reliable activation than normal participants in regions associated with cognition (DLPFC, intraparietal sulcus, insula; see Figure 13.3.B). Their reliability was comparable to that of normal participants in the primary motor cortex, better in the supplementary motor area, and worse in the lateral premotor areas (see Figure 13.3.C)—regions associated with motor function.

To summarize, task performance was reliable in both groups, and normal participants showed reasonable reliability of brain activation in four of the six regions studied. They were consistently more reliable than patients with schizophrenia in regions associated with cognition. Patients with schizophrenia showed relatively better reliability in regions associated with motor function than with cognitive function. In cognitive regions, they showed essentially no relation of activation across sessions.

The earlier study (Manoach et al., 2000) demonstrated greater heterogeneity between patients with schizophrenia in the spatial distribution of DLPFC activation. The test–retest study (Manoach et al., 2001) demonstrated decreased reliability of activation *within* patients with schizophrenia across sessions. In addition, although RT was reliable, patients with schizophrenia showed increased variability of RT both within and across sessions. Thus, the schizophrenia group was characterized by reliable, but more variable, task performance and less reliable brain activation. In addition to a possible contribution from measurement confounds that may have disproportionately affected the schizophrenia group (i.e., motion), increased variability may be intrinsic to schizophrenic pathology. It has been observed even on repeated administrations of simple manual preference tasks (Nelson, Satz, Green, & Cicchetti, 1993).

Although repeated fMRI studies have the potential to detect clinically significant changes in brain activation, it is critical to understand sources of variation (both artifactual and intrinsic) and to develop reliable measures. Despite limited test–retest reliability among patients with schizophrenia individually, averaged over the group, the identical network of structures was activated in both sessions.

Summary

Findings of both hypo- and hyperfrontality are likely valid and informative reflections of prefrontal dysfunction in schizophrenia. They are consistent with clinical findings that implicate the prefrontal cortex in a range of cognitive deficits. Whether a particular study finds hypo- or hyperfrontality may depend on a number of variables. Some of these variables are intrinsic to schizophrenic pathology. These include the degree of working memory impairment (capacity), the heterogeneity of the sample, and the variability of task performance and recruitment of critical brain regions. Other variables are methodological. These may include the type of working memory processes measured, the level of working memory load, whether or not an incentive is provided, and whether data from individual participants are considered. Related to this, the reliability of the measures used must be considered. This is especially critical for attempts to evaluate the effects of intervention on regional brain activation and working memory deficits. It is clear that neuroimaging studies of cognitive deficits in schizophrenia present formidable challenges.

The findings reviewed in this chapter suggest some directions for future research. They are consistent with reduced working memory capacity in schizophrenia, but the basis of this deficit is not well understood. Specific deficits in the components of working memory have not been identified (e.g., maintenance processes, manipulation processes, or both), and the exact anatomical substrate is unknown. In addition, variability might best be regarded as intrinsic to schizophrenia and having a neural basis that requires explanation. In this chapter I have not addressed the important issue of interactions of the DLPFC with other brain regions in subserving working memory. Working memory deficits are more likely to reflect dysfunctional neural circuitry rather than pathology at a single site (e.g., the DLPFC). Although neuroimaging identifies brain regions associated with task performance, it does not reveal which regions are critical for performance or their exact contribution. In combination with other technologies, such as transcranial magnetic stimulation and magnetoencephalography, neuroimaging can identify the anatomical components of the neural circuitry responsible for working memory deficits in schizophrenia and elucidate their contribution.

References

Andreasen, N. C., Rezai, K., Alliger, R, Swayze, V. W., II, Flaum, M., Kirchner, P., et al. (1992). Hypofrontality in neuroleptic-naive patients and in patients with chronic schizophrenia. *Archives of General Psychiatry, 49,* 943–958.

Baddeley, A. (1992, January 31). Working memory. *Science, 255,* 556–559.

Braver, T. S., Cohen, J. D., Nystrom, L. E., Jonides, J., Smith, E. E., & Noll, D. C. (1997). A parametric study of prefrontal cortex involvement in human working memory. *Neuroimage, 5,* 49–62.

Callicott, J. H., Bertolino, A, Mattay, V. S., Langheim, F. J., Duyn, J., Coppola, R., et al. (2000). Physiological dysfunction of the dorsolateral prefrontal cortex in schizophrenia revisited. *Cerebral Cortex, 10,* 1078–1092.

Callicott, J. H., Mattay, V. S., Bertolino, A., Finn, K., Coppola, R., Frank, J. A., et al. (1999). Physiological characteristics of capacity constraints in working memory as revealed by functional MRI. *Cerebral Cortex, 9,* 20–26.

Callicott, J. H., Ramsey, N. F., Tallent, K., Bertolino, A., Knable, M. B., Coppola, R., et al. (1998). Functional magnetic resonance imaging brain mapping in psychiatry: Methodological issues illustrated in a study of working memory in schizophrenia. *Neuropsychopharmacology, 18,* 186–196.

Carter, C. S., Perlstein, W., Ganguli, R., Brar, J., Mintun, M., & Cohen, J. D. (1998). Functional hypofrontality and working memory dysfunction in schizophrenia. *American Journal of Psychiatry, 155,* 1285–1287.

Carter, C., Robertson, L., Nordahl, T., Chaderjian, M., Kraft, L., & O'Shora-Celaya, L. (1996). Spatial working memory deficits and their relationship to negative symptoms in unmedicated schizophrenia patients. *Biological Psychiatry, 40,* 930–932.

Cohen, J. D., Braver, T. S., & O'Reilly, R. C. (1996). A computational approach to prefrontal cortex, cognitive control and schizophrenia: Recent developments and current challenges. *Philosophical Transactions of the Royal Society of London, 351,* 1515–1527.

D'Esposito, M., Postle, B. R., Ballard, D., & Lease, J. (1999). Maintenance versus manipulation of information held in working memory: An event-related fMRI study. *Brain and Cognition, 41,* 66–86.

Ebmeier, K. P., Lawrie, S. M., Blackwood, D., Johnstone, E. C., & Goodwin, G. M. (1995). Hypofrontality revisited: A high resolution single photon emission computed tomography study in schizophrenia. *Journal of Neurology, Neurosurgery, and Psychiatry, 58,* 452–456.

Friedman, H. R., & Goldman-Rakic, P. S. (1994). Coactivation of prefrontal cortex and inferior parietal cortex in working memory tasks revealed by 2DG functional mapping in the rhesus monkey. *Journal of Neuroscience, 14*(5, Part 1), 2775–2788.

Frith, C. D., Friston, K. J., Herold, S., Silbersweig, D., Fletcher, P., Cahill, C., Dolan, R. J. et al. (1995). Regional brain activity in chronic schizophrenic patients during the performance of a verbal fluency task. *British Journal of Psychiatry, 167*, 343–349.

Goldberg, T. E., Berman, K. F., Fleming, K., Ostrem, J., Van Horn, J. D., Esposito, G., et al. (1998). Uncoupling cognitive workload and prefrontal cortical physiology: A PET rCBF study. *Neuroimage, 7*(4, Part 1), 296–303.

Goldberg, T. E., & Weinberger, D. R. (1996). Effects of neuroleptic medications on the cognition of patients with schizophrenia: A review of recent studies. *Journal of Clinical Psychiatry, 57*(Suppl. 9), 62–65.

Goldman-Rakic, P. (1991). Prefrontal cortical dysfunction in schizophrenia: The relevance of working memory. In B. J. Carroll & J. E. Barrett (Eds.), *Psychopathology and the brain* (pp. 1–23). New York: Raven Press.

Green, M. F., Satz, P., Ganzell, S., & Vaclav, J. F. (1992). Wisconsin Card Sorting Test performance in schizophrenia: Remediation of a stubborn deficit. *American Journal of Psychiatry, 149*, 62–67.

Hellman, S. G., Kern, R. S., Neilson, L. M., & Green, M. F. (1998). Monetary reinforcement and Wisconsin Card Sorting performance in schizophrenia: Why show me the money? *Schizophrenia Research, 34*, 67–75.

Holt, J. L., Van Horn, J. D., Esposito, G., Meyer-Lindenberg, A., Callicott, J., Egan, M., et al. (1998). Variability in functional neuroanatomy in schizophrenia: Group vs. single-subject PET activation data. *Society for Neuroscience Abstracts*, p. 1238.

Holt, J. L., Van Horn, J. D., Meyer-Lindenberg, A., Esposito, G., Callicott, J., Egan, M., et al. (1999). Multiple sources of signal abnormality underlying prefrontal hypofunction and increased variability in the sites of activation within BA 9/46 in individual medication free schizophrenic patients. *Society for Neuroscience Abstracts*, p. 18.

Honey, G. D., Bullmore, E. T., Soni, W., Varatheesan, M., Williams, S. C., & Sharma, T. (1999). Differences in frontal cortical activation by a working memory task after substitution of risperidone for typical antipsychotic drugs in patients with schizophrenia. *Proceedings of the National Academy of Sciences USA, 96*, 13432–13437.

Maher, B. A. (1999). Anomalous experience in everyday life: Its significance for psychopathology. *The Monist, 82*, 547–570.

Manoach, D. S., Gollub, R. L., Benson, E. S., Searl, M. M., Goff, D. C., Halpern, E., et al. (2000). Schizophrenic subjects show aberrant fMRI activation of dorsolateral prefrontal cortex and basal ganglia during working memory performance. *Biological Psychiatry, 48*, 99–109.

Manoach, D. S., Halpern, E. F., Kramer, T. S., Chang, Y., Goff, D. C., Rauch, S. L., et al. (2001). Test–retest reliability of a functional MRI working memory paradigm in normal and schizophrenic subjects. *American Journal of Psychiatry, 158*, 955–958.

Manoach, D. S., Press, D. Z., Thangaraj, V., Searl, M. M., Goff, D. C., Halpern, E., et al. (1999). Schizophrenic subjects activate dorsolateral prefrontal cortex during a working memory task as measured by fMRI. *Biological Psychiatry, 45*, 1128–1137.

Manoach, D. S., Schlaug, G., Siewert, B., Darby, D. G., Bly, B. M., Benfield, A., et al. (1997). Prefrontal cortex fMRI signal changes are correlated with working memory load. *NeuroReport, 8*, 545–549.

Nelson, L. D., Satz, P., Green, M., & Cicchetti, D. (1993). Re-examining handedness in schizophrenia: Now you see it—Now you don't! *Journal of Clinical Experimental Neuropsychology, 15*, 149–158.

Park, S., & Holzman, P. S. (1992). Schizophrenics show spatial working memory deficits. *Archives of General Psychiatry, 49*, 975–982.

Park, S., Holzman, P. S., & Goldman-Rakic, P. S. (1995). Spatial working memory deficits in the relatives of schizophrenic patients. *Archives of General Psychiatry, 52*, 821–828.

Park, S., Puschel, J., Sauter, B. H., Rentsch, M., & Hell, D. (1999). Spatial working memory deficits and clinical symptoms in schizophrenia: A 4-months follow-up study. *Biological Psychiatry, 46*, 392–400.

Petrides, M., Alivisatos, B., Meyer, E., & Evans, A. C. (1993). Functional activation of the human prefrontal cortex during the performance of verbal working memory tasks. *Proceedings of the National Academy of Sciences, 90*, 878–882.

Rajkowska, G., & Goldman-Rakic, P. S. (1995). Cytoarchitectonic definition of prefrontal areas in the normal human cortex: II. Variability in locations of areas 9 and 46 and relationship to the Talairach coordinate system. *Cerebral Cortex, 5*, 323–337.

Schmand, B., Kuipers, T., Van der Gaag, M., Bosveld, J., Bulthuis, F., & Jellema, M. (1994). Cognitive disorders and negative symptoms as correlates of motivational deficits in psychotic patients. *Psychological Medicine, 24*, 869–884.

Sternberg, S. (1966, August 5). High-speed scanning in human memory. *Science, 153*, 652–654.

Summerfelt, A. T., Alphs, L. D., Wagman, A. M.; Funderburk, F. R., Hierholzer, R. M., & Strauss, M. E. (1991). Reduction of perseverative errors in patients with schizophrenia using monetary feedback. *Journal of Abnormal Psychology, 100*, 613–616.

Watanabe, M. (1996). Reward expectancy in primate prefrontal neurons. *Nature, 382*, 629–632.

Weinberger, D. R., & Berman, K. F. (1996). Prefrontal function in schizophrenia: Confounds and controversies. *Philosophical Transactions of the Royal Society of London, 351*, 1495–1503.

Yurgelun-Todd, D. A., Waternaux, C. M., Cohen, B. M., Gruber, S. A., English, C. D., & Renshaw, P. F. (1996). Functional magnetic resonance imaging of schizophrenic patients and comparison subjects during word production. *American Journal of Psychiatry, 153*, 200–205.

Part V

Using Temperament and Cognition as Leverage in Psychopathology Research

14

Surprise and Uncertainty

Jerome Kagan

Brendan Maher's scholarship has been distinguished by an extraordinary ability to separate wheat from chaff and to penetrate to the core of a phenomenon rather than be seduced by surface gleam. This talent is uncommon in scientists from all disciplines. Young sciences are vulnerable to dogma because the absence of a rich corpus of facts makes it difficult to uproot bad ideas. That is why these disciplines need a few scholars with courage. Maher is a member of this group. His ability to penetrate technical prose and see at once the referents, or the lack of referents, for the words would make Francis Bacon smile, for Bacon was able to sniff out the "Idols" that mislead us. What I admire most about Maher is his mood during his rich career. He did not uncover false assumptions in order to disparage or shame disillusioned advocates but to enjoy a moment of playfulness, not unlike the fictional girl who declared "The emperor has no clothes."

Among Maher's many fruitful intuitions was the belief that a hallucinating patient with schizophrenia was responding to self-generated discrepant information from bodily targets and that the hallucination was the patient's way of making sense of the signal that was piercing his or her consciousness (Maher, 1983). I wish to use that idea as the scaffolding to make two points: (a) the importance of appreciating the different structures of mind and (b) the fact that individuals differ in their susceptibility to experiencing a state of fear or uncertainty in reaction to events that are discrepant from their knowledge.

Mental Structures

Most psychologists, unlike biologists and chemists, are concerned primarily with processes, such as discrimination, memory, perception, consciousness, feeling, and action. As a result, they have generally been indifferent to the particular psychological structures that render each of these processes possible. The neural sites that are the foundation of the structure are not equivalent to the psychological forms. This lack of concern with structure would surprise biologists, who know that each life function is linked to a very particular structure. Lungs do not cross over, chromosomes do not fill with liquid, and ovaries do not have synaptic potentials. The biologist J. B. S. Haldane was insightful when he insisted that form was the fundamental riddle in biology and that function cannot reveal form. Extraordinary advances in understanding followed Crick and Watson's discovery of the structure of DNA. Neither Mendel, nor Darwin, nor Weissman could have guessed at the structure of a gene on the basis of his evidence. Unfortunately, Hochberg (1998) re-minded us that there is no consensus on the number or the nature of the elementary structures of mind, where *structure* is defined as a particular set of relations among features. Sadly, these structures cannot be inferred from the patterns of neural activity or brain sites that support the structure.

The empirical corpus of investigations of humans suggests that people possess at least four types of mental structures: (a) visceral representations, (b) sensory motor schemes, (c) perceptual schemas, and (d) semantic structures. Each has a different form and neurophysiological foundation (Kagan, 2002).

Visceral Representations

The representations of bodily activity one might call *visceral representations* contain information about the physiological state of organs and tissues. The representation of a past headache is an example. Sensory receptors in visceral targets relay this information first to the medulla, then to the amygdala, and finally to the orbitofrontal cortex. Both Rolls (1999) and Damasio (1994) have written extensively on the neural bases for this structure. The information in visceral structures is more limited in variety than the products of visual or auditory events and difficult to retrieve or to describe in words, because this information synapses on the corticomedial and central nuclei of the amygdala, which have very weak connections to cortical association areas. Visual and auditory stimuli synapse on the lateral nucleus and have rich connections to association areas. Most adults cannot re-create the pain of yesterday's toothache with the same ease and clarity that they are able to retrieve a schema for a gothic cathedral visited 20 years earlier.

One source of evidence supporting the special nature of this visceral representation is the fact that hippocampal lesions impair a rat's ability to acquire a conditioned fear response—in this case, freezing—if the conditioned stimulus is a state of hunger, but the lesion does not impair the acquisition of a conditioned freezing response to a light (Hock & Bunsey, 1998).

The motor sequences Piaget (1950) called *sensory motor schemes* in infancy and that make possible the skilled performances of musicians and athletes represent a second form of representation. Most magical rituals consist of actions with familiar objects that are seriously discrepant from the usual manipulations performed with those objects in order to alert observers. In one such ritual, in ancient Egypt, the agent pulled out two fingernails and hairs from his head and placed them near a bowl full of the milk of a brown cow. He then drowned a falcon in the liquid. After the bird was dead, he wrapped it in undyed cloth and placed it beside the fingernails and hair (Graf, 1997). A modern ritual is a mother playing a recording of Mozart's music to an infant.

Perceptual Schemas

The schemas that originate in external events, especially the structures mediated by vision and audition, comprise the third form of mental structure. These nonsymbolic representations are partially veridical with the original event and, unlike the visual stimuli, are easily retrieved and described. This definition of a schema is very similar to those offered by Vernon (1954), Gibson (1969), and Paivio (1986). The images that Kosslyn (1994) studied depend on these structures. When the features of an event match those of a schema, recognition is rapid, and the features that permit rapid recognition of an event are usually called *essential*. A pair of eyes horizontally arranged in a circular frame is a more essential feature than the ears for the schema of a human face. Infants who had seen a schematic face consisting of two horizontally placed circles in the upper part of a larger circle were alerted by and studied a vertical arrangement of the two circles but did not pay much attention to the same schematic face when it was composed of two horizontally placed squares rather than circles, because this gestalt was assimilated quickly to the infant's schema for a human face. The vertical arrangement of the circles was alerting because the horizontal position of the eyes is an essential feature (Kagan, 1984). The monsters that medieval citizens imagined usually involved changes in the essential features of the human form, for example, replacing the arms with wings or the human head with that of a dog.

Finally, the brain–mind contains semantic structures that combine lexical representations with schemas to form networks of symbolic structures that are logically constrained, hierarchical, and used to communicate information. The set of relations among the components of my schema for a neighbor's fox terrier (the spatial relation among head, ears, eyes, and tail) is qualitatively different from the set of relations among my semantic representations of this animal, which include the semantic concepts "dog," "pet," "mammal," and "domesticated."

However, semantic representations vary in their schematic contribution. Concepts such as surtax, fairness, and kernel of a matrix contain minimal schematic contributions compared with girl, cat, and table. The empirical data reveal clearly that correct perception of a visual event, as well as the evaluation of the truth or falsity of a statement, are faster if the event or sentence engages a schematic representation. For example, adults are faster at naming the category to which an object belongs if the latter is presented as a picture rather than a word (Seifert, 1997).

It is also important that schemas can be transformed without any accompanying cognitive tension. Dreams and reveries provide a clear example. The image of a smiling face can turn into a bouncing ball without any of the dissonance that would occur if a person read "A smiling face is a bouncing ball." Einstein's image of riding a light wave was supposed to be one of the origins of his theory of special relativity, but the sentence "Humans can move at the speed of light" would evoke an immediate sense of impossibility in most readers.

Some relations hold only for semantic structures. Only semantic representations possess the quasi-logical relations that take the form of hierarchically nested categories, called *hyponyms*, and antonyms. Schemas, on the other hand, do not nest into hierarchical categories; neither do they consist of antonymic pairs. My schema of William James Hall is a gestalt of a tall, white, concrete building standing close to the street. It is not a member of, or subsumed by, a more abstract schema, and it has no schematic opposite. Although the semantic representations "sweet" and "sour" are antonyms, no comparable relation holds for the visceral schemas created by these two taste sensations.

Furthermore, the essential features of the semantic representation "woman" include the biological capacity to conceive and give birth to an infant. These are not the two most essential features of the schematic representation "woman," which most often includes body build, costume, and amount and arrangement of hair. A woman with a crew cut and cowboy boots is discrepant from the schematic contribution for "woman" but not from the semantic one. The newspaper reports that Susan Smith drowned her children in a lake are inconsistent with the semantic representation of "woman" but not discrepant from the schematic one.

It is surprising that a defense of the independence of schemas from semantic representations is required given the history of Western philosophical essays on knowledge. Bacon, Descartes, Hume, and Locke were convinced that the mind's transformations of sensory information were the foundation of all knowledge. These were Locke's simple ideas. On the other hand, complex ideas were suspect, because they might not refer to real events. Many of these complex ideas are the semantic networks that have little or no schematic content. Then Kant began to brood on this issue. The advances in mathematics in 16th- and 17th-century Europe, highlighted by the insights of Newton and Leibniz, made it impossible to defend Locke's bottom-up conception of mental structures. Newton's inverse square law originated in a mind and not in sensory impressions. Kant reversed the arrow of causation by making the semantically rich ideas of negation, reciprocity, possibility, existence and necessity, and the intuitions of space and time fundamental categories. These a priori categories are implicit in the amodal representations that have become the basic constructs in contemporary cognitive theory.

The appeal of theoretical arguments in parts of the social sciences concerned with human personality and development, as well as text in the humanities, often rests on consistency among semantic networks that are not always rich in confirming evidence. The writings of Freud and Bowlby provide two obvious examples. The appeal of propositions in the natural sciences is more often based on semantic networks that are penetrated throughout with the schemas created from descriptions of relevant empirical observations. Natural events and semantically consistent texts are different bases on which to make truth claims, and the reliance on one or the other of these sources of information differentiates humanities from the natural sciences.

Semantic summaries of evidence strain toward a generality that schemas do not possess. Prose summaries of psychophysiological data, for example, often describe the reactivity of the sympathetic nervous system as if the response of any one sympathetic target in a particular context were an accurate index of the reactivity of the entire system. We know it is not. Furthermore, most functional relations in the life sciences are nonlinear, but semantic summaries imply linear relations. Scientists often report that there is a positive (or negative) relation between two variables when, in fact, the relation is significant only for the top and bottom 10% or 15% of the sample. For example, the positive relation between age and size of the corpus callosum in children between 6 and 13 years of age is due entirely to the values in the top and bottom 15% of the distributions; there is no relation for the children in Percentile 16–84. A verbal description of most natural events is analogous to a person with large, thick leather mittens trying to pick up a tiny, fragile glass sculpture without breaking anything—an unlikely accomplishment.

Although events that alter the less essential features of a schema, and are therefore discrepant, and statements inconsistent with semantic networks both recruit attention, I suggest that semantic structures that possess minimal schematic contributions produce a psychological state different from the one created by transformations of semantic structures that have a rich schematic contribution. If this claim is valid, there should be different terms for these two states. I suggest that the term *cognitive uncertainty* is appropriate for the former, whereas *surprise* is a useful name for the latter; hence, the title of this chapter. Cognitive uncertainty occurs if a person reads "Justice for a majority can never be achieved in any industrialized society." Surprise is more likely if a person reads "Eating ripe tomatoes is a major cause of acne." The persuasiveness of this claim is aided by a rich corpus of evidence based on event-related potentials. These data reveal that latency, amplitude, and site of maximal amplitude vary depending on whether a word, phrase, or sentence is rich or lean in schemas.

For example, single words with a strong schematic contribution produce a larger negative event-related potential at 200 ms over the right than over the left hemisphere (King, Gavis, & Kutas, 1998). Words with a weak schematic contribution have a larger negative waveform over the left hemisphere. Second, when a coherent narrative is composed of pictures, and the final picture is either consistent or inconsistent, a negative waveform appears at about 300 ms over frontal and central sites. When the coherent narrative consists of words, and the final word is inconsistent, the negative waveform occurs later, at about 400 ms (West, 1998). These data indicate that meaning is apprehended more quickly for events that engage semantic structures that are linked to schemas.

The state of uncertainty created by inconsistency among semantic networks, in contrast to the state of surprise following an encounter with events discrepant from a schema, has relevance for the popular term *identity*. Edward Said (1999) confessed to the confusion he felt when he realized that his first name was linked to a semantic network implying a Western European family, whereas his last name belonged to a network implying an Arabic pedigree. Said titled his book *Out of Place* to reflect the fact that the meanings of the two networks were incongruent. Erik Erikson's (1950) suggestion that adolescents try to find their identity generated a feeling of truth in many readers, because historical events had forced many young Americans born to immigrant families to recognize that they belong simultaneously to incongruent semantic categories. They wondered if they were Irish, German, Italian, or Jewish, on the one hand, or American, on the other. When Erikson wrote *Childhood and Society* after World War II, large numbers of working-class men who had returned from military service decided to train for professional careers rather than remain in the blue-collar jobs their parents and relatives held. Women who worked in plane factories, as well as those in the armed forces, had added a masculine feature to the traditional semantic network for *female*. As a result, many young women had to decide whether they would retain the traditional female traits or adopt the qualities of professionalism, ambition, competitiveness, and sexual freedom as features of the concept "woman." Third, large numbers of youth enrolled in college rather than entering the workforce. As a result, many 20-year-olds who half a century earlier would have assumed adult vocational and marital roles found themselves in an ambiguous developmental category that was neither child nor adult. Erikson's genius was to sense these semantic incongruities and to articulate, in graceful metaphors, the dissonance produced by semantically inconsistent elements of the network for self that many were trying to resolve.

Variation in Reaction to Discrepancy

The second point I wish to make involves the notion of discrepancy and exploits the research in my laboratory over the past 22 years on the temperamental categories my colleagues and I called *inhibited* and *uninhibited* to unfamiliar events.[1] The defining feature of inhibited children is an extreme reaction to events that are discrepant from their schemas. High-reactive 4-month-old infants, a category defined by display of vigorous motor activity and distress in reaction to visual, auditory, and olfactory stimuli, have a low threshold for reactivity to events discrepant from their schema due, we believe, to the inheritance of low thresholds of excitability in the amygdala, the bed nucleus of the stria terminalis, and their projections. These children are especially vulnerable to a state of surprise when unfamiliar events occur. Children classified as high reactive at 4 months are significantly more likely than others to become shy, timid, fearful, and inhibited when they encounter unfamiliar people, places, or situations at 2, 4, and 7 years of age (Kagan, 1994).

One of the clearest illustrations is these children's tendency to reflexively scream in fear when a person dressed as a clown unexpectedly enters the room. The complementary group, who are low-reactive infants and become fearless children, show low levels of motor activity and distress to the same stimuli, and these children are sociable and relatively bold in later childhood (Kagan, 1994).

My colleagues and I are now evaluating a group of these children at 11 years of age. As expected, the 11-year-olds who had been identified as high reactive are showing greater right- than left-hemisphere activation; this is in line with findings by Davidson (1995) and Fox (1991) that greater desynchronization of alpha frequencies in the electroencephalogram on the right frontal area are associated with states of uncertainty. The children also have a more subdued interactive style with an unfamiliar examiner than those who had been low-reactive infants. Finally, they display a negative waveform in the event-related potential to unfamiliar pictures that implies a special sensitivity to discrepancy.

Each child saw two long series of pictures presented through goggles attached to a computer program. Each series had 169 pictures. In the first series, 70% of the pictures were of the same object (a sunburst), 15% were of the same flower (this is called the *oddball stimulus*), and the remaining 15% were different pictures of ecologically valid objects such as chairs or plates. In the second series, which followed immediately, the frequent stimulus, seen 70% of the time, was a fire hydrant; 15% of the pictures were of a very different flower, and the remaining 15% were different pictures of ecologically invalid events (e.g., an infant's head on an adult body, a leg in a cup). The children showed a negative component in the event-related potential called Nc between 250 and 1,000 ms. This Nc waveform is analogous to the P300 or the P3A that is seen when adults are presented with unexpected or discrepant events.

The children who had been high-reactive infants had significantly larger Nc waveforms to the novel and discrepant pictures than the children who had been

---

[1]This work required the significant collaboration of many individuals, in particular Nancy Snidman, Mark McManis, Sue Woodward, Doreen Arcus, Steven Reznick, and many, many others.

low-reactive infants. This implies that this temperamental group may have retained a low threshold of cortical arousal to events discrepant from the child's schematic knowledge. However, this reactivity to discrepant events does not necessarily mean that these children are more vulnerable to states of cognitive uncertainty that might accompany recognition of inconsistent semantic categories for the self or for events or ideas about the world.

Finally, high-reactive infants show more reactivity in several sympathetic targets of the cardiovascular system. For example, they usually show larger increases in heart rate and blood pressure in reaction to stress, and greater lability of the sympathetically innervated arteriovenous anastomoses in the fingertips, and spectral analysis of their resting heart rate reveals more power in the low-frequency band, a fact that implies a brisker reaction of the baroreceptor cells in the carotid sinus.

These interesting facts imply that the high-reactive infants who became inhibited children are more likely than others to experience unexpected bursts of activity in sympathetic targets and, as a result, their consciousness is likely to be pierced more often by an unexpected change in bodily feeling that is apt to be dysphoric. As a result, they will be motivated to interpret this unexpected signal. Children growing up in U.S. society are socialized to believe in their autonomous conscience as well as the fact that they are personally responsible for their actions. Hence, they are biased to interpret the unexpected dysphoric feedback as reflecting the fact that they may have committed some ethical misdemeanor. This interpretation is a frequent first guess among those who suddenly feel dysphoric for no particular reason. The child may wonder if she has been rude to a friend, told a white lie, harbored a prejudice, or not studied enough for a test. The list of moral lapses is so long that few individuals in U.S. society, children or adults, will have trouble finding some ethical flaw to explain the unwelcome sensation and, as a consequence, may experience a moment of guilt. This argument resembles the view of emotions put forward by William James and Carl Lange. Ludwig Wittgenstein may have been a member of this category. He was a painfully shy child who experienced almost pathological tension in uncongenial settings. He was a melancholic adult and tried unsuccessfully to rid himself of the dysphoria that caused him intense suffering. Guilt over his inability to conquer this mood through willpower alone, shame over his family's denial of a Jewish relative, doubt over his talent, and regret over the fact that he struck one of his pupils may have motivated him to give away most of the money he inherited from his affluent family. On the first day of April 1942, when he was 53 years old, he confessed that "it is as though I have before me nothing but a long stretch of living death. I cannot imagine any future for me other than a ghastly one. Friendless and joyless" (Rhees, 1981, p. 174).

Leo Tolstoy, who continually berated himself for his vanity, idleness, and exploitation of women, may also have possessed this chronically dysphoric tone. The diary he began in his 18th year opens with a criticism of himself that he maintained for the rest of his life. On some days the pain was acute: "I'm a worthless, pathetic, unnecessary, creature." Even after the public acclaim of his novels, he continued to criticize himself through the seventh decade:

> What a worthless creature I must be. I cannot tear apart all those nasty cobwebs which hold me fast. And not because I haven't the strength, but because I am morally unable to ... the main thing is that I am no good. (Christian, 1985, p. 329)

The diary of Athol Fugard, a South African playwright who probably held the same standards on honesty and idleness as Tolstoy, did not contain the moral angst that permeates Tolstoy's entries (Benson, 1983).

I suspect that inhibited children may be especially vulnerable to a special dysphoric state because of a temperamental vulnerability to sympathetic lability in varied targets. However, I suggest that this feeling is very different from the emotion of shame, fear of discovery, or even guilt experienced by those who frequently cheat, lie, steal, or harbor a hostile thought.

The human mind uses qualitatively different psychological structures to perform its many functions. These forms are emergent from neuronal activity but must be described with a psychological vocabulary. One implication of this claim is that sole reliance on verbal evidence limits understanding. Moreover, events that are discrepant from perceptual or visceral schemas produce states that are different from the state created when a semantic proposition is inconsistent with a person's semantic network. Thus, scientists cannot predict an individual's reaction to a particular event unless they know the content of that person's mind. The serious challenge for psychologists and neuroscientists is to devise procedures that can detect the products of earlier encounters. It is not obvious that this goal is attainable.

References

Benson, M. (Ed.). (1983). *Notebooks of Athol Fugard (1970–1977)*. London: Faber & Faber.

Christian, R. F. (1985). *Tolstoy's diaries*. New York: Scribner's.

Damasio, A. R. (1994). *Descartes' error*. New York: Putnam.

Davidson, R. J. (1995). Cerebral asymmetry, emotion, and affective style. In R. J. Davidson & K. Hugdahl (Eds.), *Brain asymmetry* (pp. 261–388). Cambridge, MA: MIT Press.

Erikson, E. H. (1950). *Childhood and society*. New York: Norton.

Fox, N. A, (1991). If it's not left, it's right. *American Psychologist, 46*, 863–872.

Gibson, E. J. (1969). *Principles of perceptual learning and development*. New York: Appleton-Century-Crofts.

Graf, F. (1997). *Magic in the ancient world*. Cambridge, MA: Harvard University Press.

Hochberg, J. (1998). Gestalt theory and its legacy. In J. Hochberg (Ed.), *Perception and cognition ut century's end* (pp. 253–306). New York: Academic Press.

Hock, B. J., & Bunsey, M. P. (1998). Differential effects of dorsal and ventral hippocampal lesions. *Journal of Neuroscience, 18*, 7025–7032.

Kagan, J. (1984). *The nature of the child*. New York: Basic Books.

Kagan, J. (1994). *Galen's prophecy*. New York: Basic Books.

Kagan, J. (2002). *Surprise, uncertainty, and mental structures*. Cambridge, MA: Harvard University Press.

King, J. W., Gavis, G., & Kutas, M. (1998). Potential asymmetries in language comprehension. In B. Beeman & C. Chiarello (Eds.), *Right hemisphere language comprehension* (pp. 187–213). Mahwah, NJ: Erlbaum.

Kosslyn, S. M. (1994). *Image and brain*. Cambridge, MA: MIT Press.

Maher, B. A. (1983). Towards a tentative theory of schizophrenic utterance. In *Progress in experimental personality research* (Vol. 12, pp. 11–51). New York: Academic Press.

Paivio, A. (1986). *Mental representations*. New York: Oxford University Press.

Piaget, J. (1950). The psychology of intelligence. (M. Piercy & D. E. Berlyne, Trans.) London: Routledge & Kegan Paul.

Rhees, R. (Ed.). (1981). *Recollections of Wittgenstein*. New York: Oxford University Press.

Rolls, E. T. (1999). *The brain and emotion*. New York: Oxford University Press.

Said, E. (1999). *Out of place*. New York: Knopf.

Seifert, L. S. (1997). Activating representations in permanent memory. *Journal of Experimental Psychology: Learning, Memory, and Cognition, 23,* 1106–1121.

Vernon, M. D. (1954). *A further study of perception.* Cambridge, England: Cambridge University Press.

West, W. C. (1998). *Common versus multiple semantic systems.* Unpublished doctoral dissertation, Tufts University.

15

Electrodermal Hyporeactivity in Psychopathy: Does It Reflect Disinhibition, Low Anxiety, or Both?

Don C. Fowles

When I entered graduate school, I viewed myself as a Freudian. By the time I finished graduate school, my orientation was strongly behavioral, and I had developed a deep interest in the biological underpinnings of individual differences in personality and psychopathology. Brendan Maher was largely responsible for that transformation, initially through a first-year proseminar and later through exposure to psychophysiology and other biological approaches to understanding behavior. His undergraduate course "Social Relations 158: Somatic Bases of Behavior and Its Pathology," which I audited, was especially important in crystallizing my interests in this orientation. I am struck by how many of the concepts presented in that course have proved invaluable to me in understanding psychopathology throughout my career. Later, this background in behavioral approaches and biology directly contributed to my ability to understand Jeffrey Gray's work (see below) and to apply it to psychopathy (Fowles, 1980), to schizophrenia (Fowles, 1992), and to a broad range of psychopathology (Fowles, 1988, 1994). Without a doubt, Maher was the intellectual progenitor of most of my work on psychopathology. He also arranged training in psychophysiology by means of a summer placement with Tom Mulholland at the Veteran's Administration Hospital in Bedford, Massachusetts, and a postdoctoral fellowship in psychophysiology with Peter Venables (at the University of London), initiating the other major influence on my career.

The postdoctoral fellowship involved work on the skin conductance response (SCR). Over time, this background led to an interest in the phenomenon of electrodermal hyporeactivity (EDH) in psychopathy. When in 1977 I read reprints and preprints of Gray's work (e.g., 1976, 1977, 1978) on the behavioral inhibition system (BIS), it appeared to offer a possible explanation for EDH in psychopathy. The theoretical significance of this phenomenon, especially as viewed from the perspective of Gray's BIS, is the topic of this chapter.

Psychopathology, Low Fear, and Disinhibition

Lykken's Low-Fear Hypothesis

Using Cleckley's (1950) concept of psychopathy, Lykken (1957) reported that psychopathic individuals manifested poor classical aversive conditioning, more rapid extinction of the electrodermal response, or both, compared with nonpsychopathic controls. He also reported that psychopathic individuals showed a specific deficit relative to controls in avoiding punished (with shock) incorrect choices in a "mental maze" consisting of 20 choice points with 1 correct and 3 incorrect alternatives at each choice point (1 incorrect alternative was paired with shock). Lykken (1957) combined these findings of poor classical aversive conditioning and poor avoidance of punishment in proposing the *low-fear hypothesis* (see also Lykken, 1995), which posits that poor fear conditioning impairs psychopathic individuals' ability to anticipate punishment and thus leads to impulsivity or disinhibition in the form of engaging in behavior with a risk of punishment. More generally, psychopathic individuals were predicted to do poorly in any situation in which anxiety mediates behavior.

Numerous reviewers (e.g., Fowles, 1993, 1994; Hare, 1978; Lykken, 1995; Siddle & Trasler, 1981; Zahn, 1986) agree that psychopathic individuals' EDH during the anticipation of punishment is well documented. The present summary of both electrodermal and cardiac studies largely is based on my (Fowles, 1993, 1994) review, which closely followed the comprehensive review conducted by Hare (1978), with the addition of a few more recent references. Using the classical aversive conditioning paradigm, EDH has been found with a range of punishments, primarily electric shock and aversive tones or noises as the unconditioned stimulus. Similarly, using other paradigms in which punishment or threat was anticipated (e.g., a countdown to shock or a period of inactivity immediately before having to engage in a threatening task), EDH has been reported with shock, aversive tones, a mental arithmetic task, social disapproval, and even shock to another participant as punishment. Finally, psychopathic individuals show smaller SCRs to slides of severe facial mutilation. This robust association between psychopathy and EDH in anticipation of aversive stimulation most often has been attributed to low fear.

On the assumption that fear is associated with increased sympathetic nervous system (SNS) activity, one would expect that psychopathic individuals' low fear similarly would reduce the SNS-mediated heart rate increase in anticipation of punishment. In fact, psychopathic individuals show normal or enhanced cardiac acceleration in anticipation of punishment—both in classical conditioning paradigms and during countdowns in anticipation of noxious stimuli. Similar findings have been reported for noncriminal participants who scored low on Gough's (1960) Socialization scale[1] or the Activity Preference Questionnaire (Lykken & Katzenmeyer, 1973), an anxiety scale Lykken (1957) used to discriminate psychopaths from nonpsychopaths.

---

[1]The Socialization scale is from the California Psychological Inventory (Gough, 1960; Megargee, 1972).

The association between psychopathy and EDH while anticipating punishment has been well demonstrated. The nonparallel findings for cardiac responses, however, argue against a simple diminished SNS reactivity interpretation of the electrodermal data. Gray's work offers a possible explanation for the discrepancy between electrodermal activity (EDA) and heart rate (HR).

Gray's BIS Applied to Psychopathy

Drawing on the animal learning literature, in the 1970s Gray (e.g., 1978, 1979) described two systems that can be called a *behavioral approach system* or *behavioral activation system* (BAS) and a BIS. The BAS activates behavior in response to conditioned stimuli that signal response-contingent reward (simple approach paradigms) or relieving nonpunishment (active avoidance paradigms). In both paradigms the animal is faced with an aversive state (e.g., hunger in approach and fear of threatened shock in active avoidance) that can be terminated by making an adaptive response: for example, running down an alley runway to obtain food or jumping over a barrier to a safe compartment to avoid shock. The BIS inhibits behavior in response to conditioned stimuli for response-contingent punishment (passive avoidance) in the conflict paradigm or for frustrative nonreward in the extinction paradigm. For example, in an alley runway approach–avoidance conflict the animal must cross an electrified grid to reach the food, inducing a motivational conflict between approach for food and passive avoidance of shock.

A major aspect of Gray's work was his conclusion (e.g., Gray 1977) that anxiolytic drugs (alcohol, barbiturates, and minor tranquilizers) exert their anxiety-reducing effects by weakening the BIS. This conclusion, combined with the aversive quality of the stimuli that activate the BIS, led Gray to view the BIS as an anxiety system. Furthermore, the septohippocampal system was identified as the neurobiological substrate for the BIS in the central nervous system.

Although he did not discuss psychopathy at length, Gray (1970, p. 255) stated that psychopathic individuals tend toward reward seeking "with no fear of punishment" and that their chronic antisocial behavior reflects "a relative insensitivity to punishment"—implying a weak BIS and a normal or possibly strong BAS. This application of Gray's theory to psychopathy makes the role of anxiety in behavior somewhat more explicit than previous theories. It predicts that psychopathic individuals would show less anxiety to cues for punishment and failure, poor inhibition of behavior in passive avoidance and extinction situations (disinhibition), and normal or excessive approach and active avoidance behavior. Thus, the weak-BIS hypothesis accounts for both the low anxiety and the disinhibition demonstrated by Lykken and observed clinically (Cleckley, 1950). Lykken (1995, chap. 10) endorsed this modification of his theory.

I (Fowles, 1980) applied Gray's formulation to the electrodermal and HR data on psychopaths, proposing that EDH during the anticipation of punishment reflected weak BIS activity, whereas HR was more closely tied to the BAS. Although EDA responds to a wide variety of stimuli and is not specific to the BIS, I (Fowles, 1980) proposed that, when threat of punishment is involved, it is reasonable to attribute the reactivity to the BIS. HR, in contrast, appears to be influenced by conditions that would activate the BAS: A large literature had documented cardiac–somatic coupling, in which HR follows somatic activity. Obrist (e.g., 1976) had clearly demonstrated cardiac acceleration during active avoidance tasks, and a modest literature supported reward-incentive effects on HR. I later reported strong effects of monetary incentives on HR in college students (e.g., Fowles, 1988), strengthening the evidence that HR responds to the same stimuli that activate the BAS. This interpretation of EDA and HR, combined with the hypothesis that psychopathic individuals have a weak BIS but a normal or possibly unusually strong BAS, provided an explanation for the divergence of EDA and HR in psychopathic individuals.

In brief, attributing the deficit in psychopathy to a weak BIS more precisely specifies the types of behavioral deficits to be expected (problems with extinction and passive avoidance), accounts for the low anxiety seen clinically, and offers an explanation for the deficit in EDA but not HR. This hypothesis also implies that low anxiety and impulsivity/disinhibition are closely linked, being dual aspects of a dimension reflecting the strength of the BIS. EDH, therefore, should be associated with both low anxiety and disinhibition. Finally, EDH should be specific to the anticipation of punishment—that is, it should not be seen when responding to rewards or other positive stimuli. As I discuss later, there are challenges to some of these expectations. First, however, it will be useful to consider the relevance of impulsivity/disinhibition to psychopathy from another perspective

Impulsivity/Disinhibition Versus the Core Features of Psychopathy

Although Cleckley's (1950) conceptualization of psychopathy influenced a large research literature, he did not provide the explicit diagnostic decision rules that are needed for reliable diagnoses. This gap was filled by Hare, who developed the Psychopathy Checklist, now in its revised version (PCL–R; Hare, 1991). Of particular interest to the present topic is that a factor analysis of the PCL–R yielded two factors (correlated about .5). Hare (1991) described Factor 1 as reflecting personality traits associated with psychopathy and labeled it *Selfish, Callous, and Remorseless Use of Others* (p. 38). It is defined by items rating superficial charm, grandiosity, pathological lying, manipulativeness, lack of remorse or guilt, shallow affect, callousness/lack of empathy, and failure to accept responsibility for one's own actions. Factor 2, described as reflecting socially deviant behaviors, is defined by items rating need for stimulation, parasitic lifestyle, poor behavioral controls, early behavior problems, lack of realistic goals, impulsivity, irresponsibility, juvenile delinquency, and revocation of conditional release. Factor 1 is more strongly related to narcissistic personality disorder than to antisocial personality disorder (APD) as defined by the third edition of the *Diagnostic and Statistical Manual of Mental Disorders* (*DSM–III*; American Psychiatric Association, 1980), whereas Factor 2 correlates more highly with APD ratings (Hare, 1991, p. 44; Lykken, 1995, pp. 125–126). Factor 1 is generally agreed to represent the core features of psychopathy, whereas Factor 2 characterizes the broader group of individuals who meet criteria for APD (e.g., Lykken, 1995, pp. 125–127, 132). Note that impulsive behavior is an important component of Factor 2: Poor behavioral controls and impulsivity directly relate to the concept, and early behavior problems and irresponsibility could be manifestations of impulsivity. From this perspective, then, impulsivity or disinhibition is not a core feature of psychopathy.[2]

A Neuropsychological Analogue of Psychopathy

It long has been known that some lesions in the prefrontal cortex produce personality changes that in many respects resemble psychopathy, although the normal premorbid developmental history results in a more benign form (Tranel, 1994). In recent years, the work of Antonio and Hanna Damasio and Tranel (Damasio, 1994; Damasio, Tranel, & Damasio, 1990; Tranel, 1994) has demonstrated that lesions specifically in the ventromedial frontal cortex are common to this syndrome. Of special interest to the present review is that this group has shown that patients with "acquired sociopathy" (citing *DSM–III* [American Psychiatric Association, 1980] criteria) manifest EDH to slides depicting both negatively and positively valenced scenes: social disaster, mutilation, and nudity. In addition, the acquired-sociopathy patients show smaller anticipatory SCRs when making choices associated with greater losses in a gambling task (Bechara, Tranel, Damasio, & Damasio, 1996), in contrast to normal control participants, who develop large SCRs over trials for such choices. The acquired-sociopathy patients also failed to learn to avoid disadvantageous choices involving frequent high immediate reward but very large infrequent losses, reflecting insensitivity to these greater losses.

Evidence for a strong link between so-called *acquired sociopathy* and *developmental psychopathy* is mixed. On the one hand, these results appear to strengthen the association of EDH with both psychopathy and disinhibition. On the other hand, the diminished electrodermal reactivity to positive slides seen in acquired sociopathy would not be predicted by the low-fear–weak-BIS hypothesis. Space limitations preclude a discussion of this issue here, but it has been addressed elsewhere (Fowles, 2000; Fowles & Missel, 1994). In addition, Schmitt, Brinkley, and Newman (1999) failed to demonstrate poor performance of incarcerated psychopathic individuals on the Bechara gambling task (e.g., Bechara, Tranel, Damasio, & Damasio, 1996). As Schmitt et al. noted, this failure may reflect differences in their administration of the gambling task relative to studies with acquired-sociopathy patients, but that is only a speculation. An alternative possibility is that the deficit associated with acquired sociopathy relates more strongly to the behavioral syndrome reflected in PCL–R Factor 2 (see above) than to Factor 1 and that differences between the psychopathic individuals and the incarcerated controls on Factor 2 were modest in Schmitt et al.'s study. Regardless of the ultimate resolution of this question, the findings for patients with ventromedial frontal cortex damage, like the psychopathy literature, suggest that EDH and disinhibition are related—in this case being dual manifestations of a specific lesion. Thus, one would expect that EDH in normal populations would be associated with both low anxiety and disinhibition.

---

[2]Patrick, Bradley, and Lang (1993) showed that PCL–R Factor 1, but not Factor 2, was associated with a reduced potentiation of the startle response while viewing aversive slides and concluded that Lykken's (1957) low-fear hypothesis applied to Factor 1. If so, their data suggest that low fear and impulsivity are not directly related. See Fowles (2000) for a discussion of issues related to their findings.

Anxiety and Disinhibition in
Temperament Measures

A substantial challenge to viewing anxiety and inhibitory control as two aspects of a single dimension is found in the temperament literature. Tellegen's (1985) Multidimensional Personality Questionnaire serves as a current example, although the point could be made equally with other temperament measures. The key finding is that Negative Emotionality and Constraint are orthogonal second-order factors in the Multidimensional Personality Questionnaire. Negative Emotionality with loadings from the primary factors of Stress Reaction, Alienation, and Aggression would seem most strongly related to anxiety, whereas Constraint, with loadings from the primary factors of Control Versus Impulsiveness, Harm Avoidance Versus Danger Seeking, and Traditionalism, appears to relate to inhibitory control. If roughly equating Negative Emotionality with anxiety and Constraint with inhibitory control is valid, therefore, then anxiety and inhibitory control do not constitute a single dimension as expected from the BIS hypothesis.

A similar challenge comes from Rothbart's work (e.g., Rothbart & Ahadi, 1994) on temperament in 3- to 8-year-old children. Rothbart's Children's Behavior Questionnaire (Rothbart, Ahadi, & Hershey, 1994) yields orthogonal second-order factors of Negative Affectivity and Effortful Control that she suggests are the developmental precursors of Tellegen's (1985) Negative Emotionality and Constraint (e.g., Rothbart & Ahadi, 1994). Negative Affectivity is defined by primary factors of Discomfort, Fear, Anger/Frustration, Sadness, and (negatively) Soothability, whereas Effortful Control is defined by primary factors of Inhibitory Control, Attentional Focusing, Low Intensity Pleasure, and Perceptual Sensitivity. Of particular interest is that Rothbart and Ahadi (1994) attributed Negative Emotionality to individual differences in Gray's (1977) BIS but related Effortful Control to the operation of an anterior attentional system. Rothbart and Ahadi (1994) conceptualized this anterior attentional system as serving broad functions suggestive of executive functions: It is said to enable a child "to effortfully or willfully inhibit a forbidden impulse, refrain from wrongdoing, and to respond instead in an acceptable or desired manner" (p. 60) and to facilitate "modulation of approach and expressiveness according to situational demands or explicit instructions from adults" (p. 57). Thus, at an empirical level such anxiety-relevant constructs as stress reaction, discomfort, and fear load on the Negative Emotionality/Negative Affectivity factor, whereas such inhibitory control-relevant items as control versus impulsivity and inhibitory control load on the orthogonal factor of Constraint/Effortful Control. Furthermore, at a theoretical level Rothbart and Ahadi attributed only Negative Affectivity to the BIS.

Electrodermal Reactivity and Temperament
in Noncriminal Populations

Although the absence of direct assessments of individual differences in BIS activity make it impossible truly to resolve the question of whether the BIS relates to anxiety, inhibitory control, or both, one can ask a simpler question: Does the EDH first identified in psychopathic individuals relate to both low anxiety and poor inhibitory control in normal individuals? Fortunately, there are two older studies and two newer studies that provide information on this point.

Electrodermal Hyporeactivity in Normal Adolescents and Young Adults

The assessment of personality is a major problem in searching for the correlates of individual differences in electrodermal reactivity. Experimenters typically rely on a single administration of self-report measures, which may not be the best methodology. In Jones's (1950, 1960) study, 100 normal participants from the Adolescent Growth Study at the University of California were seen repeatedly from ages 12–18. At least three staff psychologists provided independent ratings of personality based on observations of playground activities and play in free situations, and peers rated classmate reputation at 6- or 12-month intervals. Thus, personality assessments were based on extensive observations and peer ratings from multiple observers. Similarly, electrodermal reactivity was based on responses to emotional words in a word association test administered 11 times, yielding a total of 10 hr of recording. Using the magnitude of the SCR to these words, Jones selected the 20 most and least reactive participants for comparison.

Jones (1950, 1960) found that the electrodermally nonreactive participants showed less controlled reward-seeking behavior (e.g., impulsive, more talkative, more animated, less restrained in social behavior, more attention seeking, and higher on drive for recognition) and more undersocialized behavior (e.g., bossy, aggressive, domineering, somewhat irresponsible, less cooperative). Furthermore, the low-reactive participants were said to be less able to tolerate tensions, discharging them immediately by a generalized motor process, and were less able to postpone the attainment of goals. In the affective domain, the nonreactive participants were easily excited, more irritable, less good natured, more labile, and less able to deal with tension—that is, the lack of inhibitory control extended to the expression of emotions. Thus, Jones reported that smaller SCRs were associated with impulsivity/disinhibition and less socialized behavior, but he did not emphasize low anxiety per se. Indeed, he emphasized greater overt emotional expression in these participants, a feature that might make it difficult to detect low anxiety as an internal state.

Jones's (1950, 1960) study inspired Block (1957) to observe 70 applicants for medical school during an 18-hr personality assessment and select the 20 least and 20 most electrodermally reactive during a simulated lie detection task. Similar to Jones's study, the personality ratings came from five to seven staff psychologists. Unlike the Jones study, Block found anxiety to be characteristic of the reactive participants. The direct indications of anxiety included being fearful, apprehensive about actual or imagined threats, prone to worry, and seeking reassurance from others. Anxiety could also be inferred from their harm-avoidant behavior: more cautious, submissive, and readily dominated by others, and likely to withdraw in the face of adversity. Finally, they were better socialized (mannerly, ethical, protective of others). In the other direction, the electrodermally unreactive participants expressed more hostility; were more independent and autonomous; and were more nonconforming, rebellious, and opportunistic. Although Block saw continuity between Jones's results and his own, he saw electrodermal reactivity as an index of anxiety or affect without any implication for discharging tension in motor activity.

Nevertheless, Block (1957) described differences in inhibitory control of behavior and emotional expression: Reactive participants turned anxiety "toward internal routes of expression," and nonreactive participants showed "visible rather than inward or covert expressions of impulses" (p. 13).

Taken together, Jones's (1950, 1960) and Block's (1957) studies support the hypothesis that in nonclinical populations (including such a highly selected population as applicants to medical school), individual differences in electrodermal reactivity are associated with anxiety, inhibitory control over reward-seeking behavior, harm-avoidant behavior, and better socialization—all features to be expected of individual differences in the strength of the BIS. In addition, electrodermal reactivity may also be associated with inhibitory control over emotional expression.

Electrodermal–Temperament Correlations in Normal Children

Scarpa, Raine, Venables, and Mednick (1997) were the first to relate electrodermal activity to the anxiety-related construct Kagan (e.g., Kagan & Snidman, 1991) conceptualized as behaviorally inhibited (anxious) versus uninhibited. Using the 40th and 60th percentiles on this dimension, Scarpa et al. divided 3-year-old children into three groups and compared electrodermal measures obtained during presentation of six 75-dB tones. Skin conductance level differentiated the groups strongly in the initial analysis, but when children who cried during the testing were excluded, the two extreme groups differed only at the .05 level. However, as the authors noted, because of the confounding of crying with behavioral inhibition, eliminating children who cry may well have eliminated those behaviorally inhibited children who would have shown high skin conductance had they not cried. In any event, this study demonstrates an association between SCR and anxious temperament in 3-year-old children.

A large longitudinal study of the contribution of temperament and parenting to the development of internalized conscience conducted by Kochanska (1997) included multiple observational assessments of both temperamental fearfulness and effortful control (see Kochanska, Murray, & Coy, 1997, for a complete description). The paradigms for the assessment of fearfulness were adapted from Kagan's work (Kagan & Snidman, 1991) and captured differences in children's fearfulness in reaction to the unfamiliar environment and mildly frightening events (see Kochanska, 1995, for a complete description). The child's behavior was coded for the latency to and extent of spontaneous exploration, proximity to mother (who remained in the room), and overall distress and approach–withdrawal to each mildly frightening event. Similarly, the behavioral batteries that assessed functions and capacities most prototypical for effortful control (or inhibitory control) were based on Rothbart's work (e.g., Rothbart & Ahadi, 1994). They included slowing down motor activity, suppressing or initiating activity to signal, delaying, lowering voice, and cognitive reflectivity. In both cases, the separate scales were standardized and averaged into one robust composite score: *Fearfulness* or *Effortful Control*. The Pearson correlation between the two dimensions of temperament was .07 at age 4.

Fowles, Kochanska, and Murray (2000) were able to exploit this opportunity by obtaining electrodermal measurements from 92 of these children at age 4. Like Jones's (1950, 1960) and Block's (1957) studies, Kochanska's (1997) study provided assessments based on extensive observations. In addition, Kochanska's study is unique in the electrodermal literature for its systematic development of multiple observational paradigms explicitly designed to assess temperament.

During Fowles et al.'s (2000) experiment, interesting events and tasks were presented to children, minimizing their distress while allowing assessment of their EDRs to a variety of standard stimuli. Specific stimuli included taking breaths, moderately loud to loud sounds (e.g., a dropped book, a party horn, a newspaper popper, etc.), and a paper-covered coiled spring that sprang from a can. More prolonged stimuli included positive, negative, and neutral film clips and slides; watching the second hand on a clock for 60 s; watching glow-in-the-dark stars and planets with the lights out; pointing to parts of the body; waiting with opaque goggles (to block vision) while the experimenter wrapped a surprise gift; and watching a jack-in-the-box.

An index of electrodermal lability was derived by computing means for the various instruction periods and task periods and then calculating an overall mean. This index reflected obvious individual differences in the responsiveness of the SCR record. Electrodermal Lability correlated .21 ($p < .05$) with Fearfulness and .25 ($p < .025$) with Effortful Control, confirming the BIS-based expectation that EDH would be related to both low fear and poor inhibitory control.

Fowles et al. (2000) took two approaches to selecting more extreme groups on the basis of the temperament dimensions in order to examine the impact on differences in Electrodermal Lability. First, when the top and bottom 20 children were selected separately for each dimension, the results were significant for both Fearfulness, $t(38) = -2.67, p < .025$, and Effortful Control, $t(38) = -2.09, p < .05$. Second, children were selected for stability of temperament at ages 3 and 4—that is, those who were above the median at both ages or below the median at both ages. Again, differences were significant for both Fearfulness, $t(53) = -2.60, p < .025$, and Effortful Control, $t(64) = -2.09, p < .05$. Two points can be made about these results: (a) All comparisons were significant with the conservative two-tailed t test and (b) the association with Fearfulness, which was weaker in the correlational analyses, improved to $p < .025$ in the two extreme group analyses for that dimension, whereas the effect of Effortful Control did not increase with selection of extremes.

Finally, because of the conceptual association between Fearfulness and Effortful Control, Fowles et al. (2000) selected 10 children who were high (above the 65th percentile) and 10 who were low (approximately the bottom 30%) on both dimensions. It was thought that the theory might apply more strongly to these "convergent" children. This selection of convergent participants produced a very strong effect, $t(19) = -3.67, p < .005$, suggesting that perhaps a BIS-based dimension of fearlessness–disinhibition is obscured in the overall data by other factors.

Electrodermal Lability as a Moderator of Paths to Conscience

Kochanska's (1997) longitudinal study was designed to test a developmental model she had proposed earlier (Kochanska, 1993). In this model, the child's biologically based temperament interacts with parental socialization practices to influence the development of internalized conscience. The form of this interaction is such that there are different pathways to internalized conscience for fearful versus fearless children. Gentle parental discipline that deemphasizes power (vs. power assertion at the other end of this dimension—essentially a dimension of good vs. poor disciplinary strategies) works well for fearful children, but it may not induce sufficient anxiety in fearless children. Increasing the severity of the discipline for fearless children appears to be counterproductive, at least with respect to promoting internalized conscience. Rather, a mutually positive mother–child relationship provides an effective pathway to internalization among fearless children.

In the longitudinal study, Kochanska (1997) provided strong support for the model. Using a median split of an index of fearful temperament based on both behavioral observations and maternal ratings at toddler age, children were classified as fearful or fearless. Conscience development at age 4 among fearful children was predicted by good "maternal gentle discipline de-emphasizing power" assessed at toddler age. In contrast, security of attachment at toddler age (presumably reflecting a trusting, close, mutually positive mother–child relationship) predicted conscience development at age 4 among fearless children. Thus, an anxiety-based pathway is effective for fearful children, whereas a reward-based pathway is effective for fearless children. The alternative combinations were not effective: Internalization was not predicted by security of attachment among fearful children or by gentle discipline among fearless children; that is, the temperament dimension of fearfulness moderates the impact of socialization.

These results provided a unique opportunity to determine whether the Electrodermal Lability score could be used as an index of anxious temperament that would moderate pathways to conscience in the same manner as Kochanska's (1997) composite index of fearful temperament. This possible substitution was all the more interesting because the correlation between electrodermal lability and anxious temperament, although .21 when anxious temperament was assessed with observational data only (as reported above), was .00 when maternal ratings were combined with observational data for the overall composite used by Kochanska (1997).[3]

Using a median split based on Electrodermal Lability, Fowles and Kochanska (2000) divided the children into reactive (cf. fearful) and nonreactive (cf. fearless) groups. A hierarchical multiple regression for the reactive children, with age and sex entered at Step 1, attachment security entered at Step 2, and gentle discipline entered at Step 3, revealed that gentle discipline but not attachment security predicted internalization at age 4. An identical regression for nonreactive children revealed the opposite pattern: Attachment security, but not gentle discipline, predicted internalization at age 4. Thus, the results paralleled those obtained earlier with an index of fearful temperament based on behavioral observations and maternal ratings.

Implications of Studies With Normal Participants

On the basis of the psychopathy literature, and especially the weak-BIS hypothesis, researchers have assumed that EDH would be correlated with both disinhibition

---

[3]In the Fowles et al. (2000) study, we wanted to keep the number of statistical analyses as small as possible and, consequently, focused on the (objective) observational data as more likely to correlate with electrodermal measures than would maternal ratings. However, to examine the role of electrodermal lability in moderating pathways to conscience, we were obliged to compare it with the overall composite including maternal ratings, as that composite was used in the original analysis of this phenomenon by Kochanska (1997).

and low fear. The studies of this phenomenon in noncriminal populations appears to confirm this expectation. Jones's (1950, 1960) study strongly documented an association of hyporeactivity with greater impulsivity and poor socialization in adolescents, and Block's (1957) study documented an association with lower anxiety and poor socialization in applicants to medical school. Scarpa et al. (1997) reported an association with low anxiety in 3-year-olds. Using Kochanska's (1997) sophisticated assessments explicitly developed to assess temperament in 4-year-olds, Fowles et al. (2000) reported an association between EDH and both low Fearfulness and low Effortful Control, even though the latter two dimensions were themselves not significantly correlated. Fowles et al. also found rather substantial differences in electrodermal reactivity when they compared convergent groups selected for extreme scores on both dimensions, suggesting that perhaps there is a dimension of anxiety–impulsivity that is obscured by the complexity of other factors influencing the assessment of the two temperament dimensions.

The success reported by Fowles and Kochanska (2000) of electrodermal reactivity in assessing a temperament that moderates pathways to conscience has several further implications. First, the similarity to the original findings using observed and mother-reported fearfulness, with which electrodermal lability was not correlated, supports the validity of both approaches. Second, the finding supports the conclusion not only that electrodermal activity reflects (to some degree) an anxious temperament but also that it reflects aspects not captured by those more traditional methods. Demonstrating this nonredundant contribution to temperament assessment highlights the limitations of validating an index of temperament by correlating it with other measures of temperament—a method that can reveal only components in common. Thus, the relatively low correlations with the temperament dimensions of Fearfulness and Effortful Control reported by Fowles et al. (2000) probably constitute an underestimate, because to some extent electrodermal reactivity captures aspects of temperament not captured by those other assessments. Third, associating EDH in an important way with the development of internalized conscience, the lack of which is a core feature of psychopathy, strengthens the hypothesis that an underlying process reflected in EDH is involved in the etiology of psychopathy.

Final Comments

Theoretical Difficulties

I have emphasized evidence supportive of the EDH–BIS hypothesis, but difficulties should also be noted. Two issues are particularly salient. First, the challenge by the temperament literature of the BIS-based assumption that low anxiety and disinhibition go together points to the complexity of these concepts. In connection with the stronger effects for the convergent children in Fowles et al.'s (2000) study, I suggested that other factors obscure this dimension. The function of the BIS is to respond to cues that making certain responses may lead to punishment or frustration. That leaves individual differences in the strength of another motivational system (fight–flight), classical conditioning, emotional expressiveness (e.g., the possibility that some low-anxious children appear anxious because of poor emotion regulation, as suggested above), the cognitive factors of demoralization and alienation as potential influences on the assessment of temperament factors such as Neuroticism, or some combination of these. Even ratings of inhibited children in Kagan's (e.g., Kagan & Snidman, 1991) paradigm, which Rothbart (e.g., Rothbart & Ahadi, 1994) and Kochanska (1997) used to assess fearfulness, may be influenced by weak approach in addition to the effects of fear (Barkley, 1997, pp. 48–49). Thus, the BIS is only one of many processes that affect behavior and ratings of temperament.

Second, the original attribution of EDH in psychopathy to a weak BIS assumed some specific responsiveness to the aversive stimuli in the punishment paradigms used in that literature. The acquired-sociopathy studies suggest a broader deficit that includes hyporeactivity to positively valenced stimuli—a question that has been little studied in psychopathic individuals. Furthermore, the stimuli used to elicit electrodermal responses in the studies of normal adults, adolescents, and children have not been highly aversive. Although one can suggest—and it might be true—that all experiments are sufficiently aversive that EDH inherently reflects a response to aversive stimuli, there is a possibility that the temperament-relevant assessment of EDH need not be limited to cues for punishment.

Deficits and the Core Features of Psychopathy

The issues raised here offer an interesting perspective on the etiology of psychopathy. Recall that Hare (1991) characterized PCL–R Factor 1 personality traits as the "selfish, callous, and remorseless use of others," underscoring the lovelessness and guiltlessness that are a core feature of psychopathy. The Fowles et al. (2000) findings and, more broadly, Kochanska's research on multiple pathways to conscience, point to a possible conceptualization of the etiology of psychopathy (see Lykken, 1995, pp. 135–144, for a highly similar conceptualization). Low fear constitutes a risk factor for antisocial behavior, because even good maternal gentle discipline is less effective in promoting internalized conscience. However, such children can become well socialized: The risk of poor socialization can be offset by a close, responsive, and positive relationship between the parent and the child—a reward-mediated alternative pathway to embracing parental values and rules. However, it is likely that a disinhibited (hyperactive, noncompliant) infant–toddler temperament, especially in the context of an unresponsive or unskilled caretaker, may have a negative impact on parental disciplinary practices, leading to coercive exchanges. These coercive exchanges, in turn, initiate a developmental trajectory of acrimonious social interactions, poor social skills, and school failure, ending in chronic antisocial behavior (Patterson, DeGarmo, & Knutson, 2000) rather than the development of those prosocial behaviors designated by the concept of conscience. Furthermore, this disruption of the normal attachment process by interpersonally aversive coercive exchanges, with subsequent rejection by peers, teachers, and other important figures, is likely to foster the development of lovelessness—that is, a disinhibited temperament decreases the probability of the positive parent–child relationship needed by low-fear children to develop an internalized conscience. Thus, the combination of low fear and disinhibition makes both pathways to conscience less likely—low fear makes maternal gentle discipline less effective, and disinhibition makes a positive parent–child relationship less likely—while at the same time increasing the probability of developing lovelessness as a result of a developmental history of interpersonal conflict. From this perspective, none of the hypothesized temperament-based deficits directly define psychopathy; rather, the core features of psychopathy reflect an outcome of a failed developmental process to which the deficits may well contribute.

References

American Psychiatric Association. (1980). *Diagnostic and statistical manual of mental disorders* (3rd ed.). Washington, DC: Author.

Barkley, R. A. (1997). *ADHD and the nature of self-control.* New York: Guilford Press.

Bechara, A., Tranel, D., Damasio, H., & Damasio, A. R. (1996). Failure to respond autonomically to anticipated future outcomes following damage to prefrontal cortex. *Cerebral Cortex, 6*, 215–225.

Block, J. (1957). A study of affective responsiveness in a lie-detection situation. *Journal of Abnormal and Social Psychology, 55*, 11–15.

Cleckley, H. (1950). *The mask of sanity* (2nd ed.). St. Louis, MO: Mosby.

Damasio, A. R. (1994). *Descartes' error.* New York: Putman's.

Damasio, A. R., Tranel, D., & Damasio, H. (1990). Individuals with sociopathic behavior caused by frontal damage fail to respond autonomically to social stimuli. *Behavioural Brain Research, 41*, 81–94.

Fowles, D. C. (1980). The three arousal model: Implications of Gray's two-factor learning theory for heart rate, electrodermal activity, and psychopathy. *Psychophysiology, 17*, 87–104.

Fowles, D. (1988). Psychophysiology and psychopathology: A motivational approach. *Psychophysiology, 25*, 373–391.

Fowles, D. (1992). Schizophrenia: Diathesis–stress revisited. *Annual Review of Psychology, 43*, 303–336.

Fowles, D. (1993). Electrodermal activity and antisocial behavior: Empirical findings and theoretical issues. In J.-C. Roy, W. Boucsein, D. Fowles, & J. Gruzelier (Eds), *Progress in electrodermal research* (pp. 223–237). London: Plenum.

Fowles, D. (1994). A motivational theory of psychopathology. In W. Spaulding (Ed.), *Nebraska Symposium on Motivation* (Vol. 41, pp. 181–238). Lincoln: University of Nebraska Press.

Fowles, D. C. (2000). Electrodermal hyporeactivity and antisocial behavior: Does anxiety mediate the relationship? *Journal of Affective Disorders, 61*, 177–189.

Fowles, D. C., & Kochanska, G. (2000). Temperament as a moderator of pathways to conscience in children: The contribution of electrodermal activity. *Psychophysiology, 37*, 788–795.

Fowles, D. C., Kochanska, G., & Murray, K. (2000). Electrodermal activity and temperament in preschool children. *Psychophysiology, 37*, 777–787.

Fowles, D., & Missel, K. (1994). Electrodermal hyporeactivity, motivation, and psychopathy: Theoretical issues. In D. Fowles, P. Sutker, & S. Goodman (Eds.), *Progress in experimental personality and psychopathology research 1994: Special focus on psychopathy and antisocial behavior: A developmental perspective* (pp. 263–283). New York: Springer.

Gough, H. G. (1960). Theory and measurement of socialization. *Journal of Consulting Psychology, 24*, 23–30.

Gray, J. A. (1970). The psychophysiological basis of intraversion–extraversion. *Behavior Research and Therapy, 8*, 249–266.

Gray, J. A. (1976). The behavioural inhibition system: A possible substrate for anxiety. In M. P. Feldman & A. Broadhurst (Eds.), *Theoretical and experimental bases of the behaviour therapies* (pp. 3–41). London: Wiley.

Gray, J. A. (1977). Drug effects on fear and frustration: Possible limbic site of action of minor tranquilizers. In L. L. Iversen, S. D. Iversen, & S. H. Snyder (Eds.), *Handbook of psychopharmacology* (Vol. 8, pp. 433–529). New York: Plenum.

Gray, J. A. (1978). The neuropsychology of anxiety. *British Journal of Psychology, 69*, 417–434.

Gray, J. A. (1979). A neuropsychological theory of anxiety. In C. E. Izard (Ed.), *Emotions in personality and psychopathology* (pp. 303–335). New York: Plenum.

Hare, R. D. (1978). Electrodermal and cardiovascular correlates of psychopathy. In R. D. Hare & D. Schalling (Eds.), *Psychopathic behavior: Approaches to research* (pp. 107–144). New York: Wiley.

Hare, R. D. (1991). *The Hare Psychopathy Checklist—Revised.* Toronto, Ontario, Canada: Multi-Health Systems.

Jones, H. E. (1950). The study of patterns of emotional expression. In M. L. Reymert (Ed.), *Feelings and emotions: The Mooseheart Symposium* (pp. 161–168). New York: McGraw-Hill.

Jones, H. E. (1960). The longitudinal method in the study of personality. In I. Iscoe & H. W. Stevenson (Eds.), *Personality development in children* (pp. 3–27). University of Chicago Press.

Kagan, J., & Snidman, S. (1991). Temperamental factors in human development. *American Psychologist, 46*, 856–862.

Kochanska, G. (1993). Toward a synthesis of parental socialization and child temperament in early development of conscience. *Child Development, 64*, 325–347.

Kochanska, G. (1995). Children's temperament, mothers' discipline, and security of attachment: Multiple pathways to emerging internalization. *Child Development, 66*, 597–615.

Kochanska, G. K. (1997). Multiple pathways to conscience for children with different temperaments: From toddlerhood to age 5. *Developmental Psychology, 33*, 228–240.

Kochanska, G., Murray, K., & Coy, K. C. (1997). Inhibitory control as a contributor to conscience in childhood: From toddler to early school age. *Child Development, 68*, 263–277.

Lykken, D. T. (1957). A study of anxiety in the sociopathic personality. *Journal of Abnormal and Social Psychology, 55*, 6–10.

Lykken, D. T. (1995). *The antisocial personalities.* Hillsdale, NJ: Erlbaum.

Lykken, D. T., & Katzenmeyer, C. (1973). Manual for the Activity Preference Questionnaire (APQ). In *Psychiatric research reports*. Minneapolis: University of Minnesota.

Megargee, E. I. (1972). *The California Psychological Inventory handbook.* San Francisco: Jossey-Bass.

Obrist, P. A. (1976). The cardiovascular–behavioral interaction—As it appears today. *Psychophysiology, 13*, 95–107.

Patrick, C. J., Bradley, M. M., & Lang, P. J. (1993). Emotion in the criminal psychopath: Startle reflex modulation. *Journal of Abnormal Psychology, 102*, 82–92.

Patterson, G. R., DeGarmo, D. S., & Knutson, N. (2000). Hyperactive and antisocial behaviors: Comorbid or two points in the same process? *Development and Psychopathology, 12*, 91–106.

Rothbart, M. K., & Ahadi, S. A. (1994). Temperament and the development of personality. *Journal of Abnormal Psychology, 103*, 55–66.

Rothbart, M. K., Ahadi, S., & Hershey, K. L. (1994). Temperament and social behavior in children. *Merrill-Palmer Quarterly, 40*, 21–39.

Scarpa, A., Raine, A., Venables, P. H., & Mednick, S. A. (1997). Heart rate and skin conductance in behaviorally inhibited Mauritian children. *Journal of Abnormal Psychology, 106*, 182–190.

Schmitt, W. A., Brinkley, C. A., & Newman, J. P. (1999). Testing Damasio's somatic marker hypothesis with psychopathic individuals: Risk takers or risk averse? *Journal of Abnormal Psychology, 108*, 538–543.

Siddle, D. A. T., & Trasler, G. (1981). The psychophysiology of psychopathic behaviour. In M. J. Christie & P. G. Mellett (Eds.), *Foundations of psychosomatics* (pp. 283–303) London: Wiley.

Tellegen, A. (1985). Structures of mood and personality and their relevance to assessing anxiety, with an emphasis on self-report. In A. H. Tuma & J. D. Maser (Eds.), *Anxiety and the anxiety disorders* (pp. 681–706). Hillsdale, NJ: Erlbaum.

Tranel, D. (1994). "Acquired sociopathy": The development of sociopathic behavior following focal brain damage. In D. Fowles, P. Sutker, & S. Goodman (Eds.), *Psychopathy and antisocial behavior: A developmental perspective* (pp. 285–311). New York: Springer.

Zahn, T. P. (1986). Psychophysiological approaches to psychopathology. In M. G. H. Coles, S. W. Porges, & E. Donchin (Eds.), *Psychophysiology: Systems, processes, and applications* (Vol. 1, pp. 508–610). New York: Guilford Press.

16

Experimental Approaches to the Recovered Memory Controversy

Richard J. McNally

The title of this festschrift volume refers directly to Brendan Maher's methodological contributions to the study of mental illness, and it alludes, more specifically, to his landmark book on the topic. Maher applied the logic and methods of experimental psychology to the realm of mental disorder, and anyone working in this tradition has been the intellectual beneficiary of his efforts. In this spirit, my colleagues and I have extended his methodological approach to a serious social controversy bordering the field of psychopathology: the problem of repressed and recovered memories of childhood sexual abuse (McNally, 2001).

Yet an emphasis on Maher's methodological contributions runs the risk of having readers miss the much broader impact he has had on those who have had the privilege of knowing him personally. Maher and I have been colleagues in the Department of Psychology at Harvard University since 1991. The intellectual rigor and integrity, embodied in his science and scholarship, are equally evident in the broader world of university life.

Few recent controversies in psychology have been as bitter as the one concerning the reality of repressed and recovered memories of childhood sexual abuse (CSA). On the one hand, some theorists hold that sexually abused children develop coping skills that enable them to dissociate and forget their abuse, only to recall it years later under special circumstances that cue retrieval (e.g., Herman & Schatzow, 1987; Terr, 1991). On the other hand, skeptics deny that there is any convincing evidence that people can repress and later recover memories of repeated CSA (e.g., Loftus & Ketcham, 1994; Pope, Hudson, Bodkin, & Oliva, 1998). These authors suggest that to make sense of otherwise inexplicable distress, some people may come to believe that they must have been molested in early childhood. Some may "recall" memories of CSA after having watched television shows about repressed memories or having read certain self-help books (Heaton & Wilson, 1998).

The recovered memory debate has been strikingly unencumbered by data on cognitive functioning in the very people at the heart of the controversy: those reporting repressed and recovered memories of CSA. To be sure, there have been published anecdotes of both recovered and false memories of CSA that vary in methodological rigor (e.g., Herman & Schatzow, 1987; Ofshe & Watters, 1994; Schooler, Bendiksen, & Ambadar, 1997), and there have been surveys of people who report periods of time when they did not think about (and perhaps could not remember) their CSA (e.g.,

Briere & Conte, 1993; Elliott, 1997). There also have been experiments documenting that false autobiographical memories of nontraumatic events can be "implanted" in college students (e.g., Hyman & Loftus, 1998). Yet experimental data on cognitive functioning in people reporting repressed and recovered memories of CSA have been entirely absent until very recently.

The purpose of this chapter is to illustrate how the methods of experimental psychopathology can be brought to bear on the recovered memory controversy by summarizing the work of me and my colleagues. Our research program began serendipitously. Several years ago, I was conducting psychiatric diagnostic interviews with women who had responded to newspaper notices requesting participation of CSA survivors for a positron emission tomography study on posttraumatic stress disorder (PTSD; Shin et al., 1999). During the course of about 10 days, I had interviewed several potential participants who believed they qualified as CSA survivors but who had no memory of their abuse. Inquiring further, I learned that they experienced a diversity of difficulties, ranging from interpersonal problems to substance abuse. Lacking any credible explanation for these problems, they assumed that their difficulties must have arisen from repressed memories of CSA. Although these women were ineligible for the positron emission tomography study, they provided the inspiration for a series of studies on repressed and recovered memories of CSA.

The chief aim of our research has been to test hypotheses about cognitive functioning in women reporting various CSA histories. Our participants have been recruited from the community, and they fall into one of the following four groups: (a) those who believe they were sexually abused as children but who have no memory for these events (repressed memory group), (b) those who report having recalled long-forgotten episodes of CSA (recovered memory group), (c) those who report always having remembered their CSA (continuous memory group), and (d) those who report never having been sexually abused (control group). We use the terms *repressed memory* and *recovered memory* merely to capture the phenomenology of these individuals. We were unable to confirm (or disconfirm) whether these participants had, in fact, been abused.

Personality Profiles and Clinical Symptoms

In addition to our laboratory experiments, we characterized our four groups on standard personality and clinical scales (McNally, Clancy, Schacter, & Pitman, 2000b). Participants completed the Multidimensional Personality Questionnaire (MPQ; Tellegen, 1982), a comprehensive inventory that includes an absorption scale predictive of hypnotic susceptibility (Tellegen & Atkinson, 1974); the Dissociative Experiences Scale (DES; Bernstein & Putnam, 1986), the Beck Depression Inventory (Beck & Steer, 1987), and the civilian version (Vreven, Gudanowski, King, & King, 1995) of the Mississippi Scale for Combat-Related Posttraumatic Stress Disorder (Keane, Caddell, & Taylor, 1988).

Several important findings emerged. First, the MPQ personality profiles of the control and continuous memory groups were strikingly similar, as were those of the repressed and recovered memory groups. Second, the repressed memory group scored significantly higher than the control and continuous memory groups on the MPQ Negative Affectivity scale, but not significantly higher than the recovered memory group. Negative affectivity denotes proneness to experience anger, anxiety, guilt, and depression. There were no significant differences among the groups on positive affectivity. Third, the control and continuous memory groups did not differ in terms of dissociative, depressive, and PTSD symptoms, whereas the repressed memory group reported more of these symptoms than both of these groups and reported more depressive and PTSD symptoms than did the recovered memory group. The recovered memory group also reported significantly more symptoms of dissociation and PTSD than did the control group, but not significantly more than the continuous memory group. Fourth, the repressed and recovered memory groups scored equivalently high on absorption and significantly higher than the control group. The repressed memory group also scored significantly higher on absorption than did the continuous memory group.

In summary, the repressed memory group was the most psychiatrically disturbed; the most prone to experience negative emotions; the most dissociative; and the most prone to absorption and, therefore, perhaps, the most hypnotizable. Participants who had always remembered their abuse were indistinguishable from those who had never been abused. Recovered memory participants tended to fall midway between continuous and repressed memory participants on most measures.

These data can be interpreted in two ways. To make sense of otherwise inexplicable dysphoria, some individuals may infer that repressed memories of CSA lie at the root of their problems. An "effort after meaning" may lead them to conclude that they harbor repressed memories of early childhood trauma. Indeed, the DES predicts false-memory formation in some paradigms (Heaps & Nash, 1999; Hyman & Billings, 1998), and the Absorption scale predicts hypnotic susceptibility (Tellegen & Atkinson, 1974). Therefore, elevated dissociation and absorption scores in the recovered and repressed memory groups may indicate their proneness for false-memory formation.

On the other hand, elevated dissociation scores may reflect the capacity to repress traumatic memories. In accordance with this interpretation, the group whose presumptive CSA memories remain inaccessible scored the highest on dissociation (repressed memory group), the group whose members perhaps were presumably unable to forget their trauma scored the lowest (continuous memory group), and the group whose members were unable to keep their memories repressed scored midway between the other two groups (recovered memory group). Unfortunately, there is no easy way to determine which of these two interpretations is correct in the absence of independent evidence bearing on the veracity of the memories.

Guided Imagery and Memory Distortion

Many psychologists have argued that therapies designed to recover suspected memories of CSA may inadvertently foster illusory memories of abuse (e.g., Poole, Lindsay, Memon, & Bull, 1995). Among these therapeutic methods is *guided imagery*, whereby patients who are uncertain about having been molested are asked to visualize what it might have been like. Unfortunately, repeated visualization of imaginary events can increase conviction that the visualized events actually occurred. Studies show that having college students imagine unusual childhood events subsequently inflates their confidence in having experienced the visualized events (Garry, Manning, Loftus, & Sherman, 1996; Heaps & Nash, 1999).

We used this experimental procedure to test whether women reporting recovered memories of CSA are more susceptible than nonabused control participants to the imagination inflation effect (Clancy, McNally, & Schacter, 1999), as predicted by the false-memory perspective. During one of their early visits to the laboratory, participants rated their confidence regarding whether they had experienced certain childhood events (e.g., getting stuck in a tree, finding a $10 bill in parking lot). None of the events were abuse related. During a later visit, they performed a guided-imagery task that required them to visualize certain of these events, but not others. Participants once again rated their confidence in having experienced the childhood events they had rated previously. The results indicated that merely having imagined certain unusual events nonsignificantly boosted confidence that the events had, in fact, occurred, but the effect size for imagination inflation was more than twice as large for the nonabused group than for the recovered memory group. This finding directly contradicts the false-memory prediction that recovered memory participants would be especially vulnerable to memory distortion following guided imagery. However, remarks by several participants, all from the recovered memory group, strongly suggested that they were on guard against exhibiting any memory distortion effects in the laboratory. Moreover, although the recovered memory group scored higher than the control group on the DES, the DES was positively correlated with imagination inflation only in the control group, which replicates the results of a previous study (Heaps & Nash, 1999), but negatively correlated with imagination inflation in the recovered memory group. Taken together, these findings imply that vigilance on the part of the recovered memory participants enables them to counteract the tendency for dissociation proneness to foster memory distortion.

False-Memory Effects in Recovered Memory Participants

We have attacked the false-memory issue in a laboratory paradigm that is far less transparent than the imagination inflation one (Clancy, Schacter, McNally, & Pitman, 2000). In our next experiment, we tested whether recovered memory participants exhibit proneness for false-memory effects in a paradigm introduced by Deese (1959) and adapted by Roediger and McDermott (1995). In the standard Deese/Roediger/McDermott (DRM) paradigm, participants hear a series of word lists during the study phase. Each list consists of semantically related items (e.g., *sour, bitter, candy, sugar*) that converge on another strongly related, but nonpresented, word—the false target—that reflects the gist of list (e.g., *sweet*). Participants later receive recognition tests for all words, plus other distracter words, including the false target. Psychologists have repeatedly found that many participants claim to remember false targets as having been presented during the study phase, and this false-recognition effect is predicted by DES scores (Winograd, Peluso, & Glover, 1998).

Because people reporting repressed and recovered memories of CSA are characterized by elevated DES scores (McNally et al., 2000b), we tested their proneness to exhibit false recognition in this paradigm. Women reporting either repressed, recovered, or continuous memories of CSA or no CSA participated. They were presented with word lists drawn from previous research, none involving trauma-related information. The results indicated that the recovered memory group was more prone than the other groups to exhibit false-recognition effects and that DES scores predicted false-memory effects across the groups. The more dissociation a participant reported in everyday life, the more likely she was to exhibit false memory effects in the laboratory. Because this experiment involved only words (and nontraumatic ones at that), one must be careful extrapolating this finding to autobiographical memories. Nevertheless, this study does suggest that recovered memory participants are characterized by an information-processing style characterized by a reliance on gist memory. Reliance on gist may render them prone to believe they experienced CSA per se when, in fact, they may have experienced other, broadly similar events (e.g., emotional neglect).

Directed Forgetting of Trauma-Related Information

Some theorists hold that molested children develop an avoidant encoding style that enables them to disengage attention from threatening cues and direct it elsewhere during abuse episodes (e.g., Terr, 1991). Impaired encoding of these and other adverse events during childhood may result in the impoverished autobiographical memory said to characterize CSA survivors (Harvey & Herman, 1994).

In one of our early experiments, we tested whether psychiatrically ill CSA survivors exhibit this hypothesized avoidant encoding style held to result in impaired memory for trauma-related material (McNally, Metzger, Lasko, Clancy, & Pitman, 1998). CSA survivors with PTSD, psychiatrically healthy CSA survivors, and non-abused control participants performed a directed-forgetting task that required them to view a series of words on a computer screen that were either trauma related (e.g., incest), positive (e.g., cheerful), or neutral (e.g., cupboard). Immediately after each word's appearance, instructions informed the participants to forget or to remember the previous item. Participants knew that their memory for the remember-words was to be tested following this encoding phase. If CSA survivors with PTSD are characterized by an enhanced ability to disengage attention from abuse cues and to forget disturbing events, then they should exhibit impaired memory for trauma words when they are subsequently asked to recall all words, regardless of the original encoding instructions—that is, if one can forget genuine traumatic events with relative ease, then one should be readily capable of forgetting trauma-related words—mere pale proxies of autobiographical memories of abuse.

Consistent with basic research in cognitive psychology (Johnson, 1994), control participants and healthy abuse survivors easily disengaged attention from trauma, positive, and neutral words they had been told to forget, thereby producing a standard directed-forgetting effect whereby remember-words were recalled more often than forget-words, regardless of word valence. However, in striking contradiction to the avoidant encoding hypothesis, participants with PTSD exhibited memory deficits, but only for neutral and positive words they were supposed to remember. They remembered trauma words all too well, including those they were supposed to forget.

However, perhaps only those CSA survivors with a reported history of having forgotten their abuse should exhibit enhanced forgetting of trauma words in this paradigm. Using the aforementioned protocol, we tested participants reporting either repressed or recovered CSA memories and compared their performance to that of nonabused control participants (McNally, Clancy, & Schacter, 2001). If anyone should exhibit superior forgetting of trauma cues, it ought to be people reporting repressed and recovered memories of CSA. The results, however, revealed entirely "normal" memory functioning in these groups. Repressed and recovered memory participants recalled trauma, positive, and neutral words they were told to remember more often than trauma, positive, and neutral words they had been told to forget. They exhibited neither impaired nor enhanced memory for trauma-related material.

Taken together, the directed-forgetting experiments show that people reporting either recovered or repressed memories of CSA do not behave like those with PTSD when it comes to the ability to forget trauma cues. None of these groups exhibit superior ability in forgetting trauma-related information.

Selective Processing of Trauma Cues

The most replicated information-processing finding in the PTSD field is selective processing of trauma cues in the modified Stroop color naming paradigm (McNally, 1998). In this paradigm, individuals view words of varying emotional significance and are asked to name the colors in which the words appear while ignoring the meanings of the words (Williams, Mathews, & MacLeod, 1996). Delays in color naming—or *Stroop interference*—occur when the meaning of the word captures the individual's attention despite the individual's struggle to attend to its color. Psychologically traumatized people with PTSD exhibit more interference for words related to their traumatic experiences than to neutral or other emotional words, and they exhibit more interference than do trauma-exposed people who do not qualify for PTSD (McNally, 1998). In fact, emotional Stroop interference may provide a quantitative index of intrusive cognition: Interference for trauma words is correlated with self-reported intrusive, but avoidance–numbing symptoms in PTSD (Cassiday, McNally, & Zeitlin, 1992). This effect has been replicated many times, including in people exposed to combat (e.g., McNally, Kaspi, Riemann, & Zeitlin, 1990) or rape (e.g., Foa, Feske, Murdock, Kozak, & McCarthy, 1991) and in children with documented CSA histories (Dubner & Motta, 1999). We tested whether women reporting repressed or recovered memories of CSA would look like PTSD patients in this paradigm, exhibiting delayed color naming for words related to abuse (McNally, Clancy, Schacter, & Pitman, 2000a).

Participants reporting either repressed, recovered, or continuous memories of CSA or no CSA history viewed a series of words on a computer screen and named the color of each word as quickly as possible while ignoring their meanings. The words were either trauma related (e.g., *molested*), positive (e.g., *elation*), or neutral (e.g., *carpet*). In contrast to results common in PTSD patients, none of our reported CSA groups exhibited trauma-related Stroop interference.

False-Memory Effects in People Reporting
Abduction by Space Aliens

Unable to confirm that our recovered memory participants had, in fact, been abused, we have been left wondering whether our data are best interpreted as indicating propensity for false-memory formation (e.g., elevated DES scores, false recognition effects in the DRM paradigm). To attack this problem from a different angle, we have endeavored to identify people reporting recovered memories of trauma that are almost certainly false: people who report recovering memories of abduction by space aliens.

In our experience, the modal "abductee" is a nonpsychotic individual who holds a range of curious beliefs, ranging from belief in astral projection to mental telepathy, prior to experiencing at least one episode of sleep paralysis accompanied by hypnopompic visual hallucinations of figures hovering around their bed. Many subsequently seek the aid of mental health professionals who hypnotize them in an effort to recover repressed memories of "what happened next" after the figures appeared in the bedroom. During these hypnotic sessions, the modal "abductee" suddenly realizes that the mysterious figures were aliens, and remembers having been whisked out of the window, and having been forced to undergo various sexual activities aboard a spaceship. Two of our research participants claimed to have fathered hybrid babies during encounters with female aliens.

We tested three groups of participants in a variant of the DRM paradigm (Clancy, McNally, Schacter, Lenzenweger, & Pitman, in press). One group comprised participants who reported having recovered memories of alien abduction; a second (control) group comprised people who denied having been abducted by aliens. A third group comprised people who believed they had been abducted by aliens but who had no autobiographical memories of abduction. These individuals adduced small, seemingly inexplicable scars on their bodies as evidence of having been probed by aliens in addition to other "circumstantial evidence" that they believe is best explained by an abduction hypothesis. Unlike our CSA participants, they did not believe they harbored repressed memories in their unconscious mind. Instead, they suspect that the aliens "zapped" the memories out of their brains.

Clancy's results indicate that people reporting recovered memories of alien abduction or who believe they have been abducted (but lack memories) exhibit higher rates of false recollection in the DRM paradigm than do control participants who deny a history of alien abduction. That is, people reporting recovered memories of CSA and recovered memories of alien abduction exhibit the same propensity for false-memory formation, at least in this laboratory task.

Conclusion

The studies summarized in this chapter constitute the first attempts to study information processing in people reporting either repressed or recovered memories of CSA. Several provisional conclusions seem warranted. First, these individuals exhibit considerable psychological distress, and they score relatively high on measures of dissociation and absorption. Whether these elevations reflect propensity for repression of traumatic memories or propensity for false-memory formation cannot be determined in the absence of independent evidence bearing on the veracity of the memory reports. Second, people reporting recovered memories of CSA appear capable of counteracting the potentially memory-distorting effects of guided visualization, but they fall prey to false-memory effects in the less transparent DRM paradigm. The same effect occurs in people who believe they have been abducted by space aliens. Third, my colleagues and I have found no evidence to support the claim that CSA survivors, with or without a history of alleged repressed memories, are characterized by skill in forgetting information related to abuse. Fourth, in contrast to people with PTSD, recovered and repressed memory participants do not exhibit the characteristic signature of PTSD on the modified Stroop test: delayed color naming of trauma-related words.

Most of the research discussed in this volume concerns people with serious mental illness. This emphasis is expectable; the experimental analysis of schizophrenia has been the main focus of Brendan Maher's career. Although not addressing mental illness per se, this concluding chapter illustrates how the experimental methods pioneered by Maher can be extended to phenomena lying at the border of psychopathology. The tools of experimental psychopathology can thereby play a role in resolving one of the most bitter controversies ever to affect our field: repressed and recovered memories of trauma.

References

Beck, A. T., & Steer, R. A. (1987). *Beck Depression Inventory manual.* San Antonio, TX: Psychological Corporation.

Bernstein, E. M., & Putnam, F. W. (1986). Development, reliability, and validity of a dissociation scale. *Journal of Nervous and Mental Disease, 174,* 727–735.

Briere, J., & Conte, J. (1993). Self-reported amnesia for abuse in adults molested as children. *Journal of Traumatic Stress, 6,* 21–31.

Cassiday, K. L., McNally, R. J., & Zeitlin, S. B. (1992). Cognitive processing of trauma cues in rape victims with post-traumatic stress disorder. *Cognitive Therapy and Research, 16,* 282–295.

Clancy, S. A., McNally, R. J., & Schacter, D. L. (1999). Effects of guided imagery on memory distortion in women reporting recovered memories of childhood sexual abuse. *Journal of Traumatic Stress, 12,* 559–569.

Clancy, S. A., McNally, R. J., Schacter, D. L., Lenzenweger, M. F., & Pitman, R. K. (in press). Memory distortion in people reporting abduction by aliens. *Journal of Abnormal Psychology.*

Clancy, S. A., Schacter, D. L., McNally, R. J., & Pitman, R. K. (2000). False recognition in women reporting recovered memories of sexual abuse. *Psychological Science, 11,* 26–31.

Deese, J. (1959). On the prediction of occurrence of particular verbal intrusions in immediate recall. *Journal of Experimental Psychology, 58,* 17–22.

Dubner, A. E., & Motta, R. W. (1999). Sexually and physically abused foster care children and posttraumatic stress disorder. *Journal of Consulting and Clinical Psychology, 67,* 367–373.

Elliott, D. M. (1997). Traumatic events: Prevalence and delayed recall in the general population. *Journal of Consulting and Clinical Psychology, 65,* 811–820.

Foa, E. B., Feske, U., Murdock, T. B., Kozak, M. J., & McCarthy, P. R. (1991). Processing of threat-related information in rape victims. *Journal of Abnormal Psychology, 100,* 156–162.

Garry, M., Manning, C. G., Loftus, E. F., & Sherman, S. J. (1996). Imagination inflation: Imagining a childhood event inflates confidence that it occurred. *Psychonomic Bulletin and Review, 3,* 208–214.

Harvey, M. R., & Herman, J. L. (1994). Amnesia, partial amnesia, and delayed recall among adult survivors of childhood trauma. *Consciousness and Cognition, 3,* 295–306.

Heaps, C., & Nash, M. (1999). Individual differences in imagination inflation. *Psychonomic Bulletin and Review, 6,* 313–318.

Heaton, J. A., & Wilson, N. L. (1998). Memory, media, and the creation of mass confusion. In S. J. Lynn & K. M. McConkey (Eds.), *Truth in memory* (pp. 349–371). New York: Guilford Press.

Herman, J. L., & Schatzow, E. (1987). Recovery and verification of memories of childhood sexual trauma. *Psychoanalytic Psychology, 4*, 1–14.

Hyman, I. E., Jr., & Billings, F. J. (1998). Individual differences and the creation of false childhood memories. *Memory, 6*, 1–20.

Hyman, I. E., Jr., & Loftus, E. F. (1998). Errors in autobiographical memory. *Clinical Psychology Review, 18*, 933–947.

Johnson, H. M. (1994). Processes of successful intentional forgetting. *Psychological Bulletin, 116*, 274–292.

Keane, T. M., Caddell, J. M., & Taylor, K. L. (1988). Mississippi Scale for Combat-Related Posttraumatic Stress Disorder: Three studies in reliability and validity. *Journal of Consulting and Clinical Psychology, 56*, 85–90.

Loftus, E. F., & Ketcham, K. (1994). *The myth of repressed memory.* New York: St. Martin's Press.

McNally, R. J. (1998). Experimental approaches to cognitive abnormality in posttraumatic stress disorder. *Clinical Psychology Review, 18*, 971–982.

McNally, R. J. (2001). The cognitive psychology of repressed and recovered memories of childhood sexual abuse: Clinical implications. *Psychiatric Annals, 31*, 509–514.

McNally, R. J., Clancy, S. A., & Schacter, D. L. (2001). Directed forgetting of trauma cues in adults reporting repressed or recovered memories of childhood sexual abuse. *Journal of Abnormal Psychology, 110*, 151–156.

McNally, R. J., Clancy, S. A., Schacter, D. L., & Pitman, R. K. (2000a). Cognitive processing of trauma cues in adults reporting repressed, recovered, or continuous memories of childhood sexual abuse. *Journal of Abnormal Psychology, 109*, 355–359.

McNally, R. J., Clancy, S. A., Schacter, D. L., & Pitman, R. K. (2000b). Personality profiles, dissociation, and absorption in women reporting repressed, recovered, or continuous memories of childhood sexual abuse. *Journal of Consulting and Clinical Psychology, 68*, 1033–1037.

McNally, R. J., Kaspi, S. P., Riemann, B. C., & Zeitlin, S. B. (1990). Selective processing of threat cues in posttraumatic stress disorder. *Journal of Abnormal Psychology, 99*, 398–402.

McNally, R. J., Metzger, L. J., Lasko, N. B., Clancy, S. A., & Pitman, R. K. (1998). Directed forgetting of trauma cues in adult survivors of childhood sexual abuse with and without posttraumatic stress disorder. *Journal of Abnormal Psychology, 107*, 596–601.

Ofshe, R., & Watters, E. (1994). *Making monsters.* Berkeley: University of California Press.

Poole, D. A., Lindsay, D. S., Memon, A., & Bull, R. (1995). Psychotherapy and the recovery of memories of childhood sexual abuse: U.S. and British practitioners' opinions, practices, and experiences. *Journal of Consulting and Clinical Psychology, 63*, 426–437.

Pope, H. G., Jr., Hudson, J. I., Bodkin, J. A., & Oliva, P. (1998). Questionable validity of "dissociative amnesia" in trauma victims. *British Journal of Psychiatry, 172*, 210–215.

Roediger, H. L., III, & McDermott, K. B. (1995). Creating false memories: Remembering words not presented in lists. *Journal of Experimental Psychology: Learning, Memory, and Cognition, 21*, 803–814.

Schooler, J. W., Bendiksen, M., & Ambadar, Z. (1997). Taking the middle line: Can we accommodate both fabricated and recovered memories of sexual abuse? In M. A. Conway (Ed.), *Recovered memories and false memories* (pp. 251–292). Oxford, England: Oxford University Press.

Shin, L. M., McNally, R. J., Kosslyn, S. M., Thompson, W. L., Rauch, S. L., Alpert, N. M., et al. (1999). Regional cerebral blood flow during script-driven imagery in childhood sexual abuse-related PTSD: A PET investigation. *American Journal of Psychiatry, 156*, 575–584.

Tellegen, A. (1982). *Brief manual for the Differential Personality Questionnaire.* Department of Psychology, University of Minnesota, Minneapolis.

Tellegen, A., & Atkinson, G. (1974). Openness to absorbing and self-altering experiences ("absorption"), a trait related to hypnotic susceptibility. *Journal of Abnormal Psychology, 83*, 268–277.

Terr, L. C. (1991). Childhood traumas: An outline and overview. *American Journal of Psychiatry, 148*, 10–20.

Vreven, D. L., Gudanowski, D. M., King, L. A., & King, D. W. (1995). The civilian version of the Mississippi PTSD Scale: A psychometric evaluation. *Journal of Traumatic Stress, 8*, 91–109.

Williams, J. M. G., Mathews, A., & MacLeod, C. (1996). The emotional Stroop task and psychopathology. *Psychological Bulletin, 120*, 3–24.

Winograd, E., Peluso, J. P., & Glover, T. A. (1998). Individual differences in susceptibility to memory illusions. *Applied Cognitive Psychology, 12*, S5–S27.

Author Index

Numbers in italics refer to listings in the reference section.

Abercombie, H., 204, *206*
Abramson, L. Y., 11, 26, 196, *206*
Adalsteinsson, E., *225*
ADAMHA Reorganization Act, *114*
Adami, H., 75, *78*
Adamo, U. H., 10, *26, 42*
Adams, N., 126, 127, *132, 134*
Adams, N. L., 127, *134*
Adelson, E. H., 184, *191*
Ader, D. N., 56, 57, *65*, 71, *81*
Adler, L. E., *105*
Agarwal, M., 25, *26*
Aggernaes, H., 216, *225*
Agid, Y., 61, *64*, 86, *105*
Ahadi, S. A., 260, 262, 266, *268*
Albert, M. L., 138, *153*
Albin, R. L., 61, *63*
Albright, T. D., 183, *191*
Alexander, G. E., 61, *63*
Alger, J., 217, *226*
Alivisatos, B., 88, *105*, 230, *240*
Allen, M., 216, *226*
Alliger, R., 85, 98, *100*, 230, *239*
Allman, J., 183, *191*
Alloy, L. B., 196, *206, 207*
Alpert, M., 33, *42*, 70, *81*
Alpert, N. M., 270, *277*
Alphs, L. D., 123, 124, *134*, 234, *241*
Alvir, J., 189, *192*
Amador, X. F., 70, 71, *79, 139, 153*, 168, *170*
Ambadar, Z., 269, *277*
American Psychiatric Association, 34, 42, 47, *63*, 71, 75, *78*, 97, *100*, 109, *114*, 139, 140, *152*, 158, 161, *170*, 258, 259, *267*
American Psychological Association, 176, *191*
Ames, D., 51, 57, 58, *64, 65*, 70, *81*
Ancoli, S., 70, *79*
Andermann, F., 138, *154*
Andersen, C. A., 20, *27*
Anderson, S. W., 130, *132*
Andreasen, A., 10, *26*
Andreasen, N. C., 70, 73, 74, *79, 80*, 85, 98, *100*, 109, *114*, 230, *239*
Angrist, B., 85, *106*
Angst, J., 203, *206*
Angus, J. W. S., 72, *82*
Annett, M., 59, *63*
Ansel, M., 109, *114*

Anthony, W. A., 108, 109, 110, *114*
Aosaki, T., 61, *64*
Aquirre, G. K., 89, 106
Arata, O., 85, *105*
Arbisi, P., 89, *104*
Arieti, S., 158, *170*
Arndt, S., 70, 74, *80*
Arntz, A., 168, *170*
Asarnow, R. F., *43*, 91, *103*
Asherson, P., *78*
Athanassopoulou, M., 196, *207*
Atkinson, G., 270, 271, *277*
Auerbach, J. G., *43*
Awh, E., *88, 103*
Azuma, M., *106*

Babb, S., 216, 217, *225, 226*
Babigian, H. M., 54, *64*
Bachevalier, J., 84, 88, *100, 103*
Baddeley, A., 84, 86, 87, 88, *100, 101, 102*, 199, *206, 229, 239*
Ballard, D., *239*
Banaji, M. R., 202, *207*
Barbaro, N. M., 183, *193*
Barber, T. X., 160, *170*
Barch, D. M., 120, *132*
Bargh, J., 196, 197, 202, *206*
Barker, P., 217, *224*
Barkley, R. A., 266, *267*
Barlow, D. H., 203, *206, 207*
Barlow, H. B., 184, *193*
Barnes, M. P., 54, *63*
Barnes, T. R. E., 72, *78*, 84, *104*
Barnhard, P. J., 195, 199, *208*
Barocka, A., 216, *226*
Baron, M., 32, *42*, 69, *78*
Bartzokis, G., 72, *82*
Bassett, A. S., *42*, 69, *78*
Bates, J. A., 127, *132*
Baum, K., 130, *134*
Baum, K. M., 10, *28*
Beam-Goulet, J., 109, *115*
Beasely, C. M., Jr., 71, *82*
Beaudette, S. M., 58, *65*
Bechara, A., 259, *267*
Beck, A. T., 195, 196, *206*, 270, *276*
Beck, L. H., 169, *171*
Becker, D. R., 110, *114*

Subject Index

vs. psychological processes, 245
Methological issues
  adaptive atypical behavior and default
    hypothesis, 10–12
  legacy of Francis Galton, 14–16
  primary heterogeneity and, 12–14
  in psychopathology research, 10–16
  secondary homogeneity and, 14
MRS. *See* Magnetic resonance spectrosctopy
  (MRS)

Narcissistic personality disorder
  vs. antisocial personality disorder
    and impulsivity/disinhibition, 258–259
Negative memory biases
  in depression
    behavioral studies of, 196–197
  encoding component of
    in depression, 200
  event-related potentials and, 197
Negative symptoms
  genetic influences on, 68–69
  in normal individuals, 69
  as indicator of genetic and neurobiological basis
    of schizophrenia, 77
  in individuals with schizophrenia and first-
    degree relatives, 69
Neuroimaging studies
  off-line bases for, 211–212
  of working memory tasks
    hypofrontality on, 89
Neuromotor abnormalities
  affective deficits and, 70–71
  in individuals with schizophrenia, 71–76
    affective deficit association and, 75
    bradykinesia assessment in, 73
    clinical measures of, 72, 75, 76
    electromechanical measures of resting and
      action tremor in, 72–73, 77
    measures of, 75
    research in participants' daily environments,
      76
    rigidity assessment in, 73
    study participants, 71–72, 75
Neuropsychological measures
  construct validity of, 122–128
  in schizophrenia research
    confounding effect of IQ and, 124, 127
    construct validity of, 122–127
    structural modeling for, 127
Neuropsychology
  definition of, 120
  in schizophrenia research, 120–121

Oculomotor delayed response paradigm
  in spatial working memory deficit, 91–92, 94

Pain insensitivity
  association with family history of bipolar
    disorder, 159
  in bipolar disorder, 159
  limitations of empirical literature, 158
  linkage with major psychopathology, 169
  in patients with mania, 158
  in patients with schizophrenia or bipolar
    disorder and relatives
    future research directions and, 168–169
    need for signal detection approaches to, 168
  in schizophrenia, 139–140
    historical perspective on, 157–158
  study of relatives of patients with schizophrenia
    or bipolar disorder
    differences in, 168
    psychological correlates in, 166–167
Pain sensitivity
  endorphins in mediation of, 169
  opioid receptors and, 169
  potential genetic foundation of, 169
  in relatives of patients with bipolar disorder
    comparison with relatives of patients with
      schizophrenia, 167–168
    non-weight-corrected scores for, 164–165
    weight-adjusted tolerance, 165–166
  in relatives of patients with schizophrenia,
    163–164
  study of relatives of patients with schizophrenia
    or bipolar disorder
    family mental health questionnaire in, 161
    pressure algometry in pain induction,
      160–161
    reliability of sensitivity measures in, 162
    Schizotypal Personality Questionnaire in,
      161
    study participants, 159–160
    weight and, 162–163
Paranoid schizophrenia
  adaptive atypical behavior and default
    hypothesis, 11
Parietal lobe
  in body image distortion, 138
  in exteroception dysfunction, 138–139
Park, S., *83*
Pathology and delusions
  irrelevance of formal rationality in real world,
    18–24
  primacy of experience over cognitive structuring
    of experience, 19
Pavlov, *13*
PEPSI. *See* Proton echo planar spectroscopic
  imaging (PEPSI)
Perceptual distortion
  in schizotypy, 137–138
Physiological arousal
  integral to emotional experience, 203–204

About the Editors

Mark F. Lenzenweger, PhD, is currently professor of psychology at the State University of New York at Binghamton, where he is appointed in the clinical (psychopathology), behavioral neuroscience, and cognitive areas. Previously a member of the tenured faculty at Cornell University for 11 years, he moved on to Harvard University in 1998. He returned to the rolling hills of upstate New York to join the Binghamton faculty in 2001. Dr. Lenzenweger conducts research and teaches on schizophrenia, schizotypy, personality disorders, and statistical methods.

Jill M. Hooley, DPhil, is currently professor of psychology at Harvard University, where she is appointed in the clinical and psychopathology area. Dr. Hooley conducts research on psychosocial processes in schizophrenia, particularly expressed emotion, and she teaches on schizophrenia, family factors in psychopathology, and clinical issues.